IN THE HOUR
of
VICTORY

BY THE SAME AUTHOR

The Hearts of Oak Trilogy

The Fighting Temeraire: Legend of Trafalgar

The Admiral Benbow: The Life and Times of a Naval Legend

The Glorious First of June: Fleet Battle in the Reign of Terror

The Fighting Ships Series

Fighting Ships: From the Ancient World to 1750

Fighting Ships 1750–1850

Fighting Ships 1850–1950

Shipwreck: A History of Disaster at Sea

Fighting at Sea in the Eighteenth Century: The Art of Sailing Warfare

IN THE HOUR

of

VICTORY

———— ◆ ————

THE ROYAL NAVY AT WAR
IN THE AGE OF NELSON

SAM WILLIS

Atlantic Books
London

Published in Great Britain in 2013 by Atlantic Books,
an imprint of Atlantic Books Ltd.

Copyright © Sam Willis, 2013

Appendix II © Nicholas Blake, 2013

10 9 8 7 6 5 4 3 2 1

A CIP catalogue record for this book is available from the British Library.

Hardback ISBN: 9780857895707

Special Edition ISBN: 9780857898302

Ebook ISBN: 9780857895721

Paperback ISBN: 9780857895738

Text design and typesetting: Carrdesignstudio.com
Printed in China.

Atlantic Books
An Imprint of Atlantic Books Ltd
Ormond House
26–27 Boswell Street
London
WC1N 3JZ
www.atlantic-books.co.uk

For Tors

absolutely irresistible

Rear-Admiral Horatio Nelson describing his attack on the French fleet
at the mouth of the Nile, 2 August, 1798

CONTENTS

ACKNOWLEDGEMENTS

I am extremely grateful to the many people who have offered their time and knowledge during the creation of this book. Nicholas Blake's work on the documents themselves was inestimable and his research for Appendix II meticulous. Oliver Walton has been a valuable sounding board and nonsense-preventer. Richard Blake helped with questions of piety; Tony Beales with Trafalgar; Sim Comfort with swords and telescopes; Andrew Bond, who is becoming something of a naval historian himself, with word-finding and grammar; Phil Weir with developments in telegraph and radio; and Andrew Little with Dutch museums. Lucy Morris did some excellent work at short notice and my father, Michael Willis, was an important shellfish and Dutch lager consultant on our 'research' trip to Rotterdam. The staff at the British Library, and particularly Dr William Frame, Curator of Modern Historical Papers, have been highly professional and helpful. Mark and David Hawkins of the Lanes Armoury in Brighton were very kind in letting me use an image of their Nile medal. And, as always with my work, this book is all the better because Michael Duffy read it through in draft and pointed out a number of howlers.

Finally I would like to thank Georgina Capel and Anthony Cheetham for believing in this project from its birth as a two-lined email, which began 'You'll never believe what I have just found …'

ILLUSTRATIONS

First section

1. The volume of dispatches (© *The British Library Board. Add. Mss. 23207*)
2. The silk banner belonging to *L'Amerique* (*National Maritime Museum, Greenwich, London*)
3. Admiral Richard Howe by John Singleton Copley, 1794 (*National Maritime Museum, Greenwich, London*)
4. 'The *Brunswick* and *Le Vengeur* after the Action on the First of June, 1794' by Nicholas Pocock, engraved by R. Pollard and J. Widnell (*Sim Comfort Collection*)
5. Sir John Jervis by Gilbert Stuart, *c*. 1782–7 (*National Maritime Museum, Greenwich, London*)
6. La Granja de San Ildefonso, Segovia, Spain (© *Paul Maeyaert/The Bridgeman Art Library*)
7. 'Nelson boarding the *San Nicolas* in the victory off Cape St Vincent, 1797' by W. M. Thomas, *c*. 1800 (*National Maritime Museum, Greenwich, London*)
8. Fragment of the naval ensign of the Batavian Republic (*National Maritime Museum, Greenwich, London*)
9. 'Duncan receiving the surrender of de Winter at the Battle of Camperdown, 11 October 1797' by Daniel Orme, 1797 (*National Maritime Museum, Greenwich, London*)

Second section

10. Lightning conductor from *L'Orient* (*National Maritime Museum, Greenwich, London*)
11. Rear-Admiral Horatio Nelson, attributed to Guy Head, *c*. 1800 (*National Maritime Museum, Greenwich, London*)

Images in the main text

The parts of the original letters reproduced on pages 23, 24, 25, 50, 67, 96, 127, 175, 191, 193, 195, 197, 218, 255, 316 all come from the volume of dispatches in the British Library (© *The British Library Board. Add. Mss. 23207*)

p. 339   Veteran of the Battle of the Nile (*Courtesy of Mark and David Hawkins*)

MAPS & BATTLE PLANS

As always, my maps and battle plans have been drawn by the extraordinarily talented artist and illustrator, Jamie Whyte. For more of his work, please see www.jamiewhyte.co.uk

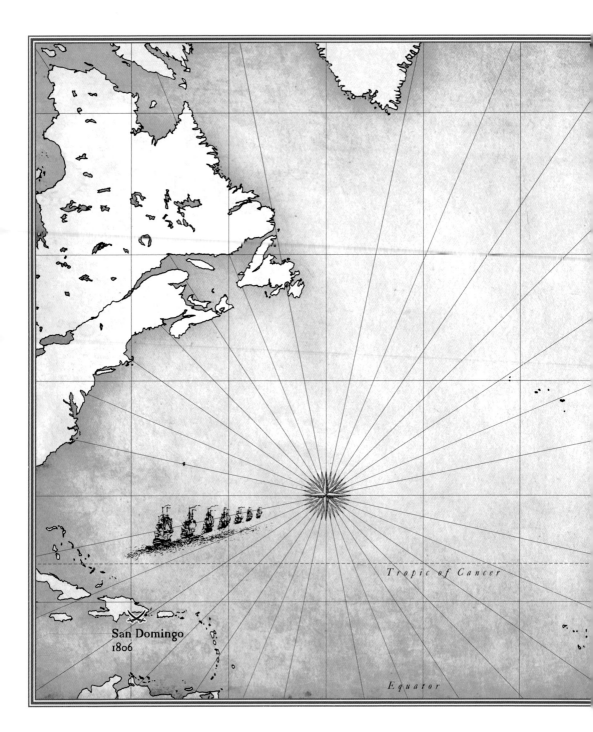

San Domingo
1806

Tropic of Cancer

Equator

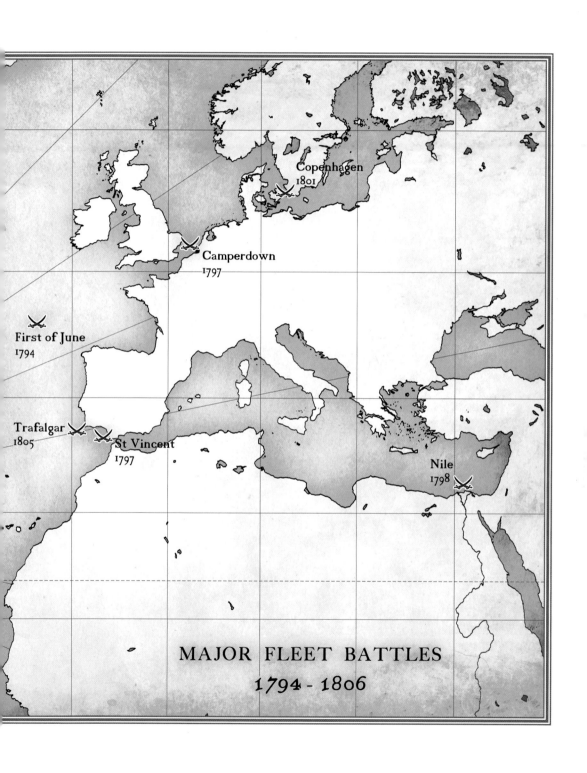

Copenhagen
1801

Camperdown
1797

First of June
1794

Trafalgar
1805

St Vincent
1797

Nile
1798

MAJOR FLEET BATTLES
1794 - 1806

PREFACE

The Finding

On a cold spring day in 2010 I made my way to the British Library and climbed the stairs to the manuscript reading room. It was just one more stop on a tour of British archives and libraries that I was undertaking as part of the research for a new book. Buried in the list of documents that I wanted to consult that day was the innocuous-sounding Add: 23207. A catalogue entry stated that it contained a number of letters written in the aftermath of a naval battle fought between Britain and France at the height of the Reign of Terror in 1794, a battle that became known as The Glorious First of June.

As is often the case with such material, I was expecting to receive several loose sheets of paper tucked inside a dull-coloured envelope made of acid-free paper. Instead, however, the archivist asked to re-check my credentials, took me to a special seating area reserved for the most precious of manuscripts and wheeled over a trolley bearing a varnished box the size of a coffin. I thought that there had been a mistake. Perhaps I had ordered the wrong document – one of those huge illuminated medieval manuscripts for which the British Library is so famous or an early copy of the Bible or the Koran. I nearly sent it back without looking inside but, when I opened the box, the glint of moulded decoration and clasps promised something sensational. Inside was a book so large and heavy that it took two people to move it from its box to a table. Straining under its weight, we rested it on a large foam wedge.

The book was over two feet long, at least eighteen inches wide, several inches thick and covered in the most gorgeous navy-blue velvet. At its head and foot were decorated silver-gilt onlays displaying themes of naval war and victory while, at the centre, another onlay displayed a fouled anchor set against a sea of rigging, ensigns, cannon and drums. The book was held shut by a clasp, beautifully moulded into the shape of a shell (fig. 1). I fiddled with it and swung the cover open as if opening the heavy oak door to a church. Inside were the original dispatches sent to London from the victorious fleets after the most significant naval battles of the French Revolutionary and Napoleonic Wars. I told myself to keep breathing.

The volume was divided by portraits of the victorious admirals. They stared out from the book, guarding their letters, as once they had stared out from their quarterdecks, guarding their fleets and their country. The letters were a national treasure. Here, immaculately preserved, were the admirals' narratives describing their victories to the King and the naval lords and politicians in London. Here also were letters from captains describing their conduct in battle to their admirals; from boatswains describing the damage to their ships; and from surgeons describing injuries to their men. Here were maps detailing the changing locations of ships as the chaos of battle unfurled; here were captured enemy narratives, here, even, were some of the original *envelopes*. History came off them all like heat.

I knew instantly that these documents had to be shared and that they would change the way that we think about naval warfare in this crucial period of British and world history. It is the aim of this book both to place these letters in the context of their battles and to examine their significance. As fascinating for what their authors leave out as for what they put in, they remain urgent and riveting more than 200 years after they were written.

INTRODUCTION

———•———

'You may rely on what I have written because it is
what I have seen.'
E. Poussielgue, Comptroller General of Napoleon's Eastern Army,
to his sweetheart, 3 August 1798

The Writing

Listen! Do you hear it? It is the sound of a quill, like an urgent whisper. It is the sound of history being written at a heavy oak desk in a low-beamed cabin; the sound of a naval officer describing one of those mighty clashes that ruptured history between 1794 and 1815, when Europe was at war and when much of the conflict was fought at sea.

Perhaps you hear nothing but frantic scribbling as the events of the preceding days come out in a desperate, instinctive torrent, the account bursting with the adrenaline that has kept its author awake for hours, perhaps even days. For some the creation of a dispatch is partially cathartic, a means of internally reconciling the recent events as much as of informing a third party of its detail. Their words pour from the quill in an endless fountain of ink. The very act of writing eases the pressure on an overburdened mind.

Others take their time. They pause, listening to the snap of the canvas or the moans of the injured and dying; they glance out of the cabin window, perhaps seeing their reflection in the few panes that have not been destroyed by enemy gunfire. They pick up their quill. They lay it down again. They shift their weight; they rub their eyes. Do not see these dispatches as *faits accomplis*, but imagine them first as blank pieces of paper, as challenges posed to shattered minds. This, after all, is far more than a private letter and the author knows it: it is an opportunity to announce, broadcast and publicise. It is also an opportunity to mislead as well as to inform; to be disingenuous as much as to be frank. This type of author has his public audience in mind and wants every word to count. He writes a first draft and then adds sentences here and there to squeeze more information between the lines. He crosses out words or phrases that fail to capture his exact meaning. He is a man wrestling with words just as he has been wrestling so recently with the enemy. His finished dispatch will be concise, well considered and articulate.

Another type of man has no time at all for the task. He is uncomfortable at his desk and worried about the ongoing repairs to his ship, the lives of his men that still hang in the balance and the gathering clouds on the horizon. He is a seaman and a fighter but no bureaucrat. He finds it difficult to express himself on paper even though he has been commanding hundreds of men in fleets 50 strong for a lifetime. He will not shirk his task but his dispatch will be nothing but a newsflash, reticent and brief.

The sound of scribbling may even be interrupted by brief passages of speech because the dispatch is being dictated to a trusted secretary. The Admiral may be uncomfortable with a quill or conscious of his poor spelling and grammar. He may, of course, simply be unable to write. Are all of his fingers intact? Have the tendons in his forearm been severed by a splinter or sabre cut? Has the loss of blood left this fierce warrior too weak to hold a bird's feather?

However it is created, the dispatch will soon assume a life and a power of its own. It will not only be read by the Lords of the Admiralty, but also by the King and the Prime Minister; it will then be published in several newspapers and journals and will become the talk of London's coffee houses before it becomes the talk of Great Britain, Europe, America and the Colonies in the East and West Indies. The author is creating both a description of the battle and a piece of journalism for a knowledgeable, critical and powerful audience that is starved of, though fascinated by, the detail of naval battle. The Admiral's letter will influence perceptions of him and his navy on a global scale. And make no mistake of the power of these dispatches; there is no greater challenge to rational thought and behaviour than sudden and powerful news. Letters like these did not just transmit news but also relief, grief, excitement, energy and opportunity. They could make or break political fortunes, launch or wreck naval careers and directly affect the lives of men, women and children with only the most tenuous links to the battle. They stopped people sleeping, made them abandon their established routines and had them rushing around in a frantic whirl. In 1798, when Napoleon was loose in the Mediterranean with a vast army bound for an unknown destination, the First Lord of the Admiralty was under such stress that, when he finally received the news of Nelson's great victory at the Nile, he collapsed in a dead faint.

Once written, the letter is added to other documents, perhaps a list of dead or injured, or one describing the fates of the enemy ships, describing in shorthand the immediate physical effects of the battle. Sometimes an exhausted surgeon describes a crew's injuries and gives the names of the victims; sometimes a boatswain's report describes the damage to his ship and her stores; sometimes a captain describes how the battle unfolded several miles from the fleet flagship; sometimes a narrative has even been captured from the enemy.

Bundled together with the Admiral's letter, this sheaf of documents becomes 'the dispatches'. They are handed to a man worthy of the great responsibility, whose body is probably bruised and his uniform scuffed but whose eyes are bright with the promise of reward and acknowledgement of the great honour bestowed. This is a man who has been entrusted with a secret that could change the world. He will carry the dispatches home swiftly and surely and will be ready to elaborate on them if requested; remember, the written dispatches are only part of the story that will be told. He is the messenger, the winged Mercury of the all-powerful naval gods who fight out of sight but whose presence and influence are immense. He will sail for home in one of the fleet's swiftest ships, making port where the wind will allow. The dispatches will be sealed in their own envelopes and protected as a bundle with a canvas wrap, perhaps even locked in a wooden case or leather satchel, but the gist of their contents will spread even before his ship makes land. Fishing boats may come alongside for news as she makes her journey and a thousand eyes will watch her drop anchor. Sailors granted leave will pass their own news ashore; those left on board will gossip with harbour labourers and merchants who come to tend to the ship's needs.

Meanwhile our maritime Mercury will race as never before to London, perhaps on horseback, perhaps in a post-chaise pulled by a team of stamping, blowing beasts. If he landed at Falmouth, the westernmost of all English ports, his journey will take him more than 270 miles up winding river valleys and across wild moorland. Plymouth, though significantly farther up Channel, will still require several days of hard riding. If he lands at Portsmouth the journey will be much quicker though just as spectacular, through the Portsdown hills, past the Devil's Punch Bowl and along the great Hog's Back in the North Downs of Surrey. And if he brings news from the North Sea, he will ride from Great Yarmouth or Ipswich across the windswept flatlands of Suffolk and Essex.

He will arrive in the courtyard of the great Admiralty building, behind the masonry screen that protects it from Whitehall. If it is night time he will knock up the porter who will scurry off to raise the Secretary of the Admiralty. Perhaps the Secretary is asleep but, more likely, he is working through a mound of papers in the dim gleam of candlelight. The Secretary will be the first to break the seals, the first to read the dispatches. He will then rouse the First Lord from his chambers upstairs and find clerks to copy the letters and messengers to dispatch them. The news must reach the King at Windsor, the Prime Minister at Downing Street, the Government at Westminster and the Lord Mayor in the City who will pass the news on to the shipping interests at Lloyds Coffee House.

And then our Mercury's job is done. He finally rests, fuddled with the exhaustion and pain that come from his battle-bruises as much as from the shattering experience of several days in the saddle after a year or more at sea. He creeps to a sofa or bed, his legs bowed, his feet shuffling. Finally he sleeps while London goes mad. Mobs prowl the streets cheering, shouting and fighting for joy. Lamps are lit all over town. Guns are fired from the Tower as rumour becomes fact, as the whisper of victory becomes a cheer and as the elusive dream of national security moves closer to reality.

The Forgetting

The National Archives in leafy Kew house the written records of the Royal Navy in boxes of dusty letters on miles of shelves, meticulously organised and filed by generations of administrators. Here are thousands of logs from the navy's ships, hundreds of thousands of letters, reports, orders and instructions, intelligence, ship plans, weapons patents and crew lists. Together they describe the story of the Royal Navy from its earliest days as a permanent fighting force under Henry VIII to the present day. The archive, however, is missing some very important documents: the original dispatches sent to London after the most significant fleet victories of the French Revolutionary and Napoleonic Wars that were fought between 1793 and

1815. Copies of a handful of the letters survive in the relevant sections of the naval records in Kew, but the original dispatches, those actually sent to the Admiralty in the aftermath of those battles, have all been removed. There is no note saying so and no clue that the archives are missing some of the most significant documents in world history. If you searched for the original dispatches here, you would leave empty-handed, safe in the belief that they simply no longer existed.

Their absence dates back to 1821, the year that Napoleon died in exile and the naval-minded Prince of Wales was crowned King George IV. It was then that the Lords of the Admiralty ordered that all of the original dispatches, and even the envelopes that they came in, be gathered together. Nearly 40 years later, in 1859, a new generation of Lords of the Admiralty decided to use the dispatches to create a magnificent display of naval heritage. They ordered the letters to be bound in an immense volume, covered in the most exquisite royal blue velvet and decorated with elaborate silver-gilt onlays. Portraits of the victorious admirals were to be carefully interspersed between the original documents. Each letter would be mounted in the centre of a much larger page of heavy-gauge gilt-edged paper so that it could be read without being touched; their preservation was as much a priority as their display. The completed volume was presented to the nation to be admired as a jewel of British history. As a permanent reminder of the sacrifices and successes of our naval ancestors it would provide incontrovertible evidence of the seapower that formed the foundation of the growth and longevity of the British Empire.

Despite these lofty ambitions, at some stage in its life, this luxurious tome was removed from the British Museum, put into a coffin-like, satin-lined box with a clasped lid and stored in the bowels of the British Library. Only a handful of people know of its existence and only six scholars have referred to it in published work in the past 51 years.[1] It has, in effect, been hidden from the passing eyes of those for whom it was conceived. This is a tragedy for many aspects of naval history, not least because there are few more direct routes into the state of mind of a naval commander than through what he wrote in the immediate aftermath of a great battle. Howe, for example, collapsed after The Glorious First of June because he had not slept properly for more than a week; Nelson believed he was going to die from a severe head wound only hours before he wrote his Nile dispatch; and Collingwood stood catatonic in the aftermath of Trafalgar and his fellow sailors feared for his sanity. Edward Codrington, captain of the *Orion* at Trafalgar, made the telling point in his memoirs that 'The battle after all, as I warned my officers, is nothing compared with the fatigue, the anxiety, the distress of mind which succeeds.'[2] It was in exactly these moments of intense stress that admirals composed their letters. Character simply bled onto the paper, the authors' souls laid bare.

The dates that the dispatches were first gathered together and then bound are themselves significant. The year when they were first collated, 1821, was one of retrospection in the face of technological advance. It was the year in which a steam engine was adopted by the Royal Navy for the very first time in the paddle ship HMS *Comet*. The Atlantic had been first crossed by steamship only two years earlier and, just a year before, the exploding shell had first come into use. Naval warfare, and the shape of seapower, was unmistakably changing. It was also the year that George IV commissioned Joseph Turner to paint a companion piece to Philippe de Loutherbourg's magnificent 1794 canvas, *The Glorious First of June*, a composition which captures so beautifully the heroic splendour of the age of sail. Turner chose as his subject the moment of Nelson's death at Trafalgar in 1805 and the resultant painting was a fitting companion and comparable achievement to Loutherbourg's.

The year the dispatches were bound together in their magnificent velvet volume, 1859, was another significant date. A new generation of warships was now in the offing. That November, the French navy had launched *La Gloire*, the first iron-clad battleship, and generated wide-eyed panic in Britain. Were the French planning to invade? Could the Royal Navy cope with the threat posed by this new breed of fighting ship? In a political attempt to assuage such fears, the Prime Minister, Lord Palmerston, instigated a Royal Commission on the defence of the country. It reported in 1860 and argued strongly that Britain's maritime defences were wholly inadequate.

The British had been unable to match the speed of French technological innovation and in 1859 the Royal Navy had nothing in service to challenge *La Gloire*. In that year, however, the Admiralty ordered the construction of HMS *Warrior*, the Royal Navy's first iron-hulled and armour-plated warship. She mounted rifled, breech-loading guns and was powered by a steam engine that could drive her through the water at more than 14 knots. She was unlike anything anyone, anywhere, had ever seen. Everything about her was extraordinary and unsettling for a generation which had known an age without steam engines, iron hulls or exploding shells. Charles Dickens described her as 'A black vicious ugly customer as ever I saw, whale-like in size, and with as terrible a row of incisor teeth as ever closed on a French frigate.'

It was unclear what the future would hold but, in 1859, what *was* clear was that the age of wooden warships, driven by sail alone and firing solid shot, was over. Some believed that this transition also heralded the end of the supremacy of British seapower and naturally turned to the past for guidance. Those Lords of the Admiralty who recognised the value of these dispatches as an educational and inspirational tool for their own and for future generations must have long been turning in their graves. They had the generosity to look forward; we have not had the grace to look back.

The Content

The 1859 volume contains the original dispatches of the Battles of The Glorious First of June (1794), Groix (1795), St Vincent (1797), Camperdown (1797), The Nile (1798), Copenhagen (1801), Trafalgar (1805) and San Domingo (1806). They represent a period of military dominance that equals any in history. In the 22 years between the start of the wars with France in 1793 and their end in 1815, the British lost five 74-gun ships, one 54-gunner, another 50-gunner and 17 frigates. Not one British three-decked ship, the most prestigious type built for the navy, was captured or sunk. Her enemies, by contrast, lost 139 ships of the line, including nine three-decked First Rates and 229 frigates. These figures include all types of naval warfare, from single-ship actions to cutting-out operations. In fleet battles alone, Howe took or destroyed seven ships of the line at The Glorious First of June, even though he let several more defeated enemy ships escape; Alexander Hood, in the smallest of these victories, took three at L'Orient; Jervis, heavily outnumbered, took four at St Vincent; Duncan 11 at Camperdown; Nelson 13 at the Nile; Hyde Parker and Nelson 15 at Copenhagen; Nelson and Collingwood 22 at Trafalgar; and Duckworth five at San Domingo.* At *none* of those battles did the British lose a single ship of any description to the enemy.

---

* These prizes are all described in detail in Appendix II.

The Royal Navy had become a more effective instrument of war than at any time in its history. During the previous conflict, the War of American Independence (1775–83), it fought no less than 16 fleet battles. Of those, the most crushing British victories were achieved at the Saints in 1782, where four enemy ships were captured and two more destroyed in the aftermath, and at the Moonlight Battle in 1780, when four enemy ships were captured and one destroyed. The remaining 14 battles say very little at all about British naval skill in fleet battle. And if one steps back in time again to the Seven Years War fought between 1755 and 1762, only two fleet battles stand out. Four enemy ships were captured or destroyed at the Battle of Lagos in 1759 and seven more were wrested from the enemy at Quiberon Bay in the same year. One can, in fact, continue back *ad infinitum* without coming across any period that matches the battles fought in the 12 years from 1794 to 1806, it was a veritable golden age of British naval success.

Before we look at the letters in detail it is important to understand exactly what they describe and represent, and what they do not. They are the dispatches sent home after the most significant[3] large-scale British naval victories won in the years 1794–1806. The battles included do not span the entire duration of the Revolutionary and Napoleonic Wars; they begin in the second year of the Revolutionary War (1793–1802) and they finish nine years before the end of the Napoleonic War (1803–15). In the middle of this period, in 1802, there was a brief year of peace. These battles, therefore, occupy a period that begins well after the wars began and that ends well before they finished.

British naval failures of all kinds are excluded, as are battles with a more uncertain identity. We do not, for example, read about William Hotham's lethargy in the Mediterranean in 1795 in what Nelson described as a 'miserable action';[4] nor about Robert Calder's lack of conviction in the summer of 1805, which ended his career; nor, again, about Gambier's neglect at Basque Roads in 1809, another poor performance which ended a commanding officer's career.[5] British naval success in other disciplines including amphibious invasion, frigate action, blockade, coastal bombardment, convoy escort and, most importantly, fleet seizure, is also excluded.

The battles described are impressive victories but other naval operations were more significant successes. At Toulon in 1793, for example, the British inflicted the worst disaster of the entire period on the French navy when they seized the entire Mediterranean fleet without a shot being fired. Twenty-two ships of the line, eight frigates, numerous smaller craft and the whole Toulon arsenal and shipbuilding stores fell into British hands. Similarly, the Royal Navy defeated the Dutch at the Battle of Camperdown in 1797 but the Dutch navy actually suffered far more severely at Saldanha Bay in 1796 when, in the twin fleet surrenders, they lost a complete fleet of nine ships of the line without a shot being fired, and at the Texel in 1799, when they surrendered eight ships of the line, four frigates and a brig.

The same can be said of the Danes. Heavily though they were beaten in fleet battle at Copenhagen in 1801, it was their entire *navy* that was seized in 1807 after the bombardment of Copenhagen: no less than 18 ships of the line, 11 frigates, two smaller ships, two ship-sloops, seven brig-sloops, two brigs, one schooner and 26 gunboats were taken by the British and five more ships of the line and two more frigates were destroyed. As for the Russians, contact between their warships and the Royal Navy in the early 19th century was sporadic and unsatisfactory. However, when Napoleon retreated from Portugal, he abandoned a Russian fleet of nine ships of the line and a frigate in the Tagus, all of which were captured by the British without a shot being fired.

These blows, all achieved without the type of fleet battles described here, and all without significant damage to British ships or injury to British crews, did far more to alter the balance of European maritime power than any fleet battle. But fleet battles captured the public imagination. They were the bright flashpoints of drama and intensity that became central to the creation of national myths.

The battles covered in these dispatches represent only a tiny fraction of the astonishing variety of British naval activity, successful or otherwise, in this period. Fleet battle was, in fact, very rare. A sailor in the Royal Navy in 1805 served aboard one of 136 ships of the line or one of 160 cruisers; he was one of 114,012 sailors entered into British ships' books.[6] He could have been stationed in the North Sea, the English Channel, the Western Approaches, the eastern or western Mediterranean, the Windward or Leeward Islands in the Caribbean, the East Indies or somewhere off the coast of North America. He would have been very lucky indeed to witness one battle, let alone more. Officers, especially talented ones, were more likely to do so because they were more likely to be sent to trouble spots, and yet only three senior naval officers, Horatio Nelson, Cuthbert Collingwood and Edward Berry, witnessed as many as three fleet battles. Indeed, the battles featured in this book were all fought in different locations and all under different commanders.

In only one year, 1797, did two battles occur. The largest gap between major victories was from the Battle of Copenhagen in April 1801 to Trafalgar in October 1805,[7] a period of four years and six months, while 20 months elapsed between Groix (June 1795) and St Vincent (February 1797), and two years and eight months between the Nile (August 1798) and Copenhagen (April 1801). Contrary to the initial impression given by this collection, British fleet victory was therefore not the 'norm' in relation to other British naval activity. Most of the time the ships sat at anchor or patrolled windswept horizons in the constant toil of blockade. Sailors were far more likely to die of disease or shipwreck than they ever were in fleet battle. It has, in fact, been calculated that only 6.3 per cent of British sailors' deaths in this period were caused by enemy action, compared with 81.5 per cent by disease or accident and 12.2 per cent by shipwreck.[8] Life was dull. Sailors cleaned, painted and sewed. From a broad perspective it is possible to view the period as one of intense activity, but in terms of the day-to-day life of a sailor, living in the cold, dark decks of a man of war, these years were long, very long indeed.

When faced with so many magnificent triumphs, with one enemy after another falling like dominoes, it is also particularly important to remember that these victories were not inevitable. Confusion begat chaos; well-laid plans disintegrated; random acts tipped battle one way or another. Such was the nature of sailing warfare. The seascapes were shrouded in so much gunsmoke that, in the midst of battle, visibility beyond a few feet was all but impossible. Incidents of friendly fire were common. Wind, swell, tide and current, light and dark all ruined the best intentions. The ships' rigs were so vulnerable to damage that a single lucky shot could cripple any man of war. The sudden death or injury of a ship's officers could bring a crew to a standstill and the sudden death or injury of a large portion of the crew could bring their officers to a standstill: neither could work without the other and both were vulnerable.

Nor were concepts of honour and duty as rigid as we might expect. One of the greatest myths of the period derives from Nelson's famous signal, hoisted as the British fleet bore down on the French at Trafalgar: 'England expects that every man will do his duty'. For make no mistake, in these letters, interwoven with the over-powering narrative of British success, are examples of British officers who did not do their duty. Captain Anthony Molloy was court martialled after The Glorious First of June and never employed again; Vice-Admiral Bridport was strongly criticised within the navy for his failure to press his victory at Groix, even if the public saw him as a hero; Jervis was furious with the conduct of Sir Charles Thompson at the Battle of St Vincent; Captain John Williamson was dismissed after the Battle of Camperdown for failing to bring his ship into action; Nelson was deeply unimpressed with the behaviour of Captain Davidge Gould at the Nile, a battle which, more than any other, is so indelibly linked with the idea of a 'band of brothers'; Admiral Hyde Parker was blacklisted by the Admiralty and never employed again after the Battle of Copenhagen; Captain Edward Berry blazed away ineffectively at both Trafalgar and San Domingo and was quickly retired from the active list; even at Trafalgar several officers, including Nelson's third in command, Rear-Admiral the Earl of Northesk, performed 'notoriously ill'; and Vice-Admiral John Duckworth never received the hereditary peerage he expected after the Battle of San Domingo, an action that, if Duckworth had been doing his job, should never even have been fought.

The dispatches also illustrate, and sometimes disguise, significant personality clashes. We know that Nelson and James Saumarez, both highly ambitious, talented and successful men, riled each other; that Duckworth was not even on speaking terms with his flag captain, Richard Keats; that Collingwood loathed Howe's flag captain, Roger Curtis; and that Jervis referred to the 'notorious imbecility' of one of his captains, Charles Knowles.

The tale is hardly one of uninterrupted British success with each captain or flag-officer behaving as he should and without exception; it is far more complex than that. At times the alternative narrative is clear in these letters, with dismay and anger bubbling irresistibly to the surface; at others it is hidden. There is a lesson here: to understand the dispatches one must learn to discern what is *not* there as much as to read what *is*. Some of the omissions are quite extraordinary. Why did Howe name some captains for their good behaviour at The Glorious First of June but ignore others equally deserving? Why did Jervis fail to mention Nelson once after St Vincent, when he had just boarded and captured one enemy ship from another, an event unique in naval history? After the Nile, why did Nelson himself fail to mention or even to identify his second in command? Why did Hyde Parker fail to offer any detailed description of the engagement off Copenhagen and why did Nelson not mention his own cunning diplomacy which actually stopped the fighting? And why did Collingwood fail to mention the unmistakably poor behaviour of several captains during the Battle of Trafalgar? There are many mysteries here.

We shall see how courageous action did not guarantee public recognition nor even that the deserving officer would be 'mentioned in dispatches'. Personal relationships, politics and sheer luck all had to be negotiated first. A commanding officer might witness an act of courage but easily choose to ignore it in his dispatch in order to strike a calculated blow against a rival. He may have looked away at exactly the wrong moment and have missed just such a courageous act. He may simply have felt unable to comment on an act that he had not personally witnessed. It all rather depended on the man writing the dispatches, his relationship with his subordinates and the logistics of the battle. These dispatches have a much more multi-dimensional character than one might suspect.

The Commanders And Their Fleets

The main dispatches were written by eight different commanding officers: Admiral Richard Howe (First of June), Vice-Admiral Alexander Hood (Groix), Admiral John Jervis (St Vincent), Admiral Adam Duncan (Camperdown), Rear-Admiral Horatio Nelson (The Nile), Admiral Hyde Parker (Copenhagen), Vice-Admiral Cuthbert Collingwood (Trafalgar) and Vice-Admiral John Duckworth (San Domingo). Each of these admirals was unique in command experience, style and personality. To lump any two or three together would be to do each man, and each battle, a grave injustice, and here the original documents do lend a hand. It is impossible to read the dispatches without becoming rapidly and acutely aware of the personalities of those composing them, if only from their handwriting.

Have you ever written a letter on board a ship? You expect it to be a normal experience but it is not; it is extraordinarily different. On a pitching or rolling ship, writing can be disorientating. To bend low and focus on a single point is to render oneself vulnerable to the dizziness of sea-sickness while the movement of the desk can make the careful formation of letters a distinct challenge. The tails of letters can suddenly shoot off in unexpected directions; 'o's can easily become lozenge-shaped or even triangular; 'i's can become 'u's; 'v's can become 'n's; 'm's so easily transform into 'w's. Sometimes, however, the sea is so calm that one could be writing at a desk in a library.

The writing technology of the age also encouraged variety. If the nib of a quill is cut too thickly, the ink pools and dribbles; cut it too thinly and it fades and dries up mid-sentence, just as it always will with an old or brittle nib. Then, of course, there is the handwriting style of each man with which to contend. Sometimes we see the unmistakable flowing hand of a trained secretary. At others we have a series of sharp, fierce darts and jabs with the nib, the writing of an exhausted, stressed man. Some handwriting, Hyde Parker's in particular (p. 218), is barely legible, as frustrating for us now as it must have been for the staff of the Admiralty then. Imagine receiving a hugely significant letter and being unable to read it. Mode of expression and grammar also varied greatly. Most correspondents were long-winded, in the style of the time, but some, like Howe, were far more long-winded than others. Others, like Duckworth, even became entirely lost in their own rambling syntax. Most of the admirals' letters describing battles were published, either in the contemporary press or subsequently in collections of correspondence, but they were usually edited, occasionally heavily, to make them more readable and, in some cases, understandable.[9] To go back to the originals therefore offers us valuable insights into the men who wrote them. Some, like Nelson and Collingwood, were talented wordsmiths; others, like Duncan, were men of deeds and not words. Some, like Hyde Parker, were clearly not at home with the physical art of writing at all and some, like Howe and Duckworth, entirely lacked the mental agility and discipline required for concise self-expression in a written form. Their dispatches necessarily reflect their personalities. Howe's text is lengthy and rambling; St Vincent's careful and clear. Duncan's is rushed and excited; Nelson's evocative and generous. Hyde Parker's is vague and uninformative; Collingwood's sombre and dignified and Duckworth's energetic and unctuous. Only the closing of their letters follows any standard form: all end with the common 'Your obedient and humble servant', although some admirals adopt a particularly grovelling or self-satisfied tone and are careful to make it clear that they are 'the most obedient' or 'very humble'.

The enemy, of course, varied. The British fought the French alone in only four of the eight battles in this period, those of The Glorious First of June, Groix, The Nile and San Domingo. They also fought the Spanish, alone at St Vincent and allied with the French at Trafalgar, the Dutch at Camperdown and the

Danes at Copenhagen. Both the Spanish and the Dutch changed sides during the period, the Spanish twice. The ships varied too. These wars involved a continuing process of navy-building and fighting. Fleets were never homogenous, comprising warships all built at the same time and to the same design, but were collections of ships, some old and some new, some small for their rate and some large. HMS *Victory* is the best known of all of the British warships but she also provides one of the best examples of career longevity. She is most famous for being Nelson's flagship at Trafalgar, but she was actually launched in 1765, forty years previously. She had served as Vice-Admiral Augustus Keppel's flagship at the Battle of Ushant in 1778 during the War of American Independence, and as Rear-Admiral Richard Kempenfelt's flagship later in the same war. She then served as Admiral John Jervis's flagship at the Battle of St Vincent in 1797. By the time that she fought at Trafalgar, therefore, she was a veteran of the Royal Navy. In fact, by 1805, many of the newly constructed Second Rates, such as HMS *Temeraire*, were of a similar size to, and some even larger than, elderly First Rates like *Victory*, while the newest generation of First Rates were significantly larger still. There was no British First Rate in the fleet at the last of these battles, San Domingo in 1806, but there was the very latest incarnation of the very largest French First Rates, *L'Impérial*. Her displacement was over a third or 787 tons greater than *Victory's*, the difference in size being equivalent to the displacement of a good-sized 32-gun frigate. *L'Impérial* was also the first three-decker to mount 18-pounder cannon on her top deck; *Victory* was only built for 12-pounders. The weight of broadside from her upper deck was nearly 50 per cent larger than *Victory's* upper deck and her total weight of broadside was larger by nearly a third. However, the ships of every nation had other individual characteristics that we must add to this variety in age, size and power. French ships were large and swift, Spanish large and beautiful, Dutch small with shallow draughts and British short and stout. Moreover, each nation's fleet comprised both ships it had built itself and ships it had captured from others.

The location of service of each ship depended on the reputation of the station, the type of service for which it was intended and the resources available. For the Royal Navy the most high-status station was the Mediterranean. The climate was good, there was a deep pool of potential prizes and there were fine resources for ship repair and maintenance at Gibraltar. The Caribbean had a similar reputation, but sickness was a real problem at certain times of year and the infrastructure was not as good as the Mediterranean. The distance from home and the constant cruising to protect or attack trade also meant that First Rate warships were rarely used as flagships in the Caribbean in the way that they were in the Channel or Mediterranean fleets. The North Sea command was the poor relation. Yarmouth was cold and windy and the ships sent there were usually elderly or poor sailers.

We therefore see a significant variety in the fleets that fought these battles. At The Glorious First of June we have the powerful Channel fleet strengthened throughout the line by huge First Rate warships; at Camperdown we have a fleet scratched together from small, elderly warships and converted Indiamen; at the Nile we have a crack squadron of beautifully maintained 74-gunners; and at Trafalgar we have a combination of the Mediterranean fleet, the Channel fleet and several ships which, if they had not recently been repaired through a novel strengthening method, would have been unserviceable wrecks.

The Demands Of Seapower

Although these powerful ships were built to fight, it is wrong to assume that this was always their purpose. Naval strategy shifted with the tides of war. At The Glorious First of June, the French Admiral Villaret's task was to lure the British away from a French grain convoy that the British had intended to seize; Admiral Córdóba's fleet, when caught off St Vincent by Jervis, was at sea to protect four ships laden with mercury; Napoleon's fleet, destroyed by Nelson at the Nile, was there to transport and supply his army; in 1806 Rear-Admiral Leissègues' fleet was in the Caribbean because it had brought troops to reinforce the beleaguered French forces on San Domingo and then had instructions to raid British trade. The very last thing that any of these fleets wanted to do was to fight the British.

Every battle was characterised by its own strategic, tactical and logistical ingredients. Some of these dispatches describe ponderous formal fleet actions in which each side was aware of the other's presence and was willing to fight. Others record dramatic chase actions in which one fleet was surprised and made every exertion to get away while the other strained every muscle to prevent their flight. There are fleet battles in mid-ocean and others in confined coastal waters; battles fought in daylight and others at night; battles involving merchant convoys and treasure ships; battles against single enemies and battles against allied fleets. There are battles in cold water, in freezing rain over iron-grey sea and battles in a tropical haze; battles fought under full sail and battles fought at anchor; battles fought at close range and others at extreme range; and battles fought against monstrous First Rates, against whippy frigates, against immobile blockships, against stout 74-gunners and against powerful bomb vessels.

The dispatches do share certain characteristics, however. As a rule they fail to reveal the human experience of naval warfare. They imply, but do not describe, pain and fear. They do not bring to life the realities of a man falling to the deck with his bones sticking out through the skin of his leg or of men's arms evaporating in a mist of gristle or their skin melting off their skulls. Nor do they mention the smell of shit as dying men voided their bowels as their lives slipped away, the pervading stench of beer that soaked the decks from shattered barrels or the reek of burned gunpowder that hung thick in the air. Some witnesses who sat down and pondered their experience later revelled in this sort of detail. One who fought at St Vincent subsequently described a defeated enemy ship 'full of dead bodies, some with their heads off, and others both their legs and arms off, and the rest knocked all to pieces, and their entrails all about, and blood running so thick we could not walk the decks in parts without going over our shoes in human blood.'[10] The official dispatches, written in the immediate aftermath of battle by admirals and captains, are not like that. They are about the business of war, though there is something chilling in that. They are written by men who are hardened to its realities to other men who are also hardened to those realities and whose imaginations are restrained by the demands of their task.

By the time that the official dispatches arrived, rumour of battle had usually reached London, in at least one case from a smuggler.[11] However, the Lords of the Admiralty needed solid information upon which they could act and prepare for the logistics of receiving a battle-damaged fleet crammed with thousands of prisoners and with their own injured and dying sailors. Hospitals and prisons had to be made ready for the men and drydocks for the ships. Vast quantities of naval stores would be needed to repair masts, hulls and sails; even sailors' clothing and bedding had to be replaced when so much was lost or destroyed in the chaos of battle. The overall war strategy then had to be considered. To what extent had the enemy been beaten? Did their fleet still pose a threat? Was the way now open for British amphibious operations or invasion?

These letters showcase how the Admiralty first heard of the actions, when the facts were still raw, stripped of any concept of glory and burdened with a business-like indifference. They are important in their own right, but they are only one type of account. They paint some aspects of the battle in glorious colour and leave others in the darkest shade. Each letter is a piece from a jigsaw puzzle, valuable on its own but also powerfully suggestive of what is absent. We have here letters from flag-officers, captains and petty officers but nothing from anyone else aboard; nothing from the people who formed the majority of a ship's company, the seamen, landsmen, artisans, marines, servants, children and women. Nor do we have the idealised and allegorical compositions of journalists, artists, poets and playwrights that helped form and then sustain the national myths that grew up around the battles. The dispatches are the evidence of historical reason, not of historical romance.

Another of the characteristics that the dispatches share is, surprisingly, inaccuracy. The letters represent the first attempts to write historical narratives of the battles when their authors were restricted in their access to descriptions from different perspectives. Battles were fought over vast areas of sea and were shrouded in smoke. They were also fought over long periods, sometimes of several days. It would be impossible for an admiral to know in detail what had happened all the time and at every location. Even when the action was right in front of him he could easily get things wrong. Ships are frequently misidentified. Casualty figures are also very fluid. The figures given here are not accurate, nor are they meant to be accurate for the entire action. They are a snapshot of a shocked and recovering fleet at a given moment. Men who are listed as injured later died, while some who were listed as dead were merely lost and later found. In almost every instance the casualty figures given in these dispatches are not the figures that are now generally accepted.

For all of these reasons, it does not necessarily follow that these documents are accurate just because they were written by men who witnessed and took part in the action. Indeed, the opposite is often the case; the fact that they took part necessarily renders their testimony flawed. It is one of the most important lessons that a naval historian can learn.

The Navy And The Nation

To understand the full impact of these dispatches one must first consider the position and reputation of the Royal Navy within its contemporary society because this has a direct bearing on why the dispatches were so revered and later collated, preserved and presented. The letters must be understood from the perspective of the public who so avidly consumed them.

There is no equivalent volume of army dispatches, and the collection was important to Britain because it described *naval* victories. Britain has always had a special relationship with the sea and with her navy. As an island nation, her security and economic health rely on an impossible dream: the 'control' of the sea. But the world's oceans are too large to control, even for the largest and most modern navy, and everything was twice as difficult in the age of sail. It was all very well trying to keep the enemy in port but no blockade was ever perfect. In fact, most of the battles in this book were fought because the enemy had eluded a blockading force. Howe was blown deep into the Atlantic by a gale in the late spring of 1794 which allowed the French fleet under Villaret to leave Brest; in 1797 the Dutch escaped the Texel when Duncan's fleet was back in Yarmouth; in 1798 Napoleon escaped Toulon unnoticed because Nelson had been blown off station; in 1806 Leissègues left Brest when the British blockaders were withdrawn to Torbay in poor weather. In a curious way, therefore, most of the opportunities for the British successes featured in this book were created by British naval failure, by her inability to control the sea, even after repeated victories.

The dispatches themselves emphasise this point, particularly those relating to the last and least well-known of the battles, San Domingo in 1806. So many assume that Britain achieved absolute 'control' of the sea after Trafalgar in 1805, but that, of course, is nonsense. The entire Brest fleet took no part at all in the Trafalgar campaign, there was another unscathed squadron in Rochefort and the British were unable to keep either in port. Just a few months after Trafalgar, French naval squadrons threatening the security of British interests in the Caribbean and East Indies led to the Battle of San Domingo.

Seapower and sea control were therefore never absolute, even after all of these victories. Fighting against this continuous threat, the Royal Navy was directly and constantly associated with notions of wealth and liberty, powerful indeed for a nation whose lifeblood was mercantilism. The army, by contrast, was burdened with a reputation for tyranny. There was no standing police force in the 1790s and the common domestic experience of the army was as a tool for crowd control. The army was also intimately associated with absolutist government and the imposition of alien rule, a reputation gained more than a century before in the English Civil War and Cromwell's subsequent military dictatorship. Its campaigns on foreign soil, deep in the heart of Europe, usually thousands of miles from British territory, did nothing to amend that reputation.

The army was therefore feared as much as the navy was loved, something neatly summed up in an article in the *St. James's Chronicle,* one of the popular London papers of the time, shortly after The Glorious First of June in 1794.

> 'The extacy of joy displayed by the public on receiving the news of Lord Howe's glorious victory, proves how much more Britons are delighted by success at sea than on land. The sea is our protecting element, and as long as *Britannia rules the waves* nothing can hurt us. A victory at sea must ever give us more heart-felt pleasure than twenty victories on the Continent.'[12]

The naval dispatches therefore carried news that was interpreted in terms of financial, personal and national security. Naval battles were celebrated for preserving the *status quo,* not for expanding the empire: there is something of the Battle of Britain about them all.

The Recipients

We must also be careful to consider the Secretaries of the Admiralty, the individual men to whom the dispatches were addressed. The contact point between the Admiralty Board and serving naval officers, they were men of immense knowledge and experience whose devotion to the service was as great as any who sailed the ships. Their renowned longevity was one of the key factors in the consistency of British seapower from the mid-17th century onwards. Although Samuel Pepys is often remembered as the most famous

Secretary of the Admiralty, many more wielded greater influence for far longer. Josiah Burchett, once a clerk to Pepys, served 28 Admiralty Boards over a career spanning 48 years; Philip Stephens was Admiral George Anson's secretary and then enjoyed 24 years as an administrator for the Navy Office and the Admiralty *before* he became Secretary of the Admiralty, a post he then held for 32 years; and Thomas Corbett served in various roles within the Admiralty for 27 years before he became Secretary.

In the century before the first of these battles, only four men held the post of Secretary of the Admiralty. There followed something of a flurry; as many Secretaries of the Admiralty served in the 12 years of these battles between June 1794 and February 1806 as had served in the 53 years between 1742 and 1795. Philip Stephens was the man in possession when Howe wrote the first of these dispatches in June 1794. He was replaced shortly afterwards, in March 1795, by Evan Nepean who served as Secretary for the next nine years. The dispatches of five of the eight battles, therefore, were first seen and dealt with by Nepean. He was then replaced in January 1804 by William Marsden, the incumbent when news of Trafalgar and San Domingo reached London. Each of these talented men lived fascinating lives in their own right, which I have sketched in an Appendix (p. 342).

The Secretaries' professional endurance was extraordinary by any standard. They worked themselves into the ground, frequently to the point of illness, to ensure that the British naval machine continued to function. These men may not have stood on a quarterdeck to brave a hail of grape shot but they risked the death of 1,000 paper cuts. It is telling that, when Lieutenant John Lapenotiere arrived at the Admiralty with the Trafalgar dispatches at 1.00 a.m. on 6 November, William Marsden was awake and working. Three months later, when Duckworth's dispatch arrived, Marsden wrote:

'I had a terrible day of it – was knocked up at three o'clock in the morning, when I had got about an hour-and-half's sleep, called up Mr Grey at four, having by that time arranged and docketed my papers, and drawn out a bulletin. I then worked till seven, and lay down in hopes of getting a little sleep – but it would not do; so I returned to the office, and worked there till Mr Grey's dinner was ready'.[13]

And these men were valued; from 1800 the Secretary received *double* the pay of the First Lord. A contemporary noted of the Admiralty Secretary:

> 'Whosoever cons the ship of the Admiralty, the Secretary is always at the helm. He knows all the reaches, buoys and shelves of the river of Parliament, and knows how to steer clear of them all. He is the spring that moves the clockwork of the whole Board, the oracle that is to be consulted on all occasions: he sits at the Board behind a great periwig, peeping out of it like a rat out of a butter firkin'[14]

A proprietorial presence still hovers rather menacingly over the dispatches. Now they are public documents but then they were private letters. They are addressed not to the Lords of the Admiralty, the Government, the King or the country but to a single man, to Philip Stephens, to Evan Nepean or to William Marsden.

One of the great paradoxes of the dispatches, therefore, is that they are private documents concerning matters of great public moment. All three Secretaries had

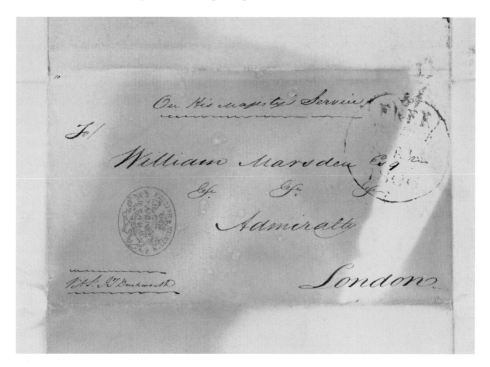

The dispatches are personally addressed to the Secretaries of the Admiralty.

The bottom left-hand corner has been folded over and the Board's decision summarized.

a habit of folding over the bottom left-hand corner where they would scribble a reminder of the Admiralty Board's decision[15] and Nepean 'marked' the letters with innumerable ticks, like a manic school teacher.

Marsden, by comparison, was remarkably restrained. The Trafalgar dispatches he received are almost unmarked, but those describing San Domingo are decorated with small ticks though sparingly, as if he was embarrassed that he had begun to mimic his illustrious predecessor.

To help them exercise their duty the Secretaries had their own private secretaries, messengers and a body of clerks. The navy that these men administered with parchment and quill was one of the largest and most complex organisations ever to have existed. The figures from a single ship alone are impressive. Consider a

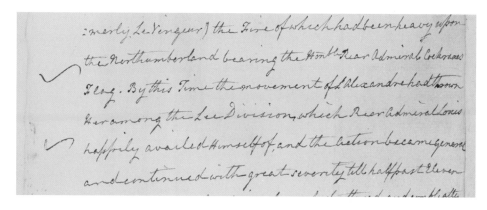

Nepean ticks relevant passages in this letter from Admiral Jervis.

74-gunner, a two-decked Third Rate warship, the backbone of most fleets during this period. She was fast and manoeuvrable but still sufficiently strong to stand in line of battle and hold her own against the leviathans of the age of sail, the three-decked First Rates of 100–130 guns. That 74-gunner contained a crew of more than 600 men and 1,200 tons of food. Cows, pigs, goats, sheep and fowl of numerous types berthed alongside the men. She was propelled by sails that blocked out two acres of sky and those sails were worked by 25 *miles* of rigging. Her 74 guns produced more firepower than all of Napoleon's artillery at the Battle of Austerlitz. And that was just *one* relatively small ship. Some of the largest had crews of 1,200 men or more and displaced at least 3,000 tons or roughly twice as much as a standard 74-gunner of the 1790s. Now consider a fleet of warships. At Trafalgar in 1805 we know that the British fleet consisted of approximately 17,000 men in 27 ships mounting 2,148 cannon. The combined Franco-Spanish fleet was larger still, with some 30,000 men in 33 ships mounting 2,632 guns. Now consider an entire navy. In 1795 the Royal Navy consisted of 123 ships of the line and 160 cruisers manned by 99,608 men. A year later the size of the navy exceeded 100,000 for the first time, and by 1806, when the last of these battles was fought, the total had reached 122,860. To maintain that force in 1795 the British Parliament voted £7,806,169, which had risen to £15,864,341 by 1806.

To see just one fleet of sailing warships come over the horizon under full sail, their canvas wings rising up as if from out of the very ocean's depths, was to witness one of humanity's greatest engineering and administrative achievements. To see two such fleets together, in a small area of sea room, one intent on destroying the other, was to witness the tension of human drama at its zenith. To witness, and survive, the subsequent battle was an experience that could damage men's souls as surely as the flying splinters could break their bones. The Lords of the Admiralty knew the power of these letters when they collected them together; and they knew that they must be shared. Now, for the first time, we can give them the audience that they deserve.

A Note On The Transcriptions

Considerations of space make it impossible to reproduce a transcription of every dispatch in the collection, although the majority are included here. I thoroughly encourage any reader to go back to the original and discover the volume in its entirety. It can be ordered through the Manuscript Department of the British Library, quoting ref: Add. MSS. 23207.

For reasons of economy I have excluded the dispatch relating to Lord Bridport's victory off Groix in June 1795. Bridport's original letter docs survive in good condition although it has none of the accompanying material that can be found in the other battles' dispatches. It did not therefore warrant a chapter of its own. Nonetheless the fact that Bridport's dispatch was included in the original collection, when James Saumarez's action of July 1801 was not, remains an interesting talking point and an important aspect of the collection's identity.

Spellings in the years 1794–1806 were not yet firm and formalised, nor were capitalisation and punctuation. Nelson, for example, wrote almost without punctuation, his text decorated with random capital letters which were his favourite way of emphasising words. Since it seems an abrupt break in continuity to call attention to such contemporary usages with a [sic], this device has been employed only in the most extraordinary circumstances.

Small omissions, where text is irrelevant, are marked by …

Some letters are truncated down one side where they have been trimmed and the missing letters or words have had to be inferred. Significant inclusions have been italicised.

The result is intended to keep the letters as close as possible to the original.

A glossary is included to help with the technical terms.

The Glorious First of June
Le Combat de Prairial

1 June 1794

'The Commander of a Fleet ... is unavoidably so confined in his
view ... as to be little capable of rendering personal testimony'

Admiral Richard Howe, 6 June 1794

AT A GLANCE

DATE:
1 June 1794

NAVIES INVOLVED:
British and French

COMMANDING OFFICERS:
Admiral Earl Howe and Rear-Admiral Villaret-Joyeuse

FLEET SIZES:
British, 25 ships of the line; French, 26 ships of the line

TIME OF DAY:
0915–1315, and sporadically to 1430

LOCATION:
400 nautical miles south west of Ushant
44° 26′58.38″N 13° 03′ 26.81″W

WEATHER:
Fresh breeze at south by west; moderate swell

RESULT:
6 French ships captured, 1 sunk

CASUALTIES:
(including battles on 28–29 May): British, 1,098; French, c. 2,654

BRITISH COURT MARTIALS:
Captain Molloy (at his request); dismissed from
command of the *Caesar*

DISPATCHES CARRIED HOME BY:
Captain Roger Curtis, Howe's flag captain

The Banner

My favourite piece of maritime heritage from the age of sail is a flag, a great silk-tasselled banner in the collection of the National Maritime Museum in Greenwich. Embroidered in gold thread in its centre is the chilling exhortation: '*Marins La Republique Ou La Mort*' – or 'Sailors The Republic or Death' (fig. 2). It was flown aboard *L'America*, a French warship which fought and was captured by the British at The Glorious First of June. It is a special object because it is so powerful; it says a great deal about the period in which it was created and about the day on which it was captured.

The words speak of a foreign country urging its sailors to fight to the death for an elusive idea. This battle was not fought over gold or for the territorial ambitions of a distant king but for the people and by the people. The flag is not addressed to officers but to 'sailors', a word deliberately chosen because it encompassed everyone aboard ship. An admiral was a sailor in the same way that a powder-monkey was a sailor; to win they all had to fight, even if it was in different ways. The words scream energy and commitment because they refer to a Republic that already existed in an age when republics were forged only in misery and fire. This is not an exhortation to create a republic but to fight on behalf of an existing republic. The banner tells of risks taken and of battles already won. It thus points to the future by recalling the past, the very essence of all history, but its message is especially merciless. There is more than a hint of double-talk about its apparently simple expression. On the one hand, it suggests that French sailors were expected to fight and to die for their cause; on the other it implies that any French sailor who did not fight with sufficient commitment would be killed – by his own side. There is no doubt that the purpose of this simple order is to threaten as much as it is to encourage.

The colour, feel and texture of the flag are also special. It can now only be viewed in the unreal stillness of an archival room but it is still possible to imagine this mighty banner curling in the wind, wrapping around a giant staff carried high by a chosen standard bearer. Its silky look and imagined movement bring to mind the multi-sensory nature of fleet battle where scarlet uniforms and shining silver belt buckles could be glimpsed through smoke which stung the eyes and choked the lungs; where sea spray ran down sailors' faces like tears and the force of explosions was so great that they were as much felt as heard. In all this confusion, the banner was as much a specific rallying point as a general exhortation to unite in a single purpose. We know that it belonged to the boarding division of *L'America* and one can imagine the sailors hustling together and brandishing short pikes and hand axes, the thrusting and hacking weapons that could be used in a crowd where there was little space to swing a sword.

The banner is utterly compelling. It is a powerful reminder of just how alien the period is generally, as much as it is a reminder of how alien 1794 was particularly. The French Republic, only two years old, was in the grip of the Terror, ruled through the threat of the guillotine by Maximillian Robespierre and his Jacobin colleagues of the Committee of Public Safety. All French sailors – officers, men and boys – were as terrified of being executed by their political masters as they were of being killed by the enemy. These unique circumstances led to a fleet battle unlike any that had ever been fought and one which would soon become renowned as the hardest fought battle of the age of sail.

The Extremists

The British thought that the French Revolution was rather a good idea until the French killed their King. In 1789, the year that the Bastille fell, the Revolution was praised by the British Ambassador in Paris and the House of Commons proposed a 'day of thanksgiving for the French Revolution'.[1] A popular poem even celebrated the new-found freedom of the old enemy.

> There is not an English heart that would not leap
> That ye were fallen at last, to know
> That even our enemies, so oft employed
> In forging chains for us, themselves were free.[2]

This all changed in January 1793 when a man called Citoyen [Citizen] Louis Capet was marched to a scaffold in the centre of Paris where his head was roughly shaved and he was strapped to a horizontal wooden board. That board was then pushed forward so that the nape of his neck was exposed as a thin target of ivory to a dark blade that never missed. Drums rolled and the vast sea of heads that bobbed together in the Place de La Révolution stilled for a moment as the audience held its breath. Then those heads saw one other head fall into a waiting basket. It was the head of a man who had once been their king but who had been stripped of all signs and symbols of monarchy. For Citizen Louis Capet was none other than Louis Auguste de France, the 16th King Louis of France, the eighth King of the Bourbon dynasty, and the thirtieth king to have reigned in the 802 years since the foundation of the Capetian dynasty in AD 987.

It is well known that France during the Revolution was unrecognisable from France before the Revolution. It is less well known that 'The Revolution' can be divided into numerous periods, each of which has its own distinct cultural flavour. Even if one takes a very broad brush, there is the Revolution at the storming of the Bastille, the Revolution at the execution of Louis XVI, the Revolution under the Jacobins and the Revolution under the Directory. The battle that became known as The Glorious First of June was fought during the reign of the Jacobins, five years after the storming of the Bastille and more than a year after the execution of Louis.

The Jacobins were an unforgiving political faction that dominated French politics during a year of utter turmoil from 1793 that became known as the Reign of Terror. It was in this period that loyalty to the Revolution was strictly defined and the populace rigidly divided into its friends and foes. Enemies or, more accurately, those who were perceived as enemies swiftly found themselves under the iron blade of the guillotine, their last view of the world the bottom of a woven rush basket stained with blood. The Terror itself can be sub-divided into the First Terror of the summer of 1793 and the Second Terror of the summer of 1794, when everything accelerated into a crazy whirlwind of baseless prosecution and inequitable persecution. Over half of all the Terror's victims died in June and July 1794 alone and, in those same two months, more were executed in six weeks than in the previous 15 months.[3]

The fact that The Glorious First of June was fought at the very height of the Second Terror is a major factor in considering the 'enemy'. French society had been whipped into a frenzy of ideological fervour by the Jacobins in a bid to unite France against her enemies, both external and internal. The survival of the Revolution was threatened by foreign nations waging wars on her borders as surely as it was by civil war dissolving France's internal order and security. The revolutionaries had succeeded in removing the monarchy with an unprecedented vision of a fair society but they were now surrounded by enemies and were fighting for survival without international allies. The ancient European monarchies that surrounded France had been horrified by the execution of Louis XVI and had united in opposition to the Revolution. With the military strength of the young Republic too weak to attract or force alliances, the enemy that faced the Royal Navy in 1794 was the French navy alone.

That navy was, however, unlike any other navy that had ever been raised by France. The Revolution had affected all sections of French society and the navy had suffered particularly severely for its close association with the *ancien régime* and the aristocracy. Before the Revolution, naval officers were not only required to be aristocratic but to demonstrate descent from four generations of aristocracy. The navy, moreover, was closely associated with the personal ambitions and desires of the King. The ships were even named for the perceived qualities of Bourbon monarchy: *Foudroyant* (devastating or stunning), *Glorieux* (glorious or proud), *Magnanime* (magnanimous or noble), *Victorieux* (victorious or triumphant) and *Courageux* (brave).

The new leaders of the Revolution simply did not trust the navy, and its officer corps suffered an unforgiving purge. Many experienced officers were forced out and, while some were imprisoned and others executed, many more simply never returned to their ships.

Things were not made any easier in August 1793 when the French Mediterranean naval base and city of Toulon surrendered to Vice-Admiral Samuel Hood without a shot being fired. The Jacobins sensed base treachery on the part of their navy, when the real reasons for Toulon's surrender were far more complex. The Jacobin response was a witch-hunt for traitors that drove yet more experienced men out of the navy. By the winter of 1793 very few naval aristocrats remained confident that their transparent loyalty to the new regime would keep them safe. One who did, however, was Louis-Thomas, the Comte Villaret de Joyeuse. Not only an aristocrat, Villaret had even worked as a member of the King's guard. Nevertheless he was promoted to admiral when it became clear that he was one of only a handful of officers who commanded the respect of his men. During a widespread mutiny at Brest in the autumn of 1793, the crew of Villaret's ship was one of very few that retained its discipline.

For all of Villaret's social skills, however, he had no experience of commanding fleets in battle and his experience of fighting at sea in any format was limited to the command of a frigate in the East Indies during the War of American Independence. To make matters worse, his captains shared his inexperience. Only one of Villaret's captains or flag-officers had commanded a ship in fleet battle before. Of the three flag-officers in the Brest fleet, two, including Villaret himself, had recently been lieutenants and the third a sub-lieutenant. Three of the captains had been lieutenants, 11 had been sub-lieutenants, nine had been captains or even mates of merchant ships, one had been a boatswain, one a seaman and the remaining captain was so insignificant that he has left no trace of a previous career of any description in the written records.[4] Few officers of any rank had more than two years' experience of their post.

Another major area of concern was at the level of gunner. Before the Revolution, a corps of seamen gunners had trained men in the exacting arts of naval gunnery but this had been dissolved because of its members' suspect loyalties and the powerful position they commanded within the ships' crews. A potential source of mutiny had been removed but at the expense of gunnery skill. Thus not only did the French navy lack experienced officers, it also lacked experienced sailors to man the guns.

However, while they may have lacked experience, the resolve of the French sailors in Brest was stiffened in the spring of 1794 by judicious use of the guillotine. In the aftermath of the surrender of Toulon, Jeanbon Saint André, a member of the Committee for Public Safety, was sent to Brest to ensure that the Atlantic fleet did not capitulate in the same way as its Mediterranean counterpart. With the Atlantic fleet now all that France had left to defend her coasts, the stakes could not have been higher and Jeanbon acted accordingly. He transformed the dockyard into a hive of industry; he harangued and threatened sailors to respect officers; he urged and encouraged officers to respect their men; he repaired ships and he requisitioned martial supplies and men. In so doing, Jeanbon built a navy to defend his Republic.

The British, meanwhile, had a very limited idea of the impact of the Revolution on the French navy. They knew, at least, that the dockyard at Brest was buzzing with activity but they did not know that the quality of the service's manpower had suffered so badly. The French navy was rotten inside but Jeanbon had polished its skin until it gleamed. A significant distinguishing factor of this battle, therefore, was the unknown quality of the enemy that the British faced. The war was already two years old and there had been several frigate actions and one recent action between two small squadrons but, as yet, there had been no large fleet action. There had not, in fact, been a fleet action between the British and French for 11 years. The French had all fought bravely in the few small actions since the start of the war but fleet warfare demanded so much more. How would the enemy captains control their ships in relation to each other? How swiftly could they form a line of battle from a cruising formation? How well could they recover their cohesion if routed by a successful attack? How swiftly and competently could they manoeuvre their ships, either individually or as a fleet? All of this was crucial information if the British were to win a fleet battle, but it could only be ascertained and then used to advantage by a man of immense naval skill and experience. In the summer of 1794 there was no finer or more experienced British seaman than Richard Howe.

The Sea Dog

Howe was a difficult man to get to know and one's reaction to him rather depended on where and how one met him. His career spanned politics and the navy and his reputation in both worlds differed wildly. He served as Member of Parliament for Dartmouth for 25 years and had enjoyed a stint as Treasurer of the Navy before being honoured with the position of First Lord of the Admiralty in the peace that followed the War of American Independence. It was a notorious time of political faction and many politicians suffered from partisan bickering. Howe suffered particularly badly and was out of his depth in the cut and thrust of the vigorous, fluid politics of the 1780s. A decade later, when he returned to sea and took command of the Channel Fleet, such was his political reputation that several high-ranking officers openly refused to have anything to do with him. Vice-Admiral

John Jervis, the future victor of the Battle of St Vincent (fig. 5), determined to 'oppose him in everything'. The impact of Howe's political naivety seems to have been increased by an inability to encourage friendship. He was fiercely private and contemporaries variously described him as silent, morose, inaccessible, strange, awkward, shy, austere and cold. His portraits, and particularly that by John Singleton Copley, reveal a man with deep bags under his eyes, standing ever so slightly stooped as if weighed down by the burdens of high rank (fig. 3).

A line must be drawn, however, between Howe's political and naval lives. At sea, social skills were less of a concern for a man who could lead by example or who demonstrably cared for his crews, and Howe was undoubtedly both. For all of his awkwardness, which led the politician Horace Walpole to declare that he 'never made a friendship but at the mouth of a cannon',[5] Howe certainly could make friends at that cannon's mouth. His earliest biographer believed that the sailors' attachment to Howe was 'unexampled'. Their loyalty stemmed from his unmatched dedication to improving their living and working conditions and his famous courage, both of which were magnified by the length of his naval service. By 1794, he had served in the navy for 59 years, having joined as a nine-year-old boy. He was famed for firing the shots off Newfoundland that led to the capture of the French 64-gunner *Alcide* and began the Seven Years War at sea. He went on to distinguish himself in that war when he attacked a shore fortification off Rochefort with such ferocity and from such a close and perilous position that he drove the French from their guns, causing his enemy to wonder in amazement that 'something more than a man must be on board that ship'.[6] Howe then fought in the American War with great facility, regularly out-foxing and out-manoeuvring his French rivals in a cat-and-mouse game played off New York in 1778. In 1782 he again distinguished himself by escorting a fleet of vulnerable transports to the besieged fortress of Gibraltar, an operation executed under the guns of a powerful Franco-Spanish fleet. When his behaviour during that operation was questioned by a fellow naval officer, Captain John Hervey, Howe called Hervey out to a duel and his opponent backed down. Howe was not a man to be provoked.

By 1794, however, his time as an active naval officer had ended. He was 68 and suffered so badly from gout that he had tried to cure it by standing on a stingray, a well-known but nonetheless extreme cure. He was then forced out of retirement to command the Channel Fleet at the insistence of the King, who was certainly fond of Howe but was also severely restricted in his choice of flag-officers. Of those with fighting experience from the previous war, the War of American Independence, George Rodney, Richard Kempenfelt and George Darby were dead, Edward Hughes was fully retired and would be dead within a year and Samuel Hood, the obvious candidate, had already been posted to the Mediterranean. Howe, languishing in Bath to cure his ills, was summoned by the King and sent back to sea. How would the elderly, unwell and reluctant Howe fare against the youthful determination and inexperience of Villaret?

A major problem that Howe faced was the manning of his fleet. The traditional view of this period emphasises the difficulty with which the French fleet was manned in the chaos of revolution and under their archaic manning system, the *system de classes*, which required all men from the coastal provinces of France to serve one year in three, four or five, depending on the size of the province and the needs of the fleet. However the British system was also straining under the burden of war. The pick of the navy's men and ships had already sailed to the Mediterranean under Samuel Hood and Howe failed to make up the shortfall. Some of those raised were mere boys, many with no experience of ships, let alone of fighting. Rear-Admiral Thomas Pasley of the *Bellerophon* was furious that some of his marines were too young and weak even to carry a musket. When he eventually left Spithead to cruise in Biscay, all of Howe's ships, with the exception of one, the 98-gun *Glory*, were undermanned. The seven First and Second Rates of the fleet were 766 men short while the 18 Third Rate ships, those powerful 74-gun two-deckers that formed the backbone of the fleet, were no less than 1,629 men short. We also know that the British crews were not exercised at the guns or sails as systematically or as regularly as has long been assumed. Some ships, Howe's flagship being the best example, practised regularly in the days before the fleet left Spithead, but we know from their logs that nine of the fleet, that is just under a third, had either no practice or had practised just once when they left to face the French.

In comparison with the French captains, however, the British captains were highly experienced. All 23 had experience of fleet action, six of them more than four times. The most experienced had fought in three wars, the War of the Austrian Succession (1739–58), the Seven Years War (1756–63) and the War of American Independence (1775–83). Nine had fought at the most decisive actions of the previous 50 years, the two Battles of Finisterre (1747), the Battles of Lagos and Quiberon Bay (1759) and the Battle of the Saints (1782). For all that experience, however, Howe was still concerned about how they would react under gunfire. We know that he confided to a midshipman of his flagship that he would refuse any opportunity of action at night as he needed daylight 'to see how my own captains conduct themselves'.[7] His concern was based on a well-established tradition of British captains failing to do as their admiral ordered.

Nevertheless the British public bayed for, and expected, naval success. News of the activity in Brest flew across the Channel as surely as the rumours of butchery in the streets and entire families being carted off to the guillotine. The populace was terrified that the French would invade and pollute British society with their extremism and horror. And they placed their faith in the navy. The expectation heaped upon Howe and his fleet was not entirely justified by recent form, however. The navy had enjoyed convincing victories against the French at the Battle of the Saints in 1782 and at the Moonlight Battle of 1780 but they had been a full 12 and 14 years earlier respectively and were but two of the several battles fought during the War of American Independence. The rest of them had been either hard-fought draws or British losses. It had been during the war before that, the Seven Years' War, that British victory had first become regular, sustained and in any way 'expected'. And that war had ended in 1762, 32 years before Howe took charge of his fleet and set sail in May 1794 to meet the navy of the nascent French republic.

The Convoy

France had been starving since the early spring of 1794. In the previous year the Committee of Public Safety had launched a programme of enforced conscription to raise a vast army, intended to be some 750,000 strong. The young men who worked the fields now learned to work muskets; the carts that once carried crops now carried army victuals; and the horses that once worked the fields now pulled gun carriages. To make matters worse, spring was always a time of want. The year's supply of grain had been consumed and the barns lay empty, waiting for the new harvest.

The only solution was to import the necessary food. Failure to do so would increase internal disorder and threaten the survival of the Republic itself. The stakes could not have been higher. And so Robespierre looked for a trading partner and found one in America. The American colonies had recently won their independence from British rule with their own revolution and a significant portion of Americans, though by no means all, were sympathetic towards the French struggle. Although the Americans remained officially neutral in the conflict, the French found in them a willingness to trade.

Throughout April a vast convoy of French merchantmen gathered in Chesapeake Bay under the wings of an escorting force commanded by Rear-Admiral Pierre-Jean Vanstabel. When the convoy was ready to leave it consisted of no less than 156 ships, worth in total some £1.5 million. The ships' holds contained 67,000 barrels of flour, hides, bacon and salt-beef, 11,241 barrels of coffee and 7,163 barrels of sugar, cotton, cocoa, rice and indigo. There was so much to carry that even the warships loaded trade goods. None of this could be carried out in secret and soon the British came to hear of the convoy. It offered an extraordinary opportunity to weaken the French war machine by depriving it of vital foodstuffs and thus of threatening the political position of the tottering Robespierre. Its capture was considered by the British government to be 'an object of the most urgent importance to the success of the present war' and it was perfectly clear that the French would do everything in their power to protect it. The arrival of the convoy would therefore also provide an opportunity to bring the main French fleet to battle.

The British assault was two-pronged. To the south, deep into Biscay, sailed Rear-Admiral George Montagu with a squadron of six 74-gunners and three frigates. His orders were to find the convoy and return with it to Britain. Howe, meanwhile, was charged with preventing the French fleet from protecting the convoy and, if possible, destroying it. So, while Montagu headed south, Howe headed for Brest and sent fast frigates ahead to discover the location and strength of the French fleet. He found them in Brest but he was driven off station by a severe westerly wind. When he finally returned to the French coast, Brest harbour, so recently full of the clank and rattle of maritime industry, was empty except for a few sorry hulks too rotten to sail or too ill-equipped to fight. Villaret had seen Howe's frigates in Brest Roads as surely as the frigates had seen Villaret in Brest, and the Frenchman had quickly reached the conclusion that the British fleet was out in force. He had had no choice but to sail to protect his convoy.

Howe sailed west, hunting desperately for the French. Not only could they now protect their convoy but they could also overwhelm Montagu's far smaller squadron; it had become essential to intercept Villaret. Although initially three days behind, Howe soon began to find evidence of the French as he came across merchantmen who had seen them pass or others who had been captured by the French fleet and were being taken back to port as prizes of war. All were mopped up by the British and most burned so that Howe did not have to sacrifice any of his weakened warship crews to man the prizes. Combining intelligence of their rough location with his seaman's sense of where a fleet might be after three days in the extant sea and weather conditions, Howe began to sense Villaret's location. He headed north and then dramatically east after receiving new intelligence that he had already passed him. Villaret, meanwhile, had heard rumours of Howe's position and headed east to avoid contact. On 28 May 1794, therefore, we find both Howe and Villaret heading east along almost the same line of latitude, Montagu heading back to Plymouth having been unable to locate the convoy and Vanstabel rapidly closing from the west on both Villaret's and Howe's location.

The Dispatches

There are more dispatches for this battle than for any other and by some margin. No less than 147 pages of the 300-page volume are dedicated to the dispatches produced in the aftermath of 1 June. Three explanations suggest themselves. First, the battle was far longer than any other. Its name is actually misleading: The First of June was the third of three major actions fought over a five-day period. There were also significant clashes on both 28 and 29 May, both of which are described, together with the events of 30 and 31 May. Second is Howe's particular dispatch technique. As can be seen from his letter dated 2 June (p. 48), he was extremely reluctant to offer any opinion about the behaviour of British captains in those numerous areas of the several battles which he did not himself witness. To solve the problem he enclosed with his own dispatches a significant number of other reports, including lengthy dispatches from his subordinate flag-officers. The dispatches from The First of June are unique in this respect. No other battle is described in so many different accounts from so many different perspectives and in so many different ways. And third, there is Howe's work ethic. He was a man of immense industry, both as a sailor and as an administrator, and his work was always coloured by great professional pride and an eye for detail. He therefore sent to the Admiralty the documents that he would have liked to have read in their situation. And that meant everything.

Rear-Admiral G. Montagu to P. Stephens, 3 June 1794

This letter from George Montagu was the first hint that the much-anticipated battle with the French had finally happened. It was written aboard Montagu's flagship, the *Hector,* as she lay in Plymouth Sound on 3 June, two days after the main battle and a week after the two fleets' first contact. Montagu was in Plymouth because he had been forced to abandon his search for the convoy in Biscay and revictual his ships. So while news of the engagement was good news for the Admiralty, it was not good news for Montagu. If his estimate of the size of the French fleet, 30, was correct, then Howe's fleet of 26 would have been outnumbered and his force of six 74-gunners could have made all the difference. Had Montagu's decision to return home left his Admiral outnumbered in the face of the enemy?

The letter is typical of the way that news trickled through to the Admiralty. It is vague, comes third-hand and relates to only one part of an engagement that lasted several days. Montagu has not seen the battle, but has heard news of it from Captain Curzon of the *Pallas* who has, in turn, heard news of it from Captain Parker of the *Audacious*. Montagu has nothing at all to add to Curzon's account other than the fact that the enemy fleet consisted of 30 ships, which was wrong.[8] This letter has very little to say but, with the benefit of hindsight, it is particularly powerful because this rather loose report heralded such an extraordinary period of British victory. Indeed, when news first arrived, nothing was certain. At this early stage, ignorance grew faster than knowledge.

HECTOR IN PLYMOUTH SOUND 3ᴰ JUNE 1794

Sir,

Be pleased to mention to the Lords Commissioners of the Admiralty that His Majesty's Ship Pallas joined me this morning & that the Honble Captain Curzon reports having fell in last Evening off the Lizard with the Audacious belonging to the Fleet under the Command of the Earl Howe & that he had received from Captain Parker the Intelligence which I now transmit for the information of their Lordships, esteeming it of sufficient Importance to have it forwarded to you by Express. The Audacious is gone on for Portsmouth, the Wind being too scanty to allow of her fetching this port. I beg also to add to the Intelligence, that Captain Parker relates that the Enemy's Fleet consisted of Thirty Sail of the Line.

I am

  Sir

   Your most obedient humble servant

    Geo Montagu

PHILIP STEPHENS ESQ^ᴿ SECRETARY ADMIRALTY

Montagu enclosed Curzon's brief account of Parker's engagement, which made it clear that there had been a significant battle. He described an engagement fought 'in the closest manner' by the *Audacious*; a Frenchman's mizzen mast, main yard, main topsail yard and fore yard being shot out of the sky; a near-collision as the crippled Frenchman surged towards the *Audacious*; the *Audacious* soon being too crippled to control her movements; a desperate chase as the *Audacious* was discovered the next day by nine French warships; and finally a lucky escape through a fog bank. But the Admiralty had to wait until they received Parker's own description of the battle for the detailed account that they craved.

Capt. W. Parker to Philip Stephens, 3 June 1794

Parker begins his letter by describing the initial chase as Villaret drew the British fleet away from the anticipated arrival location of Vanstabel's convoy. Several British ships, including the *Audacious*, then engage the rearmost ship of the French fleet, the mighty First Rate *Révolutionnaire*. With a complement of 1,200 men and a battery of 110 guns, she was far larger than any ship in the British fleet and a monster compared with the Third Rate *Audacious*. The French ship withstood hours of battering before she was silenced but Parker reveals his uncertainty over her fate. Had she struck? His uncertainty was shared by the rest of the British ships nearby and the *Révolutionnaire* eventually escaped, unclaimed by any British warship. It was a major mistake and a reminder that the ultimate tally of seven ships captured or sunk in this battle could have been significantly better with this mighty three-decker added to the list.

The *Révolutionnaire* had fought well, however, and the *Audacious* was severely damaged and in great danger. The next morning nine Frenchmen bore down on her and her crew tried to bend the foresail and maintopsail and set several studding sails on their injured masts. They even had to hoist false colours to disguise themselves, a ruse which appears to have failed. Parker and his crew were extremely lucky that the Frenchmen chose only to engage at a distance before escaping.

Parker thanks his crew and makes particular note of the inexperience of some of his sailors. He is also careful to pass on the name of the ship they engaged, the *Révolutionnaire,* and he even refers to her previous name, the *Bretagne.* This highlights the French practice of re-naming their ships during the early years of the Revolution, erasing any reference to the fleet of the *ancien régime.* Such intelligence was of great value to the Admiralty and it serves as a reminder that the enemy now was not the enemy of old, but an entirely new breed of Frenchman.

His Majesty's ship Audacious
Plymouth Sound June 3ʳᴰ, 1794, In the Eve.

Sir,

I have the honour to acquaint you for their Lordships information that on the 28ᵗʰ ult. in the morning about 8 oclock, His Majesty's Fleet under the command of the Earl Howe, then in the Lattᵈ: 47" 33' N° Longᵈᵉ: 14" 10' West got sight of that of the Enemy.

The wind blew strong from the Southward and the Enemies Fleet consisting of about Thirty Two Sail directly to windwᵈ.

Every thing was done by His Majesty's Fleet per signals from the Earl Howe (preserving them in Order) to get up with the Enemy, who appear'd to be forming in order of Battle: but as I apprehend His Lordship consider'd their conduct began rather to indicate an intention of avoiding a general action; at fifty five minutes after One OClock, He directed a general Chace.

Twas just becoming dark when His Majesty's Ship under my Command arriv'd up with the Rear Ship of the Enemies Line; I immediately commenced a very Close Action which continued near Two hours, without intermission; never exceeding the distance of half a Cables length, but generally closer, and several times in the utmost difficulty to prevent falling on Board, which as his last effort to appearance, at about 10 oclock he attempted to effect, at this time his Mizzen Mast was gone by the Board, his Lower Yard and Main Top Sail Yard shot a way, his Fore Top Sail being full, (though flying out from the Top Sail Yard the Sheets being shot a way,) he fell a thwart our Bows, But we separated without being entangled, any time, he then directed his course before the wind, and to appearance pass'd through, a close a stern of the Ships in the Rear of our Line.

When the Enemy separated from athwart our Bows, the company of His Majesty's Ship under my command, gave three cheers from the Idea taken from the People quartered forward that his colours were struck; this I cannot take upon me to say, though think it likely from his situation obliging him to pass through or near to our line; But certain it is he was compleatly beaten, his fire slacken'd towards the latter part of the Action, and the last broadside, (the ship's sides almost touching each other) he sustain'd without returning more than the fire of two or three guns.

His Majesty's Ship under my command at the time we separated, lay with her Top Sails a back, (every brace, bowling; most of her standing, and all her running rigging shot away) in an unnavigable state, t'was some time before I could get her to wear, to run to Leeward of the French line, under cover of our own Ships, which by what I could judge by their Lights, were all pretty well up, and tolerably form'd.

This being effected, I turn'd all hands to the repairing our damages to get into readiness (if possible) to resume our station at day light.

The Rear of the French line had been engaged at a distance by Rear Admiral Pasley's Division, and some other ships that did not fetch so far to Windward, a considerable time before I arriv'd up with them; and this very Ship was engag'd by the Leviathan at some distance to leeward, the time I did.

The night being very dark I could form but little judgment of the situation of our fleet with respect to the French in point of distance, other, than not hearing any firing after our own ceas'd, I concluded they were scarcely far enough to Windward.

Soon after day light the next morning to our utmost chagrin and astonishment we discovered Nine Sail of the Enemies Ships about three Miles to Windward.

The Audacious then with her standing rigging but very indifferently stopper'd, her Fore Sail and Top Sails unbent, Main Top Sail in the Top in the act of bending, we put before the wind with the main and Fore Top mast stay sails only, ill set, from the sheet being shot a way; but it being Haze with rain and soon became thick, we for a time were cover'd from their view, and before, as I apprehend, they had form'd a judgment of what we were.

The greatest exertion was used by every Officer and Man in the ship to get the other Fore Sail and Main Top Sail Bent, the Fore Top mast being so badly wounded, the Fore Top sail was of but little moment, however the People brought the damag'd sail to the yard a gain though it could not be hoisted; But before we got the Fore Sail and Main Top Sail set, the haze clear'd off, and we soon discovered ourselves to be chaced by two of the Enemies Ships: at this period we saw the Ship we had engag'd without any mast standing and pass'd her at a bout a mile and a half Distance. The Ships coming up with us very fast our situation became very alarming, untill we got the Main Top Gallant Sail, Main Top M[ast] and Top Gallant Studding Sails set, when it was judged we nearly preserv'd our Distance, however from the Fore Mast being in a tolerable state of security, at half past nine we were about setting a lower studding sail, when three Sail that had been discover'd to the E' ward some time before viz two Ships and a Brig coming pretty near us we hoisted French colours.

The state of our Masts did not admit of making alteration in course, they observing our shatter'd state, and two Ships in chace of us, stood a thwart us boldly in fire, and shot were exchang'd, the one a Large Frigate and the other Two, Corvett's, But as We had so much Sail out, they fell a stern for a considerable time, at length the Frigate came within shot of us again and harrass'd us by a distant canonade upon the quarter upwards of an hour, but without doing us any material injury, we only firing some of our after Guns upon each Deck at her, she was observ'd to make a Signal to the Ships a stern and soon after viz a bout half-past 12 oclock with the two Corvett's haul'd her wind, and by its becoming hazey the whole were soon out of sight.

Having been chaced twenty four Leagues directly to Leeward, and the crippl'd state of the Bowsprit being such as judged impossible to stand if the ship was haul'd to the wind, I considered the endeavouring to find the fleet again, might put His Majestys Ship (in her defective state) to too much risque, and therefore judged it most advantagious for the Service to proceed to Port without loss of time to refit; which I hope may meet their Lordships approbation. I must beg you'l be pleased to represent to their Lordships, that the conduct of the lieutenants of His Majesty's Ship under my Command, during the Action, merits all the praise I can bestow upon them. As also that of Lieutenant Crofton of the 69th Regiment whose alertness and activity with his Men at Small Arms, in supporting the seamen arm'd to defend the Boarding (which occurr'd twice during the Action) gave me perfect satisfaction.

The conduct of my Ship's Company from the greater part of them never in His Majesty's Service before, and scarcely any ever in Action, exceeded every possible expectation: as also the soldiers of the 69th Regiment who were all young recruits a twelve month agoe when they were embark'd on board.

In fact the whole of my Ships Company Officers and Men in their different departments Behaved in a most exemplary manner.

Tis wonderfull after such an action that I have the happiness to say the whole number kill'd and wounded are but Twenty two, three were kill'd on the spot, one died soon after, and the life of two more is despair'd of.

The Captain and some of the Officers of a French Corvette which we took possession of and burnt a few mornings before by the Earl Howe's Order, view'd the Ship we had engag'd while passing her in the morning and were of opinion she is called Le Revolutionaire formerly the Bretagne.

In case their Lordships should have any enquiries to make further, I have dispatch'd Lieutenant Joseph Bingham my Senior Lieutenant on board with the charge of this letter who is a very excellent Officer, and an intelligent young Man, and I trust capable of giving every requisite information.

Sir

I am

Your Most Obedient

& most Humble Servant

Wm Parker

Philip Stephens Esqr.

Taken together, however, Montagu's and Parker's letters were nothing more than a tantalising promise of more to come. If one closes one's eyes to the subsequent decade of British success, Parker's letter is actually quite troubling. It describes nothing more than a skirmish between a few isolated ships and reveals a resolute enemy. There is also some suggestion of muddle in the minds of the British captains who had failed to secure a valuable prize. So many questions still remained. Had Howe achieved anything more on 28 May than the disabling of a single ship? It was also clear that the *Audacious* was severely damaged and only narrowly escaped capture. Had her experience been shared by other British ships? Had Howe secured the grain convoy or was the contact restricted to this skirmish? Which sailors lay in the darkness of the orlop decks under the knives of surgeons, squinting at pale lanterns swinging from the deck beams above while knives and saws separated muscle from bone, limbs from torsos? Which ships had been damaged, which captured, which sunk? Answers to these questions and to so many more came in Howe's first dispatch.

Admiral R. Howe to P. Stephens, 2 June 1794

This was the first official news of British naval victory in the Revolutionary War. The letter is written aboard the *Queen Charlotte* on 2 June, deep in the Atlantic a full 140 leagues, or 420 nautical miles, south west of Ushant. This anonymous location is the reason for the battle's curious name. Because there was no headland or bay nearby to identify it, it is named after a date.

The letter is a classic example of Howe's meandering style of expression: he gives the reader no idea of the battle's outcome until the third page. His elaborate prose does not reflect the way that his mind worked at sea. In command he was incisive; at his desk he was tortuous. Nelson once described a letter from Howe as 'a jumble of nonsense' but he also described Howe, and with some justification, as 'the first and greatest sea officer the world has ever produced'.[9] Howe was exhausted when he wrote this letter. When the fleets finally came together on 1 June, he had been awake for eight days, his only rest taken slumped in a chair behind a canvas screen in his cabin. At the end of the battle he had to be helped from the deck.

He sketches over the action of 28 May in one line, and there is no mention at all of the major action fought on the 29th or the two days of intermittent contact on 30 or 31 May. His description of the engagement on 1 June mentions his confrontation with the French flagship but otherwise is brief. Given that the letter was written so soon after the action, this comes as no surprise. Howe was not deliberately withholding information but simply had no idea what actually happened elsewhere. The result of the battle, however, is clear. Howe reports that seven ships were taken from the enemy, one of which, the *Vengeur*, sank. He also mentions the escape of 'two or three' dismasted ships at the end of the action, a failure that must be added to the escape of the beaten *Révolutionnaire* on 28 May.

THE CHARLOTTE AT SEA
2ᴰ JUNE 1794.
USHANT E ½ N 140 LEAGUES

 Sir

Thinking it may not be necessary to make a more particular report of my
proceedings with the Fleet for the present information of the Lords Commissioners
of the Admiralty I confine my communications chiefly in this dispatch, to the
Occurrences when in presence of the Enemy yesterday. –

Finding on my return off of Brest on the 19ᵗʰ past, that the French Fleet
had a few days before put to Sea; and receiving on the same evening, Advices
from Rear Admiral Montagu, Copies of which are herewith enclosed; I deemed
it requisite to endeavour to form a junction with the Rear Admiral as soon as
possible; and proceeded immediately for the Station on which he meant to wait for
the return of the Venus. –

But having gained very credible intelligence on the 21ˢᵗ of the same Month,
whereby I had reason to suppose the French Fleet was then but a few Leagues
farther to the Westward, the course before steered was altered accordingly. –

On the morning of the 28ᵗʰ the Enemy were discovered, far to Windward:
And partial Actions were engaged with them, that Evening and the next day. –

The Weather Gage having been obtained in the progress of the last mentioned day,
and the Fleet being in a situation for bringing the enemy to close Action the 1ˢᵗ instant,
the ships bore up together for that purpose, between 7 and 8 oClock in the Morning.

The French, their force consisting of twenty six Ships of the Line, opposed to
His Majesty's Fleet of twenty five, (the Audacious having parted Company with
the Sternmost Ship of the Enemys Line, captured in the Night of the 28ᵗʰ:) waited
for the Action, and sustained the attack, with their customary resolution. –

In less than an hour after the close Action commenced in the Centre, the French
Admiral engaged by the Queen Charlotte, crowded off: And was followed by most
of the Ships of his Van, in condition to carry Sail after him: Leaving with us, about

ten or twelve of his totally crippled or totally dismasted Ships, exclusive of one sunk in the Engagement. The Queen Charlotte had then lost her Fore Topmast; And the Main Topmast fell over the side very soon after. –

The greater number of the other Ships of the British Fleet, were at this time so much disabled or widely separated, and under such circumstances with respect to those Ships of the Enemy in a state for Action, and with which the firing was still continued, that two or three, even of their dismasted Ships attempting to get away under a Spritsail singly, or smaller Sail raised on the Stump of the Foremast, could not be detained. –

Seven remained in our possession, One of which however, sunk before the adequate assistance could be given to her crew: But many were saved.

The Brunswick having lost her Mizen Mast in the Action, and drifted to Leeward of the French retreating Ships, was obliged to put away large to the Northward from them. Not seeing her chaced by the Enemy in that predicament, I flatter myself she may arrive in safety at Plymouth. – All the other twenty four Ships of His Majesty's Fleet, reassembled later in the day: and I am preparing to return with them, as soon as the Captured Ships of the Enemy are secured, for Spithead. –

The material injury to His Majesty's Ships I understand, is confined principally to their Masts and Yards, which I conclude will be speedily replaced. –

I have not been yet able to collect regular Accounts of the Killed and Wounded in the different Ships. Captain Montagu is the only Officer of his Rank who fell in the Action. The Numbers of both description I hope will prove small, the nature of the Service considered: But I have the concern of being required to add on the same subject, that the Rear Admirals Bowyer and Pasley, and Captain Hutt of the Queen, have each had a Leg taken off. They are however (I have the satisfaction to hear) in a favorable state under those Misfortunes. – In the captured ships, the numbers of Killed and Wounded appear to be very considerable. –

Though I shall have on the subject of these different actions with the Enemy distinguished examples hereafter to report, I presume the determined bravery of the several Ranks of Officers, and the Ships Companies employed under my authority, will have been already sufficiently denoted by the effect of their spirited exertions.

And I trust I shall be excused for postponing the more detailed narrative of the other transactions of the Fleet thereon; for being communicated at a future opportunity: more especially as my first Captain Sir Roger Curtis, who is charged with this Dispatch, will be able to give the farther information the Lords Commissioners of the Admiralty may at this time require. — It is incumbent on me nevertheless now to add, that I am greatly indebted to him for his Councils as well as Conduct in every branch of my Official duties: And I have similar assistance in the late occurrences, to acknowledge of my second Captain Sir Andrew Douglas.

    I am with great consideration
        Sir
            Your most obedient Servant

                  Howe

    P.S.
The names and Force of the captured French Ships with the Fleet, is transmitted herewith.

PHILIP STEPHENS ESQR
&C &C &C

Admiral R. Howe to P. Stephens, 6 June 1794

Four days later Howe wrote to the Admiralty again, this time offering more detail of the major engagements fought on 28 and 29 May. He noted how the French seamanship was so poor on 28 May that they took several hours to form into line, valuable intelligence that suggested either that the French ships were undermanned or that they were crewed by inexperienced sailors or that the sailors were crippled by sickness, all of which, in fact, were true. Howe goes on to describe the action between Pasley's advance squadron, of which the *Audacious* (p. 43) was a part, and he mentions her Captain, William Parker, by name for his spirited conduct. Howe then admits to his ignorance of subsequent events as night fell, which is further exposed by his inaccurate claim that the *Révolutionnaire* struck to the *Audacious*.

The complex engagement on 29 May is then described in some detail and Howe devotes particular attention to his signal to pass through the enemy line, which could not be seen by the rest of the fleet. He is also careful to mention the conduct of the *Caesar*, commanded by Anthony Molloy, a man with a poor reputation. Molloy was in the van of the fleet and should have initiated Howe's intended manoeuvre, but his failure to act crippled Howe's tactical plan; Howe had no choice but to tack his flagship, the *Queen Charlotte*, and head for the enemy line himself. Howe's bold example was copied and three British ships cut through the French line.

Howe is also careful to mention several successful manoeuvres made by the enemy. These were significant. In contrast with the poor French seamanship implied earlier in his letter, these manoeuvres were complex, performed under the guns of the enemy and in very poor visibility. This was clear evidence of impressive French seamanship, but where did the truth lie? In the woolly incompetence of 28 May or in the skilful professionalism of 29 May? Which enemy were the British sailors fighting?

Howe finishes his letter by carefully refusing to mention the good conduct of any deserving captain or flag-officer. This ran against the grain of tradition but Howe argues that, because he was unable to see every ship in his fleet all of the time, he could not possibly comment on the behaviour of all of his captains. He therefore allowed them to speak for themselves and included several other reports along with his dispatch. This final paragraph created a world of trouble for Howe and his captains. The Admiralty and the public did not want to hear from the captains but from Howe; they wanted the Admiral to honour those who most deserved it. Howe was eventually forced to name those he considered to have been conspicuously brave and some of those captains who were not named took their absence from his list as a sign of displeasure. Among the latter was Cuthbert Collingwood, then Rear-Admiral George Bowyer's flag captain. Bowyer was injured early on and Collingwood commanded the *Barfleur* throughout the battle as if she were his own. He was so cross at being ignored by Howe that, when he was offered a medal for his subsequent gallantry at the Battle of Cape St Vincent in 1797, he refused it until he was given a medal for The First of June. The Admiralty swiftly caved in to his demands in a clear acknowledgement that Howe's list of gallants from 1794 was by no means comprehensive.

THE CHARLOTTE AT SEA
THE 6TH OF JUNE 1794

 Sir

In the Extract of the Journal herewith enclosed, the proceedings of the Fleet are stated from the time of leaving St Helens on the 2ᵈ of last Month, to that of the first discovery of the French Fleet on the 28ᵗʰ of the same. For the information of the Lords Commissioners of the Admiralty, I have now therefore to relate, the subsequent transactions not already communicated in my Dispatch of the 2ᵈ instant, to be delivered by my first Captain Sir Roger Curtis. –

Early in the morning of the 28ᵗʰ the Enemy were discovered by the advanced Frigates far distant on the Weather Bow. The Wind then fresh from the SbW – with a very rough sea. –

They came down for some time, in a loose Order: seemingly unapprized that they had the British Fleet in view. After hauling to the Wind when they came nearer, they were some hours before they could completely form in regular Order of Battle upon the Starboard Tack: The British Fleet continuing as before, in Order of Sailing. –

The time required for the Enemy to perfect their Disposition had facilitated the nearer approach of His Majesty's Fleet to them; And for the separately appointed and detached part of it, commanded by Rear Admiral Pasley, to be placed more advantageously for making an impression on their Rear. –

The Signals denoting that intention being made, the Rear Admiral near upon the close of Day, led his Division on with peculiar firmness, and attacked a three-decked Ship (the Revolutionaire) the Sternmost in the Enemys Line. –

Making known soon after that he had a Topmast disabled, assistance was directed to be given to him in that Situation. The quick approach of Night only allowed me to observe, that Lord Hugh Seymour (Conway) in the Leviathan, with equal good judgement and determined Courage, pushed up alongside of the three-decked French Ship: And was supported as it appeared, by Captain William Parker of the Audacious, in a most spirited manner. –

The darkness which now prevailed, did not admit of my making any more accurate observations on the conduct of those Ships and others concerned in the same Service. But I have since learnt, that the Leviathan stretched on farther ahead for bringing the second Ship from the Enemys Rear to Action, as soon as her former Station could be occupied by a succeeding British Ship. Also, that the three-decked Ship in the Enemy's rear as aforesaid, being unsustained by their other Ships, struck to the Audacious: And that they parted Company together soon after. –

The two opponent Fleets continued on the Starboard Tack in a parallel direction, the Enemy still to Windward the remainder of the Night. The British Fleet, appearing in the morning of the 29th when in Order of Battle, to be far enough Advanced for the Ships in the Van to make some farther impression on the Enemys Rear, was tacked in succession with that intent. –

The enemy wore hereupon from Van to Rear And continued edging down in Line ahead to engage the Van of the British Fleet. When arrived at such distance as to be just able to reach our most advanced Ships, their headmost Ships as they came successively into the Wake of their respective seconds ahead, opened with that distant fire upon the headmost Ships of the British Van. The Signal for passing through their Line, made when the Fleet tacked before, was then renewed. –

It could not be for sometime seen through the fire from the two Fleets in the Van, to what extent that Signal was complied with. But as the Smoke dispersed at intervals, it was observed that the Cæsar the leading ship of the British Van, after being about on the Starboard Tack and come abreast of the Queen Charlotte, had not kept to the Wind; And that the appointed movement would consequently be liable to fail of the purposed effect. The Queen Charlotte was therefore immediately tacked: And, followed by the Bellerophon her second astern, (and soon after joined by the Leviathan) passed through in Action, between the fifth and sixth

Ships in the rear of the Enemys Line. She was put about again on the Larboard Tack forthwith, after the Enemy, in preparation for renewing the Action with the advantage of that weathermost situation. —

The rest of the British Fleet being at this time passing to Leeward and without the Sternmost ship mostly of the French Line, the Enemy wore again to the Eastward in succession, for succouring the disabled Ships of their Rear: Which intention, by reason of the then disunited state of the Fleet, and having no more than the two cripled Ships the Bellerophon and Leviathan at that time near me, I was unable to obstruct. —

The Enemy having succeeded in that operation, wore round again, after some distant cannonading of the nearest British Ships occasionally returned, and stood away in Order of Battle on the Larboard Tack: Attended upon by the British Fleet in the same Order, (but with the Weather gage retained) as soon as the Ships coming forward to close with the Queen Charlotte, were suitably arranged. —

The Fleets remained separated some few Miles, in view at times on the intermission of a thick Fog which lasted most part of the two next days. —

The Commander of a Fleet, their Lordships know, is unavoidably so confined in his view of the Occurrences in Battle, as to be little capable of rendering personal testimony to the meritorious services of Officers who have profited most extensively, by the opportunities to distinguish themselves on such occasions — To fulfill that part of my public duty, in the best manner I am able; after having acquainted you in my Letter of the 2ᵈ instant (a duplicate of which is now added) with the principal incidents during the Action of the preceding day; I herewith likewise transmit, the Reports (those from Rear Admiral Bowyer in his present state excepted) which I had called for from the several Flag Officers and Captain of the Fleet: Whereby the Board will become informed of those meritorious Services of the Commanders, and animated intrepidity of their Ships Companies, to which the defeat of the Enemy with every advantage of situation and circumstance in their favor, is truly to be ascribed. To that purport also, I beg my testimony in behalf of the Officers and Company of every description in the Queen Charlotte, may be accepted.

I am with great consideration
    Sir
      Your most obedient
        Humble Servant

Howe

Sir Philip Stephens esqr
Secretary &c &c
13 June
at ¾ past 9 p.m.

Survey of the French fleet, 31 May 1794

All of the other battles in this book were fought on a single day and between two fresh fleets. The Glorious First of June is unique, therefore, because it was the third of three significant engagements fought over five days. After the first two engagements of 28 and 29 May there was a two-day break as the fleets shadowed each other through the Atlantic fog, biding their time until the moment for battle came again. This gave both fleets time to repair and also time for a little maritime espionage, beautifully captured in this document, a survey of the condition of the French fleet made on the day before the main battle. Seven ships were missing one or two masts and one was so shattered that she was being towed.

A note at the bottom of the page is instructive because it records that some of these repairs had been made good by the morning. It is an important reminder that these ships carried a great many spare parts, and if an appropriate piece could not be found, one could be made from other parts of the rig or from other spares. Topgallant yards could thus become jibbooms or spritsail yards; a spare topmast could become a main yard; a topsail yard could become a topgallant mast. Cracked masts and yards could be 'fished' by tying splints around the broken section. Even if an entire mast had been lost, a ship could still be given sufficient headway, using her surviving sails, to maintain steerage. In short, it was very difficult indeed to disable a sailing warship for any significant period of time. The process of repair therefore became a crucial factor that could influence the outcome of a battle, and never more so than on 30 and 31 May as both fleets raced to repair for the major action that they both knew was coming. Not since the very first contact on 28 May, when Villaret had lured Howe away from the convoy rendezvous, had the French attempted to run from the British. Villaret was prepared to fight and Howe knew it. When this list was made, therefore, much still hung in the balance. The French repairs were continuing and so were the British. Who would be in the best condition to fight on the following day?

The French Line of Battle, May 31st 1794.

Van

1st	Ship.	A Two Decker compleat.
2	–	Ditto
3	–	Ditto
4	–	Ditto without a Mizen Topmast
5	–	A Three Decker without a Foretopgallant Mast.
6	–	A Two Decker compleat
7	–	Ditto
8	–	Ditto
9	–	Ditto
10	–	Ditto
11	–	Ditto without Topgallant Masts, Foretops¹ and Cross Jack Yards, and towed by her Leader.
12	–	A Two Decker compleat.
13	–	A Three Decker
14	–	A Two Decker without a Mizentopmast
15	–	A Two Decker compleat
16	–	A Two Decker, Maintopsail close reeft, her Top Gallant Masts & Mizentopm¹ down
17	–	A Two Decker compleat
18	–	Ditto
19	–	Ditto

20	–	Ditto
21	–	A Two Decker Foretopsail close reeft
22	–	A Two Decker, her Foretopgallant Mast, & Jib Boom gone.
23	–	A Three Decker, without a Mizentopgallant Mast
24	–	A Two Decker compleat
25	–	Ditto
26	–	Ditto

They were in the same Order the next morning but some of their Defects, apparently made good.

CHRST. NICHOLLS

Signal Lieutenant's Log of the *Royal Sovereign*

Howe enclosed with his letters numerous documents and reports including this extract from the signal lieutenant's log of the *Royal Sovereign*, flagship of the van division. It is useful because it provides an alternative view of the events and does so in a format which includes the timing and detail of signals. The signalling system is particularly significant in this battle because it was actually invented by Howe and he was using it to signal his own tactical ideas. Howe didn't just win this battle; he did so using his own ideas expressed through his own signalling system, which was quite some achievement.

That he was fond of signals is made rather obvious by this log. According to this, Howe made his first signal at 04.00, well before dawn, so that it could be seen as soon as the lookouts were able to see. At 05.50 he then made his next signal, to alter course, and then a flurry of signals which included signal number 34, 'to engage and pass through the enemy's line', and then signal 36, made at 08.24, 'for each ship of the fleet to steer for, and independently engage the ship opposed to her in the enemy's line'. This was the essence of Howe's tactics on 1 June. He did not intend to cut through the enemy line in one body but for every ship of his fleet to cut though the line astern of the ship opposite them in the French line.

The French line would thus not be broken once, but at every link in its chain. It was an entirely novel tactic designed to disrupt the enemy's line and then prevent

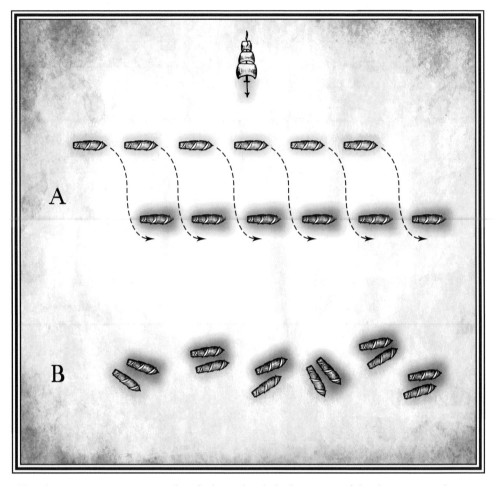

Howe's innovative tactics required each ship to break the line astern of the ship opposite them in the French line.

his ships from escaping to leeward. What this log does not reveal is that, in spite of these very clear signals, only five British captains actually did as Howe had ordered. This has been taken as clear evidence of Howe's poor style of command or of his subordinates' poor response to his signals. But we also know that these explicit signalled orders were protected by a cartilage of unwritten rule and convention and were boosted by verbal and written orders passed between captains and their commanders. In this instance we know that Howe's signalled order to break through the line co-existed with an understanding that, in the confusion of battle, it might not be possible. Although generations of historians have condemned Howe or his captains for failing to execute his plan, Howe, after several days of contact and with a fleet of damaged ships, made no such criticism of his men nor is there any evidence of confusion among his subordinates.

At 08.00 Admiral Graves ordered Captain George Berkeley of the *Marlborough* to swap places with him in the line so that the three-decked *Sovereign* would line up against a three-decker in the enemy fleet. This was standard practice and a matter of honour as much as of practicality. Flag-officers wanted to engage flag-officers and the best way of occupying an enemy three-decker and preventing her from savaging weaker ships was to keep her engaged with a ship of similar size. This was a particular concern for the British in this battle because the French three-deckers were enormous, far bigger in every dimension than their British counterparts and armed with more, and heavier, guns. The master of the 100-gun *Royal Sovereign* lined her up with the appropriately named 110-gun *Terrible*, an absolute brute of a ship of 2,500 tons, 325 tons larger than the *Sovereign* and no less than 13 feet deeper in the hold. If she was fully manned, she would have had 389 more men than the undermanned *Sovereign*, enough to crew two frigates.

The *Caesar*, under Captain Molloy, receives several mentions, all for failing to do what was expected, and other ships are reprimanded with her: the *Russel*, *Marlborough*, *Impregnable* and *Barfleur*. It is evidence that several captains were not behaving as their Admiral expected, of whom the worst offender was Molloy.

At 09.50, just 27 minutes after opening fire, Graves was injured and taken below to the surgeon. From this moment on Collingwood was in command of the *Royal Sovereign*. The log then gives a vivid description of a French three-decker rolling so heavily that water poured into her lowest gunports. This was quite a common occurrence because the lowest gunports were often no more than three feet above the waterline. It was certainly not a problem experienced by the French alone; we know that the lowest deck of Howe's flagship was also awash and that the water had to be drained by opening the lee gunports.[10]

At 11.17 the *Sovereign* was hit by gunfire from another British ship, the *Valiant*. Such accidents were common in sailing warfare because the guns generated such a thick cloud of smoke that entire ships would vanish from sight. The French then grouped together and rallied, forcing the *Sovereign* to flee to the protection of other British men of war. This was more evidence of impressive French seamanship in the heat of battle, as had already been demonstrated on 29 May.

By 14.40 the battle was over and the *Sovereign* had secured a prize. The *America* took aboard no less than 301 prisoners, a large and potentially dangerous number for a ship that began the action with 762 men, but whose numbers were now reduced by 58 dead or injured.

At the bottom of the page is a poignant reminder of the inaccuracy of these logs: the Master freely admits that the timings may not be accurate because the sailor allotted that task was killed at 09.40, only 17 minutes after the engagement began and a full five hours before it finished.

Hour	Minute	PM or AM	Number of Signal	Signification and Observations. Sunday 1st of June 1794.
				The Fleet formed on the Larboard Line of Bearing.
4	..	AM	61	The Charlotte. For the Fleet to keep in closer order to The Van.
5	50		18	The Charlotte. To alter the Course together to NW.
6	30		18	The Charlotte. To alter the Course together to No.
6	35		61	The Charlotte. For The Van to keep in closer order
7	8		4	The Sovereign. For The Van Squadron to take their Stations
7	9			Furled the Mainsail
7	10		84	The Charlotte. To prepare to come to the Wind together on the Larboard Tack.
7	17		49	The Charlotte. To form the Larboard Line of Bearing.
7	26		34	The Charlotte. To Engage and pass through the Enemy's Line.
7	35		4	The Sovereign. For the Impregnable to take her Station.
7	46		61	The Sovereign. For the Van Squadron to close to the Center.

8	.		53	The Sovereign. For the Marlborough to prepare to interchange places in The Line, that the Sovereign might be opposed to the Three decked Ship in the Van of the Enemy.
8	11		73	The Charlotte. To make Sail after lying by.
8	19		4	The Sovereign. For the Leviathan to take her Station.
8	24		36	The Charlotte. For each Ship of the Fleet to steer for, and independently Engage the Ship opposed to her in The Enemy's Line.
8	35			The Preparative being hawled down, and the purport of the preceding Signal not being immediately attended to, threw out The Cæsar's and Russels Pendant.
8	37		4	The Sovereign. For the Cæsar and Leviathan to take their Stations.
8	38		36	The Sovereign with the same Pendants for those Ships to Steer for, and independently engage the Ships opposed to them.
8	42		60	The Sovereign. For the Marlborough, Impregnable, Cæsar and Russel to make more Sail.
9	8		73	The Sovereign. For The Van to make Sail.
9	18			The French Van began to fire as we approached and several Shot struck The Sovereign.
9	23		5 with red pendant over	The Sovereign began to fire edging towards the Enemy, and made the Signal for close action.
9	30			Threw out the Cæsars, Impregnable's, Barfleur's and Russels Pendants, the Signal for close action being flying; the Russels pendant was soon after hawled in, but the others were kept flying during the action.
9	50	AM		Admiral Graves was badly wounded and obliged to leave the Deck.

John Blake Signal Lieut.

Approved

Chs. Nicholls captain for the Admiral

10	38			The Three decked Ship we were opposed to lost her Main Mast and Mizen Mast, bore up, and Yawed much by which we had frequent opportunities of raking her.
10	39		7	The Sovereign for a General Chace as there were Several other Ships of the Enemy running besides the Ship she was opposed to.
10	40			Set the Courses, Spritsail, Jib and Staysails and continued to pursue the three decked Ship that was first opposed to us, until a Second three decked Ship and also a two decked Ship neither apparently much hurt in her Masts or Sails came to her assistance. The three decked Ship we first engaged took the water in at her lower deck Ports, and rolled so heavily as to make us conceive she was Sinking: had either of the large Ships then lying to Windward (apparently not disabled) came down, that Ship must have fallen for she had ceased firing
11	38			One of the two decked Ships opposed to our Van ran past us, we manned our larboard Guns and gave her two or three broadsides
11	40			Observed a ship lying a considerable distance to Windward which we supposed to be the Thunderer. Threw out her Pendant, the signal for chace and close action being flying.
11	50			Began a close action with the Second three decked Ship
	17	PM		The Valiant came down brought too to Windward and fired a shot now and then over us or but just ahead.
	18		73	The Sovereign for the Valiant to make sail after lying by.
	18			Observed the Cæsar coming down with her Foresail set but she hawled it up and brought too to Windward.
	25			The three decked Ship bore up, we continued to follow her until the French Ships began to rally, and there being no Ship to support us, we hawled as much up as the shattered state of our Masts Sails and Rigging would allow.

	32	PM		Left off firing and hawled down the Signals for Chace and Close Action, and hawled in the Barfleur's Impregnable's Cæsars and Thunderer's Pendants.
	36		55	The Charlotte. To form the Line as most Convenient.
	40			The French Ships to leeward not dismasted wore round and formed a Line on the Starboard Tack apparently with an Intention to protect their dismasted Ships.
	42		81	The Charlotte. To come to the wind together on the Starbd. Tack.
	44		55	The Charlotte. To form the Line taking the most convenient Stations. Wore round and Set all the Sail we could to take our Station in the van; lashing the Cringles in the Leech of the Foresail and Foretopsail together where the Rope was shot away.
2	40		64	The Charlotte. A General Signal to Stay by Prizes. Hawled up as much as we could and after firing several Shot at the French Ship America of 74 guns she struck, and we took possession of her; As the other Ships did of six others. One of which we observed to go down. Sent an Officer and twenty Men on board the America and received from her 301 Prisoners. Ordered the Niger to take her in Tow. Employed Securing the Masts. Bent new Courses and a Main topsail.

NB. The time after 40 minutes past nine is probably not very correct as the Person appointed to take minutes was then killed.

| | | | | |

John Blake Signal Lieutenant

Approved. Christ. Nicholls

Rear-Admiral T. Pasley to Admiral Howe, 6 June 1794

This is one of the captains' reports that Howe enclosed with his letter to the Admiralty. It is written by Thomas Pasley of the *Bellerophon*, a man renowned for his courage and a ship renowned for her speed. His letter is dated 6 June, a full five days after the main battle and more than a week since he fired the first shots of these engagements when he opened fire on the *Révolutionnaire*. The delay in writing is explained by Pasley's loss of a leg on 1 June which he refers to in the first paragraph as 'my unfortunate situation'. The letter has been written by a secretary and Pasley is barely able to scrawl his name at the end (p. 67).

He comments on the conduct of his own ship and others that he could see. He begins with a brief discussion of the *Bellerophon's* conduct on 28 May with specific reference to his clever manoeuvre which brought the *Bellerophon* into contact with the enemy long before any other British ship. It was an inspired and extremely courageous piece of seamanship. The *Bellerophon* was a 74-gun Third Rate, similar in size to the *Audacious*, and was thus dwarfed by the 110-gun *Révolutionnaire*. Like Parker of the *Audacious* and Howe himself, Pasley believes erroneously that the *Révolutionnaire* has been captured.

His comments on the conduct of the van division on 1 June confirm the observations made in Howe's second letter (p. 52) and in the log of the *Royal Sovereign* (p. 60). Pasley singles out the *Russel*, *Leviathan* and *Caesar* as ships which did not act as expected, an uncomfortable observation that caused a man who had just lost a leg 'great pain'. Pasley also draws attention to the curious behaviour of the *Tremendous*. Although she appeared to Pasley to be undamaged, her rig, in fact, was so shattered that she was immobile while her hull was leaking so much that the pumps were in constant use. Adequate excuses were also discovered for the behaviour of the *Russel* and the *Leviathan* but Molloy of the *Caesar* was court martialled. He claimed in his defence that his ship was too damaged to comply with his orders, an excuse that was not accepted by the court. Even after all these years, Molloy reeks of incompetence.

The letter finishes with a characteristic Pasleyan flash of splendid language, praising the 'steady coolness and determined intrepidity' of his crew. A magnificent letter, it rings with pride and zeal even though it was dictated by a man wracked with exhaustion and pain. It will come as no surprise that Pasley was loved deeply by his crew and widely admired by his fellow professionals. He was a consummate 18th-century fighting sailor and his loss to the service at the start of this war was a grievous blow to the Royal Navy.

BELLEROPHON AT SEA
THE 6TH JUNE 1794.

My Lord

It was not my intention to have made any Publick report upon the proceedings of the ships that came within my observation until I should have been able to have done it in Person; but as from my present unfortunate situation it may be some time before I shall have that satisfaction and your Lordships order of the 5th instant puts it out of my power to suppress my sentiments I cannot but lament what I am called upon in honour to relate.

With respect to the attack made upon the Enemies rear on the evening of the 28th ultimo I have but little to observe upon, except to remark, that, on that day and for some days before the Bellerophon was the worst sailing ship of the flying squadron; yet by embracing the moment for tacking after the Enemy, she was enabled to bring their Rear Ship to action, with which she was engaged alone near an hour and an half. As from the situation of the Queen Charlotte your Lordship had a full view of the conduct of the Captains who were able to get up with the Enemy, I shall forbear to make any strictures, as I conceive the intention of your Lordship was effected by the enemies progress being retarded. I feel it my duty however to remark that I made the Gibraltars signal to assist the ships engaged at 14 min: past and at 9, I ordered the Marlborough to make sail for the same purpose – It is a duty I owe to the Captains of the Leviathan and Audacious to observe, that in their attack upon the enemies rear, they behaved most nobly, and, that through the steady conduct of the latter, their Rear ship was captured. the Bellerophon had been obliged to take in her main topsail a shot having upset the Main Cap and totally disabled it.

In regard to the proceedings of the 29th, the situation of the Bellerophon being next astern of the Charlotte, nothing of moment came within my view; but what must have been remarked by your Lordship.

I have now my Lord to make my remarks upon the division of the Van squadron under my more particular direction on the 1st inst. the Marlborough having exchanged situations with the Royal Sovereign I have only to observe upon the behaviour of the Russel, Leviathan and Cæsar, and it gives me great pain in being obliged to report that Admiral Graves made Cæsar's signal to make more sail when we were going down to the attack, and, that I felt myself under the disagreeable necessity of throwing out her pendant twice for close action, while in battle, viz: at 23 min: past 10 and at 12 min: past 11 o'clock, at which times she was laying near half a mile to windward and not before the Bellerophons beam – neither of these sig^{ls} were complied with – and Captain Hope reported to me that he thought it his duty, after I was taken off the deck, to make the Cæsars signal again for close battle – to Chace the van ship of the enemy, then veering and making off – and when they hauled upon the starboard tack, signal was made for the Cæsar to do the same, the Cæsar hauled her wind; but the other signal to chace was not complied with – I make no doubt, but Captain Molloy will explain to your Lordship his reasons for his conduct.

Lord Hugh Conway and Captain Payne demand my warmest praise, particularly the former, who supported me most gallantly during the whole of the battle.

How it came to pass I cannot tell; but as the Tremendous was observed from the Bellerophon laying upon the Leviathans quarter and near three quarters of a mile to windward of that ship, I made her signal at 35 min: past 10 for close battle, which she answered at 54 min: past 10 by signal of inability – the Tremendous did not appear to be damaged either in Masts Sails or Yards.

Before I close my Letter permit me my Lord to pay the tribute due to Captain Hope and the Officers and Crew of the Bellerophon who supported me during the several actions with a steady coolness and determined Intrepidity.

I have the honour to be
My Lord
Your Lordships
most faithful and Obed
Humble Servant

Thos. Pasley

Boatswain's damage report of HMS *Brunswick*

In the midst of battle on 1 June, two ships, the British *Brunswick* and the French *Vengeur du People*, fought the battle in microcosm, the might of the British and the determination of the French playing out in a private duel. And what a duel it was (fig. 4).

John Harvey, captain of the *Brunswick*, was determined to break through the French line and headed for a tantalising gap which had opened up between *Le Patriote* and *Le Vengeur*, three ships astern of the French flagship. However, his intention was as clear as the defensive response was simple. Captain Jean-François Renaudin of the *Vengeur* increased his speed to close the gap. Harvey was too committed to stop quickly and the starboard bow of the *Brunswick* smashed into the bow of the *Vengeur* with such force that both ships were driven out of the line.

In the collision the starboard anchors of the *Brunswick* hooked into the larboard fore shrouds of the *Vengeur*, locking the two ships together. Harvey was delighted and the British set about reducing their enemy to kindling by firing their guns alternately high and then low, catching the French gun crews in a deadly crossfire and tearing the ship apart from the inside.

As this document shows, however, the *Brunswick* did not escape lightly. It is a damage report compiled by her boatswain, the warrant officer in charge of the ship's maintenance. It reveals the astonishing scope of the damage, not all of which was inflicted by the French. The 10 gunports on the starboard side that are listed as being 'carr[ie]d away' were destroyed not from the outside but the inside. After the ships collided the British guncrews on the lowest deck found that they could not open the gunport lids and, not willing to let this get in their way, fired all the guns with the lids down, blasting them away so that they could more easily get at the French.

When the ships finally broke apart, the *Vengeur* was in a shocking state and water poured into her lowest gunports. She was boarded by a British officer who swiftly left as the state of the ship became clear. Some British ships sent boats but several others, including the *Brunswick* herself, deliberately did not, in spite of the *Vengeur*'s obviously distressed condition. The *Brunswick*'s crew were particularly aggrieved at the French use of heated shot, 'raw ore' and 'sulphur pots', which 'scalded our people so miserably that they wished for death to end their agony'.[11] Indeed, one of the things that this damage report does not mention is that, at one stage, the *Brunswick* was on fire in four different places: she survived one of the fiercest duels of the entire age of sail but had a very lucky escape.

The *Vengeur* soon sank by the stern with as many as 365 dead and injured still aboard. The *Brunswick*, meanwhile, was still in a very dangerous situation. More British sailors were killed or injured on her than on any other British ship. She was crippled, far behind the French line and some distance from any British ship. It is not surprising that Howe was concerned about her fate in the days after the battle (p. 49). She eventually made it home after a limping voyage that took 11 days. Her captain, John Harvey, also made it home but died shortly afterwards. He has a memorial, which he shares with Captain John Hutt, who was captain of the *Queen* at The Glorious First of June, in the north aisle of the nave of Westminster Abbey.

The Defects of His Majestys Ship Brunswick John Harvey Esqr Commander in the Action of the 29th May & 1 June 1794

Lower Deck Starbᴰ Side

The starbᵈ fore hause piece and knight head above the Hause hole much wounded
The Ports 1.2.3.4.5.6.7.8.10.13 Shot & Carrᵈ away
One Shot between 3ʳᵈ & 4ᵗʰ ports & two half Beams carrᵈ away
Shot between the 9ᵗʰ & 10ᵗʰ ports

Larboard Side

Spare Tiller Shot. – Spungiton* under the 10ᵗʰ Gun shot thro'
9ᵗʰ Gun the Port Timber & Clamp shot thro'
between the 8ᵗʰ & 9ᵗʰ a Shot in the End of the Beam & the Clamp Shot thro' in two places and hangᵍ knee shot away
Head of the Rider between the 5ᵗʰ and 6ᵗʰ Port Shot
Foremast beam – the lodging knee broke by a Shot

Upper Deck Starbᴰ Side

5ᵗʰ Port the lower Cele and Spungiton shot thro'
The 4ᵗʰ Beam from Aft Shot
Clamps after pieces upper and lower wounded between 12ᵗʰ & 13ᵗʰ gun
Between the 10ᵗʰ & 11ᵗʰ gun a Shot below the Clamp
9ᵗʰ Gun the Clamp & upper Cele Shot away
Over the 8ᵗʰ Gun the Clamp & upper sheer shot away
7ᵗʰ Gun the port timber & sling shot thro' 8ᵗʰ Gun Ditto
Beak Head Beam much wounded
4ᵗʰ Beam of the Forecastle Shot. Hanging knee betwⁿ 3ʳᵈ & 4ᵗʰ port Shot
Between the 2ⁿᵈ & 3ʳᵈ the Head of the Top rider shot
Between 1ˢᵗ & 2ⁿᵈ Port one Hangᵍ & 2 Lodg Knees Shot

---

* This word is spelt very clearly and is repeated in the original document, though it is unclear what this is. From its location, it probably means Spirketting – the name given to the timbers between the decks and the gunports.

The Clamps and Spungiton cut under the Forecastle
The Fore Topsail sheets bits wounded
Plank Boards, Plank Sheers & the Skids much cut

Upper Deck Larb^d Side

The Clamps of the Forecastle much Wounded
Hanging Knee of the 3rd & 4th Gun Shot & port timber of the 5th Shot
A shot between 8th & 9th Gun
Upper piece of sling shot thro
Upper & Lower Clamp & Hanging Knee of the 10th Gun shot away
Skids & Gangboards much cut Iron stantions shot away
Larboard Quarter Gallery shot away
Limber Heads of the Forecastle many shot away
The Mizen Mast Shot Overboard Main Mast much wounded
Main T^p mast sprung. Fore Mast wounded. Fore Yard shot thro'
Main & Main topsail y^d wounded one Shot & lost overboard
The bow spreet much wounded. The Decks much cut
The Channells much Shot and cut
All the Boats spare Masts & Booms & Spars cut to pieces
The starboard Bumpkin Shot away
The starboard Cat Head and Supporter Shot & carried away
Head Rails and Timbers Shot to pieces. Figure [head] much cut
A number of shot in the sides not through
A number of Chain Plates shot & Damaged

Wm Yelland Carpenter

Boatswains Department

BOWSPRIT

Gammoning
Shrouds
Bobstays
Spritsail Yard
Braces & Lifts
Halliards & Slings
Clew Lines & Sheets
Jibb Boom
Jibb Stay
Jibb Halliards
Jibb Sheets

FORE TOPMAST

Shrouds
Backstays
Topsail Cluelines
Do. Bowlines
Reef Tackle Pendants
Fore Topsail Halliards
Studdingsail Halliards

MAIN TOPMAST

Main Truss
Shrouds & Backstays
Main Topmast & Preventer
Stay all gone
Main Topsail Halliard & Lift
Main Topsail Braces
Do. Clewlines
Do. Buntlines
Do. Bowlines
Do. Reef Tackle Pendants Fall

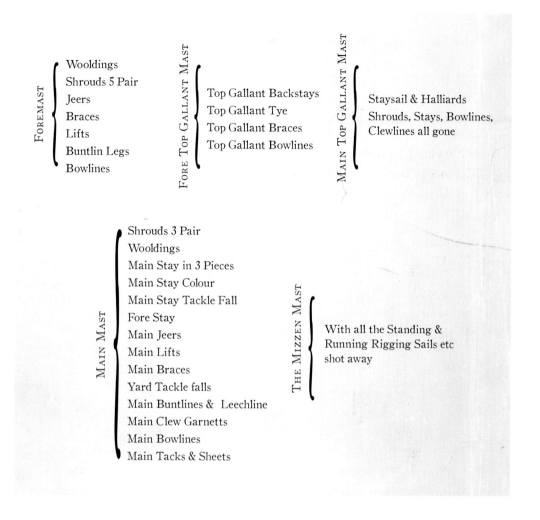

FOREMAST
- Wooldings
- Shrouds 5 Pair
- Jeers
- Braces
- Lifts
- Buntlin Legs
- Bowlines

FORE TOP GALLANT MAST
- Top Gallant Backstays
- Top Gallant Tye
- Top Gallant Braces
- Top Gallant Bowlines

MAIN TOP GALLANT MAST
- Staysail & Halliards
- Shrouds, Stays, Bowlines, Clewlines all gone

MAIN MAST
- Shrouds 3 Pair
- Wooldings
- Main Stay in 3 Pieces
- Main Stay Colour
- Main Stay Tackle Fall
- Fore Stay
- Main Jeers
- Main Lifts
- Main Braces
- Yard Tackle falls
- Main Buntlines & Leechline
- Main Clew Garnetts
- Main Bowlines
- Main Tacks & Sheets

THE MIZZEN MAST
- With all the Standing & Running Rigging Sails etc shot away

Admiral R. Howe to P. Stephens, 13 June 1794 enclosing an account of the casualties in the British fleet

The battle over, Howe turned his mind to the manpower issues and other logistical headaches that were raised by such a battle. He thus wrote once more to the Admiralty when his ship was off Dunnose Point on the eastern side of the Isle of Wight. His first priority was to get his fleet operational but there were too many damaged ships for them all to be repaired in Portsmouth. He therefore divided his fleet and sent one half to Plymouth. The rest, with the captured French ships which he now named for the first time, sailed with him to Portsmouth.

Howe enclosed a detailed account of the killed and wounded compiled in the days following the battle. The casualty figures of Molloy's *Caesar* are particularly interesting. He lost 55 men dead or injured, by no means a particularly low figure and one that suggests Molloy did see a far greater share of the fighting than his critics suggested (pp. 51, 59, 64).

The significant missing figures are those of the *Brunswick*, a significant omission considering that her crew suffered more than any other, losing 41 killed and 114 wounded. Howe's total of 904 British casualties is therefore 155 short of the total of 1,059 for the entire fleet. More men subsequently died from their wounds, raising the final total to 1,098. Compared with the subsequent battles, this is a particularly large figure; only the casualty figures from the Battle of Trafalgar are higher; but the problem was exacerbated in 1794. We know from this letter that Howe was concerned that his crews would become sick. He was right to be worried. Many of the French crews were already depleted by typhus, a sickness which could spread with terrifying speed through a crowded ship, and Howe's victorious ships certainly were crowded. He estimates in this letter that there were 2,300 French prisoners crammed into his holds, an estimate that we now suspect to be at least 2,000 too few. They were making each other sick and, if they stayed aboard for much longer, the British crews would suffer too.

Howe's warnings and concerns were received and given the appropriate attention and priority by the Admiralty. However their orders to prepare prisons and prison ships were not carried out as they should have been. The result was everything that Howe had feared. The British fleet became infected with typhus and the manning problem became so serious that, between June and December, the Channel Fleet was at sea for less than a month. By failing to cope with their success, the British were unable to capitalise on the victory they had won.

THE CHARLOTTE OFF OF DUNNOSE
13ᵀᴴ JUNE 1794

Sir

Queen Charlotte
Royal George
Queen, Barfleur
Glory
Bellerophon
Cæsar
Leviathan
Defence
Invincible
Valiant
Ramillies
Russel
Majestic
Thunderer
Latona
Niger
Aquilon
Pegasus

~

FRENCH SHIPS

Le Juste
Le Sans Pareil
L'Amerique
L'Impetueux
L'Achilles
Le Northumberland

~

R Sovereign
Impregnable
Marlborough
Tremendous
Gibraltar
Culloden
Orion
Alfred
Montagu

Being arrived off of Dunnose on the passage to Spithead with the Ships of the Channel Fleet, and captured French Ships of War named in the margin; I send enclosed the account of the Killed, and Wounded, not able to resume their Stations at Quarters, in the Actions of the 28ᵗʰ and 29ᵗʰ of May, and 1ˢᵗ of this Month: as far as they have been collected. Also an abstract of the principal Damages to the ships on those occasions. Concluding it will be judged necessary to have the Ships made ready for service with all possible expedition, I would submit my opinion, that the greater part of the absolutely necessary repairs, besides replacing their lost or defective Masts and Yards, may be adequately done afloat. –

It will however be requisite that the french prisoners (about 2300) should be taken out of His Majesty's Ships the most Speedily: for preventing the infection, which is to be apprehended from the unprovided condition, and confined situation wherein several of them unavoidably remain at this time: The Seamen of the Fleet being otherwise, for the most part, now in a very promising State of permanent good health.

On the arrival of the Fleet off of the Lizard I gave directions for Admiral Graves to proceed with the other Ships named also in the margin to Plymouth Sound, where I conclude he arrived yesterday. –

The Defects of the Ships I have brought to Spithead, will be reported to the Yard; And the commands of the Lords Commissioners of the Admiralty waited for thereon.

I am Sir
Your most obedient
humble servant

PHILIP STEPHENS ESQR
&Cᵒ &Cᵒ &Cᵒ

A RETURN OF THE KILLED AND WOUNDED ON BOARD THE UNDERMENTIONED SHIPS OF THE CHANNEL FLEET IN THE ACTIONS WITH THE FRENCH FLEET ON THE 28TH 29TH OF MAY, AND 1ST OF JUNE 1794. –

SHIPS NAMES	KILLED		WOUNDED		TOTAL
	SEAMEN	MARINES OR SOLDIERS	SEAMEN	MARINES OR SOLDIERS	
CÆSAR	18	~	37	~	55
BELLEROPHON	3	1	26	1	31
LEVIATHAN	10	~	32	1	43
SOVEREIGN	11	3	39	5	58
MARLBOROUGH	24	5	76	14	119
DEFENCE	14	4	29	10	57
IMPREGNABLE	7	~	24	~	31
TREMENDOUS	2	1	6	2	11
BARFLEUR	8	1	22	3	34
CULLODEN [NO ENTRY]					
INVINCIBLE	9	5	21	10	45
GIBRALTAR	1	1	12	~	14
THE CHARLOTTE	13	1	24	5	43
BRUNSWICK PARTED COMPANY ON THE 1ST OF JUNE. –					
VALIANT	1	1	5	4	11

Queen	30	6	57	10	103
Orion	5	~	20	4	29
Ramillies	2	~	7	~	9
Alfred	~	~	6	2	8
Russel	7	1	24	2	34
R: George	18	2	63	9	92
Montagu	4	~	13	~	17
Majestic	3	~	4	1	8
Glory	13	~	31	8	52
Thunderer none Killed or Wounded					
Audacious parted company on the Night of the 28th of May					
Grand Total	203	32	578	91	904

Account of the casualties in the captured French ships

The true scale of the British victory is best indicated by the next document, a return of the killed and wounded in the captured French ships. As we have seen, a figure of 1,098 is an acceptable figure for the entire British fleet of 25 ships. In the six captured ships alone 1,270 were killed or injured, to which can be added the approximate figure given here of 320 who sank in the *Vengeur*, bringing the total to 1,590 for just seven ships. In other words, 18 fewer ships suffered 492 more casualties. The full return of the French fleet is unknown but it is estimated to be somewhere around 4,200 dead and 3,300 wounded or 10 per cent of all of the seamen in France. Not only had so many experienced French seamen and particularly officers already been driven out of the navy by the ideological zealots of the early Revolution, but this new navy was now crippled at birth.

The claim that the *Jacobin* was sunk is incorrect. Numerous British sailors in this battle claimed to have seen ships sink when they did not. One can assume that the sight of a giant sailing warship well over 150 feet long and with masts nearly as high being swallowed by the sea is not one that can be mistaken, so it is likely that those sightings were occasions when an enemy ship simply vanished into the dense gunsmoke that we know hung over the battle.

An Account of the Numbers Killed and Wounded on board the French Ships Captured and sunk on the 1st of June 1794. –				
Le Juste	100	Killed	145	Wounded
Sans Pareil	260	"	120	"
L'Amerique	134	"	110	"
L'Achilles	36	"	30	"
Northumberland	60	"	100	"
L'Impeteuex	100	"	75	"
	690		580	

Le Vengeur ——— 320 sunk
Le Jacobin sunk in Action not a Man saved –

Report on the condition of the British ships that returned to Portsmouth

This is a report on the condition of the British ships that returned with Howe. Information on those that returned to Plymouth is not included. The document tells us several important things. The *Queen Charlotte* received numerous shot in her hull, clear evidence of the French firing low which explodes the enduring myth that the French 'always' fired high. Those shot, however, did not break through. Even though there were several shot below the waterline, the ship made no water. This was common. The sides of a British warship were immensely thick, 3 feet at some points, and enemy shot would often lodge in the side. The velocity of that shot, moreover, was dependent on the quality of the powder, which we know was very deficient at this early stage of the war. This meant that injuries to British sailors in the gundecks were more likely to have been caused by splinters exploding off the inside of the hull than by direct hits from enemy shot.

The scale of the damage was also important. All of the ships with the exception of the *Barfleur* had damaged masts and the *Marlborough*, the worst of all, required nothing less than 'A General outfit of everything above the Deck'. But the British yards, sailors and shipwrights could cope. The necessary expertise and labour were readily available and the stockpiles of naval matériel adequate. In contrast, the

1. The volume of dispatches.

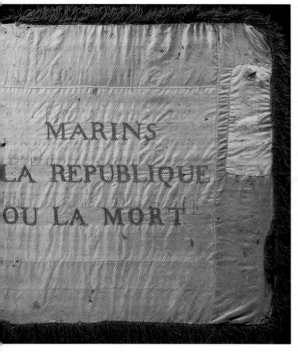

2. Silk banner belonging to the boarding division of the French 74-gunner *L'Amerique*, captured on 1 June, 1794.

3. Portrait of Admiral Richard Howe by John Singleton Copley, 1794.

4. 'The *Brunswick* and *Le Vengeur* after the Action on the First of June, 1794. The first totally disabled, the latter dismasted, water-logged and sinking'. Painted by Nicholas Pocock, engraved by R. Pollard and J. Widnell.

5. Portrait of John Jervis as a young captain by Gilbert Stuart, *c.* 1782–7.

6. La Granja de San Ildefonso, Segovia, Spain.

7. 'Horatio Nelson boarding the *San Nicolas* in the victory off Cape St Vincent, 1797' by W. M. Thomas, *c.* 1800.

8. Fragment of the naval ensign of the Batavian Republic (1795–1806).

9. 'Duncan receiving the surrender of de Winter at the Battle of Camperdown, 11 October 1797' by Daniel Orme, 1797. A dull composition, but the portraits of Duncan and the members of his crew were taken from life by Orme, a skilled portrait painter, shortly after the battle. It is an eerie and accurate snapshot of the British North Sea fleet.

French stores had been stripped clean to get their fleet ready for sea and, when the French fleet returned, many of the ships could not be repaired.

The arrival of the crippled ships in Portsmouth with their prizes in tow was a wonderful spectacle and thousands of people travelled to witness it. The King even came with his family, a unique example of a royal visit in the aftermath of battle during these wars. Numerous artists also made the trip because images of such maritime glory could be lucrative. Several sketches and prints of the damaged ships still survive.

STATEMENT OF THE PRINCIPAL DEFECTS IN THE SHIPS OF THE CHANNEL FLEET JUNE 3RD 1794. –

QUEEN CHARLOTTE	Lower Masts and Yards want inspection. All the Shot in the Hull may be covered without stripping the Timbers, – and those under water are of no consequence as the Ship makes no Water. Fore and Mizen Tops wanting. –
R. SOVEREIGN	Most of the Principal Masts unservicable and some of the standing Rigging. –
ROYAL GEORGE	Lower Masts and Rigging wanting: also some Spars. 13 Shot in the Bottom under Water. Hull wants inspecting.
BARFLEUR	Fore Yard, a few spars and Main Capstern to be examined. –
IMPREGNABLE	Fore and Mizen Masts, Fore, Main and Mizen Yards wanted. – Some Spars and standing Rigging wanted. – 2 Guns and three Carriages disabled. –
QUEEN	Lower Masts, Bowsprit and Yards, Rigging &c and various parts of the Hull want refitting. –
GLORY	Lower Masts and Bowsprit to be examined, Main Trussell Trees, Fore Yard and Cat-heads. –
CÆSAR	Rudder, Fore Yard, Mizen and Main Masts to be inspected. –
GIBRALTAR	Head of the Main Mast wants inspection and a little standing Rigging.
MONTAGU	Lower Masts either to be shifted or fished, as may appear necessary upon inspection. Lower yards and standing Rigging much damaged. –
INVINCIBLE	Lower Masts may be found to be wanting upon inspection. Lower Yards and some other Spars.

THUNDERER	Fore Mast, Mizen Mast and Fore Yard to be inspected. Trussle Trees of the Main Mast shot away. –
DEFENCE	A General outfit of Lower Masts, Spars and Rigging. –
MARLBOROUGH	A General outfit of everything above the Deck. –
LEVIATHAN	Lower Masts and Yards wanting. –
MAJESTIC	Fore Mast and Mizen Mast to be examined, a Lower Yard and a few Spars wanted. –
ALFRED	Some standing Rigging, Mizen Mast and Bowsprit to be inspected. – A Cat-head and the Gun Carriages to be examined on board. –
TREMENDOUS	Quarter and Stern of the Ship damaged by a Ship getting on board. Main Mast, Mizen Mast and Bowsprit to be inspected. –
RAMILLIES	Fore Mast, Bowsprit, Fore Yard, Main Top, Mizen Mast and Mizen Yard to be inspected. Some Spars and standing Rigging wanted. –
RUSSEL	Main Mast, Bowsprit, Main Yard, Knee of the Head to be inspected. Some Lower Deck Gun Carriages wanted. –
BELLEROPHON CULLODEN VALIANT ORION BRUNSWICK AUDACIOUS	no Report. –

Memo.
Most of the Ships are in want of Sails and Rigging to replace those lost in the late Actions.

Howe

While The Glorious First of June was a major victory for British seapower, it had a sting in its tail. The French battlefleet had been mauled and thousands of French sailors killed, disabled or captured, but British seapower also suffered, at first from the battle casualties but later, and to a much greater extent, from the typhus that the French crews brought into English ships.

The French fought well and none of the captured ships surrendered until there was no hope of succour. For all of the destruction suffered and inflicted in the battles on 28 and 29 May and 1 June, however, the British failed to intercept Vanstabel's convoy. The merchant ships, holds brimming with grain, arrived in Brest unharmed, having passed directly through the site of the battle on 29 May and only a little to the south of that on 1 June.

French politicians did their best to celebrate the battle and applaud the navy for achieving its strategic goal. They had done so by outfoxing the British and fighting with sufficient resolve to occupy them for five full days. For many French politicians and naval officers, however, the evident beating that the navy had taken was too bitter a pill to swallow. The battle thus became one of several political weapons wielded by enemies of the Jacobins that eventually ended their short but intense period of tyranny.

Robespierre and many of his supporters were beheaded within two months of the battle. Their deaths brought an end to the Reign of Terror but by no means an end to the Revolution. On the contrary, the Jacobin excesses re-invigorated popular enthusiasm for the original humanistic and democratic ideals of the Revolution while The First of June was seen by many as proof that the new Republic could survive by defending her coasts and maritime trade from the British 'leopards'. The battle also coincided with numerous significant French land victories to east and south that both expanded the territory of France and made the Revolution secure from a landward threat. Many in Britain had hoped that a significant naval victory would bring an end to the war but it did no such thing. In fact, things soon became much worse for the British.

St Vincent
Cap San Vincente

St Valentine's Day 1797

*'I would much rather have an action with the
enemy than detail one'*

Admiral John Jervis, 1797

AT A GLANCE

DATE:
14 February 1797

NAVIES INVOLVED:
British and Spanish

COMMANDING OFFICERS:
Admiral Sir John Jervis and Admiral Don José de Córdoba

FLEET SIZES:
British, 15 ships of the line; Spanish, 23 ships of the line

TIME OF DAY:
11.00 – 16.00

LOCATION:
Off Cape St Vincent, Portugal. 37°01′30″N 8°59′40″W

WEATHER:
Light west-southwesterly breezes and cloudy

RESULT:
4 Spanish ships captured

CASUALTIES:
British, 300; Spanish 1,484

BRITISH COURT MARTIALS:
None

DISPATCHES CARRIED HOME BY:
Captain Robert Calder, Jervis's flag captain. Nelson, however,
sent home his version of events, which arrived first,
via Lieutenant William Pierson

The Palace

Fifty miles or so north of Madrid, lies one of the world's finest royal palaces. La Granja de San Ildefonso nestles in the cool northern slopes of the Sierra de Guadarrama (fig. 6). It sits within a vast landscape of formal gardens whose lines drag you hither and thither to fountains, sculptures, rare specimens of trees, vistas and dead-ends. More often than not the features you see are in some way deceptive, seeming farther away, closer, larger or smaller than they really are. You are constantly manipulated by the garden's designers and the men who have worked there for centuries. Here you are as much in the heart of Spain as it is possible to be, at least 200 miles from the nearest coastline or from the Pyrennees, and yet it is impossible not to notice how convincingly foreign – how *un-Spanish* – the entire establishment is. Compare it to another palace nearby, El Escorial. Radically different in appearance from La Granja, the latter oozes the majesty and arrogance of 16th-century Spain. Both palace and fortress, it is convincingly austere as the residence of the normally black-clothed Philip II (1527–98), a Spanish raven in an age of peacocks. The most distinctive feature of La Granja, by contrast, is that it appears so *French*. It was, in fact, built by Philip V of Spain (1683–1746), who was the grandson of Louis XIV of France (1638–1715). Philip had even been born in France, at the magnificent French royal palace of Versailles. Just like Versailles, La Granja lies only a short distance from the nation's capital in magnificent landscaped gardens and with its symmetrical wings dominating the landscape. Philip built himself a replica of the house in which he was born: La Granja is his Versailles.

La Granja is also important, however, because it reminds us of the strong family ties that united France and Spain in an age of shifting alliances and loyalties. When Catholic France and Catholic Spain were separated, Protestant Britain could rest more easily. In 1794 they had been divided because the Spanish King, Charles IV, had been as outraged by the murder of Louis XVI as every other European monarch. By 1796, however, things had changed. The French Revolution had failed to self-destruct in the fierce heat of Jacobinism and the Republic seemed if anything to have grown stronger for the experience. There was certainly no doubting the scale or capability of its armies. Moreover the memory of Louis's regicide had begun to fade, its pain dulled by the intensity of the events that had followed his execution.

So much had changed. The men who now governed France were not the men who had executed Louis and many of the countries which had formed the first coalition against France had been concerned not about Republicanism *per se* but about regicide. To complicate matters further, Charles IV of Spain was weak and unstable and his prime minister, Manuel de Godoy,* who held the reins of power, was a Francophile. With thousands of the French soldiers who invaded through Catalonia and the Basque Country between 1793 and 1795 still encamped in Spain, it had become easier for the Spanish to remember ancient ties, even if they were now based on a shared fear and hatred of a common enemy rather than a shared royal bloodline. They had, after all, suffered at the hands of the British in both of the previous two wars and the former enemy still occupied Gibraltar, that strategic key to global seapower at the southern tip of Spain.

So it was that the Spanish swapped sides on 19 August 1796 when, in a symbolic gesture of Franco-Spanish unity and shared history, they signed the treaty of San Ildefonso at La Granja. In that magical Gallic enclave in the heart of Spain and so many miles from the sea, naval warfare was turned on its axis.

The Allies

On 11 October 1796 Spain declared war on Britain. The British now had to contend at sea not only with the French but with the Spanish as well. When combined, the French and Spanish naval forces outnumbered the British 132 to 123. While it would be impossible for all the ships of both navies to meet at any one time, this discrepancy in numbers made it more likely that a combined Franco-Spanish fleet would outnumber a British fleet. If naval officers knew one thing about fleet warfare, it was that numerical superiority won fleet battles.

However, while on paper the alliance between the French and Spanish was bad news for the British, they did have one thing in their favour. During their time as

---

* His rather impressive full name was Don Manuel Francisco Domingo de Godoy (di Bassano) y Álvarez de Faria, de los Ríos y Sánchez-Zarzosa.

allies under the First Coalition, the British had gained a detailed understanding of the capabilities of Spanish seapower. On the one hand, the Spanish ships, as they always had been, were magnificent. Much larger than their British counterparts if compared rate for rate, their tropical hardwood hulls made them almost impervious to rot. The British wooden walls were made from English oak but the Spanish built theirs in dense, beautiful, nut-brown, oily mahogany from the New World and lined the ships' interiors with cedar. Have you ever smelled a freshly sawn cedar plank? It is one of the most aromatic of all woods and, for someone who is not accustomed to the smell, quite overpowering in confined spaces. All Spanish ships not only looked exotic; they smelt exotic.

For all of their visual and aromatic appeal, however, it was clear that Spanish warships were, in the words of Horatio Nelson who visited Cadiz early in the war, 'shockingly manned',[1] ill equipped and badly provisioned. They were no match for the British, and Admiral John Jervis, commander of the Mediterranean fleet, certainly knew it. In October 1796 he wrote to the First Lord, Earl Spencer, 'Be assured I will omit no opportunity of chastising the Spaniards, and if I have the good fortune to fall in with them the stuff I have with me in this fleet will tell.'[2] The Spanish knew this too, but only some of them were prepared to face up to the problem. These are the words of Antonio de Escaño, head of the general staff of the Mediterranean squadron, in the winter of 1796:

> ' … it has come to my notice that all the ships, with few exceptions, are in a bad state of repair and without the means to change the situation. Even the weakest of enemies could destroy them with ease … If we have to enter into battle this squadron will bring this nation into mourning, digging the grave of the person who has the misfortune to command it.'[3]

The reasons for the Spanish fleet's poor condition were in part economic and in part political. The Spanish economy, weak at the best of times, had been shattered by its membership of the First Coalition and the disastrous war against Revolutionary France. By 1797 the Spanish treasury had a deficit of 820 million *reals*. To make matters worse, Prime Minister Godoy was no friend of the Navy. Those courageous few who pointed out its deep flaws were ignored, bypassed or simply removed from office. Thus the Spanish navy found itself burdened with yet another problem; in the New Year of 1797 it was commanded by its third flag-officer in six weeks, Teniente General José de Córdoba y Ramos, a man with no experience of senior naval command. The previous incumbents had either resigned or been sacked for complaining about the shocking state of the fleet. Just how shocking it was can be judged from the fact that, when the Spanish fleet fought at St Vincent, there were less than 80 skilled hands aboard the flagship, out of a crew 900 strong.

The Stickler

The man who was hoping to find the Spanish was Admiral John Jervis, a most intriguing character. In the New Year of 1797 he was already an officer of immense experience but one with a decidedly mixed reputation. He had joined the navy as a young boy, aged only 13, in 1748, 49 years before he met the Spanish at Cape St Vincent. Almost his entire life had been lived in or around warships. He just missed the War of the Austrian Succession (1739–48) but went on to play a major role in the Seven Years War (1755–62). In 1759 he commanded the ship which led the British fleet up the St Lawrence River, an important preliminary to the subsequent capture of Quebec. During that assault he became intimate with, and was deeply impressed by, the young and impetuous General James Wolfe. Jervis then enjoyed a significant role in a number of campaigns during the War of American Independence (1775–83), including the Battle of Ushant (1778) and all three reliefs of Gibraltar (1780, 1781, 1782). In the peace that followed he finally became an MP and, broadly speaking, a supporter of the Whig Prime Minister, William Pitt, having been fiercely partisan throughout the war. His political single-mindedness and taste for faction coloured his behaviour for the rest of his life. He was utterly and aggressively committed to his own point of view and unwilling to compromise on anything, ever. An experienced and talented seaman maybe, he nonetheless leaves a distinct impression of being bigoted and thoroughly annoying.

The early years of the French Revolutionary war had provided Jervis with an extraordinary opportunity when he was sent to the West Indies, a land of treasure and vice. The war had swiftly overflowed to the Caribbean colonies, the source of both British and French wealth, and the British seized French territory as soon as they could. Several quick British victories gave Jervis the chance to make himself very rich if the rules that governed prizes, seizures and fines were followed, and wealthy beyond anyone's wildest dreams if they were ignored. Jervis wholeheartedly and dogmatically ignored all of the rules to make himself as rich as he possibly could in as short a time as possible. His behaviour embarrassed the British, outraged the French and annoyed the Americans, whose trade became caught up in his thievery. He was even the subject of a vote of censure in the House of Commons.

One of the most important things to realise about Jervis in February 1797, therefore, is that he was 'only' an admiral: his curious behaviour in the Caribbean had prevented him from being elevated to a peerage, a reward which he could reasonably have expected to receive after a successful military campaign. It is certain that this episode left a deep scar upon both Jervis and his political masters who had been deeply unimpressed by his exploits. Similarly, it should be emphasised that his reputation is largely founded on events that occurred *after* the battle of St Vincent, the battle which gave him his title. While 1797 is famous in British naval history for that battle, it is equally notorious as the year that mutiny crippled the Channel and North Sea fleets at Spithead and the Nore. In the aftermath of the mutinies Jervis acquired a reputation for coldness, harshness and an extreme commitment to the maintenance of discipline. One of his stunts was to hang mutineers on a Sunday, which many saw as a breach of the Sabbath. Jervis believed it demonstrated the relentless nature of naval punishment and discipline on his watch; men found guilty of mutiny were hanged the next day, regardless, even, of God. His Mediterranean fleet became a byword for naval discipline.

Four years after his victory, Jervis became First Lord of the Admiralty and his reputation for having an iron fist was only reinforced. He now waged war against corruption and indiscipline in the dockyards, an approach which won him few friends at the time and few admirers since. Dockyards, like ships' companies, were sensitive bodies that required careful handling by a knowledgeable master. While Jervis knew how far he could push ships' companies, he was comparatively ignorant of the curious culture of naval infrastructure ashore. His methods outraged the dockyard workers and drove a wedge between the Admiralty Board and the Navy Board, creating animosity and tension between those twin pillars of

British seapower at a time when that relationship needed to be harmonious. On 15 March 1804, Pitt attacked the policies of St Vincent, as he now was, and declared him 'less brilliant and less able in a civil capacity than in that of a warlike one',[4] a telling opinion that had been harboured by many politicians and professional naval officers for some years.

These, therefore, are the threads of narrative that have attached themselves to St Vincent and they almost entirely define his modern reputation. In February 1797, however, as he paced his quarterdeck enjoying the warmth of the winter sun in the latitude of Gibraltar, his mind was free of the troubles of mutiny or of administrative corruption. His Mediterranean fleet was a highly polished weapon, bristling with energy and excitement. Nelson, one of his subordinates, summed up the prevalent culture.

> 'They at home do not know what this fleet is capable of performing; anything and everything ... of all the fleets I ever saw, I never saw one, in point of officers and men equal to Sir John Jervis's, who is a commander able to lead them to glory.'[5]

If there was any crack in Jervis's confidence, then it was to do with the make-up of his fleet at exactly that time and in exactly that location, because five of his 15 ships had suddenly become unavailable through a series of accidents and had been replaced by five ships from the home fleet.[6] Jervis knew his own ships and his own men, and he was exceptionally proud of them, but how would these newcomers perform?

The Storms

Within four months of the treaty of San Ildefonso, the British had abandoned the Mediterranean and withdrawn their forces on Corsica and Elba to Gibraltar, which remained firmly in their hands. It would be difficult to overestimate the scale of this blow. Corsica had only been taken from the French after a very hard-fought campaign in the spring of 1794, a matter of days before The Glorious First of June. It had provided the British with territory deep in the Mediterranean from which they could launch military operations. Without it, the Mediterranean was a French and Spanish lake.

Corsica was abandoned on 2 November 1796 and the fleet arrived in Gibraltar nearly a month later after an exhausting voyage that had shown the Mediterranean at its worst. Unrelenting westerly winds and fierce squalls whipped it into a tearing, treacherous maelstrom. When Jervis eventually made it to Gibraltar, a fierce hurricane smashed his already weakened squadron, forcing it even further west. He eventually took refuge in Lisbon, dangerously short of supplies.

England, meanwhile, was gripped by the fear of Franco-Spanish invasion. In December 1796 a powerful squadron had sailed from Brest for Ireland, where they planned to establish a bridgehead for an invasion of England via the rugged but poorly policed western coasts. They were only turned back by a succession of relentless Atlantic storms. The attempted invasion rattled both the government and the public, and the navy was at the centre of contemporary criticism. Why had British seapower, celebrated for being so powerful in the aftermath of The Glorious First of June, failed to protect British coasts?

Thus in February 1797, the momentum of the war was firmly with the French and Spanish, and the Royal Navy had come under serious scrutiny. Jervis found himself in a situation where risk was acceptable because it was necessary. It had been made clear in 1794 that a naval victory could unite the British in a way that nothing else could. A naval victory was now essential, if only to absorb the pressure imposed by a united France and Spain and to sustain the British through this low period of the war.

One of the ingredients of the mixture that brought about the eventual battle was mercury. Mercury was essential to 18th-century processes for the refining of silver which, in broad terms, involved crushing the ore with water, salt, magistral (an impure form of copper sulphate) and mercury. The resultant slimy mixture was either spread thinly and left in the sun or placed in heated vats to enable the mercury to form an amalgam with the silver. The Spanish economy of the time, which relied so heavily on the silver extracted from the vast silver mines in Spanish South America, was therefore equally reliant on mercury. Without it, the Spanish could not extract the silver from their mined ore.

Mercury was mined in South America but there were also significant domestic deposits in the hills of Almadén in Southern Spain. In early February 1797, the

Spanish fleet was at the Mediterranean naval base of Cartagena, the closest base to the Almadén mine. Some sense of the importance attached to mercury and the fear of British attack can be gained from the fact that the entire fleet was instructed to escort four mercury ships from Malaga to Cadiz before heading north and meeting up with a French fleet. If united, the combined Franco-Spanish fleet would be in a position to dominate the Western Approaches and, theoretically at least, allow the long-planned invasion of England to be launched.

Things quickly started to unravel for Córdoba when he found himself at the mercy of the unpredictable Mediterranean winter. His fleet was blown by another storm through the Straits of Gibraltar like a cork out of a champagne bottle and left scattered deep in the Atlantic, eight days' sail from home. Jervis was in exactly the same location, waiting for Nelson to rejoin the fleet from Elba, where he had been sent to evacuate the remaining British forces. Thus the pieces fell into place: a poorly manned, disordered Spanish fleet struggling to get back to Cadiz with its precious mercury ships and a well-disciplined British fleet, in desperate need of a victory, patrolling a few miles to the north.

The Dispatches

In the collections of the National Maritime Museum in Greenwich is a very fine mid-18th-century telescope that once belonged to John Jervis and was used by him at the Battle of Cape St Vincent. It is a beautiful piece. A little over 65 centimetres long when closed, it is roughly the size and shape of a rolling pin, with at one end a sliding eyepiece made of brass and at the other a snugly fitting brass cover for the objective lens. It is very plain. There are no engravings, names, dates, waves, flowers, animals or any number of the other curious engravings that you find on nautical curiosities. It is entirely functional and thus convincingly authentic; it has been built to be looked through, not to be looked at.

It is important for two reasons. First, very few commanders-in-chief's telescopes have survived from this era. It is a very rare, and possibly unique, example of a telescope that was used in fleet battle. More importantly, however, it raises the question of what Jervis actually saw on Valentine's Day in 1797. His experience matters more than one might suspect because what he saw differed from what he later described in his dispatches. In fact, Jervis's is one of the most curious battle dispatches that has ever been written. To understand why, however, one must first understand how the battle unfolded.

By two o'clock in the morning on 14 February, Jervis had already known for an hour that something curious was afoot because he had heard the sound of signal guns. Half an hour later he heard from a Portuguese frigate that the Spanish fleet was nearby, a report that was confirmed in ever-increasing detail as the day dawned. By half past six in the morning, a fleet of strange ships could just be made out with the naked eye from the decks of Jervis's flagship and seen quite clearly through his telescope. The first thing to realise about the Battle of St Vincent, therefore, is the time. If you count 06.30 as the beginning of their contact, and you consider that the prizes were secured at sunset, then the entire day, from dawn until dusk, was taken up by the battle. A lot can happen in 12 hours of contact with the enemy and this battle was no exception.

Several stages of the battle stand out as important and several events as unique. The Spanish fleet was taken by surprise when it was discovered and was split into two significant sections. This was a godsend for any attacking admiral, as had been definitively proven by the difficulty of Howe's attack on the well-formed French line on 1 June 1794. Then, several ships had been unable to break through and those that did had been so devastated by French fire that they had become vulnerable to counter-attack. A pre-existing gap, on the other hand, could be exploited by a skilful commander to divide the enemy fleet with comparative ease, though it demanded a high degree of seamanship from both the commander and his captains.

Thus the first part of the British attack at St Vincent entailed Jervis's fleet, in perfect order, attacking from the north-east and cutting the Spanish fleet in two, with the larger section, containing Córdoba's flagship, to the north and the smaller section, containing the mercury ships, of which the British were unaware, to the south. This was no easy feat. Jervis had to get his fleet in good order and then thread it through the eye of a moving needle whilst under fire. Once through, he changed course by tacking the entire fleet under the guns of the enemy, a tricky manoeuvre even on a calm day with no one else in sight and an opportunity for the Spanish to counter-attack. The Spaniards' southern division made three spirited attempts to break Jervis's line at this point and, though each attempt was beaten off, their efforts damaged many British ships and disrupted the British line.

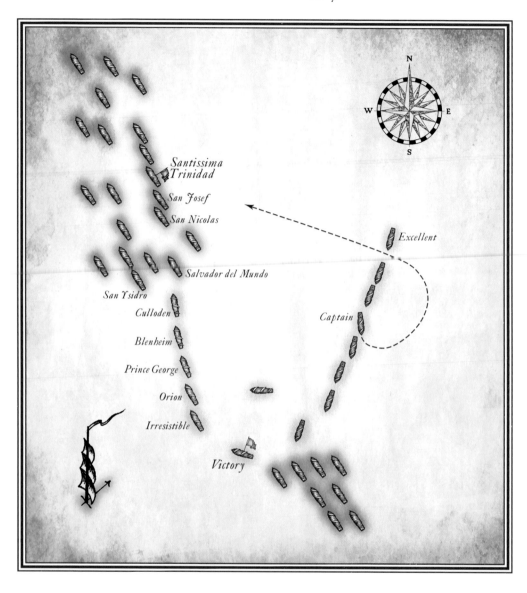

Jervis then led those British ships that could still manoeuvre in an attack against the northern division of the Spanish fleet, which was doing everything in its power to reunite with the southern section. If they had been successful, they could have turned the tables on the damaged and divided British and made for Cadiz in a single body. It was at this stage that Jervis signalled the British rear division to tack, and thus to counter the attempt of the Spanish to reunite. However, Vice-Admiral Sir Charles Thompson, leader of Jervis's rear division, failed to respond. We do not know why the signal was ignored, or perhaps missed, but we do know that Jervis was later furious with Thompson. The rest of the ships in the rear division were presented with a professional conundrum for which there was no right or wrong answer. Should they follow their divisional leader, who was clearly not following the Admiral's instructions, or break out of their own division and act as Jervis had signalled? It was a dilemma that was frequently posed in fleet battle when smoke and limited signalling systems created confusion.

It was Nelson in the 74-gun *Captain,* a few ships astern of Thompson, who acted according to his Admiral's orders rather than to the behaviour of his divisional leader. Significant time had been lost and wearing, rather than tacking, was now the most appropriate, as well as the more reliable, method of changing course and intercepting the Spanish northern division, as Jervis clearly intended. Nelson therefore wore ship and, as soon as he had broken the spell cast by Thompson's curious behaviour, other ships followed suit and prevented the junction of the two sections of the Spanish fleet.

Nelson's manoeuvre was particularly courageous because it brought his relatively small ship into action at the head of the British line and into the heart of the cauldron of huge ships surrounding the Spanish Admiral, who had yet to open fire. The engagement then became general and several British ships found themselves in the thick of it, particularly Thomas Frederick's *Blenheim*, Horatio Nelson's own *Captain*, Cuthbert Collingwood's *Excellent*, Thomas Troubridge's *Culloden*, George Martin's *Irresistible* and James Saumarez's *Orion*. And then something quite extraordinary happened: Nelson led a boarding party from the diminutive two-decker, Third Rate HMS *Captain*, onto a powerful Spanish 80-gunner, the *San Nicolas*, and secured her as a prize. Then he did it again, this time attacking from the decks of the ship he had just captured, onto a three-decker, the 114-gun First Rate *San Josef,* which he also captured.

It was the first time that a British flag-officer had led a boarding party in person since Sir Edward Howard in 1513, although Howard had lost his life when he had been thrown overboard in full armour. It was also the first time in any 18th-century fleet battle that a Spanish First Rate had been captured[7] and it was the first time that one captured ship had created a 'bridge' to another. Moreover, it had all been achieved by a man who was experiencing fleet battle for the very first time. Nelson had fought in many previous single-ship actions and amphibious operations, but he had never before experienced the unique carnage and chaos of a fleet engagement.

The British also captured another Spanish First Rate, the 112-gun *Salvador del Mundo* as well as another Third Rate, the 74-gun *San Ysidro*. Jervis saw some of these remarkable events from his quarterdeck and immediately after the battle personally congratulated Nelson; in fact, he hugged him. He knew that the British, outnumbered 27 to 15, had won a convincing victory and, more importantly, he knew how it had been achieved.

Robert Calder, Jervis's flag captain, was given the honour of taking the dispatches back to London in the frigate *Lively*. Calder arrived in the Scillies on 27 February and then headed to St Ives, the sooner to reach London overland because of foul weather in the Channel. He was extremely careful to keep the news to himself and prevent any other news of the battle from reaching the public before his. Only he, his letters and his servant were allowed ashore. Calder travelled across the endless wastes of Bodmin Moor, Dartmoor and Salisbury Plain before dropping down into the Thames Valley and proceeding on to London. He arrived at the Admiralty and handed over the letter to Evan Nepean, the Secretary of the Admiralty, who had replaced Philip Stephens in March 1795.* And this is what it said.

Admiral J. Jervis to E. Nepean, 16 Feb 1797

VICTORY IN LAGOS BAY
16TH FEBRUARY 1797.

The hopes of falling in with the Spanish Fleet, expressed in my letter to you of the 13th instant, were confirmed that night, by our distinctly hearing the report of

---

* For a biography see Appendix I.

Victory
Britannia
Barfleur
Prince George
Blenheim
Namur
Captain
Goliath
Excellent
Orion
Colossus
Egmont
Culloden
Irresistible
Diadem

	Guns
Salvador del Mundo	*112*
San Josef	*112*
San Nicolas	*80*
San Ysidro	*74*

their signal guns, and by intelligence received from Captain Foote of His Majesty's Ship the Niger, who had with equal judgment and perseverance, kept company with them for several days, on my prescribed Rendezvous (which, from the strong South East winds, I had never been able to reach) and that they were not more than the distance of three or four leagues from us: I anxiously awaited the dawn of day, when, being on the Starboard tack, Cape St. Vincent bearing EbN. eight leagues, I had the satisfaction of seeing a number of Ships extending from South West to South, the wind then at West and by South. At 49 minutes past ten, the weather being extremely hazey, le bonne Citoyenne made the Signal that the Ships seen were of the Line, twenty five in number. His Majesty's Squadron under my command, consisting of the fifteen Ships of the Line named in the margin, happily formed in the most compact Order of Sailing in two lines: by carrying a press of sail I was fortunate in getting in with the Enemy's Fleet, at half past eleven o'clock, before it had time to connect and form in regular Order of Battle: Such a moment was not to be lost, and, confident in the skill, valour, and discipline of the Officers and men I had the happiness to command, and judging that the honor of His Majesty's Arms, and the circumstances of the war in these Seas required a considerable degree of enterprize, I felt myself justified in departing from the regular system, and passing through their Fleet, in a line formed with the utmost celerity, tacked, and thereby separated one third from the main body, after a partial cannonade, which prevented their rejunction 'til the evening; and by the very great exertions of the Ships, which had the good fortune to arrive up with the enemy on the larboard tack, the ships named in the margin were captured, and the Action ceased about five o'clock in the evening.

I enclose the most correct list I have been able to obtain of the Spanish Fleet opposed to me, amounting to twenty seven sail of the Line; and an account of the killed and wounded in His

Majesty's Ships, as well as in those taken from the enemy: The moment
the latter (almost totally dismasted) and His Majesty's Ships the Captain
and Culloden, are in a state to put to sea, I shall avail myself of the first
favourable wind to proceed off Cape St. Vincent in my way to Lisbon,
notwithstanding the intelligence contained in the accompanying letter, which I
have just received from Captain Berkley of His Majesty's Ship the Emerald.

    I am

      Sir

      Your most Obedient humble

    servant *Jervis*

P.S. Captain Calder, whose able assistance has greatly contributed to
the public service during my Command, is the Bearer of this, and will more
particularly describe to My Lords Commissioners of the Admiralty the
movements of the squadron on the 14th and the present state of it.

Jervis

EVAN NEPEAN ESR.

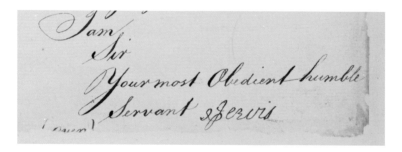

That's it! There is no mention of the vigorous Spanish attack against the British
fleet as they tacked in the gap between the two groups of Spanish ships, or of the
subsequent British attack against the northern section of the Spanish fleet. There
is no mention at all of Nelson or, indeed, of any other captain, many of whom
performed quite brilliantly. In fact the only person mentioned at all in relation to

his performance is Jervis's flag captain, Robert Calder. Jervis wrote another, private, letter to Lord Spencer on the following day in which he was a little more detailed and even slightly apologetic for the reticence of his official dispatch, beginning with an attempt at explanation: 'The conduct of every Officer and man in the Squadron on the 14th inst. Made it improper to distinguish one more than another in my public Letter …'8 In this second letter, Troubridge, Nelson, Collingwood, Berry, Hallowell, Lieutenants Spicer and Noble and Jervis's Rear Admiral, William Parker, were singled out, but very briefly indeed, and the letter was never published.

So how were the details of the battle discovered? The answer lies with Nelson. Just as he insisted, contrary to all tradition, on boarding those Spanish ships himself to share in the glory, so did he now insist on taking control over the telling of the tale. This was by no means a matter of sudden inspiration. Nelson was well practised at writing descriptions of engagements in his own hand, and he did so in a style that was colourful, fluent and generous to those with whom he had fought. His description of his then most recent battle against two Spanish frigates is a case in point. He wrote those dispatches with publication in the *London Gazette* in mind because, in his own words, 'It is what I know the English like [in a *Gazette*]'.9 He certainly knew how to play to a crowd and lavished praise on his men.

'Lieutenant Culverhouse, the first lieutenant, is an old officer of very distinguished merit. Lieutenants Hardy, [William Hall] Gage, and Noble deserve every praise which gallantry and zeal justly entitle them to, as do every other officer and man in the ship. You will observe, sir, I am sure with regret, amongst the wounded, Lieutenant James Noble, who quitted the *Captain* to serve with me, and whose merits and repeated wounds received in fighting the enemies of our country entitle him to every reward which a grateful nation can bestow.'10

Nelson's description of his action at St Vincent was in much the same vein and is one of the most detailed and extraordinary contemporary narratives of a battle. It captured the public's imagination, and rightly so. He gave it the wonderfully modest title 'A few marks relative to myself in the *Captain*, in which my pendant was flying, on the most glorious Valentine's day, 1797'. Here is an excerpt, which seems positively outlandish when compared with Jervis's austere and brief dispatch.

'The soldiers of the 69th Regiment with an alacrity which will ever do them credit, and Lieutenant Pierson of the same Regiment, were among the foremost in this service. The first man who jumped into the enemy's mizzen chains was Captain Berry, late my First Lieutenant; (Captain Miller was in the very act of going also, but I directed him to remain;) he was supported from our spritsail yard, which hooked into the mizzen rigging. A soldier of the 61st regiment having broke the upper quarter-gallery window, jumped in, followed by myself and others as fast as possible. I found the cabin door fastened, and some Spanish officers fired their pistols; but having broke open the doors, the soldiers fired, and the Spanish Brigadier (Commodore with a distinguishing pennant) fell, as retreating to the quarter deck, on the larboard side, near the wheel. Having pushed onto the quarter deck, I found Captain Berry in possession of the poop, and the Spanish ensign hauling down. I passed with my people and Lieutenant Pierson on to the larboard gangway to the forecastle, where I met two or three Spanish officer prisoners to my seamen, and they delivered me their swords.

At this moment a fire of pistols or muskets opened from the admiral's stern gallery of the *San Josef*; I directed the soldiers to fire into her stern; and, calling to Captain Miller, ordered him to send more men into the *San Nicolas*, and directed my people to board the First Rate, which was done in an instant, Captain Berry assisting me into the main chains. At this moment a Spanish officer looked over from the quarter-deck rail and said "they surrendered"; from this most welcome intelligence it was not long before I was on the quarter-deck, when the Spanish Captain, with a bow, presented me his Sword, and said the Admiral was dying of his wounds below. I asked him, on his honour, if the ship was surrendered? he declared she was; on which I gave him my hand, and desired him to call his Officers and Ship's company, and tell them of it — which he did; and on the quarter-deck of a Spanish First Rate extravagant as the story may seem, did I receive the Swords of the vanquished Spaniards; which, as I received, I gave to William Fearney, one of my barge-men, who put them with the greatest sangfroid under his arm.'

Here is compelling description, and its detail gives the reader a fine perception of the events unfolding and the names of the actors. Here is bravery, astonishment, a little humour, bashfulness, pride and courage, all presented as a flowing narrative. Nelson even wrote a comic 'recipe' for cooking Spaniards, which included advice on '*battering and basting them for an hour*' to make certain that they were '*well seasoned ... stewed and blended together*'. This was brilliant stuff; no wonder the public loved it. In obvious contrast with Jervis, and more than any other admiral, Nelson was a wordsmith. It is a major, but often overlooked, factor in his subsequent fame.

Nelson was also exceptionally cunning in the way that he ensured that his version of events was seen first, and then by the largest audience, beautifully outmanoeuvring Robert Calder, the bearer of Jervis's dispatch. On board the *Lively*, the frigate which was carrying Calder to England, was one Gilbert Eliot, a friend of Nelson's and a talented career politician. Before she left, Nelson visited the *Lively* and hatched a plan with Eliot. One of Eliot's influential friends was William Windham, the Secretary for War. Windham was also the MP for Norwich. Nelson, who was himself from Norfolk, sent the sword of the captured Spanish Rear-Admiral Don Xavier Francisco Winthuysen to the city of Norwich as a gift, thus allowing the bearer of the sword, a Lieutenant Pierson, to make contact with Windham. Nelson, of course, ensured that Pierson also took with him a copy of his personal narrative. As a result Nelson's version of events was seen by Windham in London, discussed by him with Lord Spencer, the First Lord of the Admiralty, and then shown by the latter to the King, all before anyone had seen Jervis's version, carried by Calder. Nelson had pulled off a perfectly executed and quite deliberate PR coup and his fame grew exponentially thereafter.

For all its comparative lack of colour, however, Jervis's dispatch raises numerous important questions. We know from several sources that his fleet was bound together by great comradeship and that he was warm towards his fellow sailors, so why did he neglect to name any of the men who were so deserving? His dispatch is not completely dry, because he does pay lip service to his fleet by showing how he was 'confident in the skill, valour, and discipline of the Officers and men I had [the] happiness to command', but he fails to name anyone in particular. We may never know the exact reason for this omission, but several things could have influenced him.

The most obvious and most easily proved explanation is that Jervis hated writing dispatches. 'I would much rather have an action with the enemy than detail one,'[11] he later wrote in a huff and was careful to empower Robert Calder in his dispatch to 'more particularly describe to My Lords Commissioners of the Admiralty the movements of the squadron on the 14th and the present state of it'. Perhaps, however, his reluctance stemmed also from a distaste for bureaucracy or from a desire to avoid the trap into which Howe had fallen after The Glorious First of June, when he had given some captains but not others the blessing of his written word. Jervis therefore tried to avoid potential upset by naming no one in his battle dispatch, but only after he had first made quite certain that his sailors knew the depth of his pride and the extent of his gratitude. Indeed, in the immediate aftermath of the battle the following eloquent message was passed to every captain:

> 'No language I am possessed of can convey the high sense I entertain of the exemplary conduct of the flag officers, captains, officers, seamen, marines and soldiers, embarked on board every ship of the squadron I have the honour to command, present at the vigorous and successful attack made upon the fleet of Spain on the 14th instant. The signal advantage obtained by His Majesty's arms on that day is entirely owing to their determined valour and discipline; and I request that you will accept yourself, and give my thanks and approbation to those composing the crew of the ship under your command, I am, Sir, your most humble servant, J. Jervis.'[12]

Jervis was always supportive of anyone who had performed well for him, in any guise. He once said himself, 'I have never forsaken a man who served well under me,'[13] and there is plenty of evidence to support that statement. On one occasion, a sailor spoiled £6 in notes whilst washing his clothes, the equivalent of a full five months' pay, and Jervis replaced the money from his own pocket. We also know, of course, that he not only thanked Nelson but did so by taking him 'in his arms'.[14] That is not the act of a cold man.

Jervis's dispatch to the Admiralty, though surprising, must not, therefore, be read as evidence that he was an uncaring or ungrateful commander. On the contrary, this battle stands out from so many in the Age of Sail because there is no hint that Jervis was angry with any of his captains. As Nelson's flag captain, Ralph

Miller, declared, 'I will only say that among the pleasant things of this glorious day one considerable one is there being no drawback, nobody against whom there is a breath of Censure.'[15] And that is the sign of a fleet sailing in harmony under strong and compassionate leadership. Collingwood, who had suffered so much as a result of his omission from Howe's dispatch, praised St Vincent. He wrote: 'What is particularly happy to this great event is that there is no drawback, no slander – though all were not equally engaged, all did what was in their power to reduce them, and I understand the Admiral has wisely avoided all partial praise of those whose ill luck prevented their getting into conspicuous situations.'[16]

It is possible that another influence on Jervis's composition was Robert Calder. One contemporary explanation argued that Jervis actually *did* write a detailed narrative of the battle, but was pressured by Calder into rewriting it to leave out any names.[17] There is no evidence to support this, though there is an interesting parallel with The Glorious First of June when, it was rumoured, Howe, at the instigation of his flag captain, called off the chase of the French fleet when they were beaten, resulting in the escape of several French ships. Both of these examples make the Admiral look weak by suggesting that he acted under pressure from a junior officer, and it is possible that they were manufactured for political reasons.

Jervis's dispatch made some readers very angry because it was unsatisfying, and perhaps because it was deliberately crafted to be so. Furthermore, Nelson's account irritated other captains because it magnified his role at the expense of others. Most irritated was Rear-Admiral William Parker of the *Prince George*, who firmly believed that the mighty First Rate *San José* was actually his prize. Parker had beaten her to silence before she crashed into the *San Nicolas*, allowing Nelson to secure the prize without a fight. It is another reminder that Nelson's rise to the status of hero was not achieved without casualties, one of which was the truth. Parker was by no means alone in his criticism of Nelson, and the First Lord even waded in with this attempt to calm tempers:

> 'The variation in the accounts of an action at sea by different persons are so easily and naturally to be accounted for by the different situations in which the writers are at times placed ... that it is neither necessary nor fair to draw an inference from them that any intention has existed of disparaging the conduct of others.'[18]

This dispatch-writing business was trouble from start to finish.

For all that Jervis's dispatch fails to mention, however, it does tell us three important things. First, we learn from it that Jervis knew that the Spanish were out, that he was actively searching for them and that he had 'hopes' of falling in with them. We know from his journal that he had been prepared for battle for more than 24 hours, since 14.10 p.m. on 12 February, long before Nelson joined him on the morning of the 13th after the heart-stopping experience of accidentally sailing through the middle of the Spanish fleet in the night. By then Jervis was so convinced there would be a battle that the final toast at dinner in the *Victory* on the 13th was 'Victory over the Dons in the battle from which they cannot escape tomorrow!'[19] From the early morning of 12 February, therefore, Jervis's fleet was well formed while his network of frigates worked overtime to locate the enemy. The Spanish, in contrast, had no idea that Jervis was nearby; indeed, they thought he was in Lisbon. They were completely unaware that they were sailing into a trap.

Second, Jervis makes no mention at all of the mercury ships or, indeed, of any type of merchant ship. This is not so surprising; such valuable merchantmen would have been armed and may even have been made to look exactly like warships to discourage any nosy captain with piratical instincts. The implication is important, however. Jervis genuinely believed that he was facing 25, and he later says 27, warships, a fleet that far outnumbered his own 15. And what warships they were. One was the *Santissima Trinidad,* the largest warship in the world, armed with 136 guns on four decks, and there were *six* three-deckers of 112 guns. All seven of these Spanish First Rates were larger than any British ship in the fleet. Lieutenant Henry Edgell of the *Victory* climbed aloft to have a good look at them. 'They loom like Beachy Head in a fog,' he said. 'By my soul, they are thumpers.'[20]

We now know that the size of the Spanish fleet differed from what Jervis believed and consisted of 23 warships.[21] Jervis was ignorant of this, however, and attacked anyway. That moment is wonderfully caught in an apocryphal exchange between Calder and Jervis.

'There are eight sail of the line, Sir John.'

'Very well, sir.'

'There are 20 sail of the line, Sir John.'

'Very well, sir.'

'There are 25 sail of the line, Sir John.'

'Very well, sir.'

'There are 27 sail of the line, Sir John … near twice our own number.'

'Enough, sir,' exclaimed Jervis. 'No more of that. The die is cast, and if there are 50 sail I will go through them.'[22]

The British attack was bold enough, given what we now know about the size of the opposing fleets, but it was bolder still, given that Jervis believed that he was outnumbered almost two to one, even if the real ratio was nearer three to two. His attack demonstrates powerfully his contempt for Spanish sailors, his belief in British skill and his conviction that a naval victory was crucial. That contempt no doubt stemmed in part from his recent, first-hand experience of the Spaniards' ability but would have been reinforced by what he saw on the day of the battle itself. As one witness described it, their behaviour was 'confusion worse confounded'[23] and the Master of the *Prince George* could not see 'any plan' in their movements 'nor did it appear … there was sufficient skill or discipline to execute any orders their commander might have given'.[24]

The third key message that emerges from Jervis's dispatch is that he mentions that he 'departed from the regular system' in his style of attack. In Jervis's mind there obviously was a 'regular system' but we know from studying the tactics employed in previous battles that the shared characteristic of these engagements was variety, not similarity. There were chase battles where the enemy was enveloped from the rear, defensive battles when the fleets stretched the length of each other's lines and aggressive battles when one fleet divided another. Jervis did nothing unusual or unexpected at St Vincent, so what *exactly* did he mean by a 'regular system'?

The answer lies in the mismatched sizes of the fleets. In such a situation the accepted tactic was for one fleet to stretch the full length of the other until van matched van and rear matched rear. This was the default defensive position assumed when two fleets first met, particularly when the two fleets were unmatched. By stretching the full length of the enemy, Jervis would prevent his enemy from doubling his van or rear. As it was, however, this tactic was inapplicable on this occasion and Jervis, not afraid of the Spanish, saw an extant gap that he could exploit. Only the most incompetent commanding officer in his situation would have overlooked such an obvious opportunity to keep a larger enemy divided. For all of Jervis's syntax, therefore, it can be argued that he did, in fact, act according to the 'regular system' by choosing the appropriate tactic for the given situation. Anything else would have been a fundamental mistake and his contemporaries would have known it.

Casualty list from the British Fleet, 14 Feb 1797

The next dispatch is a straightforward list of killed and wounded in the British fleet that gives numbers for the fleet as a whole and the names of the wounded officers.

LIST OF KILLED AND WOUNDED IN THE SQUADRON UNDER THE COMMAND OF ADMIRAL SIR JOHN JERVIS, IN THE ACTION WITH THE SPANISH FLEET 14TH FEBRUARY 1797. –

		KILLED				WOUNDED				TOTAL OF KILLED AND WOUNDED
		Officers	Seamen	Marines	Soldiers	Officers	Seamen	Marines	Soldiers	
VICTORY	Admiral Sir John Jervis	.	1	.	.	.	2	3		6
	1st Captain Robert Calder									
	2nd Captain George Grey									
BRITANNIA	Vice Admiral Thompson	.	.	.	.	.	1	.	.	1
	Captain Thomas Foley									
BARFLEUR	Vice Adml Honble Wm Waldegrave	.	.	.	.	.	7	.	.	7
	Captain James Richd Davies									
PRINCE GEORGE	Rear Admiral Parker	.	7	1	.	.	7	.	.	15
	Captain John Irwin									
BLENHEIM	Captain Thos Lex Frederick	.	10	.	2	2	40	.	7	61
NAMUR	" James H. Whitshed	.	2	.	.	.	5	.	.	7
CAPTAIN	Commodore Nelson	1	20	.	3	2	50	.	4	80
	Captain Ralph Wt Miller									

GOLIATH	Captain Sir Chs H, Knowles	.	.	.	.	.	4	4	.	8
EXCELLENT	" Cuthbert Collingwood	1	8	2	.	.	10	2	.	23
ORION	" Sir Jas Saumarez	.	.	.	.	.	7	2	.	9
COLOSSUS	" Geo: Murray	.	.	.	.	.	4	1	.	5
EGMONT	" John Sutton	-	-	-	-	-	-	-	-	-
CULLODEN	" Thos Troubridge	1	7	2	.	.	39	8	.	57
IRRESISTIBLE	" George Martin	.	4	1	.	1	12	1	.	19
DIADEM	" G: Hy Lowry	.	.	.	.	.	1	.	1	2
		3	59	6	5	5	189	21	12	300

OFFICERS KILLED AND WOUNDED			
BLENHEIM	Mr Edward Libby,	Acting Lieut,	Wounded.
	Mr Peacock,	Boatswain,	Wounded.
	Mr Josh Nixon,	Master's Mate,	Wounded, since Dead.
CAPTAIN	Major Wm Norris,	Marines,	Killed
	Mr James Goderich,	Mid.,	D°.
	Commodore Nelson,	bruised, but not obliged to quit the Deck.	
	Mr Carrington,	Boatswain,	wounded in boarding the San Nicolas.
	Mr Thomas Lund,	Mid.	Wounded.
EXCELLENT	Mr Peter Peffers,	Boatswain,	Killed.
	Mr Edwd Augts Down,	Masrs Mate,	Wounded
ORION	Mr Thomas Mansel,	Midshipman,	D°.
CULLODEN	Mr G. A. Livingstone,	Lieut: Marines,	Killed.
IRRESISTIBLE	Sergeant Watson,	Marines,	Killed.
	Mr Andrew Thompson,	Lieut.,	Wounded.
	Mr Hugh McKinnon,	Masrs Mate,	Wounded
	Mr Willm Balfour,	Midshipman,	Wounded

Several things stand out. These figures provide an important statistical reminder that, although Nelson's *Captain* does have the highest casualty return, his was by no means the only ship in the thick of the action. The *Blenheim, Excellent,*

Prince George and *Irresistible* all had their fair share of the engagement. We must, however, be careful that we do not fall into a trap here. In the aftermath of The Glorious First of June, Collingwood realised there was a problem with analysing casualty returns. He had fought well but his ship was little damaged and his crew relatively intact. He complained:

> 'I considered the conduct of the *Barfleur* had merited commendation
> when commendation was given to zeal and activity and that any
> insinuation that either had been wanting was injurious and unjust, nor do
> I believe any ship was more warmly or effectively engaged than the *Barfleur*
> from the beginning of the action to the end of it. That the Frenchmen
> did not knock our masts away was not my fault.'[25]

With limited source material available, the casualty return lists may seem like a good way of judging the performance of the ships in question. However, it does not of course logically follow that the ships with the highest casualty returns were necessarily conducted with greater skill or courage by their captains. It may merely be that the enemy fire had a greater effect on their crews, perhaps because of the enemy gunners' skill or, equally, through complete chance. The fundamental problem is that we do not know how these men died; it is quite possible that some died from exploding guns, from friendly fire or by falling overboard. Nor do we know why men on other ships did not die in such numbers.

The return for Jervis's *Victory* blows the cobwebs off one apocryphal tale long associated with the battle.[26] The story goes that, as Jervis stood viewing the action on his quarterdeck, a shot fizzed through the air inches away and took the head clean off a marine standing beside him, drenching Jervis in his brains. George Grey, the captain of Jervis's flagship, immediately rushed up to the Admiral to check that he was unharmed and Jervis, with a wonderful sense of calm, replied, 'I am not at all hurt … but do, George, try if you can get me an orange.' The story is certainly plausible. Jervis had for some time been cruising off southern Spain, a land full of over-sized, delicious and juicy oranges and the sang-froid seems pure Jervis. However, the casualty list clearly shows that no marine actually died, only one sailor. It's a cracking story, so let's leave it as it is, but change the identity of the victim from a marine to a sailor, poor chap.

By a curious quirk of fate we also happen to know that, aboard the *Orion*, was a woman named Nancy Perriam who was serving alongside her husband, a gunner named Edward Hopping. Women were not officially allowed on board naval ships but some captains allowed wives of petty officers to live aboard where they made themselves useful. Nancy normally performed domestic tasks for the captain and officers, and we know she was mending one of Captain Saumarez's shirts as they approached the Spanish fleet. While in battle she tended the wounded. It is likely, therefore, that the *Orion*'s wounded midshipman, Thomas Mansel, was nursed by Nancy Perriam, who was also later present at the Battle of the Nile. Perhaps he found a woman's touch comforting.

The important name in the list of officers is that of Nelson, who is described as being 'bruised, but not obliged to quit the Deck'. It was not the first time that Nelson had been wounded in action, but it *was* the first time that he officially reported a wound. Most recently, his right eye had been damaged in an explosion during an attack on Corsica. He had had no intention of making a fuss and had not filed an unofficial report or even entered the detail into his log. As a result, he was to be prevented from receiving any of the compensation[27] he was due when the wound worsened, eventually leaving him blind in that eye.

This time he was not so casual, though there is still a hint of nonchalance in the description of the wound. He was actually hit in the stomach by a splinter that had burst off a rigging block. He was struck with such force that he collapsed and was caught in the arms of Ralph Miller, Nelson's captain, who was horrified. Modern surgeons can deduce a good deal from Nelson's subsequent symptoms. If you are squeamish, look away now. He had been hit so hard that the internal wall of his abdomen split in a great fissure. When he coughed, his intestines spilled out, creating a hernia 'the size of a fist' that protruded from his stomach. He described this wound as 'trifling'. It is unlikely that the hernia became strangulated, that is, cut off from the blood supply in a condition that can kill, because Nelson makes no reference to such trauma. We can therefore deduce that he would have been able to 'push' his intestines back in whenever they popped out. We also know that the wound occasionally prevented him from urinating, probably because of swelling of the bladder wall near the mouth of the urethra, the swelling itself being caused either directly by the blow or, more likely, by resultant bleeding inside the bladder. Blood clots could easily form and thus block the urethra. The symptom would only pass when Nelson passed the clot, a traumatic and painful experience. Nelson was a very private person when it came to such matters and only ever mentioned this symptom once, in a letter to his close friend William Suckling.

Although Nelson made certain that his wound at St Vincent was officially recorded in the dispatches, he was damned if he was going to tell his wife. He wrote nine letters to Fanny in the aftermath of the battle and didn't mention his wound once, just as he failed to mention in any letter to Fanny the back wound he had received at Bastia or the eye wound sustained at Corsica. As it was, the stomach wound troubled him for the rest of his life. It is a reminder that it is all too easy to view these figures as cold statistics, when even a non-fatal wound could still be a crushing event that might affect the victim physically and mentally for the rest of his life. Oliver Davis, one of those 30 wounded seamen aboard the *Captain*, wrote as he lay with a broken arm, 'I often … think how uncertain a man's life is … I compare it to a flower in the field; in the morning growing and in its full bloom, but before night is cut down and never more seen.'[28] This is not just a list of men who had been wounded, but a list of men who had been changed.

Finally, we can see which British ships were *not* there. Jervis fought very well against a larger Spanish fleet but his fleet should have been larger by five ships. On 10 December the 74-gun HMS *Courageaux* was lost on the Barbary Coast along with 464 members of her crew. Eleven days later another 74-gunner, the *Bombay Castle*, grounded on a sandbar at the mouth of the Tagus and was abandoned, and six days after that, the Second Rate, 98-gun *St George* was badly damaged when she grounded on the Cachopos Shoals. In the same month the 80-gun *Gibraltar* and 74-gun *Zealous* also both grounded, the *Gibraltar* being forced to return to Britain for repairs and the *Zealous* to Lisbon. These extra ships might well have turned Jervis's victory into a rout.

Casualty List from the Spanish fleet, 14 Feb 1797

LIST OF THE KILLED & WOUNDED ON BOARD THE SPANISH SHIPS TAKEN BY THE SQUADRON UNDER THE COMMAND OF ADMRL. SIR JOHN JERVIS, K.C.B., ON THE 14 FEBY 1797.

SHIPS NAMES	RANK	KILLED	WOUNDED
SAN YSIDRO	Officers	4	8
	Artillerists, Seamen & Soldiers	25	55
		29	63
SALVADOR DEL MUNDO	Officers	5	3
	Artillerists, Seamen & Soldiers	37	121
		42	124
SAN NICHOLAS	Officers	4	8
	Artillerists, Seamen & Soldiers	140	51
		144	59
SAN JOSE	Officers	2	5
	Artillerists, Seamen & Soldiers	44	91
		46	96

KILLED – 261
WOUNDED – 342

603

NOTE – AMONG THE KILLED IS THE GENERAL DON FRANCISCO XAVIER WINTHUYSEN, CHEF D'ESCADRE

When compared with the British figures, this makes shocking reading. The Spanish fleet lost 15 officers dead, including a flag-officer, and 24 wounded on these four ships alone, the British only six officers killed and 10 injured in their entire fleet. The current and future command structure of the Royal Navy was little affected by the battle, whereas Spain's was ruined.

If one considers the numbers as a whole, more than twice as many Spaniards died on these four ships than on the entire British fleet. In the aftermath of Nelson's capture of the *San Nicholas*, 144 men lay dead on her decks. There were so many dead in the Spanish fleet that they would have lain in great piles, arms and legs sticking out at impossible angles, heads buried, some of the corpses with eyes open and some with eyes shut. Some lay with weapons still clasped in their hands, others with hands clasped to gaping wounds. The pools of dark blood found their way to the seams between the planks and painted the length of the decks in cruel stripes. This was a massacre caused by far superior gunnery. One contemporary believed that the British fired five or six broadsides to each from the Spanish.

There is, however, one very important ship missing from this list of captured vessels, the giant four-decked, 136-gun *Santissima Trinidad*. Howe could have secured more prizes than he did at The Glorious First of June and the same can be said of Jervis who let one of the finest of them all slip through his grasp at St Vincent. The *Santissima Trinidad* was unique. Built as a three-decker in Havana in 1769, she was converted between 1795 and 1796 to carry 136 guns on four decks. She was the world's first four-decker and no British sailor had ever seen her like before. British ships fired repeatedly into her hull and at her rigging until she wallowed in the swell with 300 casualties littering her decks. The man who came closest to taking her was James Saumarez of the *Orion*.

Saumarez knew fleet battle. As a 24-year-old lieutenant, he had fought against the Dutch at the Dogger Bank in 1781 and the following year had taken part in Rodney's impressive victory over the French at the Saints. The French had been as poorly manned and dispirited then as the Spanish were now, and the scale of that victory had been equally shocking. Saumarez was always keen for glory and at the Saints had played an important part in capturing the French Admiral's flagship, the mighty *Ville de Paris*. He had missed The Glorious First of June but had taken part in a fierce single-ship action, the capture of the frigate *La Réunion* in October 1793, that was renowned for the scale of the British victory: 120 Frenchmen killed or wounded for only one British sailor hurt. Saumarez went on to fight with Nelson at the Nile but their relationship was never as easy as that between Nelson and some of his other senior officers. He had a thirst for glory at least as great as Nelson's and they seem to have considered each other a threat to their own advancement.

There is some confusion in the sources over the fate of the *Santissima Trinidad* at St Vincent. This is not surprising since to claim such a big fish would have been to secure one's position in British naval history. Some witnesses claimed that they did not see her strike, others that they did and Saumarez that she struck to him. His Master's log, at least is clear:

'... we got abreast of the Spanish Admiral, Commander-in-Chief of
a four-deck ship, opened a heavy fire on her, as did the *Blenheim*; both
her fore and mizzen masts went over the side being totally disabled. 55
minutes past 4, she struck and hoisted English colours, but we was obliged
to abandon her, as several of their 3-deck ships which had been but little
in action came down to their assistance, and the day being far spent, we
discontinued the action ...'[29]

Saumarez later became irate at insinuations that he had been mistaken, just
as Nelson and his followers became irate that he had been ignored in Jervis's
dispatch. Indeed the absence of credit and lack of detail in Jervis's dispatch
effectively led to a race to self-proclaim that credit among his captains, a race
which was handsomely won by Nelson.

The escape of the *Santissima Trinidad* reminds us that the Spanish were not
sufficiently beaten that they would abandon the pride of their navy, and that several
Spanish ships remained in sufficiently good condition to save her. The *Santissima
Trinidad* lived to fight another day and the narrative of St Vincent was dominated
by Nelson rather than shared with Saumarez. Things could easily have turned out
differently however. A change of wind could have blown the shattered *Santissima*
towards the British fleet or a concerted, combined effort could have wrested her
free from her Spanish saviours. Nelson, moreover, was fortunate to have been
at the battle at all; he had rejoined the fleet only 17 hours before. The results of
fleet battle were malleable and easily changed. As it was, the battle provided an
important foundation for the Nelson myth that eventually led to his statue being
raised in granite 100 feet above Trafalgar Square. The dispatches remind us of the
ghosts that surround him on invisible pillars of their own.

Admiral John Jervis became Baron Jervis of Meaford and the Earl of St Vincent,
a title he disliked because he believed that it lacked modesty. Jervis would have
preferred Yarmouth because of his personal links there, but the final choice lay
with the King who insisted on St Vincent. Nelson chose to become a Knight of
the Bath rather than a Baronet like the rest of the junior flag-officers, because the
title came with a gaudy star and shiny ribbon that he could wear on his uniform.

The Spanish sailors were roundly chastised for their performance. There was no
attempt to conjure victory from defeat as there had been in France after The Glorious

First of June. Córdoba and his officers were pilloried for inefficiency, misguidance, incompetence and a lack of honour. Córdoba was sacked and banished from royal and political favour and five of his captains were suspended. The dregs of Córdoba's fleet returned to Cadiz where they were blockaded with great success. Jervis proudly declared to Nepean that the blockade was 'the compleatist thing in Naval History'.[30] In June, he wrote to his brother with nothing short of glee that he had been 'riding triumphant one hundred and seven days in the entrance to the Port'.[31]

The Spanish navy lost any position of favour it may have enjoyed in the royal court and government and its strength was sapped as the political focus waned. Of a formidable fleet of 75 warships in 1791, only 53 remained by 1802 and only 20 of those were seaworthy. The likelihood of an invasion launched by combined Franco-Spanish seapower evaporated. The British regained the faith in their navy they had lost in 1796. That navy had now fought two opponents, the French in the summer of 1794 and the Spanish in the new year of 1797, and had beaten them both. Unfortunately for the British, however, just as the Franco-Spanish threat from the south and west receded, so a new threat appeared from the east. It was now the turn of the Dutch, so recently a willing member of the First Coalition against Revolutionary France, to change sides.

The British had won momentum at St Vincent but they now faced two major problems. The first was that the Royal Navy was rotten in its core. A matter of weeks after news of St Vincent had arrived, the navy suffered two crippling mutinies, one at Spithead, the other at the Nore. The second problem was the Dutch. When Howe had fought the French at The First of June there had been a convincing, albeit distant, history of decisive fleet victories over his opponents. So too with Jervis and the Spanish, but the Dutch were an altogether different proposition. The most recent action with them had been at the Dogger Bank in 1781 and that had been a real tussle; no ships were captured and the British suffered nearly as many casualties as their foe. Long before then, the British and Dutch had repeatedly locked horns in some of the longest and fiercest battles of the Age of Sail during the Dutch Wars of the 17th century. There was history between these two great maritime nations and that history was far from encouraging for any British fleet, let alone one that was crippled by mutiny.

And there were more setbacks and they were significant. Only eight days after St Vincent, the French actually managed to land 1,500 men on British soil at

Fishguard in Wales. Although the 'army' was a ragged bunch of men and the threat posed minimal, the panic they caused was real and widespread. There was even a run on the banks and the government was forced to come off the Gold Standard. The naval victory off southern Spain had done nothing to prevent an economic crisis that, as things stood in the spring of 1797, could have forced Britain out of the war. Then Austria, Britain's most significant European ally, chose this moment to withdraw from the war. Yet again, while a British fleet had won a great victory over one of its most powerful rivals, control of the sea remained a distant dream and the future of the war a bleak nightmare.

Camperdown

Camperduin

11 October 1797

'My attention was so much taken up by finding we were in 9 fathoms water … that I was not able to distinguish the number of Ships captured'

Admiral Adam Duncan, 13 October 1797

AT A GLANCE

DATE:
11 October 1797

NAVIES INVOLVED:
British and Batavian Republic

COMMANDING OFFICERS:
Admiral Adam Duncan and Vice-Admiral Jan de Winter

FLEET SIZES:
British, 14 ships of the line and 2 50-gunners; Dutch 11 ships of the line
and 4 50-gunners

TIME OF DAY:
11.30 – 16.30

LOCATION:
Off Camperduin, Holland. 52°45′N 4°12′E

WEATHER:
North-northwesterly winds, squally, occasional rain

RESULT:
7 Dutch ships of the line, 2 Fifth Rates and 2 frigates captured

CASUALTIES:
British 823; Dutch 1,160

BRITISH COURT MARTIALS:
Captain Jon Williamson of the *Agincourt* demoted to bottom of captains'
list, never employed again

DISPATCHES CARRIED HOME BY:
Captain William Fairfax, Duncan's flag captain

The Replica

I am in Rotterdam. I have come to look at a ship under construction, a ship that will become one of the largest and most authentic 18th-century warship replicas in the world.

The Nieuwe Maas River stretches from left to right in front of me, swept by the north-westerly winds that race up the delta from the North Sea. River tramps, tankers and tourist boats flow past on the tides of the modern global maritime economy, but I feel detached from that world. I am standing deep in the chest cavity of a Dutch warship that is being built by hand to the exact measurements of the 56-gun *Delft*, originally built in Delfshaven in 1782.

The physical sensation of being in a shipyard is overpowering. To my left is the bow, to my right the stern. I am standing on the keel. The completed, twisted frames tower above me, marking out that distinctive, wine-glass shape of a sailing warship. The aroma of freshly sawn oak is everywhere. Oak sawdust flies thick through the air and gets in my eyes. I am downwind of a shipwright sanding a 'knee', a vast piece of timber, the trunk of an oak, that has a lower branch coming off it at just the correct angle to reinforce vertically the ship's side and also take the horizontal weight of a deck. It is nature's very own shelf support.

Perhaps only half of the ship's frames are now in place but, although the hull is by no means finished, it has reached its finished height. Even unfinished it is awesome. Historians often compare a ship in this state to the skeleton of a giant whale but that is nonsense; the scale is wrong by too many factors. The only way to get any sense of the size is to imagine a large church or cathedral and its timber roof turned upside down. Now delete the walls in your mind and stand on the ground, in the middle of the roof. The effect would be similar. Indeed, ancient timber roofs are as close as you will now get to gaining some sense of what the hull of an ancient ship would look like from the inside. The ship is made of *hundreds* of trees, each mature and massively thick. It is that intrinsic strength, the sheer density of this ship, that captures, and boggles, the mind.

The scale of the investment of time is also so clear because the trunks are so immense. Some of the oaks used to build the new *Delft* have come from Northern France. It has taken a century for them to reach the requisite size; so long, in fact, that many of the trunks, once sawn in half, show the scars of fire damage inflicted in the ravaged landscape of the First World War. The massive frames are, in turn, supported by unsawn trunks to stop the ship from toppling over. These supports and the age of her timbers make her look curiously old and young at the same time: young because of the freshly sawn frames at this embryonic stage of construction; old because the frames are gnarled with age and their supports look like the crutches of a wounded naval veteran. She is fascinating, at once helpless and potent, young and old, weak and strong.

At her bow is a magnificent roaring-lion figurehead but otherwise the ship has yet to acquire any real character, any real personality. That will come much later in the construction process, when the bulkheads and companionways, the stern galleries and cabins are fitted and, crucially, when her masts are stepped and her yards swayed aloft and she can fly her ensign.

We do, at least, know what that ensign is going to look like. She will fly the ensign that the original *Delft* flew in 1797, when she fought against the British at the Battle of Camperdown and when she subsequently sank to the bottom of the North Sea.* She will fly the ensign of the Batavian Republic.

Depicted on her ensign and seated in a posture that suggests both repose and vigilance will be the unmistakable revolutionary figure of Liberty. In her left hand she will grasp a Liberty Pole adorned with a hat, both powerful symbols of the pursuit of liberty. Liberty herself will wear a helmet, or perhaps a Phrygian Cap, with magnificent plumage in the red, white and blue of the tricolour of the French Republic. Gripped in her right hand will be a shield that depicts the fasces, the bundle of sticks with an axe's blade emerging from the centre that deliberately recalls the ancient Roman republic which first used it as a symbol of power. Lower to her left and deliberately 'at her feet' will be the lion of the Netherlands which will grasp the Liberty Pole as it roars.

This motif of the Batavian Republic drips with iconography and symbolism. A splendid example survives at the National Maritime Museum in London (fig. 8). At the foot of this fragment of flag is a dash of red. If one did not know that it came from the top left-hand corner of a flag with red, white and blue *horizontal* stripes,

---

* Where she still lies. She was discovered by a fisherman in 1977, 20 nautical miles from Schevningen. Only a handful of artefacts have been recovered including two splendid bronze cannon which can be seen at the Rotterdam and Amsterdam Maritime Museums.

one would be forgiven for assuming it fitted into the top right-hand corner of the French Tricolour with its blue, white and red *vertical* stripes. The flag shouts 'France' at us as much as it does 'Netherlands' and in that confused symbolism lies the confused identity of the enemy that faced the British fleet in the North Sea in October 1797.

The Invasion

French Revolutionary ideology and French armies reached the Netherlands in the New Year of 1795. In January a 70,000 strong French army crossed the Waal, the southern branch of the Rhine Delta, and began to occupy the country. The Princess of Orange fled on 15 January with the younger members of her family and a great deal of treasure. Utrecht surrendered on 16 January, Rotterdam on 18 January and Dort on 19 January, the same day that William V, Stadtholder of the Dutch Republic, fled his country for England. Landing in Harwich he made his way to London and thence to Hampton Court, where he whored himself into oblivion. On 20 January Amsterdam fell to General Pichegru and the rest of the country followed in its wake. The French now controlled the Dutch navy of 28 ships of the line and had unrestricted access to the North Sea.

Many of the Dutch welcomed the French and their new ideology with loud acclamation. Revolutionary clubs and committees sprang up all over the Netherlands fêting the French as liberators. This was a boon to the overstretched and exhausted French armies. French politics had changed in the aftermath of the Thermidorian Coup, which had ended the reign of Robespierre and the Jacobins. France was now led by the Directory, with far less focus and aggression. The conquered powers now enjoyed an easier relationship with France and the Dutch show of support was rewarded with nominal independence. The Netherlands were permitted to retain their own identity as the 'Batavian Republic' if a number of terms were met, not least of which was an indemnity of 100,000,000 florins and open support for the war against Britain.

The Dutch were openly encouraged in their own revolution by the French, but its nature was significantly different from the French revolution, as were the popular and political aspirations in its aftermath. The Batavian Republic was heavily influenced by France and French ideas but one of the central issues that dominated its politics was the question of continuing independence from France, albeit in the new conditions imposed by its conqueror. The Dutch navy, in particular, was far more than an instrument of French warfare and could be used by the Batavian Republic for its own ends, either to make political points or to impose military pressure. In spite of the recent French conquest, the political machinations that led to the Dutch navy being sent to sea in October 1797 were Dutch, not French.

By October 1797 the Batavian Republic had enough good reasons of its own to fight Britain. One of William V's first actions in exile had been to encourage his allies to fight for his crown. He therefore sanctioned the British occupation of several significant Dutch colonies, including the Cape of Good Hope and others in the East and West Indies. In August 1796 a Dutch attempt to retake the Cape failed spectacularly when they surrendered nine ships to Vice-Admiral George Elphinstone without a fight at Saldanha Bay north west of modern day Cape Town. Not only were the British therefore unmistakably the enemy, but the Dutch navy had every reason to want to fight and to fight well. They needed to erase the shame of the surrender at Saldanha Bay in exactly the same way that the French in June 1794 had wanted to erase the shame of their own fleet surrender at Toulon in 1793. With the British now in control of valuable Dutch colonies, even William's own supporters began to see the necessity of a naval war, or at the very least a show of naval strength, against Britain. How else could those colonies be reclaimed? Even if they could not be won back by force, force could certainly lay the foundation for political reconciliation.

One further ingredient of this mix was the confusion surrounding the new Dutch national identity. Throughout the 17th century the Dutch, in their military and mercantile heyday, had, in part, identified themselves through maritime hostility directed towards Britain. Now, faced with a period of great uncertainty, they looked to their past where they found naval heroes such as Maarten Trompe and Michiel de Ruyter, men who defined themselves and their nation in terms of naval victory over the British. War with Britain was therefore viewed as politically expedient from both ends of the Dutch political spectrum, from the perspective both of those who supported the Batavian Republic and those who prayed for its demise. Without this consensus, the decision to send the Dutch fleet to sea in the autumn of 1797 would be entirely baffling.

The Battle of Camperdown is unlike almost any other naval battle ever fought and certainly unlike all others in this period because there is no apparent strategic motivation. There was no merchant convoy to protect as at The Glorious First of June; no treasure ships to shepherd as at St Vincent; no army to protect and supply as at the Nile; no strategic advantage to win as at Copenhagen; no army to reinforce as at Trafalgar; and no enemy merchant ships to raid as at San Domingo.

If the battle had been fought three or four months earlier, however, everything would have made sense. Then the Dutch fleet had been crammed with French and Dutch soldiers intent on an invasion of the vulnerable east coast of England. The invading force had been under the command of the vigorous proselyte General Herman Daendels and his astute adjutant Wolfe Tone, an Irish nationalist who had sided with the French in his war against Britain. Moreover, the British fleet had been crippled by mutinies at Spithead and the Nore. All had been ready and the timing auspicious for the longed-for strike against Britain. But the weather had been horrendous. The Dutch sailors had practised repeatedly at their cannon and muskets but the wind never relented. On 18 July Wolfe Tone erupted, 'The wind is as foul as possible this morning; it cannot be worse. Hell! Hell! Hell! Allah! Allah! I am in a most devouring rage.' Eight days later and he wrote again, 'I am today eighteen days on board and we have not had eighteen minutes of fair wind.'[1]

As time passed, so opportunity faded. The British resolved the mutinies through a mixture of understanding and brutality. The French commander, Lazare Hoche, was summoned back to Paris for political reasons and died very suddenly shortly afterwards. Rumours of poison were never proven, though the sudden death of one of the revolution's finest generals remains suspicious. The invasion force ran out of food and became sick and, by the beginning of October, the threat of invasion had vanished and even a Dutch sortie was no longer anticipated by the British.

The commander of the Dutch fleet, Willem de Winter, dreaded the prospect of such a sortie just as much as the British had fretted about a possible invasion. Like the French before it, the Dutch navy suffered in the aftermath of revolution. Many Orangist sympathisers fled, leaving a great dearth of trained men that could only be filled by rapid promotion. The resultant shortage of experienced crew was acute and de Winter himself, at only 36 years old, had never commanded a fleet before. Despite that inexperience, however, he had the eye of a seaman and quickly came to realise that his fleet would be no match for the British. There were few high-quality men to crew the ships, fewer officers to lead them in battle, no recent, shared fighting experience to calm nerves and encourage confidence and no weight of expectation from recent victory.

The Scotsman

The man who had been trying to deal with the constantly shifting threat posed by the Dutch navy, with or without its cargo of French soldiers, was the Scottish Admiral Adam Duncan. In early October 1797 Duncan left a small force under Sir Henry Trollope to watch the Dutch coast and returned to the fleet base at Yarmouth to revictual and repair his ships and enjoy a rare moment of calm. The summer had been utterly exhausting.

The discord in the British fleet that had begun at Spithead and then spread eastwards along the south coast to the Nore, the fleet anchorage at the mouth of the River Medway, had found its way by June to Yarmouth, the base of Duncan's North Sea fleet. Mutiny had broken out at the most critical moment possible. As the Dutch fleet, its holds crammed with an invasion army, waited for the briefest of weather windows in which to launch the invasion, just two of Duncan's ships, his flagship *Venerable* and the *Adamant,* were uninfected by mutiny. The British blockade was nothing more than a pretence, maintained by those two ships sailing back and forth within sight of the Dutch coast and signalling to imaginary ships beyond the horizon.

Duncan, meanwhile, had worked feverishly to rid his fleet of mutiny, a feat which he achieved, as the best commanders always did, through a mixture of understanding and aggression. Duncan had both in spades. He was well-loved by his men for his open commitment to improving their health and well-being but he was also fearsome. Very tall for the time, he towered above most of his men. On one occasion he dangled a mutineer over the side of the ship one-handed, roaring his defiance all the while: 'My lads! Look at this fellow who dares to deprive me of the command of the fleet!'[2] A contemporary description certainly makes him sound rather impressive. 'Imagine a man upwards of six feet four inches in height, with limbs of proportionate frame and strength. His features are nobly beautiful, his forehead high and fair, and his hair as white as snow. His movements are all stately and unaffected, and his manner easy though dignified.'[3] The mutineers certainly bore no grudge against Duncan as a commander; their grievance was against the faulty and unfair system of payment that saw British sailors risking their lives for a pittance that never materialised.

To add to his other problems, Duncan had been faced with the troubling prospect of making an alliance with Russia work to his advantage. Catherine the Great had joined the First Coalition against Revolutionary France in 1795 and had sent 12 ships of the line and six frigates to the North Sea to assist the British fleet. The Russians continued their naval commitment when, in 1796, Catherine was succeeded by Tsar Paul I, a determined enemy of the Revolution. The Russian presence, however, created a diplomatic nightmare. Both navies bristled. How should they salute each other? Who, exactly, was in charge? How should they communicate? How should Russian sailors caught smuggling gallons of illicit booze into Chatham dockyard be punished?

Duncan proved a natural diplomat, flattering the Russians through gritted teeth while assuming and maintaining control of the combined naval force. He used the sickly Russian squadron of poor ships as best he could in his blockade of the Dutch coast. The battle he longed for never materialised, however. The Dutch stayed safely in the Texel while the British and the Russians struggled to stay at sea. Very little happened. This was not a campaign of constant sniping against frigates dashing around the sandbanks; nor was it a cat-and-mouse game between battlefleets bursting out of the North Sea fog. Duncan, therefore, did not have the opportunity to test any of his numerous tactical ideas or to improve his skill as a commanding officer in battle. And he desperately needed to do both.

While Duncan was undoubtedly competent, his abilities as a commander had never been tested in fleet battle. In fact, he had only ever experienced fleet battle once, at the Moonlight Battle of 1780, when Rodney had chased and defeated a Spanish squadron off the coast of Portugal. That was now 17 years ago. Duncan had certainly enjoyed a lengthy and varied career, but its highlights were the mighty amphibious operations of the Seven Years War (1756–63) and the great relief of Gibraltar in the subsequent War of American Independence (1775–83).

He had risen by seniority rather than by repeated shows of dashing behaviour in the face of the enemy, but this was through no fault of his own, nor was it for lack of raw talent. He had contracted malaria as a young man while serving in the West

Indies and subsequent recurrent bouts in hot climates had forced him to refuse plum commands that would have brought him into more regular contact with the enemy. The very fact that he was in command of the North Sea fleet in 1797, an uninviting prospect if ever there was one, was a case in point. He had already been offered, and had refused, the enviable Mediterranean command, recommending Jervis in his stead.

The challenge he now faced was immense, however. The North Sea, particularly around the Dutch Coast, is a unique environment that favours detailed local knowledge and utter commitment. It is characterised by shallow waters, grim weather, cold winds, an iron-grey sea and, in 1797, a relatively small area of operations. If Duncan was ever going to catch de Winter and then keep him in his clutches long enough to inflict a defeat, he would have to think and act quickly and his men would have to follow him without blinking. The political pressure was also intense. Duncan was well-connected and was married to Henrietta Dundas, niece of Henry Dundas, the then Minister of War. The First Lord, Earl Spencer, kindly wrote to him shortly after news of Jervis's victory at St Vincent had reached England: 'Sir John Jervis with fifteen of the line has just beat twenty-seven Spaniards and taken four of their best ships; I hope soon to be able to congratulate you upon as brilliant a day.'[4]

Duncan's inexperience was not the only factor likely to prevent that happening. The North Sea command, which stretched all the way from Selsey Bill in Sussex to Cape Wrath in Scotland, was the least favoured theatre. The finest and newest ships were always snapped up by the most prestigious commands and the most dashing commanders. Duncan's North Sea fleet was a ramshackle collection both of men and ships. Throughout his command his letters are littered with complaints about the seaworthiness of his ships, most of which were old and leaky and a curse for any commander. He needed his men to have confidence in their ships as machines of war before he could begin to rely on those same men to perform in battle.

What Duncan's crews did have, however, was a confidence in each other forged, curiously, in the summer months of mutiny. The surviving mutineers' letters from Duncan's fleet record their grievances alongside a careful and explicit commitment to serving the navy by defeating the enemy as soon as their complaints were addressed. Mutiny was a shameful act and the British sailors were now desperate to redeem their mutinous conduct through heroic action and to demonstrate their loyalty to their commander, to the navy and to their sovereign. One mutineer's letter to Duncan read:

> 'We cannot omit this opportunity to express our gratitude and affection to you, our Commander-in-Chief, for your paternal care, attention and salutary advice in every stage of that unhappy event which has stained the character of the British tar, but which we hope and trust may be redeemed by future bravery and a steady perseverance in their country's cause. We sincerely wish the enemy may give us an opportunity of manifesting our loyalty to our King, our steady attachment to the Constitution, and our personal regard for the best of Commanders.'[5]

On the one hand, therefore, Duncan was inexperienced and the men of the North Sea fleet sailed in rotten ships; on the other, they were bursting for a fight. The Channel fleet had won a great victory over the French at The First of June, the Mediterranean fleet had won a great victory over the Spanish at St Vincent and now it was their turn, the turn of a fleet which had become renowned for nothing but mutiny. All eyes were turned north. The sailors knew it and they were not going to let themselves or anyone else down.

The Coercion

The strategic situation in the autumn of 1797 was relatively straightforward. The Dutch fleet was in the Texel and Duncan was in Yarmouth. Henry Trollope was patrolling the Dutch coast but the threat of a combined Franco-Dutch invasion had long since passed. The campaigning season was over. Bitter winds regularly howled from north and west. It was so cold that there was snow on Dartmoor, hundreds of miles to the warmer south and west. And yet de Winter started to feel the irresistible force of politics. Members of the Batavian Committee for Foreign Affairs agreed that their navy should be sent to sea to lure Duncan out and to defeat him. It would be a demonstration of Batavian strategic independence from France, an important counter to the dishonour of the surrender at Saldanha Bay and an affirmation of Dutch identity. It would be a conscious hark back to the glory days when the Dutch had repeatedly defeated the British at sea and their empire had grown fat on the fruits of maritime trade. De Winter, who had measured the competence of his men and had found them wanting, knew that battle with the British was madness. On 6 October, however, the weather finally turned and the Dutch were blessed – or perhaps cursed – with a brief window of south-easterly winds that allowed them to leave the Texel. Two days later, the British lugger *Speculator*, sent direct from Trollope off the Dutch coast to Duncan in Yarmouth, flew a signal that, at first, seemed impossible. The Dutch, it appeared, were at sea with 16 of the line, five frigates and five brigs.

The Dispatches

A. Duncan to E. Nepean, 12 October 1797

Duncan's first dispatch is one of the most powerful of this collection. He wrote it on board his flagship the very moment that firing ceased, and he would still have been surrounded by the chaos of battle, ears ringing from cannon shot, clothes damp from sweat and sea spray. We know from other sources that he was one of only two men left unhurt on his quarterdeck, and it is worth remembering that this was only his second fleet battle and his first for 17 years. He writes with adrenaline coursing through his body, with his heart pumping too fast. He forces himself to sit at his desk and write even as he is desperate to attend to everything else that demands his attention in the aftermath of battle. The words do not keep to any rigid line; they gush across the page. Duncan can barely control his quill. He has to go back to the letter and cram more words in between lines. He simply cannot contain himself or delay telling the Admiralty of his victory. He is confident that people will want to know his news before the detail of it is certain.

He is clearly overjoyed at the victory as much as he is relieved to be alive. The details are minimal. The letter is classic Duncan, the expression of a man of deeds and not words. He is, however, careful to explain how he passed through the enemy line, something that he is clearly proud of, something that tells of aggression,

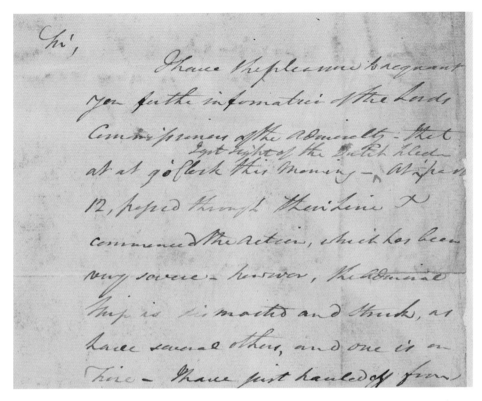

Duncan fits more words into his letter in an attempt to make it more comprehensible.

commitment and tactical nous. There is a nod to the tenacity of his opponents and the courage of his men in his description of the severity of the action. He mentions that nothing is yet decided, that a possibility even exists of renewing the action. He is not prepared to wait until he knows if he can destroy the remaining Dutchmen, which would make his victory greater, his achievement yet more impressive. He won't even spare the time to cross out one of the repeated 'at's.

It is a fiery, energetic letter, full of personality. It is written by a likeable man bursting with pleasure; by a man who knew that the reputation of the navy desperately needed a victory after the shame of the mutinies; and by a man who was proud to have provided it. It is also a curious letter because it fails to describe the action but simply places the author at its location. That immediacy makes it startlingly modern. Not only does it say 'Look at what I have done' but also 'Look at what I am *doing*'. This is not a proper battle report as much as a hastily scribbled postcard, an 18th-century battle Tweet.

VENERABLE OFF THE COAST OF HOLLAND 12 OCT (BY LOG) 1797
3 PM CAMPERDOWN ESE 8 MILES – WIND NbE

I have the pleasure to acquaint you for the information of the Lords
Commissioners of the Admiralty – that at at [sic] *9 o'clock this morning* I got sight of the Dutch Fleet *– At*
½ past 12, passed through their line & commenced the action, which has been very
severe – however, the admiral ship is dismasted and struck, as have several others,
and one is on fire – I have just hauled off from the shore to get my ships refitted they
having suffered much in masts & rigging – and shall renew the action and try to
distroy the rest if possible –
I am Sir,
> *your most obedient humble servant*

Adam Duncan

P.S. I shall send Captain Harisfaye with particulars the moment I can spare him –

EVAN NEPEAN ESQR

Admiral A. Duncan to E. Nepean, 13 October 1797

Duncan provides much more detail in his next letter, written the following day
and still off the coast of Holland. He describes how he set a trap for de Winter
by placing his fleet in between de Winter's estimated position and his home port.
He makes careful reference to the behaviour of Vice-Admiral Onslow, who led the
lee division. This is important because the British fleet did not attack as one body
but in two separate divisions, one to windward and one to leeward; the attack at
Camperdown, which was at right angles to the enemy line, was therefore almost
identical to that which was later made famous at Trafalgar.

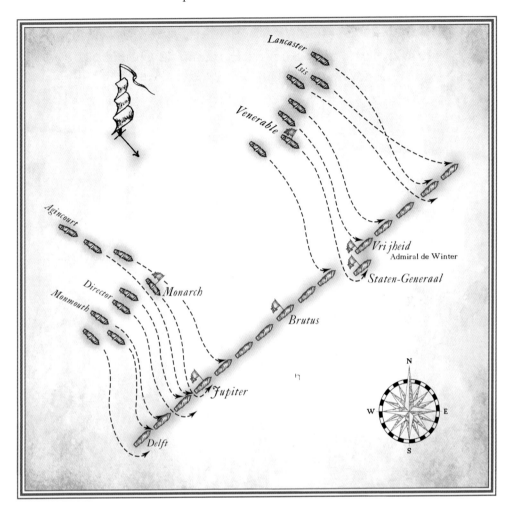

Duncan describes capturing the Dutch admiral but fails to mention that de Winter was the only man left alive on his quarterdeck. Duncan is also rather nonchalant about the significance of his capture: de Winter was the only Dutch admiral ever to have surrendered to an enemy in battle and Duncan had, in fact, actually captured three Dutch flag-officers: Admiral de Winter, Vice-Admiral Reuter and Rear-Admiral Meures. Duncan does, however, provide more information about the location of the battle and how, at one stage, they were no more than five miles from land. We know from other sources that the guns' smoke was visible from the coastline at Den Helder, a reminder of how close the shallow-drafted Dutch ships came to escaping.

The scale of the victory remains unclear. Duncan is still unaware that seven of the 11 Dutch ships of the line and 11 Dutch ships in all have been captured or that 540 Dutch sailors are dead and 620 wounded and that no less than 3,775 prisoners have been taken. In short, Duncan had no idea that he had achieved a quite extraordinary victory, for no British fleet had hitherto so completely defeated another of similar size.

VENERABLE AT SEA 13TH OCTOBER 1797.
OFF THE COAST OF HOLLAND.

 Sir,

Be pleased to acquaint the Lords Commissioners of the Admiralty, that judging it of consequence their Lordships should have as early information as possible of the defeat of the Dutch Fleet under the command of Admiral De Winter, I dispatched the Rose cutter at 3 PM on the 12th instant with a short letter to you immediately after the Action was ended. I have now further to acquaint you for their Lordships information, that in the night of the 10th instant, after I had sent away my letter to you of that date, I placed my Squadron in such situation as to prevent the Enemy from returning to the Texel, without my falling in with them. At 9 o'clock in the morning of the 11th I got sight of Captain Trollope's Squadron with signals flying for an Enemy to Leeward; I immediately bore up and made the signal for a general Chace, and soon got sight of them, forming in a Line on the Larboard Tack to receive us, the wind at N.W. As we approached near, made the signal for the Squadron to shorten sail in order to connect them; soon after saw the land between Camperdown and Egmont about 9 miles to Leeward of the Enemy, and finding there was no time to be lost, in making the attack, made the signal to bear up, break the Enemy's Line and engage them to Leeward, each Ship her opponent, by which I got between them and the Land; whither they were fast approaching – My signals were obeyed with great promptitude and Vice Admiral Onslow in the Monarch bore down on the Enemy's Rear in the most gallant manner, his Division following his

example and the Action commenced about 40 minutes past 12 o'clock: the Venerable soon got thro' the Enemy's Line and I began a close Action with my Division on their Van, which lasted near two hours and a half, when I observed all the Dutch Admirals Ships masts come by the board; she was however defended for some time in a most gallant manner, but being overpressed by numbers struck her Colours, and Admiral De Winter was soon brought onboard the Venerable. On looking around me, I observed the Vice Admiral's Ship also dismasted and had surrendered to Vice Admiral Onslow – and that many others had also struck. My attention was so much taken up by finding we were in 9 fathoms water and not farther than 5 miles from the Land, and also in getting the disabled Ships' heads off shore, that I was not able to distinguish the number of Ships captured, and the wind having been constantly on the Land since, we unavoidably have been much dispersed so that I have not been able to gain an exact account of them, but there are eight or nine taken possession of; more of them had struck, but taking advantage of the night coming on, and being so near their own Coast, succeeded in getting off, and some of them were seen going into the Texel the next morning.

It is with the greatest pleasure and satisfaction I make known to their Lordships the very gallant behaviour of Vice Admiral Onslow, the Captains, Officers, Seamen and Marines of the Squadron who all appeared actuated with the truly British Spirit, at least those that I had the opportunity of seeing.

One of the Enemy's Ships caught fire in the Action and drove very near the Venerable, but I have the pleasure to say it was extinguished and she is one of the Ships in our possession. – The Squadron has suffered much in their Masts, Yards and Rigging, and many of them have lost a number of Men; however in no proportion to that of the Enemy; the carnage onboard their two Admirals Ships has been beyond all description, they have lost no less than Two hundred and fifty men each, killed and wounded: and here I have to lament the loss of Captain Burges of His Majesty's Ship the Ardent, who brought that ship into Action in a most gallant and masterly manner, but was unfortunately soon after killed. – however the Ship continued the Action close, until quite disabled – The Public have lost a good and gallant Officer in Captain Burges, and I with others a sincere friend. Captain Trollope's exertions and active good conduct, in keeping sight of the Enemy's Fleet until I came up, is truly meritorious, and I trust will meet a just reward.

I send this by Captⁿ Fairfax who was slightly wounded, by whose able advice I profited much during the Action; and who will give their Lordships any further particulars they may wish to know.

As most of the Squadron are much disabled, and several of the Prizes dismasted, I shall make the best of my way to the Nore with them; and purpose leaving a Frigate on my Rendezvous, to collect such ships, as may have been sent thither, in order to form a Squadron, and watch the further purposes of the enemy in the Texel.

I herewith transmit you a List of killed and wounded onboard such of the Squadron as I have been able to collect, a List of the Enemys Fleet opposed to my Squadron, and my Line of Battle on the day of action. I am, Sir,

Your most obedient, humble servant

Adam Duncan

Evan Nepean Esqre

Duncan has freely named his gallant officers here – Onslow, Burges, Trollope and Fairfax – and he is careful to acknowledge the 'truly British Spirit' of everyone in his squadron. A marked omission is any mention of the suspect behaviour of Captain John Williamson of the *Agincourt*, who was later court martialled for negligence, evidenced by his abject failure to engage the enemy at any stage. He was found guilty, demoted to the bottom of the post captains' list and denied any chance of further service at sea.

Duncan's claim that 'My signals were obeyed with great promptitude' also gives a rather unrealistic view of events because other evidence suggests that many of his captains understood none of his tactical intentions. Captain John Inglis of the *Belliqueux*, a fiery Scot, was so exasperated by Duncan's signalling that he cried, 'Damn … Up wi' the hel-lem and gang into the middle o' it'.[6] A study of Duncan's log shows that he made no less than 44 signals between 06.15 and 11.49, when the fleets finally clashed, enough to confuse any captain.

It is also important to realise that Duncan's attack in two squadrons at the centre and rear of the enemy was by no means deliberate, but the result of his cancelling an original order to form into a line of battle. Seeing that time was too limited to complete the formation of a line, Duncan simply ordered his captains to engage their opposite number and break through the enemy line. Receiving no further orders regarding their formation, the ships necessarily remained roughly in their pre-existing sailing order of two divisions advancing at right angles to the scattered Dutch line. In the midst of all this, an erroneous signal to concentrate on the enemy centre was flown on the *Venerable* but no annulling signal was hoisted. Onslow, and some others, believed that Duncan's plan had changed again and that he now intended to invert the line. The result was that the British fleet concentrated on the rear of the Dutch in spite of, rather than because of, Duncan's intentions. There is also no mention of the numerous examples of friendly fire; we know that the *Agincourt* fired into the *Monmouth*, and the *Lancaster* into the *Isis*. This dispatch, in short, offers a clinical, and false, view of a battle that was in fact riddled with confusion.

The man Duncan sent back with the dispatches was the injured William George Fairfax, his flag captain. Fairfax had served with Duncan throughout the difficult summer and had been a particular help during the mutinies. He was knighted for his service at Camperdown.

The British Order of Battle, 11 October 1797

Duncan enclosed with his second, more detailed description of the battle, this breakdown of his fleet,

The fleet is clearly divided into two divisions, one to larboard, the 'lee' division, and the other to starboard, the 'weather' division. Each division is led by its own commander, consists of eight ships and has its own 'repeaters' attached to it. These last were ships that, stationed some distance away and parallel to the line of battle, repeated commanding officers' signals, thereby reducing, but by no means eliminating, the problems of communication up and down the line of battle. Flags were used to signal during the day, but often their colours were difficult to make out in fog, mist, rain, poor light or glaring sun.

Notice the size of the ships, measured by the number of their guns. All are armed on two decks. They are, therefore, relatively small compared with the giants that fought at The Glorious First of June or at the Battle of St Vincent. In the line of battle at The First of June no ships were armed with fewer than 74 guns and only

DISPOSITION OF THE SQUADRON IN ORDER OF BATTLE, ON THE 11TH OCTOBER 1797.							
Repeaters		No.	Ships	Captains.	Guns	Men.	Divisional Commanders.
Beaulieu Frigate.	Larboard or Lee Division.	1	RUSSELL	Henry Trollope	74	590	Richard Onslow Esqre Vice Admiral of the Red &c &c
Rose Cutter		2	DIRECTOR	William Bligh	64	491	
King George Dº.		3	MONTAGU	John Knight	74	590	
Active Dº.		4	VETERAN	George Gregory	64	491	
Diligent Dº.		5	MONARCH	Vice Admiral Onslow Capt. E O'Bryen	74	599	
Speculator Lugger		6	POWERFUL	W. O'Bryen Drury	74	590	
		7	MONMOUTH	James Walker	64	491	
		8	AGINCOURT	John Williamson	64	491	
Circe Frigate.	Starboard or Weather Division.	9	TRIUMPH	W. H. Eysington	74	640	Adam Duncan Esqre Admiral of the Blue and Commander in Chief &c &c &c
Marin Sloop.		10	VENERABLE	Adml. Duncan Captn. W. G. Fairfax	74	593	
		11	ARDENT	R. R. Burges	64	491	
		12	BEDFORD	Sir Thos. Byard	74	590	
		13	LANCASTER	John Wells	64	491	
		14	BELLIQUEUX	John Inglis	64	491	
		15	ADAMANT	William Hotham	50	343	
		16	ISIS	Wm. Mitchel	50	343	
						Adam Duncan	

one was at St Vincent; in Duncan's fleet more than half of the ships have fewer than 74 guns. At The First of June seven ships were armed with 90 guns or more and at St Vincent six; in this fleet *no* ships have more than 74 guns. However, the ships of the North Sea fleet were lightly armed and had shallow draughts for a very good reason: they were specifically selected for warfare in the shallow waters, shoals and sandbanks off the Dutch coast.

The Dutch fleet also consisted of small warships and they had even shallower draughts, but the British retained one huge advantage that is not revealed by this list. The given number of guns disguises a significant fact, the type of guns. The British ships were all armed with carronades, a type of cannon designed to be hugely destructive over a very short range, and they sailed into battle at Camperdown armed with 86 of them. The Dutch had none.

Notice also the differing sizes of the ships: there are 74-gunners, 60-gunners and 50-gunners. Such variety made it hard both to achieve and retain cohesion. Station keeping was challenging since ships of different sizes sailed at different speeds even under similar sail plans. It was extremely difficult to get such a fleet into a compact order and then keep them there, however talented the fleet commander. It is not surprising, therefore, that Duncan's order to form a line at 09.30 on the morning that the Dutch were sighted was never enacted, nor is it fair to criticise the British fleet for that failure. A significant part of the reason for Duncan's pell-mell attack was that he had no choice. He simply couldn't get his fleet into a compact formation.

Another important factor was the age of these ships. The newest purpose-built warship in the fleet was the appropriately named *Veteran*, already a decade old. The oldest ships were the *Triumph* and the *Russell*, both 33 years old, while Onslow's flagship the *Monarch* was only a year younger. The global demands of the maritime war in 1797 rendered Britain so lacking in warships that Duncan's fleet also included four hastily converted East Indiamen, the 64-gunners *Monmouth*, *Agincourt*, *Ardent* and *Lancaster*. Two other ships were 50-gunners, an obsolete class of ship that had been withdrawn from all respectable lines of battle years before and were therefore not considered ships 'of the line'.

The age and poor condition of the ships available to Duncan resulted in a high turnover of those actually available at any one time because they were constantly rotating to and from port to be patched up. On the day of the battle, Duncan was even worried that his flagship could not be kept free from the leaks that constantly threatened to flood the bilge. The list is important, therefore, because it is markedly different from the order of sailing that Duncan had issued just four days previously and which included three ships which were not at the battle and left out one, the *Adamant*, which was. Such uncertainty made it very difficult for Duncan to plan, and even more difficult for him to rely on his captains. By no means was his fleet formed of men who had forged a close-knit brotherhood through constant contact with each other and with their commander-in-chief.

There is another important factor here conspicuous by its absence. Where was the Russian fleet? Duncan had received Russian help from the summer of 1795 in the form of a nominally powerful, though practically weak, Russian squadron of 12 ships of the line and six frigates. Their absence is indicative of the poor co-operation between the British and the Russians. The latter refused to acknowledge Duncan's overall command or to salute his flag and they came and went at will from their bases in the Baltic. With their ships ill-disciplined and dirty, it is unclear exactly how much help they would have been in battle, but it remains significant that they were not there. Nevertheless, five years after the battle, they put in a claim for a share of the prize money on the basis that they were then allied with the British. The claim irritated everyone and was roundly ignored.

Despite its deficiencies, however, this was a fleet that could boast an unusual number of noteworthy captains. Henry Trollope, the man to whom Duncan had entrusted the blockade of the Dutch coast whilst the main fleet recovered in Yarmouth, was an officer of undoubted professional ability. By 1797 he had already been in the navy for 26 years, having entered just before the outbreak of the previous war, the War of American Independence. He was renowned for his reliability, energy and particularly his commitment to gunnery improvement.

John Knight of the *Montagu* was another man of vast experience who, by 1797, had been in the navy for 39 years. He was noted for his skill as a surveyor, which had been nurtured and used by Howe to great effect on the North American coast during the American War. A great number of Knight's published charts survive. He was easily the most experienced of Duncan's officers in terms of fleet battle, having fought at the battles of Martinique (1780), the Chesapeake (1781), St Kitts (1782) and the crowning achievement of the American war, the Battle of the Saints (1782). His reputation was such that, during the American War, he had been made personally responsible for the education of Prince William Henry, the future King William IV, who was serving as a midshipman in the *Barfleur*, the flagship of Samuel Hood in which Knight served as Hood's flag captain.

Vice-Admiral Richard Onslow was another man of immense experience. It is unclear exactly when he joined the navy but by 1758, 41 years before the Battle of Camperdown, he was already a Fourth Lieutenant. He had some experience of fleet warfare, the defence of St Lucia in 1778 being the highlight of his career, and he had a great deal of experience of strategic fleet operations in the American

War. He was unflamboyant and dependable. Little personal material survives but one of the most revealing things about Onslow was written in his will: he explicitly ordered no more than £20 to be spent on his funeral 'to prevent any unnecessary ostentation; the funeral of a brave and honest sailor costs a much less sum'.[7] Onslow was a good man to have serving under you.

In contrast to these experienced officers was William Hotham, the nephew of the more famous Admiral William Hotham. This William Hotham was, in comparison to his fellow captains, startlingly new to the service, having joined the navy only 11 years before. He had served under Nelson at the siege of Bastia in 1795 but was otherwise very green, albeit with the finest possible patronage. He was a competent naval officer and a career of glittering promise was cut short by poor health but he still reached the rank of admiral. This was to be his only fleet battle.

The captain of the *Director* was none other than William Bligh, the man who had won infamy on the *Bounty* in 1789. When mutineers had set him adrift in the middle of the Pacific in a 23-foot launch with 18 crew, he had reached Kupang in Timor two months later after a 3,500-mile voyage, having lost only one man. Bligh had been honourably acquitted of responsibility for the mutiny at his court martial, although his presence in a small, elderly ship in the North Sea fleet suggests that his reputation had by no means recovered. We know, however, that he acted with great courage and resolution during the mutiny at the Nore when he did everything he could to protect his men from the Admiralty's wrath. Bligh had joined the navy in 1761 as a ship's boy and had steadily risen through the ranks in the following 36 years. He became renowned for his ability as a sailor and navigator, and was personally chosen by Captain James Cook to serve as the Master of the *Resolution* on Cook's third and final voyage of discovery. Two years after his return from the Pacific, Bligh fought at the Battle of the Dogger Bank in 1781, a vicious drawn engagement with the Dutch during the American War. Bligh was, therefore, unique in this fleet, and very rare in the Navy as a whole, because he already had experience of fighting the Dutch. He went on to make Vice-Admiral of the Blue in 1814, 53 years after joining the Navy. That is some career.

James Walker of the *Monmouth* was another man with a mixed reputation. He had already served for 21 years and had experienced fleet battle at two of the most significant and largest engagements of the previous war, the Chesapeake (1781) and the Saints (1782). Earlier in 1797, however, he had been court martialled and dismissed from the service for convoying vulnerable British merchantmen back from Spain without specific orders to do so. This curious event probably had more to do with Britain's political relationship with Spain than Walker's sense of professional duty, but it is significant that Walker had only just been reinstated into the service when the Battle of Camperdown was fought. In fact, although he is listed here as the ship's captain, his appointment was so new that it was not actually confirmed until 17 October, a week after the battle.

John Williamson of the *Agincourt* was yet another man with a mixed reputation. He had been Third Lieutenant of the *Resolution* on Captain James Cook's third and final voyage of exploration in the Pacific. When Cook was murdered on a beach by a mob of Hawaiian tribesmen in 1779, Williamson had been in charge of the ship's launch. Cook, realising that the tribesmen were aggressive, had gestured for Williamson to bring the launch to the beach but Williamson misunderstood the gesture and took her further out to sea. With no escape, Cook was clubbed and stabbed to death on the shoreline along with four of his marines. Some witnesses blamed Williamson directly for Cook's death. Williamson would obviously have known William Bligh, who had been the *Resolution*'s sailing master.

There are, therefore, two significant themes to this series of brief biographies. First, many of Duncan's captains had already enjoyed extraordinarily long careers that simply could not be matched by the majority of the Dutch captains and, second, a significant number of British captains had mixed reputations. The North Sea fleet not only included some rag-tag ships but also some rag-tag men.

A. Duncan to E. Nepean, 15 October 1797

Two days after Duncan wrote his first detailed description of the battle, he was back in British waters, off Orfordness, and he wrote again to the Admiralty, describing some of the difficulties that his damaged fleet had suffered after the battle. We know from his previous dispatches that the British fleet had been severely disabled and that the wind had continued to blow towards the Dutch shoreline after the battle. Making ground to windward was the most demanding of all points of sailing and a ship's windward capability was the first to suffer when her rig became damaged. Duncan, therefore, had been in real danger of losing a number of his ships after the battle. He describes how the *Venerable*, which went into battle leaking, was now in such a state that her men could only keep her free of water by working constantly at the pumps. Nor were the British ships the only ones to suffer. The captured *Delft*, the replica of which is now being built in Rotterdam, sank on the same day that Duncan wrote this letter and the 74-gun Dutch prize *Jupiter* did not arrive back until 23 October, a full eight days later.

VENERABLE, OFF ORFORDNESS,
15TH OCTOBER 1797

Sir,

    In addition to my letter of the 13th instant, giving the particulars of the action of the 11^h and which I have not been able to send away until this day, have to acquaint you for the information of the Lords Commissioners of the Admiralty that from the wind continuing to blow on the Dutch Coast the ships have had great difficulty in keeping off the shore and which has unavoidably separated us. On Friday last the wind blew strong from WSW to WNW – which continued till Saturday morning when it shifted to North – Made the signal to Wear; stood to the Westward and fortunately anchored here last evening, the Venerable being so very leaky, that with all her Pumps going we could but just keep her free. This morning I observed the ships named in the margin at anchor near us – Three near the Kentish Knock and three in Hosley Bay. The wind is at NW and much against the disabled ships. I have therefore sent the Lancaster and Beauliueu out to render them assistance.

Monarch
Powerful
Lancaster
Bealiueu

    Sir Thomas Williams in the Endymion who joined me the day after the action – I also sent in shore to keep by and assist the disabled ships, and am informed he fell in with a Dutch Ship of the Line off the Texel, in the night, and had engaged her, but have not heard the particulars.

I beg leave to suggest to their Lordships whether it would not be proper to order any ships that may be in port to the assistance of the disabled ships. I shall proceed to the Nore with such ships as I can get together. Herewith I transmit you a Copy of an Order given to Captain White of the Vestal and am

   Sir

     Your most obedient humble servant

P.S. I request their Lordships will be pleased to give directions for accomodating the wounded.

                   Evan Nepean Esq.

Thomas Williams of the 40-gun *Endymion* frigate had indeed engaged a Dutch ship the day after the main action but had been unable to take her. Williams found the 74-gun *Brutus* anchored close inshore and, in spite of the major discrepancy in size between the two, fell on her. But the captain of the *Brutus* had chosen his position well and the *Endymion* was forced to withdraw. The next day she sailed in company with the 40-gun frigate *Beaulieu* to renew the action but the captain of the *Brutus* had managed to take his ship safely into the harbour at Goree. She was one of seven Dutch ships that escaped. The *Endymion* is not listed in Duncan's Order of Battle (p. 134) because she joined the fleet the day after the battle and was immediately sent after the escaping Dutch ships.

Monarch's List of Officers, and Men Wounded, in action with the Dutch Fleet, 11th of October 1797

This document is one of the gems of this era's naval history. It is a list of the men wounded on board the *Monarch*, Vice-Admiral Onslow's flagship. It is important because it is so rare. Surgeons' journals of any type from the Age of Sail are scarce but those kept by surgeons who witnessed fleet battle are even more so. This list gives the name of the sailor, his rank, described here as 'quality', the nature of his wounds and the name of the hospital ship to which he was sent.

A note on 'Quality':

LM – Landsman: An unskilled deckhand.

Ab – Able Seaman: A skilled seaman.

Ord^y/O^y – Ordinary Seaman: A trainee seaman with some experience.

Boats^n – Boatswain: Warrant officer responsible for sails, rigging and ground tackle.

Bo^n M^{te} – Boatswain's Mate: A petty officer assisting the boatswain.

Msr Mate – Master's Mate: A petty officer assisting the Master.

Mids^h – Midshipman: A young gentleman training to be a commissioned officer.

q^r. mast. – Quartermaster: A petty officer assisting the master to handle the ship.

q^r. m^{sr} mate – Quartermaster's Mate: A petty officer assisting the Quartermaster.

q^r. gunn^r Quartergunner: A petty officer assisting the gunner.

Carp^s Crew – Carpenter's crew

Yeo^n Sheets – Yeoman of the sheets: A petty officer working under the boatswain responsible for the ship's stores.

Priv^{te} – Marine Private: A soldier of the Royal Marines.

No on S Books	Mens Names	Quality	Nature of Wounds	To what Hospital or Ship sent for cure
1746	Adam Ross	LM	compound fracture of ye leg	Spanker Hosl Ship Sheerness
1789	William Finlay	Ab	dangerously by splinters	D°.
388	William Bathe	Ab	D°. by D°. arm	D°.
1783	Danl Shewin	Midn	D°. by D°. legs	Tigress Sheerness
1264	John Curtie	qr gunnr	amputd arm other by splinters	Spanker Hosl Ship
1468	Antonio Arns	Ab	Thigh & arms by D°. severely	D°.
1635	Robt Hennin	LM	Thigh & arm slightly by D°.	D°.
646	Wm Sirappin	Oy	musqt ball thro ye arm	D°.
247	John Herbert	Ab	compd fracture of ye leg splinters D°.	D°.
1075	William Cooper	Ordy	blown up by powder	D°.
1697	John Toan	LM	Foot severely by splinters	D°.
1787	George Lewis	Ab	a musqt ball right shoulder	D°.
1704	John White	LM	contusd back dangerously	D°.

1302	William Peters	Ab	Thigh musqt ball & splinters	D°.
1776	Chas Mc Berth	ym sheets	Arms & legs severely by splinters	D°.
1524	Mat Raminger	Ab	Head dangerously by splinters	D°.
219	Samuel Platt	Ab	Leg a musqt ball thigh splinters	D°.
1677	William Fuller	LM	Head by splinters severely	D°.
505	Robert Hoare	Ab	Leg a musqt ball dangerously	D°.
1236	Thomas Wetton	Bon Mte	compd fracture of ye leg	D°.
1272	William Rogers	Ab	amputd finger arms splinters	D°.
307	Thomas Hollidge	Ab	amputd Thigh ⎫ Both carried	D°.
834	Nicholas Rich	Ab	D°. D°. ⎬ away by Cannon Ball	D°.
				23
1693	Richd Blenman	LM	Amputd arm. Leg by splinters	Spanker Hosl. Ship Sheerness
1221	John Barbary	Ab	Arm & Hands by splinters	D°.
1174	John Rice	Ab	Arms by splinters slight	D°.
1679	Wm Dyer Allen	Ab	Blown up by powder	D°.
1802	Benjh Clements	MIdsh	Head & thigh splinters slight	Tigress Sheerness
1631	James Holihan	Ordy	For not usd clavicle	Spanker Hosl. Ship
676	Herbert Stanfields	Ab	Blown up by powder	D°.
791	Thomas Dalton	Ordy	Arms by splinters severe	D°.
199	Thomas Pedder	Carps Crew	amputd. thumb & arm splintered	D°.
1254	William Meyers	Ab	Back & thighs splinters severe	D°.
691	Jno Sullivan /2/	Ab	Breast by splinters severely	D°.
1540	Peter Hunter	Yeon Sheets	Fracturd leg	D°.
1684	John Cook	LM	Legs severely by splinters	D°.
338	George Davis	Ab	Hand & arm splinters slight	D°.

1788	Archd Campbell	Ab	Legs by splinters slight	D°.
1554	Lars Peters	Ab	Legs by splinters severely	D°.
MARINE LIST				
211	Archd Bailes	Privte	Legs by splinters dangerously	D°.
209	Edw Webster	D°.	Thighs by D°. D°.	D°.
163	Josh Bond	D°.	Thighs & leg by D°. severely	D°.
162	Wm Kelson	Drummr	Cheek & Eye ball by splinters	D°.
276	Jno. Php. Theme	Privte	Shoulder dangerous by ball	D°.
278	Derrick Bakker	D°.	Amptd arm Breast splinters	D°.
273	Johans Kroues	D°.	Eye & back splinters slight	D°.
288	Jno Clarke	D°.	Leg severely by D°.	D°.
230	Robert Lloyd	D°.	Leg musqt ball dangerously	D°.
				48
154	John Cockrell	Ab	Thighs & legs splintirs severely	Spanker Hosl Ship
1279	William Ireland	Boatsn	Contusn thigh slight	Mohauk
1801	John Chinley		Head by splintirs slight	D°.
290	J. S.] Smith	2d lieut. Marines	Foot by D°. slight	D°.
1805	Hy: Geo: Massie	Midsh	Head & Foot by D°. Severely	D°.
1814	James Retalick	3d Lieut.	Arms by D°. slight	D°.
1792	Joseph Ballard	qr. mast.	Head by D°. slight	D°.
1824	James Taylor /2/	D°.	D°. slight	D°.
1212	William Madley	D°.	Arm by D°. slight	D°.
1703	John White	LM	Slightly splinters	D°.
Error	John Clarke	————	————————————	D°.
773	John Dennis /2	Ordy	Legs by D°. slight	D°.
842	Heny Harris	Ab	Slightly arm	D°.
987	John Hogan	Ab	Leg slightly	D°.
1665	Geo Monks	Ordy	D°. slight	D°.

1109	John Langley	Ab	Face by splinters slight	D°.
1117	Lewis Grant	Ab	Head by D°. slight	D°.
1146	Thomas Lee	Ab	Arm by D°. slight	D°.
1224	Joseph Matthews	qr. msr mate	Foot by D°. slight	D°.
244	Robert Green	qr. gunnr	Mard by small shot severely	D°.
1262	Will Mc Carty	Ab	Hands splinters slight	D°.
1326	James Clarke	Ab	Legs splinters slightly	D°.
1408	Arthur Osborne	Ab	D°. by D°. slight	D°.
641	Patk Monegan	Oy	Foot & Leg by D°. severely	D°.
521	William Smith	Ab	Shoulder by D°. slight	D°.
522	Jonas Boosner	Ab	Thigh D°. slight	D°.
593	Jas Briggs	Ab	D°. by D°. slight	D°.
				75

1627	William Taylor	Ab	side splinters slight	D°.
1632	James Sidhall	qr mastr.	Hand & leg by D°. slight	D°.
1639	John Meadows	LM	Leg slight	D°.
1660	Owen Malone	LM	D°.	D°.
1666	Jno Proudfoot	LM	Fingers much contusd	D°.
1669	James Killeck	LM	Hand slight	D°.
1673	John Pond	LM	D°. D°.	D°.
1689	John Beare	LM	arm D°.	D°.
1717	Jno Neal	LM	Thigh musqt ball	D°.
1738	Archd Petterson	LM	Leg slight	D°.
1730	Patk Lawidge	LM	D°. D°.	D°.
1798	John Ayres	Coxn	Breast severely	D°.
1800	James Thompson	Midsh	shoulder slight	D°.
1816	John Marchioni	Ordy	arm slight	D°.
1822	William Stiling	Armor	Nose slight	D°.
MARINE LIST				
178	Thomas White	Privte	Face slight	D°.

214	John Spencer	"	Head splinters severely	D°.
226	William Neild	"	Thigh by D°. slight	D°.
S Books				
1208	Robt Primincomb	Ab	Back slight	D°.
1497	John Haft	Ab	Leg slight	D°.
1621	Dan Flocker	Ab	D°. slight	D°.
1482	John Beardoe	Ab	Head slight	D°.
770	John Diamond	Ab	Arm slight	D°.
1774	Walter Hamilton	qr gunnr	Hands D°.	D°.
1644	John Hardman	LM	D°. D°.	D°.
776	Patk Tonor	Ordy	Leg slight	D°.
				101
1619	Thos. Lampin	Gunnr	Back & thigh much bruised	Monarch
[illeg]	Robt Thursby	Pilot	Thigh slightly bruised	D°.
				TOTAL 103

THESE ARE TO CERTIFY THAT THE MEN NAMED IN THE WITHIN LIST, WERE WOUNDED ON THE 11TH OF OCTOBER 1797, IN ACTION WITH THE DUTCH FLEET

Edm O Bryson CAPTAIN   *Thos Middon* MASTER

Heny Berness PURSER   *Wm Ireland* BOATSWAIN

John Magin SURGEON

One hundred and three sailors, from a complement which we know to have been 599 (p. 134), are injured, at just over 17 per cent of the crew a relatively high proportion for a British warship in battle. By comparison, the 102 sailors wounded aboard HMS *Victory* at Trafalgar represented only 12 per cent of her registered complement while HMS *Temeraire* recorded 76 wounded at the same battle out of a complement of 720 men, a fraction over 10 per cent. Even HMS *Brunswick*, so shattered in her fierce engagement with the *Vengeur* at The Glorious First of June (p. 69), suffered no more than 114 wounded or a little over 20 per cent of her reduced complement of 552. We know that 622 British sailors were wounded at Camperdown and so the *Monarch's* figures represent approximately one sixth of the entire British casualties. In comparison with the unreciprocated slaughter at St Vincent, the British paid heavily for their victory at Camperdown.

The types of injuries are revealing. Many sailors have suffered from 'splinters'. The wooden walls of the largest warships in this period were a full three feet thick and it was quite rare for a cannon ball to penetrate right through a ship's hull. Rather, the ball embedded itself in the hull or even bounced off, back into the sea. The impact, however, tore off vicious daggers of timber that cut flesh to the bone and shattered limbs.

The next problem that the surgeon encountered was that these 'splinters', which came from the inside of the ship's hull, were often encrusted with the filth of hundreds of men living together. Bacteria of one type or another mixed with salt water in the wounds. In an age without antisepsis such a wound could quickly mortify and become fatal. These wounds, therefore, were by no means minor injuries but required careful management if the patient was to recover.

The fact that so many of the wounds are from splinters, with only the occasional wound caused by a musket ball, suggests that the ship was only ever engaged in a gunnery duel. A boarding action, either defensive or offensive, would have returned an entirely different list of injuries: we would see more chopping and stabbing wounds to arms, neck and torso caused by tomahawks and cutlasses as well as deep puncture wounds from pikes.

Several amputations are recorded in this list. The Royal Navy had a particularly good record with amputation, though the survival rate depended greatly on which limb was being amputated and the exact location of the amputation. We know, for example, that lower limbs posed a much greater risk to the patient than upper limbs and that the death-rate of mid-thigh amputees was between 40 and 50 per cent, of below-the-knee amputees between 30 and 35 per cent and of foot amputees 25 per cent. Thomas Pedder, whose thumb was amputated, no doubt survived to tell the tale, though it is doubtful whether he would have resumed his job as a member of the carpenter's crew: just try using a hammer without your thumb.

Even with these typical mortality figures, there is some suggestion that surgeons at Camperdown performed particularly well. A volume of the medical journal *The Lancet*, published in 1848, claimed that, at the Battles of Camperdown and the Nile combined, a total of 30 British sailors suffered amputation and not one died. That is an astonishing achievement for an era without either antisepsis or anaesthesia and with only vinegar as a disinfectant and oil of turpentine to seal stumps.

The surgical procedures took little time, perhaps 15 or 20 minutes in total for a thigh amputation, with most of that taken up preparing the wound site for the cut and then tidying the loose tendons, securing the blood vessels with silk ligatures, trimming the stump and sewing shut the wound. All of this was performed and endured in the most appalling conditions. The surgeon set up his operating table in the orlop deck. Here in the bowels of the ship, far below the waterline, the injured would not get in the way of the men still fighting and were in little danger of further injury. Lighting was poor, with no more than a dull orange glow cast by tallow candles shining through thick horn lanterns. There was no system of triage. The men lay cradling their wounds, damp with their own blood, as they waited their turn. We are particularly fortunate in this instance because one of the very few descriptions of surgery during battle to have survived was written by Robert Young, a surgeon in Duncan's fleet.

Young was serving aboard the *Ardent* and, once battle commenced, operated non-stop from 1.00 p.m. until 4.00 the next morning, treating no less than 90 patients. Throughout that entire period, 'Melancholy cries of assistance were addressed to me from every side by wounded and dying, and piteous moans and bewailing from pain and despair.' But Young kept his head. 'In the midst of these agonising scenes, I was able to preserve myself firm and collected, and embracing in my mind the whole of the situation, to direct my attention where the greatest and most essential services could be performed.' Young berated those who were noisy but 'cheered and commended the patient fortitude of others, and sometimes extorted a smile of satisfaction from the mangled sufferers, and succeeded to throw momentary gleams of cheerfulness among so many horrors'. At one stage their suffering was made worse when an explosion in the cockpit hatchway, where many of the wounded were waiting, knocked '14 or 15 wretches … down upon each other, their faces black as a cinder, their clothes blown to shatters and their hats on fire'. Young saved some but others died, including a corporal of marines 'with all the gluteal muscles shot away so as to excavate the pelvis'.[8]

There was no school of military surgery providing training in the treatment of battle wounds and surgeons required no official qualifications, although they were required to pass an oral examination by the Admiralty before they received their commissions. Some surgeons, but only those on the very largest of ships, had mates to assist them. One commentator, writing shortly after Camperdown, began a treatise on the state of medicine in British ships with the potent phrase: 'To the life of a navy surgeon there are, God knows, no seductions.'[9]

There are three hospital ships named here: *Spanker*, *Mohauk* and *Monarch*. By 1797 the Royal Navy had established large shore hospitals in both Portsmouth (Haslar) and Plymouth (Stonehouse) and these were augmented by hospital ships such as these in various locations around the country.

A list of persons who have lost their Beds & Apparel in the Action of the 11th of October

The aftermath of any battle was miserable for the survivors. Even those who had come through unscathed would be cold, wet and exhausted once the adrenaline had stopped flowing. The food was often destroyed and beer barrels burst. Livestock was often thrown overboard before action so that it wouldn't get in the way of the guns. This list suggests powerfully the physical discomfort of some of Duncan's victorious sailors.

DIRECTOR AT THE NORE 3RD NOV^R 1797

Sir

According to a Memorandum dated Octr 25th in Yarmouth Roads. – I beg leave to inclose a list of persons who have lost their Beds & Apparel in the Action of the 11th of Octo^r.
    I am Sir
      Your most obedient very humble Servant

Willm Heatherby	1 Bed & Bedding, 1 Outside Jacket & 1 Hat.
Jona Swan	1 Bed & Blanket & 1 Rug
Jas Cummings	2 Beds & 2 Blankets.
Walter Hewen	1 Bed & Bedding, 1 Cotton Shirt, 1 pair White Trowsers, & 1 Black Silk Handkerchf.
Josh Daniel	1 Bed & Bedding, 1 pr Blue Trowsers, 1 Hat & 1 pr Shoes.
Lawce Burrage	1 Bed & Bedding & 1 Pea Jacket
Willm Norris	1 Bed & Bedding & 1 Pea Jacket.
Wm Todd	1 Bed & Bedding, 2 Shirts & 1 Outside Jacket
Jno Batty (Boy)	1 Bed & Bedding, 1 pr Blue Trowsers & 1 pr Shoes.
Willm James	1 Bed, 2 Blankets.
Heny Napier	1 Bed, 2 Blankets.
Willm Glanville	1 Bed & Bedding
Thos Garrison	1 Bed & Bedding, 1 Outside Jacket, 1 pr Blue Trowsers, 2 pr Woollen Stockings & 1 Bag
Jno Jones (3rd)	1 Bed & Bedding 1 pr Shoes.
Saml Lawrence	1 Bed & Bedding, 1 pr White Trousers 1 pr Musquito Do. 1 pr Shoes, 1 Black Silk Handkerchief & 1 Bag.
Jno State (Boy)	1 Bed, 2 Blankets.
Geo: Peat	1 Bed & Bedding, 1 pr Blue Trowsers.
Jno Hay	1 Bed & Bedding.
Jno Todd (Boy)	1 Bed & Bedding.
Jas Paddely	1 Bed & Bedding
Heny Smith	1 Bed & Bedding, 2 Shirts, 1 pr Stockings, & 1 pr Shoes.
Jas Johns	1 Bed & Bedding, 3 Shirts, 2 pr Woollen Stockings & 1 pr Nankeen Trowsers.

VICE ADMIRAL

Sir Richd Onslow Bart.

Bedding and rugs could be easily replaced but the loss of a pair of shoes, well-worn and soft-fitting, would have been a bitter blow. The very existence of this list suggests that these items were either replaced or that the sailors were compensated for their loss. An important distinction here is that hammocks were issued to sailors by the navy but beds, bedding and clothes were bought from the purser out of the sailors' wages. This, therefore, is a list of personal loss and the fact that the navy is taking an active interest is evidence of the service at its benevolent best. The man who wrote the letter to Vice-Admiral Onslow certainly knew about discomfort. William Bligh, once captain of the *Bounty*, had survived that epic 3,500-mile open boat journey across the Pacific.

'Beds' are not to be confused with hammocks. Sailors all slept in hammocks but each sailor was also issued with a 'bed', a thin mattress that fitted inside his hammock. Each bed was 5 ft 10 in long and 2 ft 1 in wide and stuffed with rags, wool or, the best, with goat's hair. Each bed usually came with its own blanket 6 ft 10 in long and 5 ft 4½ in wide, a good size to get cosy in. Each sailor should also have been issued with a bolster or pillow, though none appears to have been lost on board unless they were included in the term 'bedding'.

'Nankeen' was a distinctive pale yellow cloth. 'Musquito' – or mosquito – trousers were a particular style of close-fitting canvas legwear. The 'pea' jacket was the classic navy blue woollen coat, known by sailors as a 'bum-freezer' because, unlike the landsmens' long coat, it was cut short to ease work aloft. These 'short' coats were one of the reasons that sailors were instantly recognisable when ashore.

J. Walker to E. Nepean, 16 October 1797

Written in Yarmouth Roads several days after the battle, this next letter is from Captain James Walker of the *Monmouth*, one of the three converted East Indiamen in Duncan's fleet. Walker had just arrived in Yarmouth with one of the seven Dutch prizes, the *Alkmaar*, and did not yet know that the *Delft*, which also struck to the *Monmouth*, had sunk.

Walker describes his 'good fortune' in being able to bring the *Alkmaar* safely back to Yarmouth roads. It was clearly a close-run thing and was only achieved by throwing 21 of her guns overboard. Such drastic action was only taken in the direst circumstances. Guns were exceptionally heavy but also very valuable. The *Alkmaar* was a 56-gunner and her heaviest guns would have been no larger than 24-pounders. Nevertheless a 24-pounder cannon still weighed as much as two tons. Throwing 21 guns overboard, even if they were not all 24-pounders, would therefore have lightened the ship by some 30 or 40 tons. She would thus have drawn significantly less water, reducing the pressure on her hull and hence the rate of her leaks, thereby easing the task of the sailors at the pumps.

Walker is keen to emphasise to the Admiralty how his men were so anxious to 'expunge from the records of their Country the remembrance of their ever having forgot their duty', a reference to the recent mutinies. It is worth noting, however, that his sailors did not necessarily do this spontaneously. We know that Walker made a conscious effort to remind them of their recent behaviour moments before the battle. At battle stations he roared: 'My lads, you see your enemy; I shall lay you close aboard and give you an opportunity of washing the stain off your characters in the blood of your foes. Now, go to your quarters and do your duty.'[10] Walker had every reason to encourage his men: we know that he was 70 men short of his full complement.

His Majesty's Ship Monmouth in Yarmouth Roads the 16th October 1797

Sir

I beg You will be pleased to inform their Lordships of my arrival at this Anchorage with His Majesty's Ship under my Command and the Alkmaar Dutch Man of War in Tow, I send likewise a Journal of our proceedings from the morning of the 11th ins.t (as we unavoidably parted Company with the Admiral,) and the state and condition of the ship.

Two ships struck to the Monmouth in the Action, the Delft of 60 Guns and 375 Men, and the Alkmaar of 56 Guns and 350 Men: we were engaged with them both for Fifty minutes, when the weathermost one having lost his Main Topmast and Mizen Mast, and being otherwise so much cut up as to prevent her escaping we attatched ourselves more closely to the other; after exchanging three Broadsides with him, observing that he kept away, we bore round up, ran athwart his Hawse, rak'd Him and backing alongside of him to Leeward, engaged him very Closely for Forty minutes, when he struck, I immediately sent the First Lieutenant Mr Bullen with a party of Men who took possession of the Delft, and Lieut. Caley with another

Party on board the Alkmaar, having made the signal, twice that we were ready to renew the Action which remained unanswered, I thought it my duty to secure the Prizes, and the Alkmaar being the most disabled took her in Tow, and we have had the good Fortune, neither to be obliged to cast her off, nor have the Hawsers broke although we were two days on a Lee shore, which we could not get off, and on the 13th had a heavy Gale of Wind in which the Prize had nearly foundered, and was obliged to throw 21 of her Guns overboard.

All the Officers and Men of His Majesty's Ship did their duty as became British Seamen; the Brave exertions and active Abilities of Mr. Bullen the 1st Lieut were conspicuous as were also those of Mr. Murray the Master, and Captain Clark of the Marines, while the exertions of the Men strongly evinced how much they wished to expunge from the records of their Country the remembrance of their ever having forgot their duty.

We had Five Men Killed and Twenty two Wounded amongst the former we have to lament Lieut. Ferret a Brave and worthy officer, who has left a Wife to Deplore his loss — the Alkmaar had 29 Men Killed and 62 wounded, I have not spoke the Delft since the Action therefore cannot state her loss but believe it to be considerable. I have the Honor to be

> *Sir*
>> *Your most obedient*
>> *Humble Servant*

James Walker

Evan Nepean Esq

Walker's letter is proof that the influence of the 1797 insurrection had, by now, become powerfully positive. It is also proof that British sailors were aware of the weight of their own history and were consciously influenced by past events. Too often British success in these wars is associated only with British triumphs in battle, the energy of pride and expectation snowballing from one victory to another. We must, however, also acknowledge the impact of shame and failure, whether caused by mutiny or by outright British naval failures such as the attempted French landing at Bantry Bay in December 1796 or the real French landing in Wales a few weeks later. Both of these enemy naval operations were entirely unopposed by the Royal Navy. The reputation of British tars in this period traced a series of peaks and troughs and the relationship between the British public, politicians and the navy was by no means always healthy. Only in the brief afterglow of a victory was it uniformly positive and successes could be forgotten as easily as failures could be remembered.

The *Alkmaar* was taken into British service along with the other captured Dutch ships but none was coppered or considered of sufficient quality to serve in a British line of battle.[11] The *Alkmaar* became a troopship before being converted first into a hospital ship and then a storeship; the *Gelikheid* became a prison ship, then a guard ship and finally a sheer hulk; the *Haarlem* became a troopship and then a receiving ship; the *Admiral de Vries*, the largest of the Dutch 68-gunners, became a troopship, then a prison ship and finally a receiving ship; the *Wassenar* became a troopship and then a powder hulk; the *Jupiter* became a prison ship and then a powder hulk; and de Winter's 74-gun flagship, the *Vrijheid*, shared an identical fate. The British careers of these captured ships are one of the most telling indicators of the superiority of British warship design. Some French, Dutch and Spanish ships were exceptionally beautiful or notably swift but, when it came to fleet battle where robustness was key, none could withstand as much fire as a British warship.

The Battle of Camperdown did not on its own destroy Dutch seapower. However, along with the surrender of the Dutch squadron at Saldanha Bay in 1796 and the subsequent capitulation of another powerful Dutch squadron at Den Helder in 1799, it contributed to the breaking both of Dutch naval capability and of the will of Dutch politicians to wage an aggressive war against Britain. Confusion and recrimination after the battle tore Dutch politics apart and the country became paralysed by disagreement and indecision. The French insisted that the Dutch rebuild their fleet, a burden that crippled a Dutch economy already shattered by the 100,000,000-florin indemnity imposed by the invading French in 1796. Dutch maritime, economic and political power collapsed to the extent that, by 1806, Napoleon had had enough. On 5 June he crowned his brother Louis King of Holland.

Camperdown deserves its place as one of Britain's most impressive naval victories because it embodied so many of the ideals that came to characterise

British naval success. It was dashing and impulsive; it was hard-fought and ferocious; it was a fleeting opportunity seized and exploited. Duncan was created a viscount and given the title Camperdown and, although some considered the reward insufficient, his reputation soared. A poem was soon popularised that celebrated the three victories of the war:

'St Vincent drubbed the Dons, Earl Howe he drubbed Monsieur
And gallant Duncan now has soundly drubbed Mynheer;
The Spanish, French and Dutch, tho' all united be.
Fear not, Britannia cries, My Tars can beat all three'

When Duncan died only six years later, Nelson wrote to his son with the telling words 'The name of Duncan will never be forgot'.[12] Duncan's precipitate attack and decisive victory was certainly a big influence on Nelson, who was recovering from the recent amputation of his arm in London* when he heard the news and exclaimed that he would have given his other arm to have been present.

The mob which prowled the streets, ensuring that everyone had lit their candles in celebration of Duncan's victory, hammered on the door of 141 Bond Street, Nelson's London home, but the windows stayed resolutely dark. The baying crowd, confronted by an irate Frances Nelson anxious to let her hero husband sleep, dutifully crept away when they discovered the identity of the man lying in the darkness, saying 'You will hear no more from us tonight.'[13]

Nelson recovered, though the pain in his arm plagued him for months afterwards, possibly as a result of a nerve being caught in the silk ligatures that secured the blood vessels in his stump. He was ready again for service the following spring, eight months after receiving the injury in the disastrous attack on Santa Cruz in Tenerife. By then, with the Dutch reeling after Camperdown and the Spanish crushed at St Vincent, the invasion threat had been lifted and the British were ready to sail back into the Mediterranean for the first time since December 1796.

In France, meanwhile, Napoleon, with his political influence growing, urged the Directory to sponsor a major operation against British India and the

---

* He was struck just above the right elbow by a musket ball in the disastrous attack on Santa Cruz, Tenerife in June 1797. His arm was immediately amputated high above the elbow.

Ottoman Empire, the first stage of which would be the conquest of Egypt. The Parisian politicians, delighted that they would see the back of this ambitious and troublesome young general, approved the idea. Thousands of men were assembled in hundreds of transports along the southern French coast but the British had no idea of their intended destination. The Admiralty turned to Nelson, equipped him with a fleet of magnificent ships and superb crews, and ordered him to find Napoleon and destroy his fleet, wherever it went. On 29 March 1798, Nelson hoisted his flag on HMS *Vanguard* and set in motion the next maritime dance between Britain and France. This one would lead to the most overwhelming battle of them all at the mouth of the mighty River Nile.

The Battle of the Nile
La Bataille d'Aboukir

1 August 1798

*'As yet we know not all the circumstances but those which we
are already acquainted with are frightful in the extreme'*

E. Poussielgue, Comptroller General of the Expenses of the Eastern Army,
3 August 1798

AT A GLANCE

DATE:
1–3 August 1798

NAVIES INVOLVED:
British and French

COMMANDING OFFICERS:
Rear-Admiral Horatio Nelson and Vice-Admiral F. Brueys d'Aigalliers

FLEET SIZES:
British, 19 ships of the line; French, 13 ships of the line

TIME OF DAY:
18.20 – c. 22.00 when *L'Orient* exploded. Recommenced sporadically
after 04.00 on the second day

LOCATION:
Aboukir Bay, Egypt. 31°20′N 30°07′E

WEATHER:
Moderate breezes and clear

RESULT:
9 French ships of the line captured, 2 destroyed

CASUALTIES:
British 896; French 3,179

BRITISH COURT MARTIALS:
None.

DISPATCHES CARRIED HOME BY:
Nelson's flag captain Edward Berry, who was captured, and Lieutenant
Thomas Capel who travelled to London via Naples and Vienna.
Lieutenant Thomas Duval carried the news to India

The Lightning Conductor

If you were a successful admiral in the age of sail, where would you keep your medals, your paintings, your battle relics and souvenirs? Nelson, in classic Nelsonian style, kept them everywhere. One visitor to his home at Merton in Surrey, where Nelson moved in 1801, remembered how ' ... not only the rooms but the whole house, staircase and all'[1] were covered with images of the admiral and littered with naval memorabilia. We know that he kept one of his most curious pieces in the hallway, so that it was the very first thing that a visitor would see, or crack their shins against, when they came to Merton. That item was the lightning conductor of the French 120-gun flagship *L'Orient* which exploded at the Battle of the Nile. Its place in such a prominent position was a clear indication of Nelson's pride in or fascination with it, a fact that bears a little consideration.

The lightning conductor is quite splendid and you can still see it at the National Maritime Museum in Greenwich. Over a metre tall, its lower half consists of a conical piece of black painted wood through the centre of which runs a sheave for a signal halyard. Resting on top is a painted metal cap to which is attached a lengthy piece of cylindrical copper, turned at the head like a bishop's crook. It looks like the fantastic contraption of a mad scientist, something that might have fallen off Chitty Chitty Bang Bang (fig. 10).

The allure of this artefact is considerable on a number of levels. First and most obviously, it came from the flagship of Rear-Admiral François-Paul Brueys, whose fleet was annihilated at Aboukir Bay and whose flagship was destroyed in the process by a cataclysmic explosion. It is therefore important both because it came from the French flagship and also because it was one of its few recognisable pieces to have survived.[*] This small object evokes the great shadowy mass of the warship that was destroyed, acting as a reminder of the incredible destructive power that Nelson brought down on the French fleet at Aboukir Bay, a fleet that was shattered as utterly as the flagship itself.

On another level, however, the artefact is important because it is a lightning conductor and the history of lightning conductors is rather interesting. Lightning

---

[*] Nelson also had a writing desk and coffin, in which he was buried, made from her timber.

strikes were always hot news in the late 18th century. In the weeks before the Battle of the Nile, strikes on Caldecot Church in Rutland and Grantham Church in Lincolnshire both made the news.[2] Strikes on churches were common because of the height of their steeples, which often towered above surrounding trees; Grantham's spire is 282 ft high. Ships were particularly vulnerable because there was nothing at sea to attract the lightning in the way that woods, hills and mountains protected houses on land. Wooden hulls, moreover, did nothing to conduct electricity safely to the sea. The result was that unprotected wooden ships struck by lightning burst into flame, a major problem for all navies whose ships were crammed with mountains of gunpowder.

The solution, a copper bar extending from the masthead through the hull and into the sea, was developed simultaneously in Europe and America in the middle years of the 18th century, the American inventor being none other than Benjamin Franklin, who was a well-respected scientist long before he became a revolutionary politician and a Founding Father of the United States. Franklin's idea was readily accepted and, by 1798, American ships had already been fitted with lightning conductors for many years. The French were slightly slower on the uptake but we know that the French scientist Jean-Baptiste le Roy toured the main naval dockyards of France in 1784, fixing copper lightning rods to ships and naval storehouses.

The British system, developed in 1762 by Dr William Watson, was significantly inferior because it was temporary and awkward. At times of suspected danger, a copper chain was rigged from the masthead, passed down through the rigging and dropped overboard. Once rigged, it got in the way of the masts, yards and sails, but the system's main flaw was that it relied on the sailors, a naturally suspicious bunch, to find the copper chain and then rig it when most believed that installing a lightning rod actually increased the risk of being struck.[3] As a result, British warships continued to suffer from lightning strikes and were hit as many as 174 times between 1793 and 1838. Those that did manage to rig the clumsy protection system found it wholly inadequate. It offered no protection against side-flashes because it was not bonded to nearby metal and the electricity would arc at the connecting links, which could easily melt.

Nelson's French lightning conductor was important, therefore, because it was an example of effective maritime technology that the British did not then have and it became a focal point for discussions among naval professionals and interested parties. There is every reason to believe that it was influential. In 1799, a year after the Battle of the Nile, an important article on French lightning conductors was published in the very first edition of *The Naval Chronicle*, the new and very popular British magazine dedicated to all matters naval. Despite this contemporary interest, however, the inadequacy of the British system was never properly addressed until 1842, when a new and impressive solution which had been invented by William Snow Harris in 1820 was finally adopted for all British naval ships. The history of lightning conductors therefore provides a rare example of British lethargy in adopting technical innovation that could improve maritime capability. Snow Harris was only six when Nelson won his lightning conductor at the Nile. In the subsequent years during which *L'Orient*'s conductor sat next to Nelson's boots and umbrellas at Merton, the science of maritime lightning protection remained a hot topic of debate.

On a more personal level, Nelson may well have cherished the artefact in his hallway as a reminder of the surprising, shockingly violent and merciless assault that he had launched on the French fleet at Aboukir Bay, an assault which was the very human embodiment of a lightning strike. Perhaps he appreciated the incongruity of its survival: the French may have been protected from nature's wrath, but they had nothing to protect them from the British.

The Prey

By 1798 four years had passed since the Jacobins had ruled France through The Terror and the Brest fleet had been shattered by Howe on The Glorious First of June. The extremism of the Jacobins had finally been tamed by the Thermidorian coup, yet many serious problems created by the way the French navy was organised, run, perceived and used still remained. The Jacobins had been replaced by the chaotic Directory which enjoyed the period of relative peace that had been won by the initial surge of the powerful revolutionary armies. The First Coalition against the Republic had been broken and the threats to French soil beaten back. French territory had then been expanded, notably in Italy where the young and aggressive Bonaparte had repeatedly defeated the Austrian armies before marching to within

100 miles of Vienna. The Austrians had crumbled and Napoleon had ruled his conquered territory as nothing less than a personal fiefdom. During this period of French victories on foreign soil, the politicians in Paris became more moderate. Peace negotiations were begun with Britain and some even spoke of reinstating the French monarchy.

Nothing could have been less attractive to men like Bonaparte and his great rival General Lazare Hoche who used their military power to back a coup on 18 Fructidor (4 September) 1797. The new government was notably more aggressive in its foreign policy and also grateful to the men who had brought it to power. However, Hoche died shortly after the coup, leaving Napoleon the principal military beneficiary of political favour. When he suggested an attack on British interests in India via an invasion of the Egyptian territories of the crumbling Ottoman Empire, the politicians seized the opportunity to send a popular and powerful general away from Paris and to occupy thousands of listless French troops brooding after their victories in Lombardy. Thus it was that Napoleon began to gather an invasion fleet of extraordinary proportions in ports all along the Mediterranean coast of France and Italy.

The man he placed in command of the fleet was Vice-Admiral François-Paul Brueys D'Aigalliers, an aristocratic officer who had survived the surrender of the fleet in Toulon in 1793 and the subsequent Jacobin death squads in the city. Compared with Villaret, the green commander of the French fleet at The Glorious First of June, Brueys was very experienced. He had cut his teeth in numerous fleet battles during the American War and had been present at the great Battle of the Chesapeake of 1781 when the British fleet had been effectively neutralised by skilled French manoeuvre. More importantly for our understanding of the Battle of the Nile, Brueys had also fought at St Kitts in 1782 when Samuel Hood had so cleverly demonstrated the potential strength of a well-defended line of anchored ships. With his ships well anchored close to each other and close to shore and with springs running to the anchor cables to allow the captains to change the direction of their ships' broadsides without setting sail, Hood had been able to protect his anchorage from persistent French attacks. He had then vanished during the night in a flawless demonstration of tactical acuity and magnificent seamanship. At the Nile Brueys would find out how well he had learned the detail of Hood's tactical lesson.

The assembly of Napoleon's invasion army in 1798 was a notable logistical achievement, but the fighting ships chosen to protect the cumbersome troop transports still lacked skilled seamen, although the situation was not quite as bleak as it had been in the tumultuous early years of the war. The end of The Terror had led to the return of some of the experienced, aristocratic officers who had fled or been expelled from the Navy under the Jacobins and the corps of seamen-gunners, which had been abolished just before The Glorious First of June, had been reinstated. Nothing, however, had been done to reform the underlying problems of the French manning system or to ease the painful effects of The Glorious First of June. Then 4,200 French sailors had died, 3,300 had been wounded and between 4,000 and 5,000 had been taken prisoner, many of whom had subsequently died of typhus in British prisons or in the holds of British ships.

With insufficient space on Napoleon's transports, the 'escorting' warships were also crammed with supernumeraries including an army of soldiers to wage the war, a chaos of children to found a colony and a ponder of philosophers to examine Egypt's treasures. Rather than a fighting squadron patrolling, the French fleet had become a substantial city relocating. It would have been torn apart if intercepted by a British fleet and what a strike that would have been. Not only was Napoleon on board *L'Orient*, lounging in an ostentatious luxury that shocked many who witnessed it, but with him were Louis Alexandre Berthier, August de Marmont, Jean Lannes, Joachim Murat, Louis Desaix, Jean Reynier, Antoine-François Andréossy, Jean-Andoche Junot, Louis-Nicolas Davout and Alexandre Dumas, the core group of generals and marshals which, in the coming years, would expand and defend Napoleon's empire.

On only a handful of occasions in history has the fate of an empire and of hundreds of thousands of lives rested on such a perilous venture. Napoleon's encumbered and poorly manned fleet would have been vulnerable to any respectable naval force. But the man who had been sent to hunt it down was Rear-Admiral Horatio Nelson and he led one of the finest squadrons that had ever sailed the seas.

The Favourite

Nelson was not particularly short[*] but he was notably frail. His complexion had been affected by the malaria and yellow fever he had suffered as a young man and, by the time he was put in command of the squadron sent to hunt down Napoleon's invasion fleet, he had one arm, was blind in one eye and suffered recurrently from the huge 'fist-sized' hernia caused by the wound he received at the Battle of St Vincent. The contrast between that physical frailty and his mental courage was an important reason why he was loved by his men, but so too was his clear fondness for them. He did not love without qualification, nor did he love without exception, but Nelson loved enough, and he made his dedication sufficiently apparent for most to love him back. His dedication to destroying the enemy, moreover, even if it was tangled up with a desire for personal glory, was contagious among men trained to fight.

By 1797 he had tasted failure as much as success. He had taken part in a disastrous campaign in the Turks Islands in the West Indies in 1783 and then in the famous calamity at Santa Cruz in the Canaries in 1797. He had enjoyed success in Corsica in 1794, in a single-ship engagement the following year and then most famously at the Battle of St Vincent in 1797, but by no means everything he touched turned to gold. He had, indeed, very nearly lost his life in battle on several occasions, often as a result of his own rashness, but his natural ability to lead was as clear to his naval superiors and political masters as it was to his subordinates. Men followed Nelson and men wanted to follow Nelson. His peculiar charm, which certainly did not work on everyone he met, worked on enough influential men to radically change his destiny.

That was why Nelson was chosen above so many others in 1798 to lead a squadron into the Mediterranean and track down Napoleon's fleet. Make no mistake of how extraordinary this selection was. Officers promoted to flag rank were put on a list of flag-officers with the youngest and least experienced at the bottom and the oldest and most experienced at the top. In reality not all Admirals wished or were able to serve and many had been advanced by the automatic promotion system

---

[*] The most accurate Nelson statue is also the easiest against which you can measure yourself. The life-size bronze by Lesley Pover is outside the Trafalgar Tavern in Greenwich.

rather than for their notable competence. The Admiralty was able therefore to reach down the list when occasion demanded to find a competent or willing flag-officer. Nelson, however, had only been a Rear-Admiral of the Blue, the most junior of all flag-officers' ranks, since February 1797, a mere 15 months before he was given command of the Mediterranean squadron. He really was exceptionally young. Of the other commanding officers in this book, Duckworth was 11 years older than Nelson, Hyde Parker 19, Jervis 23, Duncan 27 and Howe 32 years older when they commanded at the battles described. There were plenty of flag-officers who, if not destined for stardom, had nonetheless enjoyed steady careers and were above him in the list and most of them would have been desperate for such a plum command.

The ships and men in Nelson's fleet were quite exceptional too. In almost every respect his fleet was the opposite of Duncan's that had fought the Battle of Camperdown in 1797. Then, Duncan commanded small, old ships of poor quality and many of his captains had question marks over their ability, competence or commitment (p. 135). Nelson's Mediterranean squadron in 1798, on the other hand, consisted of the finest young commanders that the Navy had to offer together with the finest of its ships, which were well manned and stuffed with provisions. Admiral Jervis, by now known as Earl St Vincent for his heroics at St Vincent and commander-in-chief of the Mediterranean fleet, summed up Nelson's squadron: 'The whole of these ships are in excellent order, and so well officered, manned and appointed I am confident they will perform everything to be expected of them.'[4]

The relatively poor condition of the French fleet was also known. Back in London, Henry Dundas, the Secretary for War, declared, 'This force, tho' somewhat inferior in number, is so decidedly superior to that of the Enemy in every other respect, that should the latter be overtaken before they reach Alexandria … the most sanguine prospect of success may reasonably [be] entertained.'[5] Duncan had also been burdened with the high expectations of politicians the year before, but at least Nelson had a superb squadron upon which he could base both his tactical planning and his hopes.

Everything was set for a major confrontation and there were high expectations of British success. There was one major problem, however. No more than 65 miles off Toulon, Nelson's fleet was savagely hurled off station by one of those hideous Mediterranean summer storms, all northerly winds, sharp swells and swirling currents. When, having repaired his ships in Sardinia, he finally clawed his way back within sight of the French coast, the harbour at Toulon was empty. Thirteen ships of the line, 280 transports and 48,662 troops had simply vanished and Nelson had no idea where Napoleon had gone.

The Discovery

It is ironic that whispers suggesting Egypt as Napoleon's destination had travelled the hundreds of miles to London but had failed to reach Nelson, within earshot of the French fleet. He simply had nothing to work on. Even Ireland, a land in rebellion and its people open allies of the French, was a possible and reasonable destination; remember that the French had attempted to invade Ireland just 18 months previously. To complicate matters further, Napoleon had decided to sail to Egypt via Malta and his ultimate destination remained a secret even after the fleet had left port.

In 1798, Malta, that tiny island set in the southern Mediterranean between Sicily and the coast of North Africa, was the home of the influential and wealthy Knights of St John. They had, hitherto, remained neutral in the war but retained close links with the French and particularly with the French navy. Indeed, many of the Knights and their paid soldiers were Frenchmen, and many French sailors and naval officers had learned their trade through a system of apprenticeship in the Maltese navy. Moreover, the Knights' traditional enemies were the Turks and Napoleon was clearly intent on a major conquest of part of the crumbling Ottoman Empire. In that sense, at least, the interests of Napoleon and the Knights were aligned. The Maltese were, therefore, disinclined to fight when he arrived unannounced in their great harbour at Valetta and demanded water for his fleet. They did make a nominal stand and refused his demands but, when Napoleon landed a few troops, the Knights capitulated. They were no longer the fiercely muscled independent force which, two centuries before, had withstood one the greatest sieges in history.[*] The great gates of Valetta were opened to Napoleon who not only secured the water he needed for his fleet but robbed the Knights' vaults

---

[*] The island was besieged by a vast Ottoman horde from May to September 1565.

of the treasures of centuries. These were duly packed into the hold of *L'Orient* and the great maritime caravan headed out across the Mediterranean and towards the rising sun.

Nelson, meanwhile, was gathering what information he could, and had slowly begun to form a hunch – and at this stage it really was nothing more than a hunch – that Napoleon was heading for Egypt. He discussed the options with his captains and led them all to his own conclusion that his squadron should head east. They sailed for Alexandria and, just a day south east of Sicily on 22 June, the two fleets passed each other in heavy mist. Nelson refused to follow up a sighting of strange sails because he was convinced that the French were nearly a week ahead. In the blink of an eye he had missed an opportunity to take Napoleon's vulnerable fleet at sea, encumbered by transports, civilians and stores.

Four days later Nelson finally received confirmation from a captured French brig that Napoleon's destination was, indeed, Egypt. He raced for Alexandria, arriving on 28 June and, to his utter mortification, found the harbour empty save for a handful of Egyptian xebecs and Arab dhows plying their trade. Napoleon, who knew how close the fleets had come to colliding in the fog on 22 June, had altered course to the north and skirted the southern shore of Crete with his heavy, slow ships, while Nelson had taken a more direct route to Alexandria in his fast warships. He had not gone to the wrong place, but he had arrived there too soon. Having searched elsewhere along the coast, he headed back towards Sicily.

Three days later, Napoleon landed his troops near Alexandria uncontested, albeit in a desperate, mortal rush for fear of being caught at this most vulnerable moment. Soldiers were packed into landing craft and sailors rowed them ashore, arms burning, while their officers peered anxiously through telescopes at the horizon. The empty transports were then crammed into the safety of Alexandria harbour. Alexandria, however, is not Valetta, Toulon or Gibraltar, where the waters are deep and calm and the entrance wide. It was no place for a fleet of warships. To pass the narrow entrance, they would have had to be guided in, one at a time, and only at the very height of the flood, an operation that would have taken far too long and, even if achieved, would have left the French ships trapped. Napoleon's army may have been safe, and within three weeks of landing was rampaging past the Pyramids with the Mamelukes in utter disarray, but his fleet was not. Its choice was twofold: either to return to the safety of French-held Corfu or to anchor in the great sweep of Aboukir Bay, a 16-mile-wide indentation in the coast at the Rosetta entrance to the Nile, just to the east of Alexandria. The ensuing correspondence between Napoleon and Brueys is littered with confusion and unresolved proposals. However, Brueys eventually took the fleet to Aboukir, perhaps to keep it as near as possible to Napoleon and his army, an entirely sensible decision that we know was favoured by Napoleon himself.

Aboukir was by no means a poor location if the fleet could assume a strong defensive posture, which was certainly possible. An island, which was quickly fortified, jutted deep into the bay which, at the southern end, was defended naturally by shoals. The bay itself was shallow in places but provided good holding ground. A line of powerful battleships anchored close together near to the shore and perhaps even chained together would pose a significant challenge to any fleet.

The French never took the appropriate precautions, however. Their ships were anchored too far from the shore and too far from the fortified island and they were not prepared for defence. They were also now dangerously undermanned because all of the soldiers had disembarked to fight the land war and the crews were further weakened because parties had been sent ashore to secure water and food since almost all of the fleet's provisions had been landed with the army. The ships were nevertheless still encumbered with cargo destined for the new French colony that the army had yet to win. Moreover the frigates were anchored inshore of the main battleships rather than protecting them from the west by a screen of surveillance. So there the French fleet lay upon the topaz water in the stillness of an Egyptian summer afternoon, the gentle waves lapping against their hulls above sunken ancient ruins.

Meanwhile Nelson, after a brief stay in Sicily and with more accurate information of the French movements, had left for Egypt once more on 25 July. He headed first for Alexandria which he again found empty of warships but this time jammed with the telltale hulks of troopships. He then sent two scouts north towards Aboukir and there he finally fell on his prey. By the time that he was done, 11 of Brueys's 13 ships of the line had been captured or destroyed and the French flagship lay at the bottom of the sea in ten thousand pieces.

Her cannon and treasure rested among the sunken ruins of the Greek cities of Heracleion and Canopus while her lightning conductor, torn from the top of its mast by the explosion and bobbing past a British ship, was plucked from the water and given to Nelson.

The Dispatches

Admiral Earl St Vincent to E. Nepean, 23 October 1798

The first of the Nile dispatches is not written by Nelson. The letter comes from St Vincent, the former Admiral John Jervis, still commander-in-chief of the Mediterranean fleet and based in Gibraltar. It is addressed to Evan Nepean, Secretary of the Admiralty, and it is dated 23 October, that is 84 days or 12 weeks after the battle. St Vincent hints at the reason. The *Leander*, the ship which Nelson had sent back to Britain with the dispatches, was captured en route by the *Généreux*, one of only two French ships of the line to have escaped the carnage at Aboukir. Just before the *Leander* surrendered, the dispatches, which included not only the official letters but also many wonderful personal descriptions of the battle, were stuffed into three canvas sacks, loaded with shot and thrown overboard. The man charged with delivering them to the Admiralty, Nelson's flag captain Sir Edward Berry, was taken to French-controlled Corfu and did not manage to return to Britain for another two months. St Vincent, therefore, had no idea that one of the most decisive naval battles in history had been won by the British and in his own theatre of war.

St Vincent's description of Nelson as 'an extraordinary man' says a great deal about his utter professional faith, as well as his professional investment, in him. Remember that Nelson had fought with distinction under his command at the Battle of Cape St Vincent and that St Vincent had personally been involved in the selection of Nelson to lead the hunt for Napoleon's fleet. By nominating a man so far down the admirals' list, St Vincent had upset a great number of men.[6] He was personally relieved, therefore, that Nelson had won this great victory because his own professional judgement had been at stake.

L'Aurore Gibraltar 23ʳᵈ October 1798

Sir

 The Capture of the Leander has prevented my receiving the Account of the glorious Action of the Nile, until this moment; The Rear Admiral's modest relation, which I enclose, is a true Type of the Character of this extraordinary Man:

 The Arrival of General Mack at Naples, to take upon him the Command of the Neapolitan Army, and the Events which have taken place at Constantinople, in consequence of this decisive Victory, must be known to the Lords Commissioners of the Admiralty long before this can reach you, and there not being time to translate, or transcribe, the several papers in time for the Orion, it is impossible to send them by this Conveyance.

 I am

  Sir

  Your most Obedient

  Humble Servant

   St Vincent

            Evan Nepean Esqʳ

The letter ends with some important news. So much time has passed since the battle that the main strategic players in the war have already begun to make their next move.

General Karl Mack von Leiberich was an Austrian general who had been given command of the Neapolitan army. Nelson, meanwhile, was in Naples, acting rather strangely and conducting a wild and open affair with Emma Hamilton, the wife of Sir William Hamilton, British envoy to Naples. Just under a month before St Vincent sat down to write this letter, Emma had organised a wonderful 40th birthday party for Nelson. Together, they became a formidable couple and Emma enjoyed particularly close links with the Queen of Naples, Maria Carolina. Through this network of relationships the Neapolitan army, under Mack's command, was incited to wage war against France by invading Italy and attacking Rome.

With the British fleet in support, Rome was easily taken but the French response was too fast and too professional for the amateur Neapolitan soldiers, their corrupt officers and Mack, whom Nelson later described as a 'rascal, a scoundrel, and a coward'.[7] He was certainly incompetent: in 1805 he surrendered his entire army to Napoleon after a feeble campaign that ended in disaster at Ulm. With Mack at the helm of the Neapolitan rabble, everything turned to dust and ended, two months after St Vincent wrote this letter, with Naples itself being lost to the French and Nelson's fleet rescuing the Neapolitan royal family. This letter from St Vincent, therefore, is both news of a great victory and the harbinger of an epic fiasco.

The 'Events which have taken place at Constantinople' to which St Vincent refers were also momentous. Constantinople, modern day Istanbul, was the seat of the Ottoman Empire, of which Egypt was a part. Politics in the heart of Constantinople were not as anti-French as one might suspect. Indeed, there was a growing cabal of pro-French politicians. Napoleon's invasion of Egypt, therefore, although a direct act of war, might not necessarily have caused the Ottomans to declare war on France. Indeed, to encourage those with pro-French leanings, Napoleon styled himself throughout his Egyptian campaign as an ally of the Ottomans and a friend to the Egyptians, on the basis that he had freed them from Mameluke oppression.

Nelson's victory at Aboukir was so absolute, however, that it decided the issue politically in Constantinople. Powerful pro-French voices succeeded in postponing the declaration of war against France but were unable to prevent it. A *fetva*, a legal opinion according to Muslim religious law, was issued on 3 August, when it was clear that Egypt was under attack, but war was not officially declared by Sultan Selim III until 14 August when news of Nelson's victory arrived. Still no action was taken, however, until 2 September when the Russian fleet arrived at Constantinople after a brief voyage across the Black Sea from their base at Sevastapol. The Russians, no friends of the Turks, had been inspired to join a new anti-French coalition by Napoleon's plunder of Malta because the Russian Tsar had been created an official 'protector' of the Maltese after the Russo-Maltese Treaty of 1797. The arrival of the Russian squadron off Constantinople forced the anti-French Ottomans to take the lead. Orders were issued to imprison French merchants and advisers, and to confiscate all French property in the Ottoman

Empire. The entire French position in the Middle East, carefully nurtured over centuries and a crucial foundation of the future security of Napoleon's campaign in Egypt, was shattered at a stroke. Taken together, Nelson's victory, the arrival of the Russian squadron and the subsequent Turkish decision to declare war, ruined the prospects of Napeoleon's army in Egypt.

In purely naval terms, however, the most shocking aspect of this entire episode was the presence of the Russian fleet off Istanbul. The Russians and the Ottomans both had powerful navies and shared a mutual antipathy, having fought protracted wars between 1787 and 1792 and 1768 and 1774 that had been predated by decades of hostility and sporadic battles. To see them in alliance was quite extraordinary. The Ottomans grudgingly gave the Russians permission to pass through the Bosphorus and thence into the Mediterranean so that they could, together, drive the French out of the Adriatic.

The magnificent spectacle of the combined Russian and Turkish navies sailing through the Hellespont was a powerful symbol of the extraordinary European alliance that Napoleon's ambition had produced. A Second Coalition now stood against France, far more formidable, determined and focused than the one which had faced down the Jacobins. Russia, Austria, the Ottoman Empire, Portugal and the Kingdom of the Two Sicilies now joined Britain in a combined bid to stop Napoleon. A little over a year before, the First Coalition had collapsed and Britain had faced Revolutionary France alone. Now the tables had turned.

Rear-Admiral H. Nelson to St Vincent, 3 August 1798[8]

The next letter is Nelson's official dispatch, the 'modest relation' to which St Vincent referred (p. 170). The letter, though authored by Nelson, has actually been written by a secretary and hence is in the clearest of hands. Nelson, naturally right-handed, had taught himself to write left-handed after losing his arm the year before. By 1798 he was not struggling with the quill as he once had but his handwriting was still a distinctive scrawl. This letter, however, could not have been composed by anyone other than Nelson. Eloquent and generous, it simply overflows with the honest zeal for which he was so loved.

This is one of several copies that were sent far and wide after the battle. One went overland to India, a mighty trek indeed from the Eastern Mediterranean. The lucky man charged with that task was Lieutenant Thomas Duval of the *Zealous*. He sailed to Alexandretta in the Gulf of Scandaroon, where he was given Arab clothing. From there he went inland to Aleppo, where he was given a horse, 19 camels and 24 Arabs to guide him across the desert. Twelve days later he arrived in Baghdad, whence he sailed down the Tigris to Basra, through the Gulf of Oman, across the Arabian Sea and thence to Bombay, modern day Mumbai. He arrived on 21 October, two days *before* St Vincent in Gibraltar received his first official news of the battle.

We also know that this, St Vincent's copy, was old news when it eventually arrived in London. Nelson had sent another copy of his report to Naples by sea in the capable hands of Captain Thomas Capel. From there Capel travelled to Vienna. News of the battle had preceded him like a raging flood. In a town not far from Vienna, an expectant audience was waiting to hear the first public performance of a rather solemn new Mass, the *Missa in Angustiis* or 'Mass for Troubled Times' by Joseph Hadyn, when the news arrived. The majestic work swiftly acquired the nickname 'The Nelson Mass'. From Vienna, Capel travelled via several German States and eventually arrived in London at 11.15 on the morning of 2 October. Even then, the British already knew that there had been a battle, though not the result, having already received word from the British ambassador in Constantinople.

Capel made quite an entrance. The First Lord, Earl Spencer, who had been suffering nervous anxiety for months over the fate of Napoleon's enterprise and his own affirmation of St Vincent's recommendation to give Nelson command, fainted when he heard the news. His wife erupted in a letter to Nelson. 'Captain Capel just arrived!' she wrote, 'Joy, joy, joy to you, brave, gallant, immortalised Nelson … My heart is absolutely bursting with different sensations of joy, of gratitude, pride, of every emotion that ever warmed the bosom of a British woman on hearing of her country's glory … I am half mad and I have written a strange letter, but you will excuse it.'[9]

A third copy, this copy, was sent with William Hoste to St Vincent at Gibraltar. Hoste was a very young officer who had joined the navy only five years previously, directly under Nelson's patronage. Nelson declared him 'without exception one of the finest boys I ever met with'.[10] By 1794 he was a Midshipman and, by July 1797, an acting lieutenant; after the Battle of the Nile Nelson gave him command of the brig *Mutine*. He was only 18 and went on to enjoy a distinguished career.

This, then, is the letter that Hoste handed to St Vincent on 23 October; moments after its receipt St Vincent began to compose his own covering letter to the Admiralty (p. 170).

VANGUARD OFF THE MOUTH OF THE NILE,
3RD AUGUST 1798

My Lord

Almighty God has blessed His Majesty's Arms, in the late Battle by a great Victory over the Fleet of the Enemy, whom I attacked at Sun Set on the 1st August off the mouth of the Nile, The Enemy were moored in a strong Line of Battle, for defending the Entrance of this Bay (of shoals), flanked by numerous Gun Boats, 4 Frigates and a Battery of Guns and Mortars, on an island in their Van, but nothing could withstand the Squadron your Lordship did me the honor to place under my Command; their high state of discipline is well known to you, and with the judgment of the Captains, together with their Valour, and that of the Officers and Men of every description, it was absolutely irresistible. Could any thing from my Pen add to the character of the Captains, I would write it with pleasure but that is impossible; I have to regret the loss of Captain Westcott, who was killed early in the Action, but the Ship was continued to be so well fought by her first Lieutenant M^r. Cuthbert, that I have given him an Order to command her till your Lordships pleasure is known The Ships of the Enemy all but their two Rear Ships are nearly dismasted and those two with two Frigates I am sorry to say made their Escape nor was it I assure you in my Power to prevent them Captain Hood most handsomely endeavoured to do it but I had no Ship in a Condition to support the Zealous and I was obliged to call her in The Support and Assistance I have received from Captain Berry cannot be sufficiently expressed I was wounded in the Head and obliged to be carried off the Deck but the Service suffered no loss by that Event Captain Berry was fully equal to the important Service then going on and to him I must beg leave to refer you for every information relative to this Victory he will present you with the Flag of the second in Command that of the Commander in Chief being burnt in

L'Orient herewith I transmit you Lists of the killed and wounded and the Line of Battle of ourselves and the French

I have the honor to be

Your Lordships most

Obedient Servant

Horatio Nelson

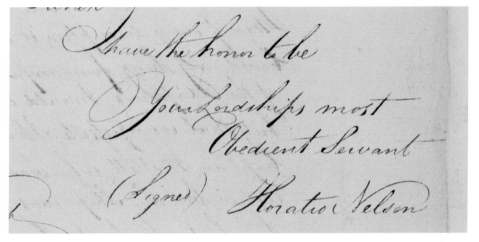

This copy of the Nile dispatch has been made by a secretary and is not in Nelson's distinctive left-handed scrawl.

The first striking aspect of this dispatch, apart from Nelson's total lack of punctuation, is his thanks given to God. The extent of Nelson's faith remains an unsettled question. We know that Victorian historians, keen to make their hero a devout Christian, over-emphasised his devotion to prayer and religious ceremony. A man of faith, maybe, but Nelson was no zealot like some of his contemporary flag-officers such as 'Dismal Jimmy' Gambier, then one of the Lords of the Admiralty. Nevertheless, the leading statement here, in a letter that he knew would become famous, reflects Nelson's more general inclination to thank God for his intervention in the engagement. Indeed, he wrote to Lord Spencer claiming that the hand of God was visible from first to last; to his brother,

William, that the hand of God had been pressed on the French; and, in a letter to William Hamilton, that 'Almighty God has made me the happy instrument in destroying the enemy's fleet.'[11] The contrast with his enemy is important here. The French revolutionaries were famous atheists who had turned Notre Dame into a Temple for the Cult of Reason. Against such an enemy, Nelson saw himself as Heaven's warrior, drawing strength from a perception that he had God's blessing. A service of thanksgiving was held on the quarterdeck of *Vanguard* soon after the battle, with Nelson in attendance, head bandaged.

Nelson's thanks to God are also a powerful reminder of his family roots. He was the son of a humble parish priest and his rise through the ranks is one of the finest examples of the Royal Navy rewarding talent with promotion. Patronage was important but its absence was not an insurmountable problem.

The second striking aspect is that the dispatch is dated 3 August and that it is lucid; in fact, it is beautifully composed. The main battle was fought in the afternoon and evening of 1 August and at roughly 20.30 Nelson was struck in the head by a piece of shrapnel which opened up a nasty wound several inches long and exposed his skull. He immediately thought he was going to die and declared, 'I am killed; remember me to my wife.'[12] There is still some debate over the immediate effects of the wound but Nelson had clearly regained his senses by 3 August when he wrote this letter. The battle, moreover, was rather longer than many suggest. *L'Orient* blew up at 21.37 on the night of 1 August and there was a notable lull in the combat after 02.00 on the 2nd, but firing began again with the dawn and the final French ships to surrender, *Tonnant* and *Timoléon*, did not haul their flags down until the morning of the next day, the 3rd.

So Nelson, in direct contrast to Duncan after Camperdown, waited until he knew the full scale of his victory before sitting down to compose his letter. It is carefully worded and gives the impression of being composed at leisure and in pleasant surroundings, but don't let that fool you. Nelson's head wound was severe enough to cause him intense pain for many weeks to come and his ship, *Vanguard*, had been battered by the French. He was bloody, bruised and exhausted from two full days of fighting and several weeks of anxious chasing around the Mediterranean. Moreover, at the time of writing, his ship was alive with the groaning of the injured and her masts and yards hung like broken wings. It is a remarkable composition.

The content is, as St Vincent says, 'modest', because Nelson does not detail the number of ships he has captured or destroyed, 11, but the ones that escaped, two ships of the line and two frigates. He could not afford to send his few undamaged ships in chase because they were needed to protect the damaged British warships from French counter-attack and to blockade Alexandria, a salutary reminder that, while the French had lost, they had put up a mighty fight.

Otherwise, the battle dispatch is remarkably undetailed. There is little information on the exact nature of the attack, the very means by which Nelson won this extraordinary victory, and only a few officers are mentioned: Westcott, who died; Cuthbert, who fought in his place; Hood, who made a valiant single-handed effort to cut off the escaping French ships; and Edward Berry, his flag captain, who caught him when he fell wounded to the deck. In direct contravention of tradition, however, he makes no mention of his second-in-command who, according to the established custom of seniority, was James Saumarez. Nelson's own appointment to command had defied those traditions of seniority, however, and now Nelson chose to ignore them himself.

Nelson was no close friend of the ambitious Saumarez and he knew that St Vincent, to whom he owed his own command, actually favoured the far younger Thomas Troubridge in this position. In defiance of convention, he chose not to mention his second-in-command at all, a calculated and significant snub that enraged Saumarez. When Alexander Ball, captain of the *Alexander*, discovered this, he burst onto deck from his cabin, proclaiming, 'Nelson says there is to be no second-in-command; we are all alike in his dispatches.'[13] The success of this battle is so often attributed to the 'Band of Brothers' which Nelson had formed and nurtured in the weeks prior to the battle and their shared understanding of his tactics is certainly impressive, but one must be careful. As this letter shows, Nelson was as calculating as he was charming and his methods could upset as much as they could gratify. He rose because he was talented and favoured, but he did so by climbing over the backs of many talented and deserving officers.

On the other hand, Nelson was careful to nurture the support of the lower deck and was deliberately profuse in his praise of 'the Officers and Men of every description'. Interestingly, he has taken such praise a little further here than the reality deserved. To praise his entire fleet, of course, reflected on his ability as a commander and he also knew, and here manipulated, the political currency of a united and successful navy. There is, therefore, no mention of Davidge Gould of the *Audacious*, whose conduct at the battle greatly displeased Nelson. When, five years later, Gould married, Troubridge sent Nelson the news: 'Davidge Gould has taken to himself a wife & I believe, & hope, left off the sea.'[14]

Although Nelson's victory at the Nile was deeply impressive, we need to remain aware that the term 'Band of Brothers' is in some senses misleading, a false construct. Nelson's rapid promotion and carefully managed self-promotion generated discord and there was a weak link in every battle fleet. At The Glorious First of June it was Molloy, at Camperdown it was Williamson and at the Nile it was Gould.

British casualty list and the English and French fleets

FORCE OF THE ENGLISH AND FRENCH FLEETS AT THE BATTLE OFF THE NILE

ENGLISH	NUMBER OF GUNS, MEN, KILLED, WOUNDED				FRENCH	NUMBER OF GUNS, MEN		How DISPOSED OF		
VANGUARD	74	595	30	75	L'ORIENT	120	1010	Burnt	Complement of Men on board the French ships burnt, taken & sunk at the Battle off the Nile as by certificate from the commissioners & officers of the different ships	
ORION	74	590	13	29	LE FRANKLIN	80	800	taken		
CULLODEN	74	590	"	"	LE TONNANT	80	800	taken		
BELLEROPHON	74	590	49	148	LE GUERRIER	74	700	Do.		8930
DEFENCE	74	590	4	11	LE CONQUERANT	74	700	Do.		
MINOTAUR	74	640	23	64	LE SPARTIATE	74	700	Do.		
ALEXANDER	74	590	14	58	LE TIMOLEON	74	700	Burnt		
AUDACIOUS	74	590	1	35	LE SOUVERAIN PEUPLE	74	700	taken	Sent on shore by Cartel including the wounded as pr Certificates from Capt. Barry of L'Alceste	
ZEALOUS	74	590	1	7	L'HEUREUX	74	700	Do.		3105
SWIFTSURE	74	590	7	22	LE MERCURE	74	700	Do.		

Ship	Guns	Crew	Killed	Wounded	Ship	Guns	Crew	How disposed of		
Majestic	74	590	50	143	L'Aquillon	74	700	D°.		
Goliath	74	590	21	41	L'Artémise	36	300	burnt	Escaped from the Timoleon	} 350
Theseus	74	590	5	30	La Sérieuse	36	300	sunk		
Leander	50	343	"		L'Hercule Bomb	–	50	burnt	Escaped – from the l'Hercule Bomb	} 50
			218	677	La Fortune	18	70	taken		
					Le Guillaume Tell	80	800	escaped		
					Le Généreux	74	700	D°.	Officers, Carpenters & Caulkers,	} 200
					La Justice	40	400	D°.		
					La Diana	40	400	D°.	Prisoners on board the Fleet	} 3705
	1012	8068				1196	11230		Killed, drowned, burnt & missing	} 5225
						1012	8068			
						184	3178 [sic]			

Horatio Nelson

Spencer Smith

The casualty list that Nelson included with his dispatch lays bare the astonishing scale of his victory. Notice in particular the column marked 'how disposed of', an extraordinary phrase that reeks of the fleet's confidence and pride in its achievement.

The British fleet lost a total of 218 dead and 677 wounded; 5,225 French sailors were either confirmed dead or had simply vanished in the tornado of battle and no less than 8,930 Frenchmen had their ships destroyed or captured. With casualty figures like these, it is hardly surprising that corpses, and parts of corpses, continued to be found washed ashore along the Egyptian coast for weeks after the battle. There were so many prisoners that the British simply could not cope and sent 3,105 ashore, back to the French army.

Such treatment of prisoners is different from that after The Glorious First of June, which was fought comparatively close to British shores. Then, the prisoners were crammed into British holds and sent to Portsmouth and Plymouth and thence to prison ships or prisons ashore.

This list presents the results of the battle in its barest form, as an unmistakable French rout. It became important, therefore, as a document that countered French claims of a moral or strategic victory. Most of the French newspapers, for example, toed the official line and published Villeneuve's account of the action, which emphasised that the job of the fleet, that of transporting the army to Egypt, had already been achieved and that the British fleet had been severely damaged in the battle. One newspaper, however, the *Courrier*, a vocal critic of the Directory and its aggressive foreign policy, acquired this list from an English diplomat in Constantinople and published it, dramatically weakening the Directory's political position.

The British ships were all, apart from the *Leander*, 74-gunners. It was very difficult to maintain cohesion in a fleet consisting of mismatched ships, as Duncan had found to his cost at Camperdown when he was unable to form a line of battle out of his rag-tag fleet. Nelson's fleet, on the other hand, had been carefully selected to be an efficient hunting squadron, while still being powerful enough to hold its own in battle against larger ships. Size has been sacrificed for speed and uniformity and the ships were even similar in age, 10 having been built within a few years of each other in the 1780s. Their captains also knew each other well, having worked together for years in the Cadiz inshore squadron.

There are, however, no frigates listed in the British fleet. There was one small ship in the fleet not listed here, the 16-gun sloop *Mutine*, which played no part in the battle but spent her time assisting the stricken *Culloden*. However the lack of small, fast ships was the single most significant reason that Napoleon ever made it to Egypt. A network of frigates, stretching to the horizon and then beyond, the ships perhaps 20 miles apart but linked like a chain by a system of signalling with flags, guns and sails, was an effective tool for finding an enemy fleet. The British and French fleets were at times so close on their voyage to Egypt that only an extraordinary stroke of luck would have saved Napoleon if Nelson had been able to make or retain contact through even a few fast ships.

Without them he was blind and always behind the game. The absence of frigates also made Nelson's approach into Aboukir far more risky than it might otherwise have been. Frigates drew less water and therefore could have sailed ahead of the ships of the line, marking out a safe route. But why the lack of frigates? The King of Naples, nominally neutral though a friend to the British, had refused to lend any of his frigates for fear of French reprisals and Nelson had to make do with those few that St Vincent could spare from the continuous burden of trade protection around Gibraltar. In the event, all of those with orders to sail with Nelson either became detached from his fleet before the battle or only joined when it was too late.[15]

The list of French ships is also revealing. The scale of the tragedy of *L'Orient's* destruction is brought home by her crewlist of 1,010. Note also the names of the French ships. *L'Orient* is named for the French port of that name on the south Breton coast, once home to the French East India Company and, over 140 years later, a base for German U-boats. *Le Franklin* is named for Benjamin Franklin, a leading figure of the American Revolution and therefore a great hero of and inspiration to the French Revolutionaries. The *Franklin* was taken into British service and would later fight on the British side at San Domingo.

Several of the French ships' names were chosen by the Revolutionaries for the myth or character that they represented. *Spartiate*, for example, refers to a warrior of Sparta, a powerful and unique city-state in ancient Greece that defined itself by its intervention in the lives and well-being of its people and its military prowess. *Timoléon* was a Greek statesman and general who subdued a Sicilian rebellion and imposed a democratic government with strong beliefs in justice. *Le Guillaume Tell* was named for the same principle but was taken from an altogether different era and location. Guillaume Tell is known to us as William Tell and the story of how the woodsman was forced to shoot an apple off the head of his son by a cruel lord was an inspirational revolutionary folk tale. Tell shot the apple with his crossbow but, before doing so, took out two bolts and kept one to kill the lord if he missed. The lord questioned Tell about the purpose of the second arrow and, when brazenly told it, arrested Tell, who later escaped, assassinated the lord and then led a rebellion. It is a classic tale of tyranny and defiance of it.

Finally, it is noteworthy how much larger the French fleet is than the British. There are five more ships in total and the French fleet has three 80-gunners, and one

120-gunner. The British fleet, on the other hand, has nothing more powerful than a Third Rate 74. Throughout the entire history of sailing warfare, comprehensive victory, with very few exceptions, was achieved by one fleet somehow achieving numerical superiority over the other. Nelson was therefore already at a significant disadvantage when his fleet discovered the French at anchor, and the fact that they were at anchor was itself another disadvantage. Another unmistakable trend in the history of sailing warfare is that it was very difficult to attack a well-defended and anchored enemy. With no sails to be set, trimmed or furled and no yards to be braced or hoisted, an anchored ship's crew could concentrate solely on gunnery. By failing to take adequate precautions, however, the French fleet was not as well defended as it could have been, a weakness that Nelson ruthlessly exploited to defy the weight of history.

French Account of the Battle of the Nile

The Admiralty had to rely on this French account to see exactly how Nelson won his victory. It was written in captivity on board the British *Alexander* on its way to Naples. The letter frequently refers to 'plans', probably the maps reproduced below.

The Battle of the Nile posed French officials quite a problem. How could they break the news of such a disaster to their professional superiors and their friends and families? For some, the battle became a focal point for political discourse in Paris. The Fructidor coup, remember, had been secured at sabre-point and there were many right-wing politicians who were ready to seize on any evidence of failure to criticise the aggressive foreign policy of the new Directory. At the same time, such battles offered a magnificent opportunity for the French to revel in revolutionary ideals such as brotherhood, sacrifice and duty. Here was a chance to stoke the fires of military myth and legend from which the increasingly militarised revolution drew its strength. French accounts of the battle, therefore, carried their own currency and were by no means shunned or cast aside.

This is an excellent example of such an account by a high-ranking administrative officer. It has been carefully constructed. The author is not afraid to explain in detail several failings and misfortunes of the French fleet. He describes how men had been sent ashore to dig wells and how they were forced to take along guards for protection from Bedouin raids. He then admits how few Frenchmen returned to their ships when the British arrived, and that orders to secure each ship to the next astern and to rig springs to the anchor cables were 'not Generally executed'. This is significant professional criticism, aimed at both officers and men, and it betrays a rotten hierarchy within the French navy.

The author reserves special favour for those who did stay to fight, however, and he emphasises the French fighting spirit, albeit in a lost cause. The courage of the mortally wounded Brueys is celebrated along with the 'bravery and intelligence' of the 10-year-old son of Commodore Casabianca. This is the child later immortalised in Felicia Hemans' poem 'Casabianca', which begins with the line known to generations of British schoolboys: 'The boy stood on the burning deck'. The poem describes the drama of *L'Orient's* destruction before returning to the quarterdeck in the penultimate verse. The boy, however, has vanished: 'The boy-oh! Where was he?' This account provides an answer: the boy who had stood on the burning deck found himself in the sea. Unable to swim, he clings to the ship's wrecked masts with his father. The subsequent explosion then killed them both 'and put an End to their Hopes and Fears'.

The surrender of the *Franklin* is described, but the author makes quite clear the scale of the carnage and destruction aboard her. This account leaves one in no doubt that the *Franklin's* crew had fought until there was no point in fighting on. A similar impression is gained from this account of the fates of the *Tonnant* and *Timoléon*. The account is carefully structured around the juxtaposition of the hopeless French position and the courage and character of the French sailors in that predicament. The author thus draws attention away from the scale of the disaster, which is not mentioned at all, and towards the principles that the revolution carried so close to its heart. It is a classic propaganda technique that was used repeatedly by French dispatch-writers seeking to deflect blame and detailed criticism of their own performance.

The 1ˢᵗ of August 1798 Wind NNW light breezes and fair weather The 2ⁿᵈ Division of the Fleet sent a Party of men on shore to dig Wells: Every Ship in the Fleet sent 25 men to protect the workmen from the continual Attacks of the Bedouins and Vagabonds of the Country.

At 2 O'Clock in the afternoon, the *Heureux* made the sig[l] for 12 sail *WSW* which we could easily distinguish, from the mast heads to be Ships of war. the sig[l] was then made for all the Boats, Workmen and Guards, to repair on board their Respective Ships, which was only obeyed by a small number At 3 O'clock the Adm[l] not having any doubt, but that the Ships in sight were the Enemy, he ordered the Hammocks to be stowed for action, & directed *L'Alerte* & *La Ruillier Brig* sloops of war to reconnoitre the Enemy whom we soon perceived were steering for Beguler Bay, under a Crowd of Canvas, but without observing any order of sailing. At 4 O'clock we saw over the Fort of Aboukad 2 Ships apparently waiting to join the Squadron: without doubt they had been sent to look into the Port of Alexandria. we likewise saw a Brig with the 12 Ships. In 2 Hours they were 14 sail of the Line and a Brig – The English Fleet were soon off the Island of Bequier.

The Brig *Le Alerte* then began to fwd the Admiral's orders into Execution Viz. to stand towards the Enemy until nearly within Gun-Shot & then to Manoeuvre & Endeavour to draw them towards the outer shoal lying off that island. but the English Adm[l]. without Doubt had Experienced Pilots on board as he did not pay any attention to the Brigs Track, but allowed her to go away hauling well round the Dangers. At 4 O'clock a small country boat dispatched from Alexandria to Rosetta, voluntarily Bore down to the English Brig, which took possession of her, notwithstanding the repeated efforts of the *Alerte* to prevent it by firing a great many shot at the Boat at 5 o'clock the Enemy came to the wind in Succession this Manoeuvre convinced us that they intended attacking us that Evening. The Admiral got the Top Gallant Yards across, but soon made the sig[l] that he intended engaging the Enemy at An Anchor, convinced without doubt, that he had not Seamen Enough to engage under sail for he wanted at least 200 good seamen for each ship. After this sig[l] each Ship ought to have sent a stream Cable to the Ship a stern of her to have made an hawser fast to the Cable, About 20 fathoms in the water & to have passed the opposite side to that intended as a spring this was not Generally executed.

Orders were then given to let go another Bow[r] Anchor, & the broadsides of the ships were brought to bear on the Enemy having the Ships heads SE from the Island of Bequier forming a line of about 1300 fathoms NW and SE distant from Each other 80 fathoms and in the Position marked Plan 1st each with an anchor out SSE.

At ¼ past I saw one of the Enemy's ships that were steering to get to windward of the headmost of the Line, Ran on the reef ENE of the Island She had immediate Assistance from the Brig and got afloat in the morning. The battery on the Island open'd a Fire on the Enemy & their Shells fell ahead of th 2ⁿᵈ Ship in the Line. – At ½ past 5 the head-most ships of our line being within Gun-shot of the English, the Admˡ made the signal to Engage, which was not obey'd till the Enemy was within Pistol Shot, and just doubling of us, the action then became very warm. The Conquerant began to fire, then Le Guerrier, L' Spartiate, L'Aquilon, Le Peuple Souverain, Le Franklin. At 6 O'clock, La Serieuse Frigate & L'Hercule Bomb cut their Cables & got under weigh to avoid the Enemy's fire they got on shore.

Le Serieuse caught fire & had part of her Masts burnt L'Artemise was obliged to get under weigh and Likewise got on shore. These two Frigates sent their Ships company's on board the different Line of battle ships. The sloop of war, two Bombs & several Transports that were with the fleet were more successfull, as they got under weigh & reach'd the Anchorage under the Protection of the Fort of Aboukar. All the van were Attacked on both sides by the Enemy, who rang'd close along our Line, they had each an Anchor out a stern, which facilitated their motions and enabled them to place themselves, in the most advantageous situation.

At ¼ 6 the Franklin opened her fire upon the Enemy, from the Starbᵈ side & at ¾ past 6 She was Engaged on both sides, L'Orient at the same time began firing from her Starbᵈ Guns. & At 7 the Tonnant open'd her fire. all the ships from the Le Guerrier to the Tonnant were now engaged, against a Superior force. This only redoubled the Ardour of our Ships, who kept up a very heavy & regular Fire. At 8 O'clock at night, the ship which was engaging the L'Orient on the Starbᵈ Quarter notwithstanding her Advantageous position was dismasted and so roughly handled, that She Cut her Cables & drove further from the Line This Event gave the Franklin Hopes that L'Orient would now be able to assist her, by attacking one of the Ships opposed to her, but at this very moment the 2 Ships that been observed a stern of the Fleet, and were quite fresh steered right for the Centre One of them Anchor'd on the L'Orient's Starbᵈ Bow, and the other Cut the Line a stern of the L'Orient, & Anchored on her Larbᵈ Quarter the action in this place became extremely warm.

Admiral de Bruey's, who, at this time, had been Slightly wounded in head &
arm, very soon after Received a Shot in the Belly which almost cut him in two, he
desired not to be carried below but to be left to die upon Deck, he only lived ¼ of
an hour, Rear Admiral Blanquet as well as his Aids de Camp were unacquainted
with this melancholy Event, until the Action was nearly over, Adm¹ Blanquet
received a Severe wound in his Face which knock'd him down he was carried off the
Deck senseless. At ¼ past 8 O'clock the Le Peuple Souverain drove to Leewᵈ
of the Line and Anchor'd a cables length abreast of the L'Orient it was not known
however what Unfortunate Event occasioned this, the Vacant space she left placed
the Franklin in a more unfortunate Position and it became very critical from a
Manoeuvre of one of the Enemy's fresh Ships which had been to the assistance of the
Ship on shore, she Anchored across of the Franklin's Bows & commenc'd a very
heavy and Raking Fire; notwithstanding the dreadfull situation of the Ships in the
Centre, they continually kept up a very heavy Fire – At ½ past 8 O'clock the
Action was general from the Guerrier to the Mercure, and the two Fleets Engaged
in the Position indicated in Plan the 2ⁿᵈ. The Death of Admiral de Breuy's, &
the severe wounds of Admiral Blanquet, must have deeply Affected the People
who fought under them; but it Added to their Ardour for Revenge, and the Action
continued on both sides with great obstinacy. At 9 O'clock the Ships in the Van
Slackened their Fire, & soon after totally ceased, & with Infinite Sorrow we
Suppos'd they had surrendered. They were dismasted very soon after the Action
began and so much damaged that it is to be presumed, that they could not hold out any
longer, against an Enemy so Superior by an advantageous Position, having placed
Several Ships against one. At ¼ past 9 O'clock the L'Orient caught Fire in the
Cabin, it soon afterwards broke out upon the Poop – every effort was made use of
to extinguish it, but without Effect, and very soon it became So Considerable, that
there were no hopes of saving the Ship. At ½ past 9, Citizen Gillis, Capitaine de
Pavillon of the Franklin was very severely wounded, and was carried off the Deck –
At ¾ past 9 the Arm Chest, fill'd with Musquet Cartridges, blew up, and set fire
to several places in the Poop and Quarter Deck, but was fortunately extinguished;
her Situation however was still very desperate, Surrounded by enemies and only
80 fathoms to windward of L'Orient who was entirely on fire there could not be

any other Expectation than that of falling a Prey to the Enemy or the Flames. At 10 O'clock the Main & Mizen Masts fell, & all the Guns on the main deck were dismounted. At ¼ past 10 The Tonnant Cut her Cables to avoid from the L'Orient, the English Ship that was on the L'Orient's Larb^d Quarter, as soon as She had done firing at her brought her broad-side on the Tonnant's Bow, and kept up a very heavy Raking Fire. The Heureux and Mercure conceived likewise that they ought to Cut their Cables, this Manoeuvre created so much confusion amongst the Rear Ships that they fir'd into Each Other & did considerable damage.

The Tonnant anchor'd a head of the Guillaume Tel, Genereux and Timolion the other 2 Ships got on shore, the Ship that had engaged the Tonnant on her Bow Cut her Cables; all her Rigging & Sails were Cut to pieces & she drove down and anchor'd a stern of the English Ship that had been engaging L'Heureux & Mercure, before they changed their Position – Those of the Etat Major & Ships Company of the L'Orient, who had Escaped Death, convinced of the Impossibility of extinguishing the fire, which had got down on the middle gun Deck, endeavoured to save themselves. Rear Adm^l Genteaume, saved himself in a Boat, & went on board the Salamine & from thence to Aboukir & Alexandria. The Adjutant General Molaud altho' badly wounded swam to the Ship nearest to the L'Orient, which prov'd to be An English Ship, Commodore Casa-bianca, & his Son only 10 Years Old, (who during the Action gave proofs of Bravery & Intelligence far above his Age) were not so fortunate they were in the Water upon the wreck of the L'Orients Masts, not being able to Swim, Seeking each other till ¾ past, 10 when the Ship blew up. The Explotion was dreadfull, and spread the Fire all round to a considerable distance. The Franklins Deck was covered with red hot pieces of Timber, Oakum and Rope on Fire. She was on Fire the 4th time but luckily got it under immediately, After the Tremendous Explotion, the Action ceased Every where, & was succeeded by the most profound Silence. The Sky was obscured by thick clouds of black smoak which Seemed to threaten the Destruction of the 2 Fleets. It was ¼ of an hour before the Ships Crews recover'd from the kind of Stupor they were thrown into. Towards 11 O'clock the Franklin, Anxious to preserve the trust confided in her, recommenced the Action with a few of her Lower Deck Guns; all the rest were dismounted, two thirds of Her Ships Company *were either kill'd or wounded, and those who remain'd were much fatigued, She was Surrounded by Enemies Ships, some of which were within Pistol Shot, & mowed down the men Every Broadside. At ½ past 11 O'clock, having only 3 Lower Deck Guns that could defend the Honor of the Flag, it became Necessary to put an End to so Disproportionate a Struggle, & Citizen Martinel, Capitaine de Frigate, ordered the colours to be struck; the Action in the Rear of the Fleet was very [illegible] till ¾ past 11, when it became very warm; 3 of the enemies Ships were engaging them, & two of them were very near, as may be seen in Plan the 3rd. The Tonnant, already Badly Treated, was nearest the Ship Engaged, and returned a very brisk Fire. About 3 O'clock in the morning She was dismasted & oblig'd to Cut her Cables a second time, & not having any more Anchors left she drove on shore.*

Le Guillame Tell, Le Genereux and Le Timoleon shifted their Births and Anchored farther down out of Gun Shot These Ships were not much damaged. At ½ past 3 O'clock the Action ceased throughout the Line. Early in the morning, the Frigate La Justice got under weigh and made Small Tacks to keep near the Guillaume Tel And At 9 Anchor'd an English Ship having got under weigh & was making Small Tacks to prevent her getting off. At 6 O'clock two English Ships join'd those which had been engaging the Rear, & began firing on the Hereux and Mercure, which ships were aground. The former soon Struck & the latter followed her Example, as they could not bring their Broadsides to bear on the Enemy (See the 4th Plan) At ½ past 7 the Ships Crew of Le Artemise Frigate Quitted her and set her on fire. At 8 she blew up. The Enemy without doubt had received great damage in their Masts and Yards, as they did not get under weigh to attack the remainder of the French Fleet. the French Flag was flying on board 4 French Ships of the Line, and 2 Frigates. At ¾ past 11 Le Guillaume Tel, Le Genereux, La Dianne, and La Justice, were under weigh and form'd in Line of Battle. The English Ship that was under Sail; stood towards the Fleet, Fearing that she might be cut off. the two other Enemy's ships got Immediately under weigh to Assist her, At Noon the Timoleon, who probable was not in a state to put to Sea, stood right for the shore under her fore sail, and As soon as she Struck the Shore her Fore Mast fell. The French Division joined the Enemy's Ship which ranged along their Line on Opposite Tacks, within Pistol-Shot, and received their Broadsides, which she returned They then each continued their Route – The Division was in sight at Sun Set – – Nothing Remarkable happened during the night of the 2ⁿᵈ – The 3ʳᵈ of August in the morning the French colours were flying in the Tonnant and the Timoleon – The English Admˡ sent a cartel to the former to know if she had struck, & upon being answered in the Negative, he directed 2 ships to against her, when they got within Gun-shot of her she struck, it being impossible to defend any longer The Timoleon was aground too near in for any Ships to approach her, in the night of the 2ⁿᵈ Inst. they sent greatest part of their Ships Company's on Shore, and at Noon the next day they Quitted her & Set her on fire.

Here ends the Journal of the 1ˢᵗ 2ⁿᵈ and 3ʳᵈ days of August which will be Ever Remembered with the Deepest Sorrow, by the Frenchmen who Possess good Hearts, and by all those true Republicans who have survived this Melancholy Disaster.

Maps showing different stages of the Battle of the Nile

Three maps, of a series of at least four, are included with the French account. They are labelled '1ˢᵗ position', '2ⁿᵈ position' and '4ᵗʰ position'. Only the first has any reference to the land while the latter two images are simply diagrams showing the ships' positions in relation to each other. They do not reflect either participant's knowledge of the area. In fact we know that Foley, in the leading British ship, the *Goliath*, had a copy of Bellin's *Petit Atlas Maritime* of 1764, complete with measured depths; that Hood had a less accurate map of English origin; and that Benjamin Hallowell of the *Swiftsure* had recently captured a rough French sketch of the bay, together with rudimentary sailing directions.

The first (p. 191) makes clear both the potential strength of the French position and its fatal weakness. Shoals are clearly marked both to the north and the south of the French position, but there is a significant gap between the southernmost French ship of the main line, *Guerrier,* at the top of the picture, and the island. It was through this gap that Captain Foley took the *Goliath*, thus leading the British fleet *inshore* of the French line. Foley had noticed that each of the French ships was only secured by a single anchor, around which the ships would swing in a full circle. He knew, therefore, that there was sufficient water for the British to sail between the French ships and the shore, and found them entirely unprepared. The inshore guns had not been run out and the decks were littered with boxes. Foley opened up a devastating fire.

Notice also how the *Culloden* is marked just inside the shoal, where she ran aground and missed the battle. She was eventually refloated but had grounded with such force that her rudder broke off and the rocks tore so many holes in her hull that she made seven feet of water every hour. The leak was only stopped by the sailmakers 'thrumming', or weaving yarn and oakum into, a topgallant sail that was then tarred, greased and used to 'patch' the hole, the pressure of water trapping the thrummed sail against the ship's hull. A new rudder was ingeniously made out of a spare topmast and other spare timber. Missing the battle was particularly painful for her captain, Thomas Troubridge, because he had also witnessed The Glorious First of June as nothing more than a bystander, in that case as a prisoner on board a French warship after his own ship had been captured a matter of days before the battle.

The French fleet is in a different order from the list that Nelson supplied with his dispatch. Brueys had stationed his flagship *L'Orient* in the centre of the fleet, protected by powerful 'seconds' either side of her, both 80-gunners. This is where Brueys expected the brunt of any attack to fall but, as soon as Foley sailed inshore of their line, the British could concentrate their force on one end of the French line by 'doubling' it, that is to say by engaging it on both sides at once. Brueys was simply not prepared for the type of attack that he received. There are several small, fast ships inshore of the main French line which could have been used as lookouts to warn Brueys of Nelson's imminent arrival but were not.

The structure of the British fleet, so well-formed, was one of the reasons that Brueys actually chose to fight at anchor. He had too few sailors to fight under sail but he also believed that, when Nelson waited for his fleet to gather and form up at the entrance to the bay, he was pausing to consider his options before attacking in the morning. Brueys therefore believed that he had time to recover his crews from shore and might even have the opportunity to escape during the night, as he had personally witnessed Hood do at St Kitts in 1782. He did not know that one of the reasons Nelson slowed down was to pass orders throughout his fleet detailing his intended attack and instructing his ships to anchor by the stern, a manoeuvre that required significant preparation, and to rig springs on their anchor cables to

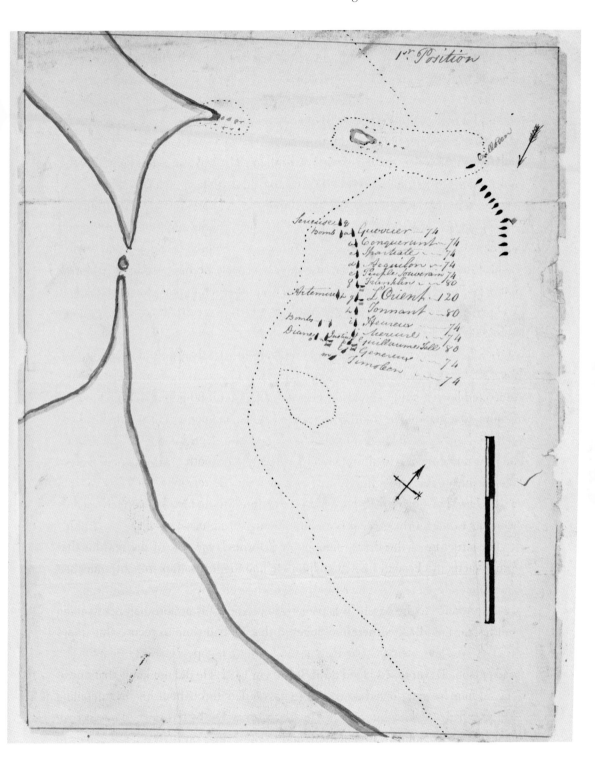

allow the British captains to manoeuvre their ships once anchored. The British forming up into a cohesive group, therefore, was not indicative of them declining battle, but of preparing for it. Brueys perceived hope in something that actually spelt doom. As a result, the subsequent attack was all the more surprising and is a reminder that Nelson was not heedlessly impulsive but carefully so, a crucial distinction if we are to understand his success.

The second map (p. 193) shows the position of the fleets after the French have been doubled by the British. Note that the *Vanguard*, Nelson's flagship, has stayed to seaward of the French line. His was the first ship of the British fleet to do so, perhaps because he did not want to run the risk of grounding his flagship and becoming helpless.

The *Goliath* finds herself where she does because her captain initially tried to anchor her by the stern alongside the first ship of the French line, the *Guerrier* (a). Anchoring by the stern, however, was a tricky business. The usual method of anchoring, and by far the safest and most reliable, was for a ship to come into the wind, drop her bower anchor and then safely drift astern until the anchor dug in and held. To anchor by the stern required a ship to come to an abrupt stop with the wind astern. If a ship attempting this manoeuvre was travelling too quickly, the anchor might not hold or, if it did, the anchor cable might part. The task that faced each ship in Nelson's fleet, therefore, was to approach as quickly as she could, before suddenly taking in all sail to reduce her speed sufficiently for her anchor to hold without endangering the cable.

To succeed in doing this at all, let alone exactly alongside another ship, was very difficult, and to do so under fire was even more of a challenge. It is remarkable that so many British ships succeeded, but three did not. The *Goliath* ran much further down the French line than she ever intended; the *Majestic* suffered the same fate and was targeted by several Frenchmen all at once; and, most unlucky of all, the *Bellerophon* failed to assume her intended position and came to rest exactly parallel to the devastating broadside of *L'Orient*, a monster ship that dwarfed her. Her captain was soon wounded and the ship entirely dismasted. The *Goliath* was lucky that her failure to anchor in her intended position had few severe repercussions. The *Majestic* and *Bellerophon* were less fortunate. Indeed, their failure to anchor as intended was directly responsible for their exceptionally high casualty figures (p. 178).

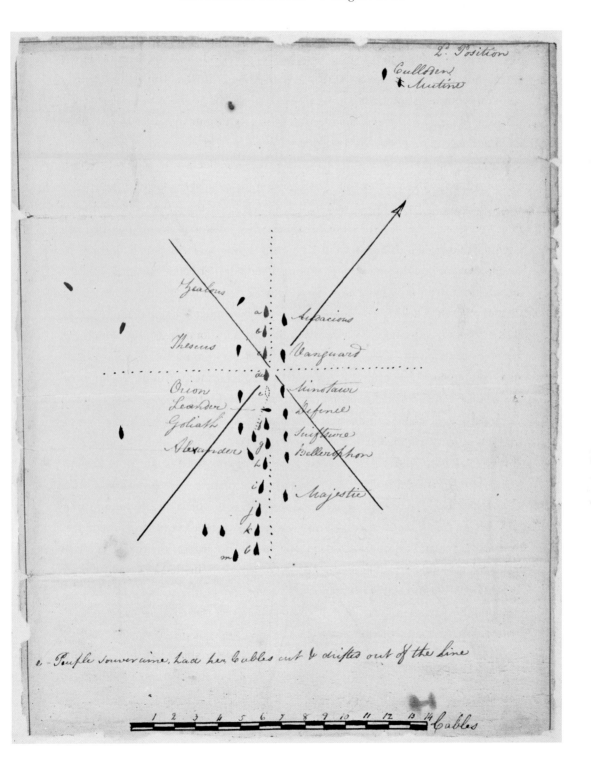

193

Ship 'e' in the French line is the *Peuple Souverain* and this clearly shows how she drifted downwind after her anchor cable was shot or cut. The resulting gap in the French line then allowed the tiny 50-gun *Leander* to position herself directly across the bows of the mighty 80-gun *Franklin*. It was a bold move but she had inadvertently placed herself directly between Saumarez's more powerful *Orion* and the *Franklin*; only quick thinking saved the *Orion* from opening fire on her.

The position and orientation of the British *Alexander* is also worthy of note. She and the *Swiftsure* were the last British ships to arrive and they joined the battle directly at the northern end of the French line, rather than sailing up the line from the south. The *Alexander's* captain, Alexander Ball, then anchored her carefully at an angle to the stern of *L'Orient* (g). She was thus ideally located to target the vulnerable stern of the Frenchman and her fire was devastating. Brueys, already wounded in the head and arm, was nearly cut in two by a shot but chose to stay on deck. There is also some suggestion, but no convincing evidence, that sailors from the *Alexander* used combustible grenades to start the fire which led to the destruction of *L'Orient*. It is a significant accusation because the use of such combustibles was generally frowned upon; at The First of June, the crew of the British *Brunswick* had been incensed when the French crew of the *Vengeur* had used chemical and combustible ammunition. Whatever the truth, the British ships *Swiftsure*, *Bellerophon* and *Alexander* are perilously close to *L'Orient*.

The third map (p. 195) shows the position of the fleets some time around 22.00, after *L'Orient* has exploded. Her wreck is marked with a red cross. The *Alexander* was badly caught up in the blast and was disabled for two hours while her crew extinguished fires and cut away damaged rigging. The *Alexander* and the disabled *Bellerophon* have now drifted well clear of the site of the explosion. The *Swiftsure*, remarkably, was undamaged. In the moments before the explosion all firing stopped from both ships. The *Swiftsure's* crew, having rescued as many as they could of the swimming Frenchmen who had dived clear of *L'Orient*, all hid below decks and shut the gunports. Her captain hoped that, by staying close to *L'Orient*, the explosion would fire the debris up and thus over her. It was a bold decision and her captain's conviction was not shared by all of her crew. As the heat became so intense that the tar between the deck planks began to melt, Captain Hallowell ordered sentries placed at her anchor cables to stop any British sailor from cutting them.

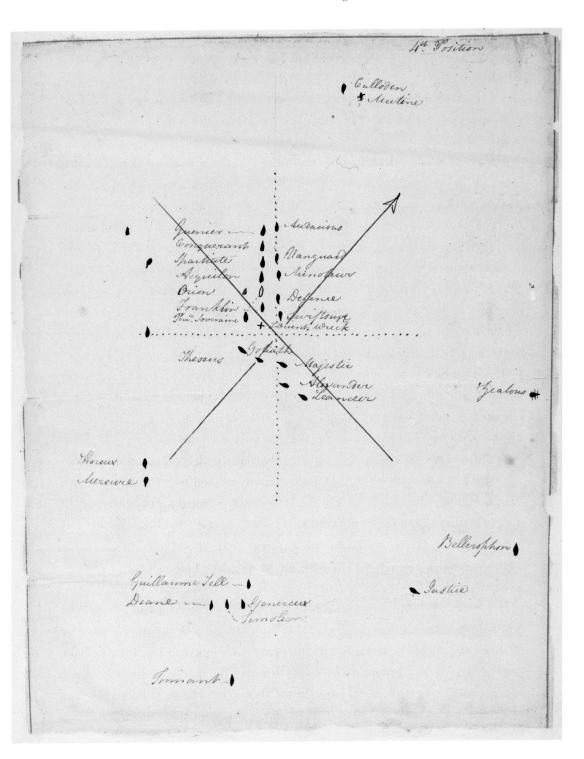

The French ships immediately astern of *L'Orient* cut their cables to escape the devastation. The *Heureux* and *Mercure* are shown inshore, where they struck a shoal in their bid to flee *L'Orient*. Others headed north (towards the bottom of the picture) in a bid to escape. When *L'Orient* exploded all firing stopped. The flash of light was seen nine miles away in Alexandria.

The only British ship near the escaping Frenchmen was now the *Bellerophon* but she was too shattered to give chase. Hood in the *Zealous*, at the far right of the map, set sail in a bid to cut them off but was immediately recalled by Nelson because there were too many damaged British ships to be left alone.

Nevertheless, of this group of isolated French ships, only four subsequently escaped: *Guillaume Tell*, under the command of Rear-Admiral Pierre-Charles Villeneuve, who would command the allied French and Spanish fleet at Trafalgar; *Généreux*, which would, within days, capture the British *Leander* together with Nelson's dispatches; and the two frigates *Justice* and *Diana*. The *Timoléon* and *Tonnant* were both in a bad way, the *Tonnant* entirely dismasted and the *Timoléon* with only her mizzen mast standing. The *Tonnant* only surrendered when surrounded by British ships and the captain of the *Timoléon* continued to fire until the last possible moment when he ran his ship ashore and burned her with her colours still flying.

At the far south of the bay and at the top of the map, the *Mutine*, a small brig and thus a ship with a shallow draught, is shown assisting the grounded *Culloden*. To lighten her, food, drink and shot were thrown overboard and more transferred to the *Mutine*. Meanwhile work at the pumps was continuous, although seamen from the *Mutine* took their turn while the *Culloden's* crew had breakfast.

Account of the Battle of the Nile by E. Poussielgue

The French Adjutant-General's account (p. 183) was acquired relatively easily by the British because it was composed on a British warship by a man held prisoner, but we are particularly fortunate with the Battle of the Nile because, in subsequent weeks, British and Turkish ships seized several French vessels bearing official dispatches as well as personal letters from the army in Egypt. The letters, which included several personal missives from Napoleon himself, were highly revealing, very personal and extremely embarrassing.

This is one of those captured letters, written by the Comptroller General of the Expenses of the Eastern Army and Administrator General of the finance to his wife or perhaps his sweetheart. It adds little to our knowledge of the battle, apart from the fact that we know it was witnessed by several Frenchman from the top of a nearby tower, but it captures beautifully the quality of description and personal touches that characterised so many of these captured letters. He starts by describing the battle but ends with a magnificent flourish, admitting to having had a portrait made but refusing to send it, before declaring his commitment to finding his way home and into her arms again: 'There is no fortune which shall retain me. I shall be contented to arrive with you naked as my hand.'

Unfortunately, the letter never reached its intended recipient but landed on the desk of a gloating St Vincent who insisted that it was sent on to Nelson's wife, a curious request that was clearly ignored because the letter remained in the Admiralty archives.

LIBERTY   EQUALITY

ROSETTA IN EGYPT 17TH THERMIDOR 6 OF THE FRENCH REPUBLIC OR 3D AUGUST 1798

FROM E. POUSSIELGUE COMPTROLLER GENERAL OF THE EXPENSES OF THE EASTERN ARMY AND ADMINISTRATOR GENERAL OF THE FINANCE.

We have just been witnesses, my dear Friend, to a Naval Combat the most bloody & unfortunate that for many Ages has taken place. As yet we know not all the circumstances but those which we are already acquainted with are frightful in the extreme. The French Squadron consisting of thirteen sail of the line one of which was a 3 decker of 120 guns and three others of 80 were anchored in Line of Battle in the Bay of Aboukar or Canope, the only one that exists on all the Coast of Egypt. For these 8 days past several Ships and Frigates belonging to the English have at different times been in sight reconnoitring the position of our Fleet, so that we have been in momentary expectation of being attacked. In a direct line from Aboukar to Bonetta the distance is about 4 Leagues and un half from the heights of the latter our Fleet is perfectly seen and distinguished. The 14th of this month at ½ past 5 oClock in the Evening we heard the firing of Cannon, this was the commencement of the Battle. We immediately got upon the Terraces the Tops of the Highest Houses & Eminences from where we plainly distinguished ten English Ships of the Line the other we could not see. The Cannonade was very heavy until about a ¼ after 9 oClock when favoured by the Night we perceived an immense light which announced to us that some ship was on fire. At this time the Thunder of the Cannon was heard with redoubled fury and at ten oClock the ship on fire was heard to blew up with the most dreadful explosion which was heard at Rosetta in the same manner as the explosion of the Grenelle was heard at Paris. When this Accident happened the most profound silence took place for the space of about ten Minutes: from the moment of the explosion until our hearing it might take up about two. The firing commenced again and continued without interruption until 3 oClock in the morning when it ceased almost entirely until five when it commenced again with as great vivacity as ever.*

I placed myself on a Tower which was about Cannon Shot from Rosetta and which is called Aboul Maudour from thence I could distinctly see the whole battle: At 8 oClock I perceived a Ship on Fire and in about ½ an hour blew up similar to the other that night; a Ship which until the moment of her explosion was not

---

* On August 31, 1794, at 7.15 a.m., 65,000 of powder exploded at the store of the Château de Grenelle, near Paris. More than 1,000 people died and the explosion was heard as far as Fontainebleau.

perceived on fire at all. The other Ship moved to a greater distance from the Shore and the fire on board her apparently diminished by which we presume that it was entirely extinguished; during this time the cannonading redoubled: a large Ship entirely dismasted was on shore on the Coast; We perceived others among the Fleet in similar manner dismasted entirely but the two Squadrons so mingled among each other that it was impossible to distinguish French from English nor on whose side the advantage was. The firing continued with unabating vivacity until about 2 oClock after midday of the 15th and at this hour we perceived two Sail of the Line and two Frigates under a press of Sail on a Wind standing to the Eastward: We perceived that the whole four were under French colours no other vessel made any movement and the firing ceased entirely.

Towards six oClock in the Evening I returned to the Tower of Abel Maudour to re connoitre the position of the two Fleets it was the same as at two oClock, the four Ships under way were abreast of the Mouth of the Nile, we knew not what to think or conjecture. Twenty four hours passed without having any person to give us any details and in our situation it was impossible to procure any by hand an account of the Arabs who were assembled between Bonatta and Aboukar, and by Sea an account of the difficulty of getting out of the opening or branch of the Nile. You may judge of our impatience and perplexity. Nothing good could be enjoined from this silence; however we were obliged to pass the whole of the night of the 15th in this incertitude and at last on the Morning of the 16th a Boat which left Alexandria in the night gave us some details though little tending to our comfort; they told us that the Officers of the French Fleet who saved themselves in a Boat arrived at Alexandria had reported that in the commencement of the Battle, Admiral Brueys had received three severe Wounds one in the head and two in the Body, that notwithstanding he persisted in keeping his Station on the Arm Chest, and that a fourth Shot took him in the Body and cut him in two, at the same moment a Shot took off the Captain of the Ship Casabianca, that at this time they perceived the Ship to be on fire in such a manner as not to be able to extinguish it, and at last that the Ship had blown up about two oClock at Night; they added that our Fleet was totally destroyed and lost with the exception of the four ships escaped, but that the remainder were entirely ruined.

I returned to the Tower where I found things absolutely in the same situation as yesterday, they were ever so yesterday Night and this Morning.

I have now to say how they appeared to our view from the Castle of Aboukar on the left sweeping the Horizon to our right.

The first Ship is without mast and under English Colours, The second and third are in good state but cannot distinguish theirs, the fourth has lost one mast, the fifth in good state and English Colours, the sixth has lost her Top Mast, this Morning she hoisted her Fore Top Mast Stay Sail and set some after Sail, seventh is without Top Gallant Masts, the 8th is dismasted, the 9th is dismasted with the exception of her Bowsprit, the 11th 12th and 13th form a kind of groupe having only seven masts between them. The 14th has only her Fore Mast, the 15th has lost her Fore and Mizen Top Gallant Masts, the 16th is entirely dismasted, the 17th has lost her Mizen Top Gallant Mast, the 18th has only a Fore Mast, the 19th 20th and 21st form a groupe with only four Masts between them and these without Top Gallant Masts. The 22nd is entirely dismasted and on shore. She has English Colours up, the people on board her are trying to get her afloat and to raise other masts, the 23rd is in a good state under English Colours the 24th is also in good state.

This is all that I can distinguish from which results that though the English have had the advantage, they have been very roughly handled since they could not follow the Vessels which went away on the 15th, for these two days these ships have been perfectly inactive and seemingly destroyed, this Morning news has arrived here from Alexandria which confirms our losses. Rear Admiral Decrest is killed also Vice Admirals Blounquet and Duchouila, five Ships have struck their Colours, the Tonant was the last Ship in action. Dupetitoir who commanded her had his two Legs carried off by a Cannon Shot, the Ships escaped are the Guillaume Tell the —— with the Frigates Diana and Justice. They say it was the Artamise which blew up the Morning before yesterday, many things relative to this Battle are yet to learn, they say that the English Admiral has sent a Flag of Truce to Alexandria demanding that they should receive and take care of the Wounded which amounts to 1500, they will send us all our Prisoners, as yet I am ignorant of what has been decided on.

You will receive in France the official news of us and of the English, I know not what they will say but you may rely on what I have written because it is what

I have seen. Communicate my Letter to Citizen Carancey, his Son who ought
to have given him these accounts is by me, otherwise occupied. He has written six
Letters and has not received one in return. I have no news of Citizen Moray whom
I have named Agent at Dunantrour.

Berancée who has been ill is quite recovered he is with me. Martin is extremely
well but has not received one line from his family. I am the only fortunate one among
them having received three Letters from you since my arrival in Egypt, one of the
2nd prairial one the 16th and one the 27th and 28th. Most certainly many are lost as the
English have taken many of our Couriers.

I have had since my arrival here my portrait in profile taken by an Able Artist
Citizen Bonoy, it is said to be very like but we have so many English around us that
for fear of its falling into their hands or going to the bottom of the Sea I dare not send
it. I could wish to be the bearer of it myself! Be assured that as soon as I can obtain
that permission which I shall not cease to solicit I shall take my departure. There is no
fortune which shall retain me. I shall be contented to arrive with you naked as my hand

As for what remains to be said, I am in good health. To morrow morning I
take my departure for Cairo in an handsome Boat with the Money and Paymaster
General, two Armed Boats with 250 men as an escort and more than 40
Passengers: I take with me a fine Arabian Horse which a Sheikh made me a present
of here. We go by the Nile. Cidri [illeg] my dear little girl, love me always, and
recall me often to the memory of all our friends. I embrace you and also my children.

E. Poussielgue

This Frenchman seems to know so much more of the Battle than I do that I
will not continue to contradict him: I am satisfied with it if he is. Send it to Lady
Nelson when read.

St. V.

In The Hour Of Victory

Numerous similar letters were captured in the aftermath of the Nile when the Mediterranean was entirely dominated by British warships. The correspondence was so revealing, and often so downright entertaining, that a selection was immediately published in Britain in the snappily titled *Copies of original letters from the army of General Bonaparte in Egypt, intercepted by the fleet under the command of Admiral Lord Nelson* (1798). The editor gleefully recorded how the letters laid bare the French tactic of 'spreading the most absurd and exaggerated accounts' of their success and warned that their campaign which 'began in wickedness and fraud' was bound to 'terminate in wretchedness and despair'.

That insight was accurate. The loss of the French fleet meant that their army was cut off in Egypt. The soldiers had no choice but to be self-sufficient in an entirely alien environment and their morale plummeted. At the same time, their enemies were encouraged by the British victory and the Bedouin lit fires all along the coast of Egypt to express their gratitude for the achievements of Nelson's fleet. Their fight against the French was renewed with vigour and cruelty. Officers moaned in their letters about everything: the climate and the country, the vicious Bedouin, the absurdity of the expedition, their lack of food, ammunition, money and medicine, and the filth and stench of the army camps in the desert heat. Moreover one of the letters, written by Napoleon to his brother, described how he envisaged himself as the 'Washington of France', a reference to George Washington who had risen from army officer to President of the United States and who had remained the single most dominant figure in American history for 24 years.

Washington was no tyrant, but such firm evidence of Napoleon's aspirations created a powerful shock wave. The author who edited the volume of intercepted French letters was confident that the Battle of the Nile would ruin those aspirations. He declared that:

> All return is now impossible, except as a fugitive, or a prisoner. He may enter into the chambers of the Pyramids, and hold conversations on the tomb of Cheops, with Imans, and with Muftis; he may organize, and conquer, and plant botanic gardens, and establish menageries; he may pass from the Delta to the Thebaid, and from the Thebaid to the Delta, with his train of tri-coloured Cheiks, and be hailed as the Ali Bonaparte

of the country – all is still but folly: his final destruction can neither be averted nor delayed...[16]

Napoleon, however, had only just begun. He was not captured, nor did he even flee, but returned from Egypt almost a year after the Battle of the Nile, seized power for himself and settled into the magnificent Royal Palace of the Tuileries. Later, when he had come to realise his ambition, when so many ancient European dynasties lay shattered, and when thousands upon thousands of soldiers and civilians lay dead at his feet, Nelson described him as 'the common disturber of the human race'.[17] The Battle of the Nile is too readily celebrated as an astonishing British victory, but it should also be remembered as the culmination of a British naval campaign that failed to catch Napoleon but which, had it done so, would have changed history far more radically than it ever did.

The Battle of the Nile, nevertheless, dealt a devastating blow to French military power both in Egypt and throughout the Mediterranean. British, Turkish and Russian warships waged an unopposed war on French Mediterranean possessions and the resulting pressure on French territory weakened the Directory in Paris. In a curious way, the battle gave Napoleon both the opportunity to return to France and the prospect of seizing power for himself. In spite of Nelson's victory at the Nile, therefore, 1798 was not the year that the war ended, but the year that it was turned on its head all over again.

Copenhagen
Slaget På Reden

2 April 1801

'I can foresee nothing but trouble and anxiety'

Admiral Sir Hyde Parker to his wife Fanny, 30 March 1801

AT A GLANCE

DATE:
2 April 1801

NAVIES INVOLVED:
British and Danish

COMMANDING OFFICERS:
Admiral Hyde Parker and Commodore Olfert Fischer

FLEET SIZES:
British 12 ships of the line; Danish 18 ships of various sizes

TIME OF DAY:
10.00 – 15.30

LOCATION:
Copenhagen Roads 55°42´10˝N 12°36´48˝E

WEATHER:
Moderate breezes, cloudy

RESULT:
12 Danish ships captured, one sunk and one destroyed

CASUALTIES:
British, 943; Danish, 1,002

BRITISH COURT MARTIALS:
None, but Hyde Parker was recalled and never employed again

DISPATCHES CARRIED HOME BY:
Captain Robert Otway, Hyde Parker's flag captain

The Manor

Tucked away in the English countryside, down narrow, leafy lanes, are the ghosts of long-vanished houses whose histories reach deep into our past. Just south of Saxmundham in Suffolk, only five miles or so from the coast, is the site of one of the finest, a house whose history is quite extraordinary for its scope. Several important houses have stood on this land, all known as Benhall Manor. The current house was built in 1810, five years after Trafalgar and five years before Napoleon was finally defeated. The land on which it stands, however, was significant enough to have been granted, in 1086, to the son of a man who had fought with William the Conqueror. The seat of the Dukes of Suffolk and the residence of two Lords Admiral, Benhall Manor was, for 500 years, central to the intrigues of the British court as it lurched from Norman to Plantagenet, Plantagenet to Lancaster, Lancaster to York, York to Tudor and from Catholic to Protestant. In such topsy-turvy times, a defining characteristic of so many of its inhabitants was that they were unable to remain in favour, or even alive, for very long.

One of the earliest owners was John de Holland, Earl of Huntingdon, half-brother to Richard II. Holland was a stout supporter of the King. When, in 1400, Richard was deposed by his cousin, Henry Bolingbroke who became Henry IV, de Holland led the failed Epiphany Uprising in an attempt to return the imprisoned Richard to the throne. Holland was subsequently captured and beheaded.

Under Henry IV, the land passed to the de la Pole family, who were unlucky in war. Michael de la Pole died at the siege of Harfleur in 1415 and his eldest son was killed at Agincourt in the same year. The land then passed to his brother, William, who deserves an entire book to himself. He was the 1st Duke of Suffolk and later became Lord Chamberlain. Having married the grand-daughter of the poet Geoffrey Chaucer, Suffolk became the most powerful figure in the realm under the weak Henry VI and, among his other titles, became Admiral of England. His eventual fall from power was followed by imprisonment in the Tower and then banishment but, on his way to exile in France, he was beheaded on the gunwale of his own ship. Many suspected that Richard of York, his arch rival and the subsequent Protector of the Realm, was responsible.

The land soon passed to John de la Pole, a strong supporter of the new House of York that was established in 1461 by Richard of York's son, Edward IV. Pole in fact married Edward's sister and thus became brother-in law to two York monarchs, Edward IV and his younger brother Richard III. When Richard was defeated at Bosworth by Henry Tudor, who became Henry VII, Pole served the new king loyally but his son, the new owner of Benhall, rebelled and was beheaded.

Under Henry VIII, the land passed to the Catholic Thomas Howard, Duke of Norfolk and Lord Admiral from 1515 to 1525. Howard was intimately involved in Tudor court life as the uncle of two of Henry's wives, Anne Boleyn and Katherine Howard. His own fall came with the fall of those wives, both of whom were executed. He was imprisoned, awaiting the blade, when the king died before sentence could be passed. Howard then helped Henry's Catholic daughter, Mary, to secure the throne for herself.

The lives of Benhall Manor's subsequent occupants proved somewhat less turbulent, however, and in December 1801 the latest grand house to be built on the site was bought by Admiral Sir Hyde Parker, a 52-year-old from an impressive naval family who had been in the navy since the age of 12. However he too, like so many of its former residents, found himself out of favour and his influence and reputation crushed, despite having been sent, in the spring of 1801, to the Baltic in command of a massive British fleet bristling with hostility. That fleet had achieved an impressive victory at the Battle of Copenhagen but, as soon as it had been attained, Parker had immediately been recalled and was never employed again. The reasons why he fell so far from grace are complex and fascinating.

The Puppet

The Second Coalition against Revolutionary France, which had been formed in the aftermath of Nelson's extraordinary victory at the Battle of the Nile, never lived up to expectations. Napoleon abandoned his Egyptian campaign and, in November 1799, returned to France to seize power from the weak Directory. He then led a bold campaign against the Austrians, who had regained much ground in Italy, and defeated them at the Battle of Marengo in the summer of 1800. The Russian Tsar, the cornerstone of the Second Coalition, had meanwhile begun to lose interest in his war against France and in his friendship with Britain, a shift in policy that was greatly abetted by the British siege of Malta.

Napoleon had seized Malta from the Knights just prior to the Battle of the Nile. When Nelson crippled the French Mediterranean navy at the Nile, the garrison at Malta was isolated and the British attacked. This campaign was initially launched with the full backing of Tsar Paul, who had been elected Grand Master of the Order of the Knights of St John in the aftermath of Napoleon's conquest; indeed the reconquest of Malta was a fundamental reason for Russian participation in the war. When the British retook Malta in September 1800, however, they refused to hand it back to the Knights. Its fine, deep harbour at Valetta was simply too valuable a strategic asset to give up.

The British-Russian alliance snapped. Paul seized British sailors in Russian ports and marched them inland, through the Russian winter, to prison camps. Napoleon, meanwhile, took the opportunity to woo the Tsar with vague and entirely false suggestions that vast areas of Italy and Germany could be restored to their monarchs and that thousands of Russian prisoners, taken in 1799, could be repatriated. Napoleon's promises may have been hollow but they are a clear indication of the extent to which Paul's foreign policies benefited the French by hurting the British.

The Russian-Austrian relationship had also crumbled during their combined campaigns to oust the French from Italy and Switzerland. The Austrians sought territorial gains of their own while the Russians, much as with their support of the British attack on Malta, were fighting to restore the traditional order shattered by Napoleon. By October 1799 the Russian-Austrian alliance had collapsed and the British were forced to choose between the two for a committed ally in their war against France. They chose Austria, which was politically more committed to a lengthy war and geographically more suited to a British alliance. The British decision to stand by the Austrians further irritated the Russians and it was not long before that irritation turned to antagonism.

Another important aspect of the fragmentation of the Second Coalition was the issue of neutral trading rights. While armies collided and navies chased each other around the world, the British conducted an economic war by flexing their maritime muscle. In 1794 this had manifested itself in the failed campaign to secure the American grain convoy which had nonetheless led to fleet battle at The

Glorious First of June. Imported shipbuilding stores were another target in the form of iron for anchors, hemp for rope, flax for canvas, pitch for seams and pine for planks. The warmongers needed a constant supply of these raw materials as much as the suppliers wanted to profit from their sale and, crucially, none of the major naval combatants was self-sufficient in any of them. Most of them had to be imported from the countries surrounding the Baltic: Russia, Denmark, which then included Norway, and Sweden. The flow of these materials therefore became a significant strategic issue.

The British insisted that they had the right to search any ship, even a neutral ship, to prevent such goods from reaching Britain's enemies. To assist them, they used a broad interpretation of the term 'contraband'. The neutral nations, meanwhile, held tight to a narrow definition of 'contraband' and insisted on their right to trade with whomever they wanted. The Tsar of Russia, the leader of the key military and diplomatic power in the Baltic, was already irritated with the British and began to assume and enjoy a role as chivalrous protector of his Baltic neighbours.

Such inherently contradictory national interests had always existed but they only became important now because of British naval success. The threat of invasion, which had been almost constant between 1794 and 1797, no longer existed. Nor, after the Battle of the Nile, was there a significant French naval presence in the Mediterranean, a sea which, in 1797, had been a French lake. During these early years British naval power had been stretched with squadrons active in numerous theatres and against numerous enemies. As a result neutral shipping had been relatively unmolested by the British; they simply hadn't had the time. Now, however, the British began to use their newfound maritime dominance to threaten their enemies' ability to rebuild their shattered fleets.

The issue of neutral rights came to a head in the summer of 1800 because the Danes began to protect their convoys with armed escorts. Soon after, a Danish convoy, escorted by the frigate *Freja*, was stopped by a British squadron. The *Freja* refused to allow the British to search the fleet and fighting broke out with men falling on both sides. The entire Danish convoy was seized.

Several similar instances of British 'interference' in neutral trade convoys gradually led to Tsar Paul hardening his stance until, in the late summer of 1800, he coerced Denmark, Sweden and Prussia into joining a 'League of Armed

Neutrality', reviving a strategy that had proved very successful during the War of American Independence. The League insisted on the rights of neutrals to trade with warring parties of any nation. Moreover the word of any of their naval officers was to be considered sufficient proof of the nature of their cargo.

The League had worked during the American War because the British had been stretched as never before and were unable to contest the neutrals' claims. Now, however, the Royal Navy was basking in the glow of repeated success while Nelson had returned from the disaster of Naples and was itching to get back to sea. He desperately needed to get away from the gossip and embarrassment that had followed him home as he had publicly waltzed through Europe with Emma Hamilton, a married lady in the arms of a married man and neither married to the other.

What Nelson most needed was a challenge and the Pitt government duly obliged by deciding to strike against the Tsar's Baltic League. Not only were the British desperate to secure access to the Baltic shipping supplies but they had also suffered two poor grain harvests and the Baltic regions were always the most accessible source of foreign grain imports. Paul knew this and insisted that, when the agreement was signed on 16 December 1800, all signatories closed their ports to all British trade. Something had to be done.

There were three navies to consider, the Russian, the Danish and the Swedish. The Russian navy was the largest by far but the Danish was the most strategically significant because of its location at the gates of the Baltic. The Swedish navy was of little concern on its own but, if joined with the Russian or Danish, would create a powerful force indeed. If all three navies united, they could send no less than 96 ships of the line to sea.

The time of year was also important. Because the harbours of the western Baltic thawed earlier than those in the east, if an attack could be launched in the early spring, the Baltic allies could be dealt with in two separate campaigns. A force was therefore gathered to strike at Copenhagen. If the Danes and Swedes could be neutralised, then the Russian naval threat could be dealt with later in the year and without an enemy still threatening in the rear.

There was, however, an alternative way of seeing things. The League of Armed Neutrality was instigated and held together by the Russians. Without the threat of Russian force over their heads, the Danes and Swedes posed no threat at all to the

British. Certainly, both countries had navies, but they existed to neutralise each other's naval threat. In 1800 Norway was part of Denmark but the Swedes were anxious to seize the country for themselves. Any viable threat to either country's naval power was therefore a threat to the immediate future of the country itself and that was far more important to both the Swedes and the Danes than their belief in neutral trading rights. If the Swedish navy was destroyed, the Danes could hold Norway; if the Danish navy was destroyed, the Swedes could take it back. It followed therefore that, with the Russians out of the picture, the issues raised by the League of Armed Neutrality would disappear. In short, the problem posed by Denmark could be neutralised by attacking Russia.

As things stood in the New Year of 1801, however, Copenhagen remained the primary target simply because it guarded the easiest and quickest route into the Baltic and because the Danes greatly feared the prospect of Russian reprisals for non-compliance in the League. The vast Russian army could, in effect, snatch Danish land at will, either by direct action or by imposing political pressure backed by military force. The Danes were also seen as being weak. They had little time to prepare to meet a British attack, nor could they rely on any help from Sweden, nominally part of the Baltic pack but in reality a lurking, lone hyena.

The Danes, however, still had the potential to stage a formidable defence, if only it could be set up in time. The approaches to Copenhagen are awkward for a single ship, let alone for a fleet under fire whose captains have little knowledge of Copenhagen Sound. To protect their fleet for a future clash with Sweden, the Danes decided that the defence of Copenhagen against British attack would be conducted by heavily armed floating batteries anchored near the treacherous shoal water scattered around the Sound. These would be supported by the powerful Trekroner battery that guarded the entrance to the harbour. Such defences could be manned by inexperienced sailors. Obviously battle experience would be an advantage but volunteers could be trained in a relatively short time to fire from a steady platform. The Danes were promised three months' wages and free medical treatment if wounded, while at the same time Prince Frederick made it clear that they would be pressed if they did not volunteer. This mixture of bribery and threat ensured that more than enough men were found to man the formidable Danish defences but it was no easy matter to get the ships into position and the men aboard.

Raising men took time, however it was done, and the particular problems of establishing a defence of floating batteries are worth considering in some detail. The floating batteries were, in fact, old warships without masts and rigging. They could not, therefore, be sailed into position but had to be dragged all the way out of Copenhagen harbour and down the King's Channel by a process known as kedging. A large warship had several anchors the largest of which, the bower anchors, weighed as much as five tons apiece and were very difficult to move at all. A ship therefore carried a variety of smaller anchors, each with a different function. The kedge anchor weighed around a ton. To kedge the ship, one of her larger boats was launched and brought around to the side. The kedge anchor was then hoisted from the deck using a tackle attached to one of the lower yards, swung over the ship's side and lowered into the waiting boat with an appropriate length of cable and secured. If there was any room left for a crew, they would row the boat a hundred yards or so ahead of the ship; otherwise another boat would tow her to the desired location where the anchor would be dropped. The cable would be run from the anchor back aboard the ship through one of the bow hawseholes and around the capstan. The ship's crew would then turn the mighty capstan, forcing the anchor to bite deep into the sea bed and dragging the ship forward. The process would then be repeated until the ship was in the desired location which, for many of the Danish warships in 1801, was two or three *miles* from where they had started.

Once in place, the ship was secured by four anchors and her position carefully adjusted until each anchor bore an equal weight and each anchor cable was a similar length. This was an exhausting and time-consuming process even for one ship, but the Danes had identified 12 such dismasted vessels to defend Copenhagen Sound. They all had to be kedged into position and a further seven ships anchored appropriately in relation to the floating batteries and shore batteries. And it was March when the temperature in Copenhagen rarely rose above freezing.

The Danes, therefore, had the makings of an impressive defence, even without using most of their own seaworthy ships or enlisting the help of any Swedish ships. It would all be useless, however, if the British could strike hard and early. Fortunately for the Danes, the man who had been sent to command the British fleet at Copenhagen was Admiral Hyde Parker.

The Newlywed

The second son of a well-respected vice-admiral, Parker was chosen to lead at Copenhagen because of the knowledge he had gained in 1791 when planning for a war with Russia during the Ochakov Crisis, another collision over British access to Baltic naval stores. Appointed fleet captain to Lord Hood, the proposed leader of the earlier expedition, Parker had helped to draw up plans for a blockade of the Russian naval bases of Revel and Kronstadt. However, the Ochakov crisis evaporated when Pitt climbed down from his aggressive stance because British public opinion shared none of his enthusiasm for a distant war. So Parker had first-hand experience not of the Baltic itself, but of planning for a war in the Baltic. In fact, George Murray of the *Edgar* and Frederick Thesiger and Nicholas Tomlinson who had both served as mercenaries in the Russian navy, were the only captains that sailed to Copenhagen in 1801 who had first-hand knowledge of that treacherous, narrow and shallow sea.

Parker nonetheless enjoyed a certain professional reputation. He was 61, he came from an established naval family and he had some experience of fleet warfare. His service history went right back to 1751 and he had served in the East Indies during the Seven Years War (1756–63), gaining his first command at the age of 21. He had then played an important role in the next war, the War of American Independence (1775–82), taking part in the fierce fleet battle against the Dutch at the Dogger Bank in 1781. He had, however, missed the four major fleet battles of the Revolutionary wars, though he had been present at Hotham's minor, indecisive, engagement with the French off Genoa in the summer of 1795. Parker also had experience of dealing with enemy fleets in harbour. He had been present at the attack in 1776 on the North River in New York, which had been defended by floating batteries, gunboats and shore batteries and again at the 1793 surrender of the Toulon squadron to Lord Hood at the very beginning of the Revolutionary war.

For all his experience, however, Parker was not widely admired. Collingwood wrote to his sister describing him as being 'full of vanity, a great deal of pomp, and a pretty smattering of ignorance'[1] and his recent marriage to the plump 18-year-old daughter of Admiral Sir Richard Onslow had made them both the object of public ridicule. Gossipers described her as 'batter pudding' and the newspapers, rather cleverly, as Parker's 'sheet anchor'. Wry smiles were shared over his commitment to service in the North Sea when his bed was kept so warm at home. Parker did nothing to help himself by remaining at home with his new wife when the fleet was ready to sail. Rumour circulated like wildfire that he did so to be present at a ball she had organised and it quickly reached the ears of the Admiralty. Nelson was furious and wrote to Troubridge: ' … what I say is in the mouth of all the old market-women at Yarmouth … Consider how nice it must be lying abed with a young wife, compared to a damned raw cold wind.'[2] Lord Spencer wrote a letter dripping with venom, 'supposing it impossible' that Parker was still at Yarmouth 'on account of some trifling circumstance'.[3] With his knuckles rapped, Parker joined the fleet and the ball was cancelled.

It is also important to realise that it was Parker, rather than Nelson, who was chosen to command the fleet. Nelson had been given command of the Mediterranean squadron in 1798 ahead of many more senior officers and had won a great victory at the Nile, but his subsequent affair with Emma Hamilton and his ill-judged interference in the Kingdom of Naples had won him few friends and had cooled the support of many powerful men who had been instrumental in his earlier rapid promotion. Although he may have been a sensible choice for the Baltic expedition, he was passed over and sailed as Parker's second in command. Parker, already faced with a thorny challenge, was thus presented with another: how to command a fleet with Nelson as a subordinate.

The Conundrum

When, on 19 March, the British arrived at the Skaw, the northernmost tip of the Jutland peninsula at the entrance to the Kattegat Sea, nothing was certain. Britain and Denmark were by no means openly at war, nor was it certain how the British would act if war proved unavoidable. Parker's instructions were to destroy the Danish navy and its dockyards if the Danes refused to leave the Baltic League, but the means by which he should do that were unclear because there were two routes to Copenhagen from the Kattegat.

The direct route passed through the Sound and approached Copenhagen from the north. The longer route was through the Great Belt and brought the attacker to Copenhagen from the south.

The alternative routes for attacking Copenhagen.

The pilotage of both routes was poorly known to the British and each was riddled with natural and man-made hazards. The Sound was heavily defended at its entrance, at a point where it is only four kilometres wide, by the mighty Kronborg fortress, known for generations after its rebuilding in the 1690s as one of the strongest fortresses in Europe. It remains today one of the finest and most important Renaissance castles in the world.

Assuming the enemy to be the Danes, therefore, it was still unclear exactly how they should be attacked. Nelson, however, was not even prepared to assume that much. From what the British knew about the natural hazards of attacking Copenhagen from north or south, combined with the limited intelligence they had recently acquired of Danish defensive preparations, Nelson decided to bypass the Danes completely. Instead he planned to strike at the heart of the Baltic League, Russia, via Tsar Paul's navy in Revel and Kronstadt. It was certainly a valid proposal, both tactically and strategically, but there were two factors against it. It went directly against Parker's specific orders to deal first with the Danes, and it wrongly assumed, because British intelligence had been wildly inaccurate, that the Danish defences were already in place. In reality only seven of the 18 Danish ships were in position, the fleet manpower was still a third under strength, the entire officer corps of the Danish naval force consisted of just 13 men, the Russians were still iced in and the Swedes had refused to help. The opportunity for a lightning strike against the Danes via the Sound was very much alive and, if seized, could have neutralised them with very little loss of life or time. The British would have then been able to sail directly for the eastern Baltic to deal with the Russians.

The Dispatches

The Copenhagen dispatches are unique for a number of reasons. First, the letters written by Parker are the least legible of all the dispatches in the entire volume. Even if one accepts that he had poor handwriting, they are hurried and scrappy, a window into a fevered mind.

Second, the most important letter of the Copenhagen collection is not, in fact, written by the fleet commander-in-chief because he was not there during

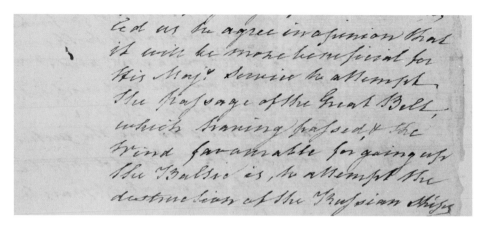

Hyde Parker's scrawled letters are the most difficult to read of all the Admirals' dispatches.

the critical phase of the action. The assault was led by Nelson, his second-in-command, and Parker defers his authority and knowledge of the attack to Nelson. Parker's letter to the Admiralty is the weakest of all of the admirals' letters in this collection. Third, the dispatches include a detailed exchange of letters between Parker and the commander of the Kronborg fortress concerning the intentions of each country. Unlike all of the other dispatches, therefore, these include and describe a diplomatic, as well as a military, tussle. Finally, of all of the dispatches, these are the least self-explanatory and consequently the most interesting.

Admiral H. Parker to E. Nepean, 23 March 1801

The first letter is important because it outlines the plans for an attack that never happened. The lead story of the Copenhagen dispatches is one of indecision and uncertainty. It is written on 23 March, four days after the British fleet arrived at the Skaw. By now Parker has sailed through the Kattegat and is anchored at the north-eastern tip of Zealand. He has a choice to make.

His first plan was simply to wait for the Danes to offer battle, which was wholly unrealistic since Danish naval strategy centred on the survival of its sailing fleet. His next plan was to attack Copenhagen via the most direct route, the Sound from the north, but in this letter Parker admits to another change of mind. He has received news of the Danes' defensive preparations from Nicholas Vansittart, a British politician of little talent or flair and no military experience, who had been chosen to act as the political brain to Parker's military muscle. Vansittart was there because Pitt's government had finally fallen after 18 years in power and Addington had taken charge and rewarded his followers. Vansittart, a conservative politician, was one of those lucky men. He arrived at the anchorage spouting unverified accounts of fearsome Danish defences and rumours of squadrons of Swedish ships of the line and gunboats descending on Copenhagen from Karlskrona.[4]

Parker then explains how, based on a subsequent discussion with Vansittart and Nelson, he has changed his mind about the attack on Copenhagen. Parker thus explicitly includes a subordinate and a politician in his command decision, preparing the ground to shift or share the blame should his new attack fail.

The new plan, he explains, is to avoid Copenhagen entirely by entering the Baltic via the Great Belt, thus bypassing all of the Danish defences, and then to see how the wind blew. If it was fair for the Baltic, he would attack the Russians; if it was fair for Copenhagen, he would attack the Danes from the south. It is an extraordinary statement for a professional seaman. Once through the Great Belt, *any* wind that was fair for Copenhagen could be harnessed to take the fleet east and north to the Russian naval bases of Revel or Kronstadt. To sum up, therefore, this letter shifts the blame for a decision that was based on unverified intelligence, which made little professional sense and which ran contrary to Parker's explicit orders to attack Copenhagen. Parker has lost his grip.

London, off the Hall
23 March 1801

 Sir,

Since writing my letter of this mornings date, I have had recourse to a consultation with Vice Admiral Lord Nelson and Mr Vansittart on the very formidable defence the Danes have made against any attack being made upon them, not only by many additional Batteries to Cronenburgh Castle but also the number of Hulks and Batteries which have lately been placed & erected for the defence of the Arsenal at Copenhagen, &

renders the attack so hazardous, joind to the difficulty of the Navigation by the passage
of the Sound as led us to agree in opinion that it will be more beneficial for His Majʸ
Service to attempt the passage of the Great Belt, which having passed, & the Wind
favourable for going up the Baltic is, to attempt the destruction of the Russian ships
at Revel which are expected as soon as the season will permit their coming down the
Baltic to co-operate with the Danes, but in the event of the Wind being contrary for
getting up the Baltic, after having passed the Belt, in this case, to attempt destroying
Copenhagen by coming down the passage from the Baltic. This measure will be
attacking them in the Rear where it is evident they do not expect an attack, nor is it in
their power to render it so defensible as by the other channel.

My intention is, should I be so fortunate as either to meet the Russian Squadron
on their passage down, or at Revel, the moment either service is performed, to return
immediately to the object of Copenhagen; and I trust, great as the responsibility I
take upon myself, their Lordships will do me the justice to believe that, I could only
be assuased, by what appears to be, for the great object my Country has in view
consistent with the peculiar situation I find myself in by the formidable disposition of
Copenhagen, and which cannot be known to their Lordships.

I therefore rely with confidence on their approbation, and am
> *Sir*
>> *Your most obedient*
>> *humble servant*

Parker

Evan Nepean Esqʳ

Nelson, meanwhile, was climbing the wooden walls with impatience. He was partially responsible for convincing Parker to sail into the Baltic via the Great Belt, but he also realised that, whatever route was taken, something had to be done immediately. He instinctively knew that indecision was unhelpful strategically and tactically and had a detrimental effect on the crews. When he eventually got to examine the Danish defences himself, he wrote with some bravado to Emma: '... I have just been reconnoitring the Danish line of defence. It looks formidable to those who are children at war but to my judgement with ten sail of the line I think I can annihilate them, at all events I hope to be allowed to try.'[5] Parker granted his wish.

Admiral H. Parker to E. Nepean, 6 April 1801

The next letter continues the theme of indecision and weakness, even if it does describe the eventual attack on Copenhagen. It is, once more, written aboard the flagship and this time 'in Copenhagen' but, as Parker makes clear, he got there neither from the south nor after attacking the Russians, the two options he proposed in his letter of 23 March, but via an attack on the Sound from the north.

This time, we know that the major, but by no means the only, influence on Parker's change of mind was Robert Otway, his flag captain, who was deeply worried about the navigation of the Great Belt and the hazards of approaching Copenhagen from the south.

The date of this letter is particularly important. It is written on 6 April, a fortnight after his previous letter, and although Parker describes a vicious storm that threatened to scatter his fleet, he fails to mention the brief window of opportunity offered by a northerly breeze, which would have allowed his ships to pass through the Sound on 23 March, the day he wrote his first letter. His failure to do so allowed the Danes to strengthen their batteries. By the time that the British eventually attacked, every Danish ship was in its allocated position, more men had been raised than was actually necessary and the green hands had been trained.

There was no false hope on the part of the Danes, however. Politicians and naval officers alike knew it was unlikely that they would win. Indeed, one member of the government who inspected the defences compared the Danes to the Spartans at Thermopylae.[*] They had done more than enough to give the British a bloody nose but if Parker *had* attacked on 23 March they might not have fought at all and the bloody Battle of Copenhagen could have been avoided entirely.

Parker describes the attack on Copenhagen in the most general terms: he cannot describe it in detail because he did not lead it himself, having left it to Nelson. He does, however, lament the deaths of Captain Mosse, a man of vast experience, and Captain Riou, an officer of immense promise. They were both

---

[*] Who held out, in 480 BC, against a vast army of Persians before being killed to the last man.

greatly mourned by the service and a monument commemorating them both can still be seen in the crypt of St Paul's Cathedral. Parker makes it quite clear that both men left dependants, whose livelihoods were then guaranteed by the navy. It does not say it here, but we know that Riou was cut in half by a cannon ball.

Parker also mentions Sir Thomas Boulden Thompson, a legend of the service who had fought so gallantly at the Nile in the tiny 50-gun *Leander*. His conduct on that day was such that he was awarded a knighthood for gallantry, a reward usually reserved for flag-officers. At Copenhagen Thompson commanded the *Bellona* and lost a leg. His active career thus came to an end but he became an important naval administrator and served as comptroller of the navy for a decade between 1806 and 1816, after which he was appointed treasurer of Greenwich hospital and director of the Chatham Chest, the pension fund for disabled sailors. Nelson later wrote personally to William Pitt, vouching for Thompson's professional ability, to secure a pension for his wife and children: 'A more gallant active and Zealous Sea Officer was not in the Service.'[6]

LONDON, IN COPENHAGEN
ROAD, 6 APRIL 1801

,

You will be pleased to acquaint the Lords Commrs of the Admiralty that, since my letter of 22ᵈ last month, I reconsiderd & weighed all the circumstances attending my going through the Passage of the Great Belt, with His Majestys Fleet under my command; and although I still think that, had we had the good fortune to have made a short passage through, Copenhagen might have been attacked from that side with less risque to the Fleet, Yet the objections and obstacles were so many, by subjecting our Communication to be cut off, by the Danes sending out two or three Ships of the Line with Frigates, and taking position & covering them with Batteries on the Islands in the narrow passage of the Navigation of

the Belt as to render their being forced very difficult, more especially by any thing coming from England. This, and the danger which must have insued from the want of Pilots in so intricate a Navigation, with such a considerable Fleet (Captain Murray, of His Maj[s] Ship Edgar and one Pilot being the only two people to be found in the Fleet who had been through that Passage) These reasons acted so forcibly on my Mind as to induce me to give up that Plan, and we have determined on the Passage through the Sound.

From the 22[d] past, no opportunity of Wind offerd for going up the Sound until the 25th when the Wind shifted in a most violent squall from SW to NW & North and blew with such violence, & with so great a Sea, as to render it impossible for any ship to have weighed her Anchor.[7] The Sea & Wind were even so violent as to oblige many of the Ships, from drifting, to let go a second Anchor, notwithstanding they were riding with two Cables an end; and by the Morning the Wind veered again to the Southward of the West.

On the 30th of last Month, the Wind having come to the North again we passed into the Sound with the Fleet, but not before I had assured myself of the hostile intentions of the Danes as to opposing our passage, as the papers N[rs]. 1. 2. 3. & 4 will prove. After this intercourse there could be no doubts remaining of their determination for War after anchoring about 5 or 6 Miles from the Island of Henuen, I, with Vice Admiral Lord Nelson & Rear Admiral Graves reconnoitred the formidable Line of Ships, Rideaus, Pontoons, Galleys, Fire Ships & Gun Boats, flank'd & supported by some extensive Batteries on the two Islands calld the Groines, the largest of which was mounted with from 50 to 70 pieces of Cannon – These were again commanded by two Ships of 70 Guns, & a large Frigate in the Inner Roads of Copenhagen, and two 64 Gun Ships without masts, were moored upon the Fleet, on the starboard side of the entrance into the Arsenal – The day afterwards the Wind being Southerly, we again examined their position, and came to the resolution of Attacking them from the S[o] Ward.

Elephant
Defiance
Monarch
Bellona
Edgar
Russel
Ganges
Glatton
Isis
Agamemnon
Polyphemus
Ardent

Vice Admiral Lord Nelson having offerd his services for conducting the attack, had, some days before we enterd the Sound shifted his Flag from the St. George to the Elephant,[8] and after having examined and buoyed the Outer Channel of the Middle Ground, his Lordship proceeded with the 12 Ships of the Line named in the margin; all the Frigates, Bombs, Fireships & all the small Vessels, & that Evening anchored off Draco Point, to make his disposition for the Attack and wait for the Wind to the Southward. It was agreed on between us, that the remaining Ships with me, should weigh at the same moment his Lordship did, & menace the Gamn Islands & the 4 Ships of the Line that lay in the Entrance into the Arsenal, as also to cover the disabled Ships, as they came out of the Arsenal.

Inclosed, I have the honour to transmit Vice Admiral Lord Nelsons report of the Action on the 2d instant; His Lordship has stated, so fully, the whole of his proceedings on that day as only to leave me the opportunity of testifying my entire acquiescence and testimony of the bravery and intrepidity with which the Action was supported throughout the Line; was it possible for me to add any thing to the well earned honours of Lord Nelson, it would be by asserting that his exertions, great as they have been, never were carried to a higher position of Zeal for his Country's Service.

I have only to lament that this sort of Attack, confined within intricate and narrow pilotage excluded the Ships, particularly under my command, from the opportunity of exhibiting their valour, but can, with great truth, assert that the same spirit animated the whole of the Fleet, and trust that, the contest in which we are now engaged, will, on a future day, afford them an occasion of shewing that the whole were inspired by the same spirit, had the Field been sufficiently extensive to have brought it into Action.

It is with the deepest concern I mention the loss of Captains Mosse & Riou, two very brave and gallant officers — and whose death, I am well informed, will be sensibly felt by the Families they have left behind; the former, a Wife & Children; the latter, an Aged Mother.

From the known gallantry of Sir T. B. Thompson on former services, the Naval Service will have to regret the loss of the future exertions of that brave Officer.

For any further particulars I beg leave to refer their Lordships to Captain Otway, the bearer of my Dispatches, who was with Lord Nelson in the latter part of the Action, and is capable of answering any questions their Lordships may think necessary to put to him.

A return of the Killed and Wounded you will receive herein.

I have the honour to be,

     Sir

        Your most obedient
        humble servant

              Parker

P.S. An account of promotions and removals which have taken place in consequence of this Action, shall be sent by the next opportunity.

The Captain of the Monarch being killd early in the Action, Lieut. Yelland continued it with the greatest spirit. I therefore cannot avoid, in justice to his merit, particularly, recommending him to their Lordships favour & attention.

              H. P.

                  Evan Nepean Esq.

Robert Otway, the man sent home with the dispatches, was in fact with Nelson during the latter part of the action. This was most unusual because Otway was Parker's flag captain, not Nelson's. He had, in fact, requested to go to Nelson shortly after Parker had made a much-criticised signal for Nelson to withdraw, which Nelson ignored (p. 233). It is possible that Otway explained to Nelson that the signal was permissive, that is that it gave him the option of withdrawing with honour if the situation demanded it. Parker, too far distant to make out the detail of the action, would not have been able to see that a stumbling British withdrawal, under fire and in damaged ships, might easily have proved fatal to the entire squadron.

Correspondence between Admiral H. Parker and the Commander of the Kronborg Castle 27–29 March, 1801

The next letters were enclosed with Parker's battle dispatch. First is the correspondence between Parker and Governor Stricker, commander of Kronborg, in which each follows the other's lead in a diplomatic dance that ends in a declaration of war.

In the first of these letters, Parker refers to the Danish expulsion of the British envoy, the politician William Drummond, and requests a definitive explanation of Danish intent. In the second, Stricker buys time by sending an express to Copenhagen; at this stage, the Danes are still scrabbling desperately to prepare their defences. In the third, Stricker gives the official response, his words coming directly from the Crown Prince of Denmark. The nature of the 'expulsion' of William Drummond is contested but a door to a political settlement remains open, though this is nothing more than another delaying tactic.

The final letter is written at two o'clock in the morning. By now Parker has been awaiting an acceptable reply for two full days and has immediately penned his irritated response. He does not declare war, but claims that the Danish letter itself is a declaration of war which leaves him with no choice but to attack.

To continue the diplomatic dance, however, Parker makes it clear that the British are anxious to restore the 'amity and friendship' between the two Courts. This is not mere bluster. This letter encapsulates the difficulties that Parker faced when he was forced to attack a country with whom the British were anxious to remain friends. Not only did the British need to retain access to Baltic grain and shipbuilding supplies but the monarchies were closely linked by blood. Crown Prince Frederick's mother, Matilda, was none other than the sister of the British King, George III. Indeed, the King had personally made it clear to Parker that he preferred a negotiated solution. These letters, therefore, are for the eyes of the King and they have been included in the dispatches by an insecure admiral who is defending his decision to attack. He later wrote to his wife, after five days without proper sleep, 'My health is tolerably well, notwithstanding all my anxiety of mind, which is beyond anything I have ever experienced.'[9]

Nᵒ 1   LONDON, IN THE CATEGAT
27 MARCH 1801

From the hostile transaction, by the Court of Denmark, of sending away His Britannic Majestys Chargé D'Affaires The Commander in Chief of His Majestys Fleet is anxious to know, what the determination of the Danish Court is, and whether, the Commanding Officer of Cronenburg Castle has received Orders to Fire on the British Fleet, as they pass into the Sound? as he must deem the firing of the First Gun a Declaration of War on the part of Denmark.

Nᵒ 2.   CRONBERG CASTLE
28 MARCH 1801

In answer to the Admiral's honour of the letter, I have to inform that, no orders are given to fire on the English Fleet. An Express is gone to Copenhagen and should any Orders be sent, I shall immediately send an Officer on board to inform the Admiral.

Stricker,
Govʳ

Nᵒ 3.   CRONBERG CASTLE 28 MARCH 1801

In answer of Your Excellencys letter which I first, the day following at 8½ received I have the honour to inform you that I am perfectly acquainted with, that His Majesty the King of Denmark has not sent away the Chargé D'Affaires, but he has according to his own Demand obtained a Passport.

As a Soldier, I can not meddle with Politicks, but it is not allowed for me, to let a Fleet, whose intention is not yet known, approach the Cannons of the Castle which I have the honour to command.

In case Your Excellency should think proper to make any proposals to His Majesty the King of Denmark I wish to be informed before the Fleet further approach the Castle. A documented answer on this is desired.

Stricker

N°. 4

ON BOARD THE LONDON
29TH MARCH 1801 AT 2 AM.

Sir

In answer to Your Excellencys Note, just now received, the Undersigned has only to reply that, finding the intentions of the Court of Denmark to be hostile against His Britannic Majesty, he regards the answer as a Declaration of War, & therefore, agreeable to his Instructions, can no longer refrain from Hostilities, however reluctant it may be to his feelings.

But, at the same time will be ready to attend to any proposals of the Court of Denmark for restoring the former Amity & Friendship which has for so many Years subsisted between the two Courts

H Parker

Rear-Admiral H. Nelson to Admiral H. Parker 3 April, 1801

The next letter enclosed with Parker's dispatch is Nelson's description of the battle. As with his Nile dispatch, this is written by a Secretary. It is not, therefore, in Nelson's distinctive handwriting.

The letter begins with a description of the British surveying the outer channel. There is no mention of the fearsome 270 guns of the Kronborg fortress because not one shot hit the British fleet which simply sailed past, out of range of the Danish guns. The Swedish guns on the other side of the strait, which could have had some impact, if only in driving the British towards the Kronborg's guns, remained silent, the Swedes betraying the Baltic alliance. Without them, the mythical bark of Kronborg fortress was more potent than its bite.

Nelson then lists the full strength of the Danish defences, a formidable array of weaponry that the Danes had gathered while the British dithered over their preferred strategy. The preparation of the Danes at Copenhagen in 1801 was everything that the French at the Nile in 1798 had not been. Against so powerful a foe, anchored in such a strong position and in unsurveyed water, the British were

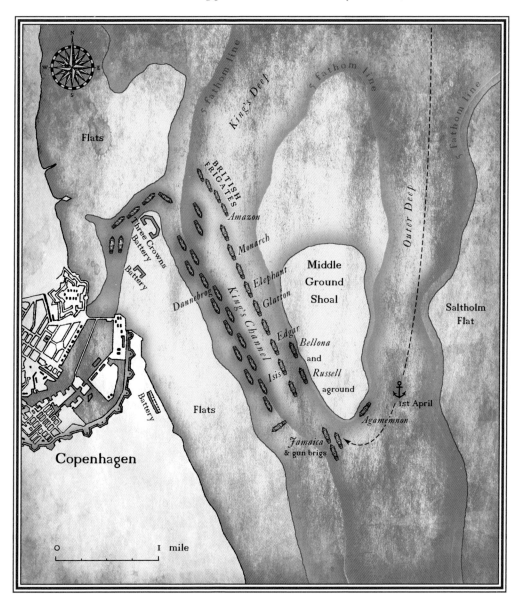

unable to avoid serious casualties. A cloud of impending catastrophe hung over the attack. Nelson brought his fleet around the Middle Ground shoal from the north, turned back on himself and sailed past the Danish defences from the south.

ELEPHANT, OFF COPENHAGEN
3 APRIL 1801

 Sir.

Defence
Monarch
Bellona
Edgar
Russel
Ganges
Glatton
Isis
Agamemnon
Polyphemus
Ardent
~
Amazon
Desirée
Blanche
Alcmene
~
Dart
Arrow
Cruiser
Harpy
~
Zephyr F.S.
Otter F.S.
~
BOMBS
Discovery
Sulphur
Hecla
Explosion
Aetna
Terrror
Volcano
&
8 Gun Brigs

In obedience to your directions to report the proceedings of the Squadron named in the margin, which you did me the honour to place under my command:

I beg leave to inform you that, having, by the assistance of that Able Officer, Capt. Rieu & the unremitting exertions of Cap. Brisbane, and the Masters of the Amazon & Cruizer in particular, buoyed the Channel of the Outer Deep, & the position of the Middle Ground the Squadron passed in safety and anchored off the Draco Fort the Evening of the first, and that Yesterday Morning, I made the Signal for the Squadron to weigh, and to engage the Danish Line consisting of 6 Sail of the Line, 11 Floating Batteries mounting from 26, 24 pounders to 18, 18 pounders & one Bomb ship, besides Schooner Gun Vessels — These were supported by the Crown Islands, mounting 88 Cannon & 4 Sail of the Line moored at the Harbour's Mouth, & some Batteries on the Island of Amaak.

The Bomb Ship & Schooner Gun Vessels made their escape, the other 17, are sunk, burnt or taken being the whole of the Danish Line to the Southward of the Gamn Islands, after a Battle of about Four Hours.

From the very intricate navigation — the Bellona and Russel unfortunately grounded, but altho' not in the situation assigned them, yet so placed as to be of great service. The Agamemnon could not weather the shoal of the Middle and was obliged to anchor — but not the smallest blame can be attached to Capt. Fancourt; it was an event, to which all the Ships were liable. These accidents prevented the extension of our Line, by the three Ships beforementioned who would I can assert, have silence the Crown Islands, the two outer Ships in the Harbours Mouth & prevented the heavy loss in the Defiance & Monarch, and which unhappily, threw the Gallant & good Capt. Rieu (to whom I had given the command of the Frigates & Sloops named in the margin, to assist in the Attack of the Ships at the Harbour's Mouth) under a very heavy Fire – The consequence, has been the death of Capt. Rieu, & many brave Officers and Men in the Frigates and Sloops. The Bombs were directed & took their station abreast of the Elephant & threw some shells into the Arsenal

Blanche
Alcmene
Dart
Arrow
Cruizer
Harpy
Zephyr
Otter

Capt Rose, who volunteered his services to direct the Gun Brigs did every thing which was possible to get them forward, but the Current was too strong for them to be of Service during the Action; but not the less merit is due to Capt Rose, and I believe all the Officers & Crews of the Gun Brigs for their exertions.

The Boats of those Ships of the Fleet who were not orderd on the attack, afforded us every assistance, & the Officers & Men who were in them merit my warmest approbation.

The Desireé took her station in raking the Southernmost Danish Ship of the Line & performed the greatest service.

The Action began at 5 minutes past ten – the Van, led by Captain George Murray of the Edgar, who set a noble example of intrepidity, which was as well followed up, by every Captain, Officer & Man in the Squadron.

It is my duty to state for you, the high & distinguished merit & gallantry of Rear Adm. Graves.

To Captain Foley, who permitted me the honour of hoisting my Flag in the Elephant, I feel under the greatest obligations, his advice was necessary, on many and important occasions during the Battle.

I beg leave to express how much I feel indebted to every Captain, Officer and Man for their Zeal & distinguished bravery on this occasion.

*Capt Stewart did me the favour to be on board the Elephant, &
himself with every Officer and Soldier under his Orders, shared with
pleasure, the toils & dangers of the day.*

*The loss in such a Battle has not usually been very heavy; among
many other brave officers and men who were killed, I have with honor, to
place the name of Captain Mosse, of the Monarch, who has left a Wife
and six Children to lament his loss; & among the wounded, that of
Captain Sir B. Thompson, of the Bellona.*

I have the honour to be with the greatest respect

Sir

Your most obedient & very humble servant

Nelson thus adds a little more detail where Parker did not. We now know that 17 enemy ships were sunk, burnt or taken in a battle that lasted for four hours, a very long period for ships to be permanently engaged and the direct result of the distance of engagement. Unlike all other battles in this book, Copenhagen was fought at very long range because the British had no idea of the location of the deep water. In fact, they thought that it was towards the Middle Ground shoal when in reality it was in the opposite direction, towards the Danish ships. The duration of the combat, therefore, is intricately linked to the fact that the *Russell* and *Bellona* both grounded on the Middle Ground early in the action. The stranding of those ships also had a significant impact on the course of the battle. Nelson's line was now no longer able to extend the full length of the Danish line as intended. This meant that the British frigate squadron faced the massive Danish defences at the north of the King's Channel alone. This was where Edward Riou's *Amazon* was anchored. Within minutes of the attack beginning, Riou and many of his sailors were dead.

Nelson also mentions the efforts of Captain Rose, who did everything he could to bring the British gun brigs into the action, but was foxed by the currents that ran through the King's Channel like a river. It is an important reminder that, not only did the British have to cope with unknown depths of water, but also with the unknown speed and direction of powerful currents in that shallow water.

Nelson carefully records the names of men who particularly distinguished themselves – Murray, Graves, Foley and Stewart – and, like Parker, he mourns the loss of Captains Mosse and Riou and the wounding of Thompson. His comment that 'not the slightest blame' could be attached to Captain Robert Fancourt of the *Agamemnon* for grounding his ship is slightly disingenuous; in fact Fancourt was strongly criticised by his fellow captains.

There is, unsurprisingly, no mention of the story that Nelson ignored Parker's order to withdraw by raising his telescope to his blind eye, a myth that has been told and embellished by historians for over two centuries. It is, nevertheless, certain that the signal was made and that it was, indeed, a general signal made to the entire fleet. The fact that it was ignored, therefore, is undoubted and it is also clear that, had the signal been obeyed, the crippled British ships would have been shattered in their attempted retreat from the Danish guns. Nonetheless, the telescope story gained traction along with several other anecdotes and unofficial accounts, all of which celebrated Nelson and ridiculed Parker and soon reached the ears of the Admiralty. Parker's reputation was crumbling.

Nor is there any mention in Nelson's letter of how the fighting actually stopped by a classic *ruse de guerre* which is still a talking point. In short, Nelson sent an ultimatum to the Crown Prince in which he threatened to burn the captured Danish prizes with the Danish sailors still inside if they did not immediately surrender. It worked. The damaged British ships, many of which were likely to have grounded in vulnerable positions had they attempted to retreat, were thus saved from further injury, destruction or even capture. In the case of one particular ship, the shattered *Monarch*, one witness was quite clear about the effect of the letter. 'The poor *Monarch* particularly suffered & is nearly a wreck – it became a positive butchery on board her, till the interchange of Ld. Nelson's flag of truce slackened & at length stopped the fire from the enemy on the Crowns.'[10]

Nelson's ultimatum has been interpreted by some as the threat of a war-crime and by others as a magnificently judged bluff to save the English fleet and secure a victory at a crucial moment in the battle. Its omission in this official report is certainly an important addition to that debate. Nelson would have us believe that the battle was won by cannon alone; in fact Copenhagen is unique in this collection of battles because it was won by diplomacy as much as by force. If, indeed, it was a clever bluff then it is surprising that Nelson did not describe it in order to receive the acclaim; perhaps, however, it was considered slightly underhand, a trick that no warrior should celebrate. Maybe Nelson was even a little ashamed of his actions.

There is, however, at least some sense of a 'result' in Nelson's dispatch that is missing from Parker's. Nevertheless, neither dispatch mentions the outcome of the battle in relation to its political, rather than its military, intention, despite Parker's letter being written on April 6, three full days after Nelson dictated his dispatch and four after the battle. The whole purpose of the battle had been to force the Danes to leave the League of Armed Neutrality by threatening to destroy its sailing fleet. However its sailing fleet still lay snug inside Copenhagen harbour and there is no indication of Danish intentions regarding the League. One can imagine the frustration back in London when these dispatches were read. A battle had been fought and the dispatches written and received but one rather crucial question remained to be answered: what on earth was going on?

The answer, when it eventually filtered back to London, did nothing to enhance the Lords' changing impression of Parker. The battle was followed by endless discussion and negotiation, most of which was carried out on behalf of the British by Nelson rather than Parker, something that Parker carefully omitted from his letter.

First, the British insisted that the Danes leave the armed neutrality, something that they could never do for fear of a Russian reprisal that might threaten the very existence of Denmark. The British, on the other hand, were loath to carry out their threat of destroying the Danish fleet or bombarding Copenhagen. No significant threat on their own, the Danes were simply caught between Russia and Britain, and the British knew it. Compromises were suggested and rejected as deadlines were reached and passed. Time slipped away.

Even as Parker wrote his letter describing the battle, he was waiting to hear the result of a final ultimatum sent to the Danes, and even when that deadline passed the British were still willing to negotiate. Two days later and a week after the battle, Nelson went to Copenhagen to hammer out a solution face to face with the Crown Prince of Denmark. During that meeting, one of the Prince's royal aides slipped into the room and whispered into his ear news that instantly changed the shape of the war and rendered the Battle of Copenhagen one of the most pitiful wastes of human life in the history of warfare. The Tsar of Russia was dead.

Paul had been murdered on 23 March, the day that Parker wrote to the Admiralty with his second plan of attack (p. 219). His domestic and foreign policies, and in particular his recent pro-French U-turn, had alienated much of the Russian nobility. He was dragged out from behind a curtain in his bedroom in St Michael's Palace in the centre of St Petersburg, given the option of signing his own abdication and, when he refused, strangled and trampled to death by a group of military officers.

With Tsar Paul dead, the Danes knew that the Armed Neutrality would fall apart. They therefore offered the British a 14-week armistice, by the end of which, they knew, the Tsar's death would be common knowledge and the strategic situation would have changed. They did not, however, share the news and the sudden Danish capitulation came as a welcome surprise. Paul meanwhile was succeeded by his son, Alexander I, who, swiftly and certainly rather suspiciously, turned Russian foreign policy on its heel to adopt a pro-British and anti-French stance. Perhaps the British had a hand in Paul's assassination, perhaps not. Either way, the moment he died, the Battle of Copenhagen became unnecessary.

British casualty list, 2 April 1801

The scale of that waste is made clear by the list of killed and wounded that Parker included in his dispatches. Written so soon after the battle, these figures increased substantially later, but the immediate numbers were still alarming. A total of 875 British sailors had either been killed or wounded on the day of the battle itself, although that figure rose to 1,200 as more than half of those listed here as wounded died of their wounds. Not listed here are the Danish figures which were higher, the lowest estimation being 1,600 to 1,800 and the total of Danish killed, wounded or taken prisoner is estimated to have been around 6,000.

A RETURN OF THE KILLED AND WOUNDED IN THE ACTION WITH THE DANISH LINE OF DEFENCE, ON 2 APRIL 1801				
SHIPS NAMES		No. KILLED	No. WOUNDED	TOTAL
EDGAR	Seamen	24	79	133
	Marines	2	17	
	Soldiers 49th Regt.	3	8	

MONARCH	Seamen	35	101	210
	Marines	12	34	
	Soldiers 49th Regt.	8	20	
DEFIANCE	Seamen	17	35	59
	Marines	3	5	
	Soldiers 49th Regt.	2	7	
BELLONA	Seamen	9	48	74
	Marines	2	10	
	Soldiers 49th Regt.	0	5	
ISIS	Seamen	22	69	112
	Marines	4	13	
	Soldiers 49th Regt.	2	2	
AMAZON	Seamen	10	16	32
	Marines	1	5	
GLATTON	– – –	17	34	51
DESIREÉ	– – –	0	3	3
BLANCHE	Seamen	6	7	16
	Marines	1	2	
POLYPHEMUS	Seamen	4	20	29
	Marines	1	4	
ELEPHANT	Seamen	4	8	19
	Marines	3	1	
	Rifle Corps	1	2	
ALCMENE	Seamen	5	12	19
	Marines	0	2	
DART	– – –	2	1	3
GANGES	– – –	5	1 missg	6
RUSSEL	Seamen	0	5	6
	Marines	0	1	
ARDENT	– – –	29	64	93
TOTAL KILLED & WOUNDED				875

There is some notable variation among the British figures. The highest casualty figures of 210, well over a third of the crew,[11] come from the *Monarch*, the 74-gunner that anchored in relative isolation opposite two very powerful Danish batteries, the *Holsteen* and *Sjælland*. Her crew also suffered when one of her guns burst. In the heat of the action one of her midshipmen, the 17-year-old William Millard, had to run the entire length of the ship to collect quills to prime the guns. He found not a single man standing on the main deck from the mainmast forward. A Danish shot blew both feet off one of his friends as he stood on the forecastle. When he returned to the quarterdeck not a man was alive. One sailor who had lost a leg managed to crawl to the cockpit to find the surgeon, but bled to death where he lay.

The *Edgar* and *Isis* also have very high figures, the *Edgar* because she was the first British ship to enter the King's Channel and therefore the first to receive much of the Danish fire. Her log records that her rigging was absolutely devastated by the Danish shot and she was lucky to get clear of Copenhagen in the battle's aftermath.

The *Isis* was the fourth into the Deep, after the *Ardent* and *Glatton*, though she ended up positioning herself just to the rear of the *Edgar* at the southern end of the Danish defences, just where the floating batteries were particularly powerful and supported by two shore-batteries under the command of Lieutenant Stricker, son of the commander of the Kronborg fortress. She was actually supposed to be behind Nelson's *Elephant*, which temporarily grounded as it entered the Channel. Captain Walker took the *Isis* past the stranded *Elephant* to get at the enemy and ended up engaging both his own allotted enemy and Nelson's. When the *Elephant* freed herself and sailed past the *Isis*, now heavily engaged, Nelson bellowed, 'Well done, brave Walker! Go on as you have begun; nothing can be better.'[12] A Fourth Rate 50-gun ship, her complement was only 350, so a tally of 112 dead and wounded was large indeed and certainly worsened by the fact that, as with the *Monarch*, one of her cannon burst. The *Bellona* also suffered from two burst cannon. It is likely that this exceptionally high instance of British guns bursting was caused by the sailors using double-charges to cope with the unusually extreme range of the combat.

Two other points are worth emphasising. Parker's flagship *London* is not listed here because she remained so distant from the action that she received no casualties; and no British ships were captured or destroyed. Yes, this was a bloody action, but it was also another display of crushing dominance.

This list also gives us a research window into the men who fought at Copenhagen, because we can find out, through the ships' musters, who was aboard. As at the Battle of Camperdown (p. 136), some of those men are worth considering in some depth.

William Bligh of *Bounty* fame, and now a recent veteran of Camperdown, was back again, this time as captain of the 56-gun *Glatton*, an experimental ship that was equipped solely with carronades. This had become possible because the great Carron Company of Scotland had recently succeeded in founding 68-pounder carronades. The *Glatton* mounted 28 68-pounders on her lower deck and 28 48-pounders on her upper deck, a mighty armament that would have been devastating at close range, that is closer than 600 yards.

She poured her fire into Olfert Fischer's flagship *Dannebrog* with such efficiency that Fischer was forced to shift his flag. The *Dannebrog* suffered some of the highest casualty figures of both fleets, with a little less than a third of her complement dead or injured. One of those injured was Commander Braun, whose right hand was blown off. Two hours after her flag was hauled down, she exploded, killing 250 men. At one stage Bligh protected Nelson's *Elephant* from a fierce and direct attack by placing the *Glatton* directly in the line of fire. After the engagement Nelson personally thanked Bligh for his conduct. His action and the relatively high casualty figures of the *Glatton* thus also account for the unusually low casualty figures of the *Elephant*.

The *Glatton* demonstrated her worth in combat but she was also symptomatic of a policy with which Nelson was decidedly unimpressed. In comparison with the slick and uniform body of ships he had commanded at the Nile (p. 178), the fleet which he took into the narrow waters off Copenhagen was both mismatched and awkward. The list of ships above consists of seven 74-gunners, two 64-gunners, a 50-gunner, a 56-gun converted merchantman, an experimental sloop and four frigates, one of which was French-built. In particular, the *Glatton*, the 56-gun converted merchantman, was found to be cumbersome and unhandy, a burden in such a tight navigation. Indeed, such ships could not only put themselves in danger but others too. The fact that she fought well must not disguise the harm she could have caused to the British operation.

One of the men aboard the flagship *London* who assisted Nelson with the post-battle negotiation and diplomacy was the Reverend John Scott, a naval chaplain and talented linguist. Nelson and Scott had crossed paths in the Mediterranean, where the latter had demonstrated his political worth through his mastery of Italian, French and Spanish. He also spoke German, was increasingly competent in Danish and had begun to learn Russian. Nelson and Scott became fast friends and Nelson personally requested his presence in 1805, officially as a chaplain but unofficially as a secretary and interpreter. Scott thus received Nelson's last wishes at Trafalgar when the Admiral lay on his deathbed, his life blood seeping through the great ship's planks.

There were also several inventors in the British fleet. Although it is not clear upon which ship he served, one of the British assistant surgeons was none other than William Clanny. Shortly after his return from Copenhagen, Clanny left the navy and went on to become famous for inventing the first safety light for miners, a crucial development that reduced the danger of explosion in collieries caused by the build-up of gas from leaking seams. James Spratt, a midshipman on the *Bellona*, went on to fight at Trafalgar where he led a boarding party onto the French *Aigle*, swimming[13] to her and climbing up the rudder chains. In the subsequent hand-to hand combat Spratt fought off numerous Frenchmen and threw one bodily from the poop to the quarterdeck. The ship was taken, but not before Spratt was shot in the leg. He refused to have the leg amputated but was crippled for life and ended up serving at the signal station in Teignmouth, Devon. There he invented the 'homograph', a system of signalling with arms, hat, oar, sword or handkerchief which formed the basis of semaphore. Another notable inventor was Captain Thomas Bertie of the *Ardent*. Bertie was an old service friend of both Nelson and Troubridge who, in 1778, had invented the lifebuoy. Bertie's *Ardent*, a relatively small ship, suffered a particularly high proportion of casualties.

George Smith, then a midshipman on the 74-gun *Agamemnon*, was not an inventor but his achievement was no less significant. He too left the navy shortly after Copenhagen to become a radical evangelical missionary and the author of more than 80 books. The plight of sailors was always close to his heart and he committed himself to raising money and awareness to ease what he described as the 'Sodom and Gomorrah of Sailors' and to found a 'marine Jerusalem'. He established endless churches and funds for crippled or destitute sailors and their dependants, as well as others caught in the economic web of dock life and in 1830 established the Maritime Penitent Young Women's Refuge for the rehabilitation of dockland prostitutes. His influence was such that it was felt worldwide and he rightly enjoys a reputation as the initiator of the worldwide movement of seafarers' missions. Today the international Mission to Seafarers offers comfort and counsel to those who pursue the peculiar, lonely and dangerous life of the seaman. Smith died in grinding poverty but 2,000 mourners, many of them sailors and their dependants, attended his funeral.

John Ward was another extraordinary man who fought at Copenhagen and was later to make a significant impact on the religious world. In 1801 he was a shipwright on the *Blanche* but left the service soon after the battle. His life then changed dramatically after a series of visions and dreams convinced him that he was none other than Jesus Christ, his conviction being confirmed by the fact that he was born on 25 December and that his mother was called Mary. He soon began to proclaim himself as the Messiah and renamed himself Shiloh. He was put in the Newington workhouse and branded as mad but promptly escaped. His followers, known as the Shilohites, grew rapidly when he took to the streets proclaiming that the Bible was a fiction, that prayer was useless, that clergymen were liars and that God did not care whether men were good or evil. Ward's writings, published in no less than 17 volumes at the turn of the 20th century, make quite extraordinary reading.[14]

Last but by no means least was John Franklin, then a 15-year-old midshipman aboard the frigate *Polyphemus*. After Copenhagen, Franklin joined Matthew Flinders'* *Investigator*, which circumnavigated Australia before being abandoned and replaced by the *Porpoise*, which duly sank, leaving the crew on a sandbank for six weeks. Franklin then fought on the *Bellerophon* at Trafalgar and after the war began a career exploring the Arctic in which he greatly expanded our knowledge of the region's geography. He famously never returned from his final voyage of 1845–6 in search of the Northwest Passage in which every member of the expedition died.

---

* Flinders himself was a veteran of naval battle. He was a Midshipman on the *Bellerophon* at The Glorious First of June and left behind a series of magnificent tactical diagrams. They are published in S. Willis, *The Glorious First of June: Fleet Battle in the Reign of Terror* (London: 2011).

There is no doubt that the Battle of Copenhagen was one of the most dangerous attacks ever mounted at sea. There was an exceptionally high risk of failure. The highly experienced Admiral Thomas Graves, who had fought in both the Seven Years War and the War of American Independence as well as in the French Revolutionary War, noted, 'Considering the disadvantages of the navigation, the approach to the enemy, their vast number of guns and mortars on both land and sea, I do not think there ever was a bolder attack.'[15] His views were shared by many. Thomas Hardy, close friend of Nelson and veteran of the Battle of the Nile, declared it 'the most daring attack that has been attempted this war',[16] and William Stewart, a lieutenant-colonel of marines serving with Nelson, declared the battle 'unparalleled in history, & for enterprise & difficulties as well as the length of the contest (for we were five hours in one incessant roar of cannon) … '[17]

However, the result of the battle had little impact on the shape of the war because the Tsar was already dead. The issues that had put Britain and Denmark on a collision cause still existed but the forces that had made conflict unavoidable had vanished. The new Tsar was conspicuously pro-British but the question of neutral rights remained and so did the powerful Danish and Russian navies. Both these navies and neutral trade would become significant problems six years later when Napoleon's extraordinary continental success allowed him to control Baltic politics.

Nor did the victory have any material benefit. With the exception of the *Holstein*, all of the prizes, 10 in number, were burned, being too elderly or too badly damaged to be of any use in British service. The Battle of Copenhagen therefore carried little weight of any kind. None of Nelson's captains received gold medals for the action in spite of his fevered pestering of anyone with influence over such matters.

For Parker, this chapter ends where it began. With the Admiralty now in possession of these dispatches to be read alongside the unofficial reports and rumour that further condemned his indecision and weak command, he was immediately withdrawn from the Baltic. He headed back to Suffolk and in December purchased Benhall Lodge, where he settled with his young wife, his reputation in tatters and his active service life over. He did not survive retirement long and was dead within six years.

Nelson, much to his horror, was given Parker's command and sent further into the Baltic. His service at Copenhagen had left him physically weak and he was struck down by a fever, possibly a recurrence of the malaria he had contracted on his early Caribbean service. He wrote to a friend, 'A Command never was, I believe, more unwelcomely received by any person than by myself.'[18] It soon became clear, however, that the Russians would not pose a threat and that the Swedes and Danes were too preoccupied with each other to cause any trouble. The British public, meanwhile, were fed up with seven years of war which had not brought about a French defeat in spite of the remarkable series of five naval victories. Pitt had imposed a painful income tax to pay for the war, which had also caused fierce inflation. Henry Addington, the new prime minister, was anxious to explore peace.

Napoleon was willing to enter into discussions but constantly shifted his position. After six months of peace on land and sea an agreement was eventually reached and on 25 March 1802 the Peace of Amiens was signed. A year after the Battle of Copenhagen, therefore, Europe was nominally no longer at war. In reality, however, Napoleon's motivations for peace were deeply suspect and both sides failed to evacuate territories as required by the treaty. When Napoleon sent soldiers into Switzerland and prepared a vast fleet to retake Haiti from rebel slaves, it became clear that his ambitious mind was still active and his appetite for conquest still unsatisfied. The great wars between Britain and France passed into yet another phase and one that would lead to the most famous naval battle in history.

6

Trafalgar
Trafalgar

21 October 1805

'As I trust you are fully aware of the great importance of those dispatches being forwarded as soon as is possible I rely on your using every exertion, that a moment's time may not be lost in their delivery'

Vice-Admiral C. Collingwood to Lieutenant J. Lapenotiere, 26 October 1805

AT A GLANCE

DATE:
21 October 1805

NAVIES INVOLVED:
British, French and Spanish

COMMANDING OFFICERS:
Rear-Admiral H. Nelson/Vice-Admiral C. Collingwood; Admiral
P. Villeneuve/Admiral F.C. Gravina

FLEET SIZES:
British, 27 ships of the line; Allies, 33 ships of the line

TIME OF DAY:
12.00 – 16.30

LOCATION:
Off Cape Trafalgar, Spain. 36°17´34.76˝N, 6°15´19.22˝E

WEATHER:
Light west north-westerly winds, heavy swell

RESULT:
21 Allied ships captured, one destroyed

CASUALTIES:
British, 1,690; French 4,530; Spanish 2,408

BRITISH COURT MARTIALS:
None. But there could have been several

DISPATCHES CARRIED HOME BY:
Lieutenant John Lapenotiere

The Relics

More relics survive from Trafalgar than from any other naval battle of the age of sail. Such a crushing victory, achieved at the loss of such a cherished naval officer, created a unique atmosphere in the battle's aftermath. The participants realised that they had been part of something special. Although we are missing so many of the mundane, everyday objects of naval life from that day in October 1805, countless objects with special significance were squirrelled and swiped, coveted and cherished, hidden and stored. The very fabric of the ships was turned into mementos, from writing desks to paper weights, from picture frames to chairs. Meanwhile, an endless array of manufactured souvenirs including cups, glasses, plates, soup tureens and clocks was produced to satisfy the enduring interest in the battle and its lessons for history.

The bicentenary of Trafalgar in 2005 demonstrated with unmistakable force the place of the battle in the cultural identities of the main participant nations and in the global perception of naval history. That interest has in turn been reflected in the careful collection, cataloguing and preservation of the relics. While some items, such as the Union Flag of the *Spartiate*, are in the hands of private collectors, and kept in unknown environmental conditions and unknown locations, hundreds of other relics are maintained by professional curators in national institutions where their continued existence is more likely to be guaranteed further into the future. When faced with the task of selecting a favourite Trafalgar relic, therefore, we are in the curious position of having to choose from an embarrassment of riches.

Something large? Well, there is nothing bigger or more impressive than HMS *Victory* herself, now restored immaculately to her 1805 appearance. She watches the world watching her from a Portsmouth dry dock where, in 1941, she was narrowly missed by a Luftwaffe bomb. To this day she remains in commission as the flagship of the Second Sea Lord. An astute observer would notice that the one thing that differs from her operational appearance is a lack of canvas on her yards. However, preserved and displayed in a building nearby is the very topsail that hung from her foretopsail yard at Trafalgar. Large? You have to see it to believe it. It is 54 feet deep, measures 84 feet at its base and covers an area of 3,618 square feet. That is a third larger than a doubles tennis court; a little more than two volleyball courts; five and a half cricket pitches; or, in nautical terms, roughly the same size as the *entire* sail area of an average Elizabethan warship.

Something atmospheric? Let's stay with *that* topsail. HMS *Victory* is impressive for her size and scale but she is too highly polished to bring one to the heart of battle. Her topsail, however, is extraordinarily powerful for its sense of history. The darkened room in which it is displayed has a unique atmosphere, the sail itself a power of its own, infused with a creeping sense of dread. The shot holes and tears caused by French and Spanish cannon and muskets are quite shocking. Nelson's uniform, at the National Maritime Museum in Greenwich, shares many of these characteristics: in the left shoulder of his coat, just below the epaulette, we see the hole made by the bullet that killed him; on his stockings we see the blood of his dead secretary that had collected in a pool by Nelson's feet; up the front of his trousers we see a jagged tear where they were cut from the paralysed legs of the dying admiral.

A weapon perhaps? A cannon-ball was removed from the hull of HMS *Victory* and is preserved in Greenwich along with numerous swords and pistols. The French officers' swords are particularly attractive with their distinctive curved shape.

Something that makes a noise to evoke the sound of Trafalgar? Then the boatswain's call from the 100-gun *Britannia* is for you, speaking the language of shrills and peeps that moved sailors hither and thither as surely as a bellowed command.

Or something a little creepy? Nelson's pigtail, cut shortly after he died, still survives (fig. 16) and so too does a miniature coffin, made from the wood of his own coffin. While for those who like a mystery or appreciate the humour in desperate attempts to associate something, *anything,* with the battle, there is a shoe buckle, preserved in a wooden box in Greenwich which, in the official words of the Maritime Museum, 'might' have come from Nelson's cabin. But then again, of course, it might not.

So what on earth happened off Cape Trafalgar that a British national institution is prepared to spend public money on the time and space to curate a shoe buckle that might, or might not, have been in Nelson's cabin, and why is a warship launched in 1765 still in commission in the Royal Navy? Anyone would think we were mad.

The Mismatch

One of the first things to appreciate about Trafalgar is the length of time that *appears* to have passed since the previous major engagement. In this collection of dispatches, the preceding battle is the Battle of Copenhagen, fought on 2 April 1801, four years, six months and 19 days before Trafalgar. Copenhagen, however, was fought against the Danes, so it would seem the last time that the British had fought the French was at the Nile on 1 August 1798. That was seven years, two months and 20 days before Trafalgar, easily long enough for Nelson to have put on a bit of weight which is noticeable in the changed cut of his surviving uniforms. Moreover, the last time that the British had fought the Spanish, at the Battle of St Vincent on Valentine's Day 1797, was even more distant at eight years, eight months and a week earlier.

This chronology is misleading, however. There were interim engagements, some of them British victories, which are not included in this magnificent collection of dispatches: an engagement with the French at Algeciras on 6 July 1801; one with the French and Spanish in the Gut of Gibraltar on 12 July 1801; and a further engagement with the French and Spanish off Ferrol on 22 July 1805. Nor were these mere minor skirmishes; the engagement in the Gut of Gibraltar in 1801 led to the destruction of two huge enemy First Rates and the capture of a further 74-gunner.[*] Yet the scale of the British victories in the preceding decade ensured that these relatively minor battles would not be included in this collection.

Nonetheless, a significant period of time had passed since the last great, decisive battle between the British, the French and the Spanish, and it had been more than enough time both for the French and the Spanish to rebuild their fleets and for the British to lose their way in this sustained maritime marathon.

What, then, were the conditions of the combatants in the autumn of 1805? It is in the British fleet that the change is most surprising. Pitt's extraordinarily long term of office ended just before the Battle of Copenhagen. Addington, his successor, representing the vociferous voters who were so fed up with the war,

---

[*] The Spanish *Real Carlos* (112) and the *San Hermenegildo* (112) and the French *Saint Antoine* (74).

began to make diplomatic moves towards peace even as Hyde Parker and his fleet set sail on their aggressive mission to the Baltic. Another of Addington's early decisions had been to replace Lord Spencer with St Vincent – the former John Jervis, admiral at the Battle of Cape St Vincent – as First Lord of the Admiralty. St Vincent had an impressive fighting record but his perception of right and wrong, of mutiny and obedience and of efficiency and corruption was ill-suited to the political subtleties demanded of the First Lord.

One of the tasks that St Vincent ploughed into was reform of the Royal Dockyards. For generations, the dockyards had produced impressive results, despite the ill-regulated and corrupt way in which they were run. St Vincent, however, had had enough. He wanted greater efficiency and he wanted to root out corruption. Fine ideals for an administrator though these may have been, St Vincent's approach, which brought 'sea' discipline to what he saw as the undisciplined hoards of idle dockies, was deeply resented and very harmful to the navy. Within two years he had reduced the yards' workforce by a fifth and severely damaged their efficiency. The cessation of hostilities following the Treaty of Amiens also gave the politicians the opportunity to save money and, in 1803, they cut the navy's budget by 27 per cent. Even in 1804, when it was becoming clear that Napoleon's peace overtures were fraudulent, naval funding was still significantly lower than it had been in 1802. This combination of St Vincent's witch-hunt for corruption and economic belt-tightening meant that, when war broke out again in May 1803, many British ships were old and weak.

Napoleon, however, was as dangerous as ever. Thousands of French troops now lined the cliffs of northern France whilst shipwrights laboured on a vast flotilla of landing craft. The paralysing fear of invasion, which had disappeared after the Battle of Camperdown in 1797, returned with a vengeance. The British were desperate to solve the problem posed by their crumbling fleet. Their saviour was Gabriel Snodgrass, who designed a way of strengthening elderly and weak ships with a system of diagonal bracing. The British fleet of ghost ships was, temporarily at least, resurrected. In the months before Trafalgar, 22 line-of-battle ships and 11 frigates were braced and given additional three-inch planking to increase their sheer strength. It was a timely intervention because, in 1803, Napoleon forced the Spanish into another alliance and, in December 1804, they declared war on Britain. The Royal Navy now had to contend with French fleets from Brest, Rochefort, L'Orient and Toulon, together with Spanish fleets from Cadiz, El Ferrol, Cartagena and Havana. Combined, the French and Spanish far outnumbered the British.

Much had changed in the years since the first naval battle of the Revolutionary Wars but 1805 shared a number of important characteristics with 1794. Then, Robespierre had ruled France with absolute authority; a decade later Napoleon had crowned himself Emperor. Both men had believed that the future of France, and the security of their own political position, lay in the prosecution of an aggressive foreign policy. Unfortunately for Napoleon, however, neither the French nor the Spanish had solved any of the significant organisational problems that continued to plague their navies.

The most basic challenge was that neither country was able to raise the same amount of money, or honour the same level of debt, as the British, whose economy was strongly supported by the growing empire which Britain had secured through its maritime trade. There were also further problems of naval logistics. British dockyards and dockyard technology, despite the problems just recounted, were far superior to those of the Spanish and French. Put simply, the British could cope with the increasing demands of naval warfare by producing excellent ships at a faster rate than anyone else and they could man them with sufficient experienced sailors to operate them effectively. The French could produce ships quickly, but they were inferior to the British, weak and with thin hulls. The Spanish had magnificent ships but they still did not have sufficient experienced sailors to crew them. Their problems had been exacerbated by the losses sustained at the Battle of St Vincent so that, when they fought at Trafalgar, almost half of their men were not seamen. The French also suffered from a lack of experienced fighting sailors, an inherent problem not helped by their significant losses at The Glorious First of June and the Nile. Making matters worse for both the French and the Spanish, in 1805 both fleets were suffering from viral sickness and scurvy and hence from plummeting morale.

The British crews, in contrast, were adequate, experienced, well-trained and healthy. The British fleets had blockaded their enemies' ports, denying them access to the fresh food that could make them strong whilst exploiting their own control of the sea lanes to keep the British fleet well stocked. The British sailors also had their confidence bolstered by an uninterrupted series of five significant naval victories. Any future contest between the two fleets would be unequal and everybody knew it. To make matters worse for the French and Spanish, Horatio Nelson, the man who disdained their seamanship and fighting skill more than any other, was in command of the fleet sent to destroy them.

The Cripple's Friend

The Trafalgar dispatches are unique in that none of the letters is written by the fleet's commander-in-chief. When considering command of the British fleet, we must therefore consider both Nelson and his second-in-command, Collingwood.

Nelson's career had been resurrected in the aftermath of Copenhagen, though his superiors remained anxious to keep him at sea and away from personal and political intrigue. On his return from the Baltic, he was immediately given command of the anti-invasion forces in the Channel and he used the opportunity to launch an attack on the fleet of landing craft moored at Boulogne. There was little glamour in the operation, however, and it was rendered insignificant by the subsequent Peace of Amiens.

Nelson spent the following weeks of peace settling into his new home, Merton Place in Surrey. During this time Emma Hamilton turned the house into a shrine to her lover, 'cramming Nelson with trowelfuls of flattery, which he goes on taking as quietly as a child does pap'.[1] Portraits, battle scenes and mementos littered the house, among them, of course, the lightning conductor from *L'Orient*, the French flagship destroyed at the Nile (p. 159). Yet, although this period of home life and his association with Emma did nothing to enhance Nelson's personal reputation, his professional stature remained unrivalled. Moreover his fame was beginning to reach extraordinary levels, fuelled by the combination of his physical frailty and the strength of his character. He had survived the Battle of Copenhagen unscathed but when he arrived to take command of the fleet off Cadiz on 28 September 1805, he was, in modern terms, disabled. Indeed, it has been calculated that he would have received a total degree of disablement at 140 per cent if assessed for a war pension today. We know that his mind had wandered to his physical state during the Peace, because he wrote a few lines that encapsulate perfectly his curious mixture of weakness, strength, sacrifice, self-absorption, understatement and indifference. He listed his wounds in the third person, as if describing somebody else, but was careful to include his title:

WOUNDS RECEIVED BY LORD NELSON

His Eye in Corsica

His Belly off Cape St Vincent

His Arm at Teneriffe

His Head in Egypt

He then added, ruefully, 'Tolerable for one war'.[2]

One man who knew the peculiarities of Nelson's character as well as anyone was Cuthbert Collingwood. The son of a Northumbrian merchant, Collingwood joined the navy at the tender age of 11. By 1805, he had known Nelson for 32 years and they had become fast friends. For all of their personal closeness, however, their command styles were notably different. Collingwood was easy on his men but cold with them too, a direct contrast with Nelson's warmth and his encouragement of friendship among his officers. Just a few weeks before Trafalgar, Nelson encouraged his squadron to knit together through constant contact and interplay. Collingwood, meanwhile, ' … never invite[d] any one to his table, nor will he allow us to visit each other'.[3] It is an important point which reminds us that command style was never taught or in any way regulated. Where Nelson could adopt one style, which was clearly beneficial to fleet efficiency, an admiral such as Collingwood, a close friend of Nelson who had witnessed his success, could adopt a very different approach. It is one of the main reasons why British naval command competence did not improve steadily over time; lessons were not learnt.

In one important respect, however, Collingwood had learnt from his past and he was determined not to repeat the mistake made by Howe at The Glorious First of June in 1794. Then, Collingwood, as flag captain of the *Barfleur*, had assumed command early in the battle when his commanding officer, Rear-Admiral George Bowyer, was wounded. When other officers enjoyed Howe's official thanks in the subsequent dispatch, and eventually received gold medals, Collingwood was ignored (pp. 51–2). He found the entire episode insulting and distressing and it made him particularly sensitive to his own subordinates' expectations. Collingwood was thus keenly aware of the need to acknowledge their contributions and that sensitivity had a significant impact on how the news of Trafalgar was received both by the contemporary public and by subsequent generations of historians.

The Desperado

By October 1805, Napoleon was exasperated with his navy and, in particular, with the commander of the Toulon fleet, the man who had had the good fortune to escape the carnage of the Battle of the Nile (p. 196) and who rejoiced in the multi-barrelled name of Vice-Admiral Pierre-Charles-Jean-Baptiste-Silvestre de Villeneuve. Through no fault of his own, Villeneuve had failed to realise Napoleon's ambition of invading England. Indeed he had failed to provide the necessary maritime foundations for any of Napoleon's eight invasion plans, none of which had been based on any realistic maritime objectives. Napoleon had by now cast his invasion plans aside. The Grand Armée had struck camp, abandoning the cliffs of the Pas-de-Calais, and had marched on Austria. A dispirited and hungry French fleet, which had just been chased halfway round the world by Nelson, lay in Cadiz alongside a sickly Spanish fleet, while Collingwood cruised off shore keeping watch. As soon as the location of the combined fleet was discovered, Nelson was summoned from Merton and sailed to join Collingwood and assume command.

Napoleon, meanwhile, had issued orders for the Allied fleet to transport troops to the Mediterranean to assist in his defence of Naples against an Anglo-Russian expedition. At the same time he sent Vice-Admiral François Rosily to replace Villeneuve. News of Rosily's imminent arrival reached Cadiz just as Rosily himself reached Madrid; deducing Napoleon's intention, Villeneuve was hurt, and the pride of this honourable officer had now been bruised once too often.

As soon as he arrived, Nelson took his fleet well out of sight of Cadiz. This was no attempt to hide; a fleet of 27 ships was far too large to be missed by allied scouts or by the net of fishing vessels and merchant ships that continually poured in and out of Cadiz harbour. With orders to take the fleet to Naples and also to stand himself down, Villeneuve sat in Cadiz, knowing full well that Nelson and his powerful fleet was waiting over the horizon. It was a golden opportunity to defy Napoleon's perception of him and his navy. This was an age in which personal reputation and honour moved men as surely as orders. In spite of a vote in a council of war held on 8 October that he should stay in Cadiz and meekly hand over his command, Villeneuve gave the order to raise anchor.[4] Thousands of people crowded the magnificent stone walls of Cadiz to watch the fleet, 33 strong, sail out to battle. And they did so in absolute silence.

In some ways Nelson was prepared for battle and in others he was not. His tactics, at least, were settled. He wanted to cut the enemy fleet in the centre and rear, and then overpower those sections before the van could come to their aid. In a further attempt to keep the enemy van out of the picture, his own division would feint towards it on the approach to lure it away from where the strike would actually fall. This plan required his ships to bear down at right angles to the enemy, exposing their vulnerable bows to enemy fire. This part of the plan, therefore, had to be executed as quickly as possible, far more so than was usual. It would also be led by the largest ships of the fleet, the flagships, whose bulk could better withstand the enemy shot. Again this was unusual; the flagships usually nestled in the centre of their divisions. Once the fighting had started, Nelson then required his captains to engage the enemy closely and to keep them there until they were beaten.

The problem he faced, however, was how to ensure that his captains understood his ideas. His fleet at Trafalgar was a motley collection of men and ships, hastily gathered from wherever they could be found; this was no 'Band of Brothers' like that which had fought at the Nile. Nelson had never even met some of his captains and 11 of the 27 had never served with him before. Indeed six of the British captains had never been in battle before, let alone in battle under Nelson's command. Moreover five of the crews had been together for less than six months and nine of the captains had only been in charge of their ships for a similar period.

In the days before the battle, therefore, Nelson held regular dinners and conversations aboard his flagship, to get to know his fellow officers and to instil in them, in very general terms, what he expected of them in the coming engagement. He had thought that three months was sufficient for such a task but now he had a matter of days. For that reason, he focused on simple, practical methods to increase the chances of cohesion and unity. He ordered the crews of all British ships to paint their mast-hoops yellow, to contrast with the black mast-hoops of the enemy fleet, and he declared, in that famous phrase, that 'No captain can do very wrong if he places his Ship alongside that of an Enemy'.[5] He later reinforced this simple message with a verbal instruction via one of his frigates: 'If, by the mode of attack prescribed, they found it impracticable to get into Action immediately, they might adopt whatever they thought best, provided it led them quickly and closely alongside an Enemy.'[6] Nelson's ideal tactics may have been innovative and subtly nuanced, therefore, but in the hours before battle he kept them as simple as possible. His final signal, 'England expects that every man will do his duty', was part of that process of simplification and encouragement.

As the masts of the Allied fleet darkened the horizon, Nelson's thoughts turned inward and then to home. He wrote a prayer and carefully amended his will.

The Dispatches

The dispatches describing the subsequent events are unique for several reasons. First and most obviously, the main dispatch is written by Collingwood, the second-in-command. Second, they include descriptions of important events after the main battle. Third, they include the dispatch sent from another British fleet commander, recounting another battle. We also have the letter written from Collingwood to Lieutenant John Lapenotiere,[7] the officer given the honour of taking the dispatches back to London. This is the only such letter to the bearer of dispatches included in this collection and it gives us a valuable glimpse into the urgent and exciting moment that news of the victory left the fleet. The letters are addressed to William Marsden, a renowned intellectual who had already been Second Secretary of the Admiralty for a decade.[8]

Vice-Admiral C. Collingwood to W. Marsden, 22 October 1805

Collingwood's missive is a masterpiece. He solved the problem of how to begin such a problematic dispatch with a phrase that echoes through the centuries: 'The ever to be lamented death of Vice Admiral Lord Viscount Nelson ... '

For Collingwood and the thousands who read this letter when it was swiftly published, the headline of the battle was not the defeat of the Allies but the death of Nelson. It is an impressive piece of writing for someone whom we know

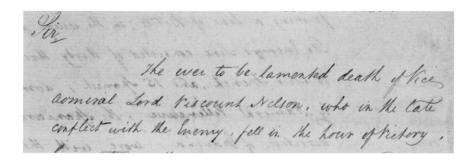

Sir,

The ever to be lamented death of Vice admiral Lord Viscount Nelson, who in the late conflict with the Enemy, fell in the hour of Victory.

to have been distracted and lost for many hours after the battle. Collingwood himself later described how he was in a 'forlorn state; my servants are killed … and Clavell [Collingwood's first lieutenant, a long-term, trusted friend and colleague] is wounded.'[9] Others described how he stood alone on the quarterdeck for hours, tugging at his clothing, nibbling at the occasional apple or biscuit and occasionally sipping wine. This was a man in shock.

The subsequent letter describes some important aspects of Trafalgar but ignores just as many others. We hear of the attack, which was not executed, as Collingwood is at pains to add, 'in the usual manner'. The British sailed quickly at right angles to the enemy in two lines, formed to save time in order of sailing rather than in order of battle, and then cut them at two points, in the centre and towards the rear.

The mode of attack was innovative but we know that Villeneuve had fully expected something of the sort. Before the battle he wrote to his captains 'the enemy will not confine himself to forming on a line of battle with our own and engaging us in an artillery duel, in which success is frequently with the more skilful but always with the more fortunate; he will endeavour to envelop our rear, to break through our line and to direct his ships in groups upon such of ours as he shall have cut off, so as to surround them and defeat them.'[10]

To counter this, the enemy *should* have met the British in a 'close and correct line' which is exactly how Collingwood describes the enemy appearance. However, this description is challenged by other accounts which emphasise the poor structure and dislocation of the enemy line, the result of an ill-judged and ill-executed manoeuvre that was attempted as the British bore down.[11]

Collingwood provides little detail of the actual engagement apart from making it clear that, as Nelson desired, the enemy van was severed from the main body in an attack that was 'irresistible'. It is an intriguing choice of word because it was

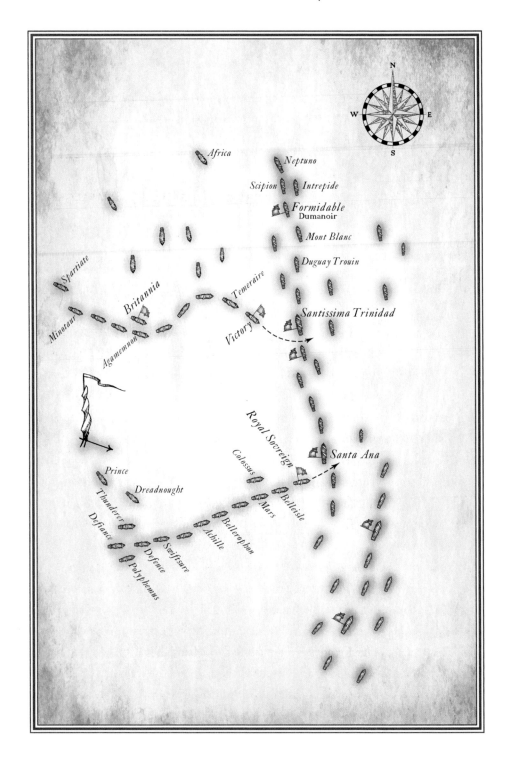

also used by Nelson in his Nile dispatch. This is Collingwood mimicking Nelson, a conscious nod to his lost friend; he is reporting Nelson's last victory in a way that Nelson would appreciate. And then, 566 words into the dispatch, Collingwood finally gets to the point: the British have won a 'complete, and glorious victory'.

The letter is written aboard the frigate *Euryalus* because Collingwood's flagship *Royal Sovereign* had suffered so much in the battle.

Euryalus, off Cape Trafalgar
22 October 1805.

The ever to be lamented death of Vice Admiral Lord Viscount Nelson, who in the late conflict with the Enemy, fell in the hour of victory, leaves to me the duty of informing my Lords Commissioners of the Admiralty, that on the 19th Instant, it was communicated to the Commander in chief from the Ships watching the motions of the Enemy in Cadiz, that the combined Fleet had put to sea—; as they sailed with Light Winds Westerly, his Lordship concluded their destination was the Mediterranean, and immediately made all sail for the Streights' Entrance with the British Squadron consisting of Twenty seven Ships, three of them sixty fours, where his Lordship was informed by Captain Blackwood (whose vigilance in watching, and giving notice of the Enemy's movements has been highly meritorious) that they had not yet passed the Streights.

On Monday the 21st Instant, at day-light, when Cape Trafalgar bore EbS. about 7 leagues, the Enemy was discovered, six, or seven miles to the Eastward, the Wind about West, and very light, the Commander in Chief immediately made the Signal for the Fleet to bear up in two Columns, as they are formed in order of sailing; a mode of attack his Lordship had previously directed, to avoid the inconvenience, and delay, in forming a Line of Battle, in the usual manner; The Enemy's Line consisted of thirty three ships (of which 18 were French, and 15 Spanish) commanded in Chief by Admiral Villeneuve, the Spaniards under the direction of Gravina, wore, with their heads to the Northward, and formed their Line of Battle with great closeness, and correctness; — but, as the mode of attack was unusual, so the structure of their Line was new, — it formed a Crescent, convexing to Leeward, so that in leading down to their Centre, I had both their Van, and Rear, abaft the beam, before the fire opened, every alternative Ship was about a cable's length to windward of her second a-head, and a-stern, forming a kind of double line and appeared when on their beam to leave a very little interval between them, and this without crowding their Ships. Adm. Villeneuve was in the Bucentaire, in the centre and the Prince of Asturias, bore Gravinia's Flag in the Rear. — but the French, and Spanish Ships were mixed without any apparent regard to order of national squadron.

As the mode of our attack had been previously determined on, and communicated to the Flag Officers and Captains, few Signals were necessary, and none were made, except to direct close order, as the Lines bore down.

The Commander in Chief in the Victory lead the Weather Column, and the Royal Sovereign, which bore my Flag, in the lee.

The action began at 12 O'Clock, by the Leading Ships of the Columns breaking through the Enemy's Line, the Commander in Chief about the 10th Ship from the Van the Second in Command, about the 12th from the Rear, leaving the Van of the Enemy unoccupied, — the succeeding Ships breaking through in all parts, astern of their Leaders, and engaging the Enemy at the muzzles of their Guns: — The Conflict was severe, — the Enemy's Ships were fought with a gallantry highly honourable to their Officers, but the attack on them was irresistible — , and it pleased the Almighty disposer of all Events, to grant His Majesty's arms, a complete, and glorious Victory; about 3 P.M., many of the Enemy's Ships having struck their Colours, their Line gave way —; Admiral Gravina with ten Ships joining their frigates to leeward, stood towards Cadiz: — the five headmost Ships in their Van tacked and standing to the Southward, to windward of the British Line, were engaged, and the sternmost of them taken — the others went off, leaving to His Majesty's Squadron, nineteen Ships of the Line, (of which two are first rates, the Santissima Trinidad, and Santa Anna,) with three Flag Officers, viz[t]. Admiral Villeneuve, the Commander in Chief, Don Ignatio Maria D'Aliva Vice Admiral and the Spanish Rear Admiral Don Baltazar Hidalgo Cisneros.[12]

*After such a victory it may appear unnecessary to enter into encomiums on
the particular parts taken by the several commanders: – the conclusion says more
on the subject, than I have language to express. – the spirit which animated all
was the same, – when all exert themselves zealously in their country's service, all
deserve that their high merits should stand recorded, – and never was high merit more
conspicuous than in the battle I have described.*

*The Achille (a French 74) after having surrendered by some mismanagement of
the Frenchmen took fire and blew up, 200 of her men were saved by the Tender.*

*A circumstance occurred during the action which so strongly marks the invincible
spirit of British seamen when engaging the Enemies of their Country, that I cannot
resist the pleasure I have of making it known to their Lordships; – the Temeraire
was boarded by accident, or design, by a French ship on one side, and a Spaniard on
the other, the contest was vigorous but in the End, the combined Ensigns were torn
from the Poop, and the British hoisted in their places.*

*Such a Battle could not be fought without sustaining a great loss of men; I have
not only to lament in common with the British navy, and the British nation, in the fall
of the Commander in Chief, the loss of a Hero, whose name will be immortal, and his
memory ever dear to his Country – but my heart is rent with the most poignant grief
for the death of a friend, to whom by many Years intimacy and a perfect knowledge
of the virtues of his friend, which inspired ideas superior to the common race of men, I
was bound by the strongest ties of affection, a grief to which even the glorious occasion
in which he fell, does not bring the consolation which perhaps it ought – his Lordship
received a musket ball in his left breast, about the middle of the action, and sent an officer
to me immediately with his last farewell, – and soon after expired.*

*I have also to lament the loss of those excellent Officers, Captains Duff of the
Mars, and Cooke of the Bellerophon. I have yet heard of none others.*

*I fear the numbers that have fallen will be found very great, when the returns
come to me; – but it having blown a gale of wind ever since the action, I have not yet
had it in my power to collect any reports from the Ships, and when their Lordships
consider that I have 23 infirm ships, 18 of them hulks, without a stick standing, and
scarce a boat in the Fleet, I am sure they will have due consideration for the slowness
with which all that kind of duty must necessarily be done, but as I feel the great*

importance of those reports to the Public, and to individuals, they may trust that I will leave nothing undone, to obtain them speedily.

The Royal Sovereign having lost her Masts, except the faltering Foremast, I called the Euryalus to me, when the action continued, which Ship lying within hail, made my signals, a service, Captain Blackwood performed with great attention; – after the action, I shifted my Flag into her, that I might more easily communicate my orders to, and collect the Ships, and towed the Royal Sovereign out to Seaward: – the whole Fleet were now in a very perilous situation, many dismasted, all shattered, in 13 fathom water, off the shoals of Trafalgar, and when I made the signal to prepare to anchor, few of the Ships had an anchor to let go their cables being shot: – but the same good Providence which aided us thro' such a day, preserved us in the night, by the wind shifting a few points, and drifting the Ships off the Land, except four of the captive dismasted Ships, which are now at anchor off Trafalgar, and I hope will ride safe until those Gales are over.

Having thus detailed the proceedings of the Fleet on this occasion, I beg to congratulate their Lordships on a Victory, which I hope will add a day to the Glory of His Majesty's Crown, and be attended with public benefit to our Country.

I am Sir

Your most obedient

humble Servant

Cuthbᵗ Collingwood

WILLIAM MARSDEN ESQᴿ

The letter is written the day after the battle, and Collingwood lists 19 enemy ships as prizes. It is an impressive amount but it is fewer than Nelson had hoped for. He had made it clear before the battle that 'it is … annihilation that the Country wants, and not merely a splendid Victory of twenty-three to thirty-six, – honourable to the parties concerned, but absolutely useless in the extended scale to bring Bonaparte to his marrow-bones: numbers can only annihilate.'[13]

When he saw the Allied fleet of 33 ships arrayed before him, he wanted to capture or destroy 20. However, when Collingwood wrote this letter, the events of Trafalgar had yet to conclude; he had not foreseen the consequences of the storm that was then starting to lash his ships or, indeed, the possibility of Richard Strachan's squadron, then cruising in the Bay of Biscay, increasing the number of prizes.

Collingwood lists the captured flag officers but, as he makes clear in a subsequent, rather embarrassing letter (p. 289), one of them, Don Ignatio Maria D'Alava, was not in his custody at all but on his way back to Cadiz. Collingwood then does something fascinating. He refuses to 'enter into encomiums' or eulogies on the behaviour of the fleet captains. This is a direct result of the pain he had felt himself when he was overlooked in the dispatches describing The First of June. He knew that, so soon after the action, he couldn't possibly comment accurately and fairly on all of his captains' behaviour. He therefore chose to comment on none of them, mentioning only those who had died and Blackwood, who was in command of the frigate squadron.

This failure to comment is particularly important because, in doing so, Collingwood deliberately chose to protect several captains who had failed to fight properly (pp. 279–80). It has taken naval historians many years to realise this and Collingwood's disingenuous dispatch is partly responsible. However, it is now known that several officers failed to engage as Nelson or Collingwood had expected. Indeed, the extent to which Nelson's indoctrination of new captains actually worked is still very much open to debate.

In this letter, therefore, Collingwood is consciously protecting the reputation of his navy in its moment of glory; he wants nothing to tarnish the public perception of the victory and the esteem in which it will be held. It is far more than a letter describing a battle; it's a press release spinning the story in the way that he wanted. Collingwood was a shrewd political operator. He understood that a navy's reputation was only partially formed by its actual deeds and that public support was essential for the success of British maritime strategy.

General Order from Vice-Admiral C. Collingwood, 22 October 1805

Collingwood included with his letter a copy of a General Order issued at the same time that he wrote his battle dispatch. Clearly proud of his 'ever to be lamented death' line, he repeats it at the start of this order which is to be repeated to his men. He congratulates and praises 'every Officer, every Seaman, and Marine' in another conscious attempt to smooth ruffled feathers and bury the evidence of poor performance.

His praise for and deliberate naming of 'Rear Admiral the Earl of Northesk' – William Carnegie, commander of the First Rate 100-gun *Britannia* – is particularly curious because Northesk's behaviour was the most suspect of all British officers.

GENERAL ORDER

The ever to be lamented death of Vice Admiral Lord Viscount Nelson, Duke of Bronte, the Commander in Chief, who fell in the action of the 21ˢᵗ, in the Arms of Victory, whose memory will be ever dear to the British Navy, and the British Nation, whose Zeal for the honour of his King, and the Interests of his Country will be ever held up, as shining Example for a British Seaman, leaves to me a duty, to return my thanks to the Right Honourable Rear Admiral, the Captains, officers, Seamen, and detachments of Royal Marines serving on board His Majesty's Squadron now under my Command, for their conduct on that day, but where can I find Language to express my Sentiments of the Valour, and Skill which was displayed by every Officer, every Seaman, and Marine in the Battle with the Enemy, where every individual appeared an Hero, on whom the Glory of his Country depended, – the attack was irresistible, and the issue of it adds to the page of naval annals a brilliant instance of what Britons can do, when their King and Country needs their Service.

To the Right Honourable Rear Admiral the Earl of Northesk, to the Captains, Officers, and Seamen, and to the officers, non-commissioned officers, and Privates of the Royal Marines, I beg to give my sincere and hearty thanks for their highly meritorious conduct, both in the action, and in the Zeal, and Activity, in bringing the captured ships out from the perilous situation in which they were among the Shoals of Trafalgar, in boisterous weather.

And I desire the respective Captains will be pleased to communicate to the Officers, Seamen and Royal Marines, this public testimony of my high approbation of their Conduct, and my thanks for it.

Euryalus, 22ᴺᴰ October 1805

Cuthbᵗ Collingwood

To the Right Honourable
Rear Admiral the Earl of Northesk
and to the respective Captains,
and Commanders.

Vice-Admiral C. Collingwood, 22 October 1805

Enclosed with this General Order is yet another that is important for its careful religious focus. Collingwood was devout and a regular attendant at his ship's divine services and, if the weather prevented a public meeting, he would read the service in the privacy of his cabin. The signal described in this order, however, appointing a day 'of general humiliation before God', is unprecedented after a victory. Other admirals, including Nelson and Duncan, had ordered general thanksgivings, but this call to repentance is quite different.

The wording is also theologically significant. Collingwood talks of offering praise and thanks to the 'Throne of Grace', which is suggestive of evangelical piety, a practice and belief system that was then being popularised in the navy by leading evangelicals known as 'Blue Lights'. No other evidence survives, however, to suggest that Collingwood was an evangelical, but his letter certainly indicates the extent to which any sense of triumphalism had been driven out by grief at Nelson's death.

Tellingly, Collingwood had great difficulty in reconciling naval discipline with his Christian belief. In one of his few letters that mention his own beliefs, he wrote: 'I cannot, for the life of me, comprehend the religion of an Officer who could pray all one day, and flog his men the next.'[14] Collingwood's personal Christian beliefs had a direct effect on his behaviour as a naval officer. He was renowned for being easy on his crew and that easiness increased as he aged.

GENERAL ORDER

The Almighty God, whose Arm alone is Strength, having of his great mercy been pleased to crown the Exertion of His Majesty's Fleet with Success, in giving them a complete Victory over their Enemies, on the 21ˢᵗ of this Month; and that all praise, and thanksgiving, may be offered up to the Throne of Grace, for the great benefits to our Country, and to mankind. —

I have thought proper, that a day should be appointed, of general humiliation before God, and thanksgiving for this his merciful Goodness —, imploring forgiveness of Sins, a continuation of his divine mercy, and his constant aid to us, in the defence of our Country's liberties, and Laws — without which the utmost Efforts of Man are nought, and direct therefore that be appointed for this holy purpose.

GIVEN ON BOARD THE EURYALUS
OFF CAPE TRAFALGAR, 22ᴺᴰ OCTOBER 1805

Cuthᵗ Collingwood

TO THE RESPECTIVE CAPTAINS
AND COMMANDERS

NB.

The Fleet having been dispersed by a Gale of Wind no day has yet been able to be appointed for the above purpose.

The Order in which the British Fleet attacked, 21 October 1805

This list of ships is actually far more important than it first appears. We know from Collingwood's letter (p. 257) that Nelson had insisted that the fleet go into battle in the order of sailing. This was designed to reduce the time lost when forming into a pre-determined order of battle, an operation that could take several hours for even the best fleets. This immediacy was central to Nelson's plan. He wanted his attack to be impulsive and fast, a demonstration of resolve, confidence and certainty. But this document, which details how the fleet *did* get into action is very different from Nelson's stipulated order of sailing. So what happened? What does this document tell us about Trafalgar?

THE ORDER IN WHICH THE SHIPS OF THE BRITISH SQUADRON, ATTACKED THE COMBINED FLEETS OF FRANCE AND SPAIN, ON THE 21ST OCTOBER 1805.

VAN.	REAR.
Victory	Royal Sovereign
Temeraire	Mars
Neptune	Belleisle
Conqueror	Tonnant
Leviathan	Bellerophon
Ajax	Colossus
Orion	Achille
Agamemnon	Polyphemus
Minotaur	Revenge
Spartiate	Swiftsure
Britannia	Defence
Africa	Thunderer
	Defiance
Euryalus	Prince
Sirius	Dreadnought
Phoebe	
Naiad	
Pickle Schooner	
Entreprenante Cutter	

Cuthb: Collingwood

The 'Van' division is more commonly known as the 'Weather' column, and the 'Rear' division as the 'Lee' column. The list of ships at the bottom left, beginning with *Euryalus*, are the small ships in the fleet – the frigates, schooners and cutters. The rest are ships of the line, of which there are 27. Faced with an allied fleet of 33 ships, the British fleet was outnumbered by six ships of the line, a significant margin.

Consider first the ships at the top of Collingwood's list. The divisions are led by flagships, followed by exceptionally powerful ships. In the 'Van' division, which attacked the formidable enemy centre, the 100-gun *Victory* was followed by two 98-gunners, *Temeraire* and *Neptune*; the 'Rear' division was not quite so powerful but it was still led by the 100-gun *Royal Sovereign*, which was followed by the *Mars* and *Belleisle*, two large 74s renowned for their sailing ability. This was central to Nelson's plan of punching through the enemy line.

It was a very risky tactic and it is reasonable to argue that it only worked because of poor Allied gunnery. Nelson had anticipated that French and Spanish gunnery would be poor but it was exacerbated on the morning of 21 October by a deep swell that made the Allied ships pitch, roll, sway and surge as they struggled to hold their line. Gunnery in such conditions was always extremely difficult but the French would have found it especially so because they didn't have gunlocks, a flintlock firing mechanism for cannon. These gunlocks made the ignition of the charge far quicker and more reliable than the alternative method of using quickmatch. A gunner using a gunlock could therefore choose the moment to fire with a much greater degree of certainty than a gunner with quickmatch. He could also stand directly behind his gun and sight along it before pulling a lanyard attached to the gunlock. The gunner with quickmatch, on the other hand, would fire his gun blind from alongside the cannon. Without gunlocks, therefore, direction and timing were both much more difficult to judge, particularly in a deep swell. The result was that, when they finally arrived at the Allied line, the leading British ships were relatively unscathed. A calm sea and an enemy equipped with gunlocks might have produced an entirely different result. But what of the other ships? What does their location in that list tell us about Trafalgar? All is not quite what it seems.

The approach to battle on 21 October was, even by the standards of sailing warfare, painfully slow. In the fluky, light winds, most British ships sailed down to the Allied line at around one and a half knots – that is, one and a half nautical miles *per hour* – but some sailed faster and some sailed slower. Moreover the distance and time involved were significant. At dawn the two fleets were eight or nine miles apart and firing did not begin until around midday. In the intervening time a difference in speed of no more than half of a mile per hour would have had a significant impact on the formation of the British fleet.

In Nelson's division the first six ships were closely engaged within 15 minutes of each other. There was then a gap of between 40 and 50 minutes before the next group engaged. The final two came into action at anything between two and two and a half hours after *Victory*. Collingwood's division was even more broken up. His first eight ships entered battle within minutes of each other but were followed by a gap of more than an hour and then another lengthy gap. The final ship in Collingwood's line did not engage for at least two and a half hours.

During the approach, not only did these large gaps appear in the British lines, but several ships also swapped places. The most famous incident of this kind involved HMS *Temeraire,* the ship later immortalised in Turner's famous painting 'The Fighting Temeraire'. As the British fleet bore down on the French, the *Victory* led the weather column, although Nelson had originally placed the *Temeraire* at its head in his original Order of Sailing.

Henry Blackwood, a frigate captain and close friend of Nelson, suggested that the *Victory* let the *Temeraire* lead to offer some protection to Nelson and his flagship. At first Nelson agreed but, as the *Temeraire* began to surge past the *Victory*, he changed his mind, realising that he could not go into battle in second place if Collingwood continued to lead his line. Collingwood, for his part, was not about to sacrifice his position at the head of the line and studiously ignored all of Nelson's signals to do so. Nelson therefore abandoned his plan to change places with the *Temeraire* and hailed her captain: 'I'll thank you, Captain Harvey, to keep in your proper station, which is astern of the *Victory*.'[15] Thus it was that the *Victory*, rather than the *Temeraire*, led the weather line into battle.

Other ships changed places too, some because their captains were ordered to, others on their captains' own initiative, and some because they were simply overtaken. Few of these instances are well known but they are far more significant than the famous exchange between *Victory* and *Temeraire*. The difficulty every captain faced was that, just as some people run faster than others, ships of the line did not sail at the same speed under the same sail plan. Their speed was the result of a complex equation of ship design, trim, sail plan and the condition of the ships' hulls, some of which were newly scraped while others were encrusted with marine growth. Some ships, such as the *Prince*, the *Dreadnought* and the *Britannia,* all of whom appear towards the end of Collingwood's list, were just downright bad sailers.

This was enough of a problem in itself but, when linked with the issue of fleet discipline, could become thorny. If you are in a speedy ship but stuck behind a lumbering one, what do you do? Do you leave your position to race into battle or hold your position to maintain the integrity of the line? Both are valid courses of action but we know that Nelson wanted his captains to leave the line in such situations, regardless of the potential consequences. Unfortunately, that message was either not understood or was ignored by several captains. The result was that some ships, although good sailers, stayed in line; some slower ships stayed in line and prevented good sailers getting at the enemy sooner; and some good sailers moved out of their allocated position to get at the enemy more quickly. By no means every captain did his utmost to get to the enemy as quickly as possible, however. As a result, there are several significant differences between Collingwood's list which depicts what actually happened and Nelson's of what was intended to happen.[16]

Van/Weather Division		Rear/Lee Division	
WHAT HAPPENED	WHAT WAS INTENDED	WHAT HAPPENED	WHAT WAS INTENDED
Victory	Temeraire (98)	Royal Sovereign	Mars (74)
Temeraire	Victory (100)	Mars	Prince (98)
Neptune	Neptune (98)	Belleisle	Royal Sovereign (100)
Conqueror	Britannia (100)	Tonnant	Tonnant (80)
Leviathan	Conqueror (74)	Bellerophon	Belleisle (74)
Ajax	Agamemnon (74)	Colossus	Bellerophon (74)
Orion	Leviathan (74)	Achille	Colossus (74)
Agamemnon	Ajax (74)	Polyphemus	Achille (74)
Minotaur	Orion (74)	Revenge	Polyphemus (64)
Spartiate	Minotaur (74)	Swiftsure	Revenge (74)
Britannia	Spartiate (74)	Defence	Swiftsure (74)
Africa		Thunderer	Defence (74)
		Defiance	Africa (64)
Euryalus		Prince	Thunderer (74)
Sirius		Dreadnought	Defiance (74)
Phoebe			Dreadnought (98)
Naiad			
Pickle Schooner			
Entreprenante Cutter			

10. Lightning conductor from the Royal masthead of the French flagship *L'Orient*.

11. Portrait of Rear-Admiral Horatio Nelson, attributed to Guy Head, *c.* 1800. Nelson, blood dripping from his head wound, is depicted at the moment that *L'Orient* exploded.

12. 'The Battle of the Nile' by Nicholas Pocock, *c.* 1808. The painting shows the start of the action, at about 6.30 p.m., looking north-west across Aboukir Bay. Nelson's fleet, led by the *Goliath*, is in the process of doubling the anchored French line.

13. Alexander Davison's Nile Medal, showing the British fleet going into action.

14. Portrait of Sir Hyde Parker by James Wallace.

15. 'The Battle of Copenhagen, 2 April 1801' by Nicholas Pocock.

16. Nelson's pigtail.

17. Portrait of Rear-Admiral Cuthbert Collingwood by Henry Howard.

18. 'The Death of Nelson' by William Arthur Devis, 1807. The painting depicts the scene in the cockpit on the *Victory* as Nelson lay dying and features accurate portraiture of the men who cared for him as he died.

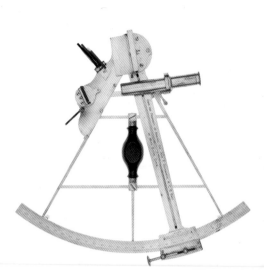

19. Duckworth's sextant. The index arm is inscribed: 'Once the Property of Admiral Sir John Thomas Duckworth, K.C.B., Bart. of Wear, B. 1748, D. 1817'.

20. Portrait of Admiral Sir John Thomas Duckworth by Sir William Beechey.

21. 'Duckworth's action off San Domingo, 6 February 1806' by Nicholas Pocock, 1808. The large ship right of centre, with her mizzenmast falling, is the 120-gun *L'Imperial*, engaging Duckworth's 74-gun *Superb*.

In Nelson's list the *Britannia* is fourth in the 'Van' division but she went into battle second to last. She was, undoubtedly, a poor sailer but the behaviour and commitment of her commander, Northesk, was certainly suspect (p. 278). In addition *Prince*, *Polyphemus*, *Agamemnon*, *Defiance* and *Defence* should all have engaged in the leading groups but did not. The reasons are only partially known. The *Defence*, in the words of one of her midshipmen, was 'one of the fastest ships in the service on all points of sailing'[17] and yet finally joined the battle roughly two hours after the leading ship. This may have been because she had found herself significantly out of position at dawn on 21 October. The *Agamemnon* was also out of station at the start of the day because she had lost a foretopmast the day before, as was the *Prince* which had split a foretopsail.

The position of the 64-gun *Africa*, last in the Van division, also deserves an explanation. She was originally intended to place herself in the *other* division, four from the end, but on the morning of battle found herself a full six miles ahead of both fleets. As a result, she entered battle on a completely different bearing from both Nelson's and Collingwood's columns. She has therefore been 'attached' to the weather column in Collingwood's list for administrative tidiness when, in reality, she was a soloist for much of the action.

Collingwood's list, therefore, is far more than it seems. It is evidence of good and bad sailing performance; of different courses taken by different captains; of obedience to or defiance of Nelson's wishes; of the scope and the limitations of Nelson's command style; and of a mixture of competence and incompetence in the British fleet.

It is also worth noting that Collingwood's list does not actually tally with other witness accounts. The *Dreadnought*, shown last in the weather column in Collingwood's list, is a good example. According to Collingwood's own journal, the *Dreadnought* actually overtook the *Swiftsure*, *Thunderer* and *Prince* on her approach to battle and then engaged six ships before the *Prince*, who engaged last. Indeed, if one compiles a list based on the *timing* that the ships engaged rather than on their location, a different order again emerges because some ships withheld their fire until at close range, others blazed away as soon as there was any chance of hitting the enemy and some even before that. We know, for example that the *Africa*, shown here as last in the weather column, actually opened fire only eight minutes after Collingwood in the *Royal Sovereign* and twelve minutes *before* the *Victory*, whereas the *Minotaur*, shown in the list as fourth from the rear, opened fire last in the weather column, no less than two hours and 28 minutes after *Victory*.

All of this, moreover, depends on how one measures time during fleet battle. Significantly, specific timings given in logs can be inaccurate, while periods within individual logs can often suggest the passage of time more accurately. Thus this 'order in which the Ships of the British Squadron, attacked the Combined Fleets' is by no means definitive and the debate over which ships engaged when, and the reasons for them doing so, continues to rage.

The discrepancy between Collingwood's list and the actual order in which the ships attacked is also valuable evidence for the difficulty of comprehending battle. Clear bird's eye images of fleets moving this way and that in perfect order are wholly fabricated. From sea level, or even from the top of a masthead, the positioning and identity of the combatants were very difficult to ascertain. It has been estimated that the overall battle space occupied by the Battle of Trafalgar was 49 kilometres square[18] and, if one remembers that the majority of the combatants were wreathed in smoke – the French Lieutenant Gicquel des Touches was adamant that, once the attack began, 'the entire fleet disappeared from our sight, enveloped by smoke'[19] – then Collingwood's inaccuracy is neither surprising nor reason for criticism.

Rear-Admiral C. Collingwood to W. Marsden, 24 October 1805

Two days after Collingwood had sat down to write his first letter in the shocking aftermath of the battle, he took up his quill again to tell the next part of the tale.

The poor weather, which had begun in the evening of the day after the battle, continued for two full days and in this letter Collingwood looks back on them. We can see his mind ranging across an ocean of chaos with dismasted ships being driven on lee shores, captured enemies retaking their ships and entire ships disappearing. One can almost hear him drawing breath; this is his first free moment for 48 hours. His crews have endured a truly horrifying experience as the helpless, shattered ships have been driven towards a lee shore while the wounded have been tossed mercilessly around inside them. Unfortunately for Collingwood, his ships and his men, the worst was still to come.

EURYALUS, OFF CADIZ
24 OCTOBER 1805

In my letter of the 22nd, I detailed to you for the information of my Lords
Commissioners of the Admiralty, the proceedings of His Majesty's Squadron, on the
day of the Action, and that preceeding it, since which I have had a continued series of
misfortunes – , but they are of a kind that human Prudence could not provide against,
or my skill prevent.

On the 22nd, in the morning, a strong Southerly Wind blew, with squally
Weather, which however did not prevent the activity of the Officers, and Seamen, of
such Ships as were manageable from getting hold of many of the Prizes (13, or 14),
and towing them off to the Westward, where I ordered them to rendezvous round the
Royal Sovereign, in tow, by the Neptune; – but on the 23rd the Gale increased and
the Sea ran so high that many of them broke the tow rope, and drifted far to leeward,
before they were got hold of again, – and some of them taking advantage, in the dark,
and boisterous night, got before the Wind, and have perhaps drifted upon the Shore,
and sunk; – On the afternoon of that day, the remnant of the combined Fleet ten
Sail of Ships, who had not been much engaged, stood up to leeward of my shattered,
and straggled charge, as if meaning to attack them, which obliged me to collect a
force out of the least injured Ships, and form to leeward for their Defence – all this
retarded the progress of the Hulks, and the bad weather continuing, determined me to
destroy all the Leewardmost that could be cleared of the Men considering that keeping
possession of the Ships, a matter of little consequence, compared with the chance of
their falling again into the hands of the Enemy, but even this was an arduous task,
in the high Sea, which was running, I hope however it has been accomplished to a
considerable extent; – I entrusted it to Skillful Officers, who would spare no pains
to execute what was possible. The Captains of the Prince, and Neptune, cleared the
Trinidad, and sunk her; – Captains Hope, Bayntun, and Malcolm (who joined the
Fleet this moment from Gibraltar) had the charge of destroying four others: – The

Redoubtable sunk astern of the Swiftsure, while in tow; the Santa Ana I have no doubt is sunk, as her side was almost entirely beat in; – and such is the shattered condition of the whole of them that unless the weather moderates, I doubt whether I shall be able to carry a Ship of them into Port: – if I had anchored such as had good Cables, they (having all their crews on board) would certainly have cut them, and run for Port in the Stormy weather, and there were ten Sail of the Line, and five frigates ready to come to their assistance in fine weather, so that I hope their Lordships will approve of what I (having only in consideration the destruction of the Enemy's Fleet) have thought a measure of absolute necessity.

I am under the most serious apprehensions for several of the Ships of my Squadron, the Belleisle is the only one totally dismasted, but the Victory, Royal Sovereign, Temeraire, and Tonnant are in a very decrepit state.

I have taken Admiral Villeneuve into this Ship; – Vice Admiral Don Aleva is dead; – whenever the temper of the weather will permit, and I can spare a frigate (for there were only 4 in the action with the fleet, Euryalus, Sirius, Phoebe, and Naiad: – the Melpomene joined the 22nd, and the Eurydice, (and Scout the 23rd) I shall collect the other Flag Officers, and send them to England with their Flags (if they do not all go to the bottom) to be laid at His Majesty's Feet.

I cannot discover what the destination of the Enemy was, but if the Bucentaure is above water, when the gale abates, I will endeavour to do it: there were 4,000 troops embarked under the command of General Contamine, who was taken with Admiral Villeneuve, in the Bucentaure.

I am

>   *Sir*
>   *Your most obedient*
>   *humble servant*

>   *Cuthb. Collingwood*

WILLIAM MARSDEN, ESQ

By now Collingwood has realised that there is another story afoot, having identified 4,000 of the captured French crew as soldiers destined for land service rather than soldiers drafted into sea service. He has clearly interrupted another of Napoleon's schemes but has been unable to confirm its details. His ignorance of Napoleon's plan, however, is not as complete as this letter suggests. We know that the *Royal Sovereign* joined Nelson's fleet off Cadiz on 9 October and brought with her accurate intelligence that the combined fleet had orders to sail for Naples. Collingwood and Nelson had even been discussing Italy as a destination for the Allied fleet on the eve of battle.[20]

His reference to anchoring matters because it suggests a measure of self-justification. He writes: '– if I had anchored such as had good Cables, they (having all their crews on board) would certainly have cut them, and run for Port in the Stormy weather.' Maybe that is so but the important point to realise is that Collingwood did *not* anchor, in spite of the fact that Nelson had repeatedly ordered his flag captain, Hardy, to do so. Indeed, some contemporaries believed that Collingwood's failure to anchor was a major factor in the loss of the prizes during the storm, while others, including Collingwood himself, stressed the shocking condition of the ships' equipment and superstructure that were crucial for anchoring. The ferocity of the subsequent storm must also be taken into consideration. It is surely unlikely that any anchor would have held in such waters and in such conditions and Nelson never lived to see the full ferocity of the weather after Trafalgar.

Rear Admiral C. Collingwood to W. Marsden, 28 October 1805

It has been estimated that, in the two days following 24 October, the date of Collingwood's last letter (p. 271), the storm rose to storm force 10 or violent storm force 11 on what we now know as the Beaufort scale, invented in 1805 by Sir Francis Beaufort who had been present at The Glorious First of June aboard the frigate *Aquilon*. Contemporary mariners did not yet know of Beaufort's scale but they knew enough to label the storm a hurricane. Edward Codrington, captain of the *Orion*, later considered it 'the most violent hurricane I was ever in'.[21]

EURYALUS, OFF CADIZ
28 OCTOBER 1805

Since my letter to you of the 24th, stating the Proceedings of His Majesty's Squadron, our situation has been the most critical, and our Employment the most arduous, that ever a Fleet was engaged in: – On the 24th, and 25th it blew a most violent Gale of Wind, which completely dispersed the Ships, and drove their captured hulls in all directions.

I have since been employed in collecting and destroying them, where they are at anchor, upon the Coast between Cadiz, and six leagues Westward of San Lucar, without a prospect of saving one to bring into Port.

I mentioned in my former letter the joining of the Donegal, and Melpomene, after the action, – I cannot sufficiently praise the activity of their Commanders in giving assistance to the Squadron in destroying the Enemy's ships.

The Defiance after having stuck to the Aigle, as long as it was possible, in hope of saving her from wreck (which separated her for some time from the Squadron) was obliged to abandon her to her fate, and she went on shore, – Captain Durham's Exertions have been very great. –

I hope I shall get them all destroyed by tomorrow, if the Weather keeps moderate.

In the Gale the Royal Sovereign, and Mars lost their Foremasts, and are now rigging anew where the body of the Squadron is, at anchor to the NW of San Lucar.

I find that on the return of Gravina to Cadiz he was immediately ordered to Sea again, and came out, which made it very necessary for me to form a Line, to cover the disabled Hulls, that night it blew hard, and his Ship the Prince of Asturias was dismasted, and returned into Port, the Rayo was also dismasted, and fell into our hands; Don Enrique McDonal, had his Broad Pendant in the Rayo, and from him I find the Santa Ana was driven near Cadiz, and towed in by a Frigate.

I am Sir

Your most obedient
humble servant

Cuthb. Collingwood

WILLIAM MARSDEN, ESQ

PS.
I enclose a list of the killed, and wounded, as far as I have been able to collect it, that
of the Victory, and Belleisle I cannot get, as they have I hope got into Gibraltar.

By now the exhausted sailors had been fighting the weather in broken ships for an entire week with just one day's respite, an achievement that did far more than simply save the British ships from destruction. In the weeks after the battle, the British achievement off Cape Trafalgar began to be appreciated in more complex terms than one might immediately suspect. The grinding British discipline deeply impressed the French and Spanish survivors. When so many of the enemy simply gave themselves up to the mercy of the weather, the British fought the storm as determinedly as they had their enemy in the battle. It was a telling lesson, that nothing at all, neither cannon nor divine fury, could drive the British from the sea.

List of Killed and Wounded in the British Fleet, 21 October 1805

This casualty list, though missing the figures from the *Tonnant*, is instructive of the way in which the British fought during the battle. It is dated 28 October and is therefore an early return. Subsequent figures[22] are different, and in most cases higher.

What is clear is that the leading six or so ships of both British columns (p. 265) suffered the majority of the casualties. Indeed, only about half of the ships on either side were involved in heavy fighting. In the weather column, *Victory* and *Temeraire* bore the brunt of the action as they smashed their way into the heavily crowded and powerful enemy centre. As they broke the line, they received the fire of at least five Allied ships, one of which was the towering *Santissima Trinidad* of 140 guns.

AN ABSTRACT OF THE KILLED, AND WOUNDED, ON BOARD THE RESPECTIVE SHIPS, COMPOSING THE BRITISH SQUADRON, UNDER THE COMMAND OF THE RIGHT HONOURABLE, VICE ADMIRAL LORD VISCOUNT NELSON, IN THE ACTION OF THE 21ST OF OCTOBER 1805, OFF CAPE TRAFALGAR, WITH THE COMBINED FLEETS OF FRANCE AND SPAIN.

Ships names	Killed				Wounded				Total Killed	Total Wounded	Grand Total
	Officers	Petty Officers	Seamen	Marines	Officers	Petty Officers	Seamen	Marines			
Victory	4	3	32	18	4	3	59	9	57	75	132
Royal Sovereign	3	2	29	13	3	5	70	16	47	94	141
Britannia	1	.	8	1	1	1	33	7	10	42	52
Temeraire	3	1	35	8	3	2	59	12	47	76	123
Prince	none	.	.	None	none		.	.	.	.	.
Neptune	.	.	10	.	.	1	30	3	10	34	44
Dreadnought	.	.	6	1	1	2	19	4	7	26	33
Tonnant	not received.										
Mars	1	3	17	8	4	5	44	16	29	69	98
Bellerophon	2	1	20	4	2	4	97	20	27	123	150
Minotaur	.	.	3	.	1	1	17	3	3	22	25
Revenge	.	2	18	8	4	.	38	9	28	57	79
Conqueror	2	.	1	.	2	.	7	.	3	9	12
Leviathan	.	.	2	2	.	1	17	4	4	22	26
Ajax	.	.	2	.	.	.	9	.	2	9	11
Orion	.	.	1	.	.	2	17	4	1	23	24
Agamemnon	.	.	2	.	.	.	7	.	2	7	9
Spartiate	.	.	3	.	1	2	16	1	3	20	23
Africa	.	.	12	6	2	5	30	7	18	44	62
Belleisle	2	1	22	8	3	3	68	19	33	93	126
Colossus	1	.	31	8	5	9	115	31	40	160	200
Achille	.	1	6	6	4	4	37	14	13	59	72
Polyphemus	.	.	2	.	.	4	.	.	2	4	6
Swiftsure	.	.	7	2	.	1	6	1	9	8	17
Defence	.	.	4	3	.	.	23	6	7	29	36
Thunderer	.	.	2	2	.	2	9	1	4	12	16
Defiance	2	1	8	6	1	4	39	9	17	53	70
Total.	21	15	283	104	41	57	870	196	423	464	1587

Cuthb. Collingwood

Furthermore, *Victory* and *Temeraire* both suffered particularly high casualties amongst their officers. Is it possible that French marksmen deliberately targeted British officers on these two ships in the centre of the battle? They were certainly sitting ducks because the *Victory* became entangled with the French *Redoutable* and the *Temeraire* fought with a French ship lashed to each side. Marksmen in the rigs of all three enemy ships could therefore take pot shots at British officers on their weather decks. As a more general observation, the proportion of British officers killed and wounded is very high with a third of the 30 British flag-officers and captains killed or wounded.

Meanwhile, more ships in the lee column bore the brunt of the fighting and more received heavy damage than in the weather column. As these figures demonstrate, *Royal Sovereign, Mars, Belleisle, Bellerophon, Colossus* and *Achille* together received the full force of the Allied rear. The highest casualty figures were sustained by the *Colossus*. She was heavily engaged for most of the action and took fire on both sides from two French and two Spanish 74s, before crashing into yet another French 74. Her complement at Trafalgar was 571 and so her casualty figure represents 35 per cent of her entire crew. The only other ship to suffer a similar casualty rate was *Bellerophon* at 30 per cent. The other heavily-damaged ships experienced casualty rates of between 10 and 20 per cent.

Although more ships in Collingwood's division shared the damage than in the weather column, the figures from the lee column are still unequal, which is partly explained by the absence of so many of Collingwood's ships from their intended positions. As he bore down to the enemy, a ragged hole appeared in the centre of his division where *Polyphemus, Swiftsure, Defence, Africa* and *Defiance* should have been. This meant that the first eight ships of Collingwood's division were heavily outnumbered and had to fight hard and hold until the rest of the line came up. Thus the first eight ships took the greater share of the casualties and the rearguard far less. Within the rearguard the exception is the *Defiance*, which threw herself into the battle where others did not.

Some ships, meanwhile, have strikingly small numbers of casualties for their size. Most notable are the 98-gun three-decked *Prince* with none, the 100-gun three-decked *Britannia* – 52, the two-decked 74-gunners *Ajax* – 11, and *Swiftsure* – 17, and the two-decked 64-gunners *Polyphemus* – 6, and *Agamemnon* – 9. The behaviour of the *Britannia*, one of the largest ships in the British fleet, was strange, even accepting that she was renowned for being a bad sailer. Rather than withholding her fire until close to the enemy, she blazed away only 10 minutes after the engagement began, although still a great distance from the enemy line. Indeed, she did not even reach the enemy line until two hours and ten minutes after she opened fire and then failed to break through. It is certain that *Britannia* had the opportunity of engaging earlier and closer, but failed to and the fact that she engaged from such a distance prevented a number of other British ships from engaging as and when Nelson had intended. Her commander, Northesk, had little fighting experience and no solid reputation. He was third in command at Trafalgar only because no more experienced and more reliable flag-officers were available. Edward Rotherham, Collingwood's flag captain, was disgusted and declared that Northesk 'behaved notoriously ill'[23] at Trafalgar, a criticism he also fired at Captain Richard Grindall of the *Prince*. Her performance was undoubtedly affected by the bad state of her hull. Her copper bottom had not been scraped recently and thus reduced her speed, but she also seems to have taken a circuitous route into battle, finding herself out of position at dawn. Nonetheless, her lack of energy was well-noted.

The behaviour of the *Agamemnon* is noteworthy because she was commanded by Sir Edward Berry who was famed for taking part in more engagements than any other British officer. Most recently, he had fought at the Nile, and had been captured while returning with Nelson's dispatches, albeit only after a fierce and prolonged battle. We must be careful, however, not to confuse fortune with talent. When Nelson once took Berry to court and the King commented on the loss of Nelson's arm, Nelson introduced Berry as 'my right hand'.[24] This phrase has been used to bolster Berry's reputation when it can just as easily be used as evidence of Nelson's conversational wit. In fact, Berry is now considered to have been wholly reliant on Nelson. He was renowned amongst his fellow officers for his company and courage rather than his intellect or seamanship. When he joined Nelson's fleet before the battle, Nelson laughed and declared, 'Here comes that damned fool Berry! *Now* we shall have a battle!'[25] From what we know of *Agamemnon's* behaviour at Trafalgar, supported by the evidence of this casualty list, the subtleties of Nelson's plan seem to have entirely escaped the 'damned fool', who ranged around the battle's epicentre firing ineffectually at long range. We know that he fired 6,781 lbs of powder and 1,145 shot without ever engaging close, an extraordinary waste of ammunition expended whilst hundreds of British sailors were dying in the thick of the action and would have greatly benefited from the nearer presence of the *Agamemnon*.

The *Ajax* was another ship that engaged ineffectually and at long range. Her experienced captain was in England, sitting in judgment at Robert Calder's court martial. In his place, she was commanded by Lieutenant John Pilford, her first lieutenant, and he had only been in post for a week. The *Thunderer*, another ship with surprisingly low casualty figures, was also commanded by her first lieutenant, John Stockham.

The behaviour of the *Polyphemus*, as reflected in her casualty figures, is also difficult to explain because she arrived late into the action, having adopted a very odd route. Her captain, Robert Redmill, retired on grounds of ill health the following year and it is quite possible that he was unwell during Trafalgar. The *Swiftsure*, like the *Polyphemus*, took a circuitous route into action and, once engaged, took little part. There is no record that her captain, William Rutherford, had ever been in action before.

The figures for *Minotaur* and *Spartiate* are revealing because they could and perhaps should have been much higher, though this was through no fault of their novice captains. Even though they entered the battle relatively late, they still suffered heavy casualties due to the arrival of Vice-Admiral Pierre Dumanoir's van division. Exactly according to plan, Nelson's attack had severed Dumanoir's division from the rest of the Allied fleet. By the time that he returned to assist the heavily engaged centre, the battle was nearly over. However, his attack, with four ships of the line, was well met by *Minotaur* and *Spartiate*, but if he had pressed his attack, as he should have done, the casualty figures of *Minotaur* and *Spartiate* would have been much higher than they were.

One of the most enduring myths about Trafalgar is that everything went to plan, yet these figures are an important reminder that, in some instances, there were large gaps between the British ships where, ideally, there should have been none, and that several captains did not engage in the manner that was expected. The subsequent scale of the victory suffered accordingly. Thomas Fremantle, captain of the *Neptune*, wrote: 'On this as on all occasions of the sort many have in my opinion behaved improperly; had all gone into action with the determination that Nelson did, it is probable few only could have escaped … '; the frigate commander Henry Blackwood 'saw the faults, or rather mistakes, on both sides … '; Captain

Edward Codrington of the *Orion* declared ' … it was all well done *errors excepted* … '; William Pringle Green, master's mate of the *Conqueror*, was certain that ' … if the officers had done their duty in every ship, the action would have been over sooner, and the whole of the enemy taken or destroyed.'[26] Once this is realised, Collingwood's fawning Order of Thanks (p. 262), naming Northesk, becomes risible and reveals instead the strength of his desire to appease his subordinates and deliberately smooth any ruffled feathers. Controversy and criticism were beyond the pale: Collingwood was utterly committed to maintaining the esteem in which the navy was held by the public.

There was, however, to be a hidden advantage in the fact that some of the British fleet were relatively unscathed. Those who played little part in the action for whatever reason soon found themselves with a crucial role to play in the ensuing storm. The *Polyphemus*, for example, towed the *Victory* back to Gibraltar and Berry's *Agamemnon* towed the shattered *Colossus*.

Perhaps the most powerful aspect of the British casualty list, however, lies in the absence of its expected companion report. Where is the Allied fleet's return? Simply put, that list did not exist because, after the chaos of battle and storm, no one had any idea how many French and Spanish soldiers and sailors had died. And we still don't know today.

It is generally accepted that at least 4,400 Allied sailors died in the battle and perhaps 2,500 were wounded and that many more perished in the storm.[27] The British casualty figures are, therefore, very high in relation to British returns for other battles, but very low in comparison with the estimated Allied return for Trafalgar. The French and Spanish fought harder than anyone expected, but the battle was prolonged and fierce and the British superiority telling.

The Allied ships and their fates.

The following documents give a powerful impression of the scale of victory. Viewed together, they are astonishing. Undoubtedly this counts as the annihilation that Nelson had sought but which he did not know had been achieved before he died.

The *Algeciras* and *Santa Ana* are listed as 'taken, but got into Cadiz', an apparently contradictory statement. The *Algeciras* was indeed taken but was then retaken by her crew when it became clear that the British prize crew, a paltry 50 strong, was unable to cope with the challenge of keeping the shattered ship clear of the Trafalgar shoal. In spite of continued signalling, no other British ship came to her aid. She was, therefore, taken by the British but she was also taken back into Cadiz.

The *Bucentaure* is noted here as being wrecked 'on the Porques', the Spanish name for the rocks at the entrance to Cadiz harbour. She, like the *Algeciras*, had been retaken by the French but they were unable to bring her to safety. A similar fate befell the *Santa Ana*, which had been captured by the British but was then recaptured by a squadron commanded by Commodore Cosmao-Kerjulien, who sortied from Cadiz. Kerjulien also saved the *Neptune* and several Allied frigates but neither he nor any of the British was able to save the *Indomptable*, which was wrecked with the loss of over 1,000 men, 500 of whom had just been saved from the wrecked *Bucentaure*. The *Fougueux* was also wrecked, her prize crew from the *Temeraire* having survived one of the most intense parts of the battle only to die in the storm with their prize.

An interesting side-effect of this extreme level of destruction in the aftermath of the battle was that the prize money, the usual reward for British sailors, was almost entirely lost along with most of the prizes, a cruel blow. To compensate, all of the captains were awarded the King's Naval Gold Medal and a special grant of money was made by the government to compensate the sailors for their loss of prize money.

The four ships at the bottom of this list are recorded as 'hauled to the Southward, and escaped', and Rear-Admiral Dumanoir is also listed as 'escaped'. The problem for Dumanoir and his ships, however, was that they had hauled directly into the path of Richard Strachan, who captured them all (p. 293).

A List of the Combined Fleets of France, and Spain, in the action of the 21ˢᵗ of October 1805, off Cape Trafalgar, shewing how they are disposed of

	Ships Names	No. of Guns	Commanders	French or Spanish	How disposed of
1	San Ildefonso	74	Brigadier Don Joseph de Vargas	S.	Sent to Gibraltar
2	San Juan Nepomuceno	74	Brigadier Don Cosme Churruca	S.	
3	Bahama	74	Brigadier Don D. A. Galiano	S.	
4	Swiftsure*	74	Monsieur Villemadrin	F.	
5	Minorca	74	Don Teodoro Argumosa	S.	Wrecked off San Lucar
6	Feugeux	74	Monsieur Baudouin	F.	Wrecked off Trafalgar, all perished, & 30 of the Temerair's men
7	Indomptable	84	Monsieur Hubert	F.	Wrecked off Rosa, all perished.
8	Bucentaure	80	Admiral Villeneuve, Commander in Chief, Captains, Prigny, & Magendie	F.	Wrecked on the Porques some of the Crew saved
9	San Francisco de Asis	74	Don Luis de Flores	S.	Wrecked near Rosa.
10	El Rayo	100	Brigadier Don Henriquez Macdonel	S.	Wrecked near San Lucar
11	Neptuno	84	Brigadier Don Cayetano Valdes.	S.	Wrecked between Rosa, and Catalina
12	Argonaute	74	Monsieur Epron	F.	On shore, in the Port of Cadiz.
13	Berwick	74	Monsieur Cames	F.	Wrecked to the Northward of Sun Lucar
14	Aigle	74	Monsieur Courrege	F.	Wrecked near Rosa

* Note that both the British and Allies had ships called *Swiftsure*.

15	ACHILLE	74	Monsieur D'Nieuport	F.	Burnt, during the action
16	INTREPIDE	74	Monsieur Infernet	F.	Do., by Britannia
17	SAN AGUSTIN	74	Brigadier Don Felipe X. Cagigal	S.	Do., by Leviathan
18	SANTISSIMA TRINIDAD	140	Rear Admiral Don Baltazar H. Cisneros Brigadier Don J. Urcartes	S.	Sunk by Prince, Neptune,&co
19	REDOUBTABLE	74	Mr. Lucas	F.	Sunk, astern of the Swiftsure, Temeraire lost 13, and Swiftsure 5 Men.
20	ARGONAUTA	80	Don Antonio Parejo	S	Sunk by Ajax.
21	SANTA ANA	112	Vice Admiral Don Ignacio D'Aleva Captain Don Joseph de Gardogui	S.	Taken, but got into Cadiz in the Gale, both dismasted
22	ALGEZIRAS	74	Rear Admiral Magon, killed Captain Monsieur Brouard	F.	
23	PLUTON	74	Monsieur Cosmao	F.	Returned to Cadiz, in a sinking state.
24	SAN JUSTE	74	Don Miguel Gaston	F.	Do., has a foremast only
25	SAN LEANDRO	64	Don Joseph de Quevedo	S.	Do., dismasted
26	NEPTUNE	84	Monsieur Maistral	F.	Do., and perfect
27	HEROS	74	Monsieur Poulain	F.	Do., lower masts in, and Adm. Rossillie's Flag on board
28	PRINCIPE DE ASTURIAS	112	Admiral Don F. Gravina Dom Antonio Escano &co	S.	Do., dismasted
29	MONTANES	74	Don Francisco Alcedo	S.	Do.

30	FORMIDABLE	80	Rear Admiral Dumanoir	F.	} hauled to the Southward, and escaped.
31	MONT-BLANC	74	Monsieur Le Villegries	F.	
32	SCIPION	74	Monsieur Berenger	F.	
33	LE GUAY TROUIN	74	Monsieur Touffet	F.	

ABSTRACT	
At Gibraltar	4
destroyed	16
In Cadiz, wrecks	6
do., serviceable	3
Escaped to the Sow^d	4
Total	0

Cuthbert Collingwood

The list also underlines the principal difference between the French and Spanish fleets; the French have no three-deckers as they did in the earlier battles of the war. Their entire fleet here consists of large, some very large, two-deckers because French shipbuilding policy had shifted away from three-deckers for reasons of economy. The Spanish fleet, on the other hand, includes some real monsters, *El Rayo* (100), *Santissima Trinidad* (140), *Santa Ana* (112) and *Principe de Asturias* (112), all magnificent prestige ships that harked back to an earlier age.

The list also encourages consideration of the identities of some of the Allied officers. In particular, it is important to realise that there was a significant difference between the French officers and the Spanish. In line with French policy since 1794, the majority of the French officers were commoners who, by default, had very little combat experience. Most of the Spaniards, in contrast, came from aristocratic backgrounds and had significant naval careers.

The Spanish commanding officer, Admiral Don Federico Gravina, had been in the navy since the age of 12, having joined in 1768, and had distinguished himself ever since. Valdés of the *Neptuno* had been in the navy for 26 years, had fought during the American War, travelled on the famous Malaspina and Galiano exploration expeditions[28] and had commanded the *Pelayo* at the Battle of St Vincent. MacDonell of the *Rayo*, a Spaniard of Irish descent, had fought during the American War and then as a mercenary in the Swedish navy against the Russians. Galiano was an experienced and talented mariner who had sailed with Malaspina and then led his own voyage of exploration before commanding a frigate at the Battle of St Vincent. Cisneros of the *Santissima Trinidad* had been in the navy for 35 years and had also fought at St Vincent. Pareja, here Parejo, was another Spanish officer with over 35 years of experience who had distinguished himself in his early career and had also fought at St Vincent. Finally Churruca had been an officer for 27 years and had fought with great courage during the siege of Gibraltar in the American War. No less than 13 of the 15 Spanish commanding officers had fought a large-scale but indecisive battle against Robert Calder the previous July.

The Allied flag-officers and their fates

A List of the Names, and rank, of the Flag officers, of the Combined Fleet of France, and Spain, in the action of the 21ST of October 1805		
Names and rank	Ships their Flags were flying on board of	How disposed of
Admiral Villeneuve, Commander in Chief	Bucentaure	Taken.
Admiral Don Federico Gravina	Principe de Asturias	Escaped, in Cadiz, wounded in the Arm.
Vice Admiral Don Ignatio Maria D'Alava	Santa Ana	wounded severely in the head, taken, but was driven into Cadiz, in the Santa Ana
Rear Admiral Don Baltazar Hidalgo Cisneros	Santissima Trinidad	Taken
Rear Admiral Magon	Algeziras	Killed
Rear Admiral Dumanoir	Formidable	Escaped
		Cuthbt Collingwood

Villeneuve was taken into captivity in England, where he settled down to a quiet life in Sonning in Berkshire and was allowed out on a day trip to attend Nelson's funeral. When he was released on parole in late 1805 he tried in vain to re-enter military service in France. On 22 April 1806, he was found dead at a hotel in Rennes with multiple stab wounds to the chest. A verdict of suicide was recorded but rumours circulated that he was murdered on the orders of Napoleon. It was certainly a sad end for a man who fought for his pride and resented the incompetence of superiors who repeatedly gave him orders that took little account of the realities.

Gravina died from his wound but enjoyed huge public affection for his conduct at Trafalgar; Alava survived to enjoy Collingwood's hospitality (p. 289), Dumanoir escaped but was soon captured by Strachan and ended up living in Tiverton in Devon, which he described as 'une petite ville, assez plaisante mais qui me parut singulièrement monotone' – 'a small town, fairly pleasant, but which seemed to me especially dull'. He did not spend his time entirely idly, however. He wrote to *The Times* to complain about rumours that criticised his performance at Trafalgar and was sorely taxed resisting the wiles of a Devon lass who offered to help him escape, but only if he promised to marry her when they reached France. He turned down her offer of adventure, waited for the slow wheels of government to turn, and was eventually exchanged after six leisurely years of captivity.

Cisneros suffered from deafness caused by a blow to the head for the rest of his life and was subsequently known as 'El Sordo' – 'the deaf'. He later became the last legitimate viceroy of the Rio de la Plata, the last viceroyalty of Spanish Southern America.

Vice-Admiral C. Collingwood to The Marquis de Solana, 27 October 1805, and reply

One of the thorny problems that Collingwood faced in the battle's aftermath was what to do with the prisoners. There were *thousands*, perhaps 8,000 in all. His solution was masterful. The French prisoners stood no chance. The state of war between Britain and France was too entrenched for Collingwood not to secure the prisoners as a bargaining tool and as a means to cripple the French navy even further. They were shipped back to England to endure years of floating misery in

British prison hulks. A lucky few made it ashore to purpose-built prisons or even ancient castles where most were held until they died. The Spanish were another matter entirely. In the soaking, crippled and exhausted prisoners Collingwood glimpsed an opportunity to change the political landscape of the war and he wrote this letter to the Governor of Cadiz.

EURYALUS, OFF CADIZ
27TH OCTOBER 1805

My Lord Marquis

A great number of Spanish Subjects, having been wounded in the late Action, between the British, and the Combined Fleets, of Spain, and France, on the 21st Ins.

Humanity, and my desire to aleviate the sufferings of these wounded men, dictate to me to offer to your Excellency their enlargement, that they may be taken proper care of, in the Hospitals on shore, provided, your Excellency will send boats to convey them, with a proper officer to give receipts for the number, and acknowledge them in your Excellency's Answer to this letter to be Prisoners of War, to be exchanged, before they serve again.

I beg to assure your Excellency of my high consideration, and that I am,
Your Lordships, most obedient
humble servant

Cuthbert Collingwood

To His Excellency,
The Marquis de Solana
Captain General of Andalusia,
Governor, etc etc etc

Cadiz

Napoleon had, indeed, allied with Spain but it is important to remember that the French and Spanish were still ideological enemies at heart. Spain was ruled by a Bourbon monarch; the French revolutionaries had executed their Bourbon monarch; and in 1805 Napoleon was attacking Naples, the throne of another Bourbon monarch who was also the younger brother of the Spanish king. This sat particularly uncomfortably with Admiral Gravina, a Sicilian by birth who had made it clear that he would never fight against his own king. There was, therefore, a good deal of uncertainty within the Spanish ranks regarding their alliance with Napoleon which Collingwood exploited.

His letter is full of humanity, magnanimity, generosity and benevolence. He offers to return the Spanish wounded to Spain, to convalesce on their own soil while retaining their status as prisoners of war, a gesture that was never forgotten by the Spanish. His offer was immediately accepted.

> *I Guillaume Valverde, having been authorized, and impowered, by the Marquis de Solana, Governor General of Andalusia, and of Cadiz, to receive from the English Squadron the wounded Prisoners and such persons, as may be necessary to their care; — which release, and Enlargement of the Wounded etcᵈ is agreed to, on the part of the Commander in Chief of the British Squadron, on the positive Condition that none of the said Prisoners shall be employed again, in any public service of the Crown of Spain, either by Sea, or Land, until they are regularly exchanged.*
>
> *Signed on board His Britannic Majesty's ship the Euryalus, at Sea, the 30ᵗʰ October 1805.*
>
> *Guillᵐᵒ de Valverde*
>
> EDECAR DE S. E.

It is widely believed that Collingwood's diplomacy in 1805 facilitated the Spanish-British alliance of 1808, formed in the aftermath of Napoleon's invasion of Spain. It is a valuable reminder that Collingwood, like his predecessors John Norris (1670–1749) and Charles Wager (1666–1743), and his contemporary James Saumarez (1757–1836), was one of Britain's most gifted naval diplomats.

Vice-Admiral C. Collingwood to Vice-Admiral I. D'Alava, 30 October 1805

Collingwood was not prepared to let his generosity towards the Spaniards go too far, however. In an earlier letter he had written of Alava's death (p. 272 – 'Don Aleva') but as soon as he discovered the Spanish flag-officer to be alive, and somehow to have escaped to Cadiz, he dashed off this letter reminding the vice-admiral of his status as a prisoner of war. Collingwood is prepared to let Alava stay in Cadiz as a British prisoner, in the same way that he has let all of the other Spanish prisoners return to Spain.

EURYALUS, OFF CADIZ
30TH OCTOBER 1805

It is with great pleasure that I have heard, the wound you received in the Action is in a hopeful way of recovery, and that your Country may still have the benefit of your future service. –

But, Sir, you surrendered yourself to me, and it was in consideration only of the state of your wound that you were not removed into my Ship.

I could not disturb the repose of a Man supposed to be in his last moments: – But your Sword the Emblem of your Service, was delivered to me by your Captain, and I expect that you consider yourself a Prisoner of War, until you shall be regularly exchanged by Cartel. –

I have the honor to be,

Sir,

Your most obedient humble servant

Cuthbert Collingwood

To VICE ADMIRAL
DON IGNATIO MARIA D'ALAVA

Alava's reply is not included in this collection of dispatches but we know that he disputed the details of his surrender, claiming that his ship was surrendered without his knowledge and that his weapons, symbols of his office and status, remained in his power. He argued that his flag captain, Don Francisco Riguelme, surrendered his own sword as Alava lay below. Alava put the confusion down to Riguelme being unable to speak good English and sent Collingwood a large cask of particularly fine wine to help matters along.

Collingwood was rather unimpressed by Alava's response but did not press matters. Instead, he sent the Spanish Admiral a large English cheese and a cask of porter, both of which were very rare in Cadiz and were consumed by a delighted party at Alava's house. Alava generously returned the gesture with 60 melons and 'some baskets' of grapes, figs and pomegranates. The two remained in regular contact for some time, another important contact point with the Spanish that undoubtedly contributed to Spain's change of sides in 1808. In these unpredictable wars, the exchange of fruit and cheese could be as important as the exchange of blood and bullets.

Vice-Admiral C. Collingwood to Lieutenant J. Lapenotiere, 26 October 1805

This is a wonderful letter. Written by Collingwood, it is addressed to John Lapenotiere, commander of the *Pickle* and the man sent back with the dispatches. The urgency and excitement are tangible.

By Cuthbert Collingwood Esqr
Vice Admiral of the Blue
commanding a squadron of His
Majesty's Ships, off Cadiz

You are hereby required, and directed to proceed in His Majesty's Schooner under your Command to England, and on your arrival at Plymouth, you are immediately to forward the accompanying dispatches to the Secretary of the Admiralty, by taking them yourself express to him, or (if the Quarantine Law prevent it)[29] *by sending them the moment of your arrival, to Vice Admiral Young, for the same purpose.*

Should you be prevented by an Easterly Wind, from fetching so high up as Plymouth, you are to make the first port you can in England and act as is above directed; taking care to obtain a receipt for the dispatches with which you are charged, and which are of the highest importance.

As I trust you are fully aware of the great importance of those dispatches being forwarded as soon as is possible I rely on your using every exertion, that a moment's time may not be lost in their delivery.

Given on board the Euryalus off Cadiz, 26ᵗʰ October 1805

Cuthbt. Collingwood

To Lieutenant Lapeniotiere
Commanding His Majesty's Schooner
the Pickle
by Command of the Vice Admiral

C. H. Cosmay

If necessary, these dispatches are to be thrown overboard, and for which you are to be prepared.

This was not the *Pickle's* only big moment. The small ships of the fleet always kept well clear of the fighting but they had come into their own in the chaos of the battle's aftermath. The *Pickle*, in particular, had performed heroically and had gone to the rescue of the French *Achille* when she erupted into an inferno and her crew threw themselves into the sea to get clear of the flames. The *Pickle* darted in and her crew dragged around 100 Frenchmen and one woman, named Jeanette,[30] from the water.

Over the following days, the *Pickle* worked tirelessly to prevent damaged ships of both nationalities from driving ashore. It is possible that Collingwood chose the *Pickle* to take the dispatches back because she was exceptionally fast, a Bermudan-built schooner of only 127 tons and no more than 73 feet long, but it is less clear why he chose Lapenotiere. In every other battle the bearer of dispatches was a senior naval officer, usually the admiral's flag captain.[31]

We know very little about Lapenotiere. He was born of a Huguenot family that had come to Britain with William of Orange in 1688 and his career up to 1805 had been unremarkable. He had joined the navy in 1790 very young, aged only 10, and had missed every major battle since. Something of a specialist in small boats, he had taken part in a number of minor skirmishes on the French coast and had played an important part in saving the crew of the wrecked *Magnificent* in 1804. He had no known significant political contacts.

The strangeness of Collingwood's choice therefore suggests the repayment of a debt and one such story has survived, although its authenticity is unproven. Collingwood and Lapenotiere are on deck, on an unnamed warship, in an unnamed location, when an order is given that will take the ship onto the rocks. Lapenotiere immediately counters the order and saves the ship. Collingwood is said to have commented, 'If ever I have the opportunity, I will do you a service.' When Lapenotiere was summoned to the *Euryalus* after Trafalgar, Collingwood said to him, 'Now take these dispatches to England; you will receive £500 and your commander's commission. Now I have kept my word.'[32] Although Collingwood is prepared to entrust the dispatches to Lapenotiere, he still orders him to get a receipt.

We do, however, know the details of his 1,000-mile journey. He left two days before the storm reached its height and had a filthy passage past Cape Finisterre. But after a voyage of nine days he arrived in Falmouth. It took a little over two hours to tie up, get ashore and source a post-chaise and, as soon as it was ready, Lapenotiere headed for London, flying a tattered French tricolour from a broomstick. He went like the wind. We even know the 21 locations where he stopped to eat or change horses in his 271-mile journey: Truro; the Blue Anchor[33] posting-house at Fraddon near present-day Penhale; Bodmin; Launceston; Okehampton; Crockernwell; Exeter; Honiton; Axminster; Bridport; Dorchester; Blandford; Woodyates; Salisbury; Andover; Overton; Basingstoke; Hertford Bridge; Bagshot; Staines; Hounslow; and finally, the Admiralty.

The journey normally took a week, but after only 37 hours of hard driving in a post-chaise Lapenotiere arrived at the Admiralty building in London's Whitehall. It was one o'clock in the morning. The Admiralty secretary, William Marsden, was still awake, finishing off work on the latest documents he had received. Lapenotiere met him with words that would unite the nation in both celebration and mourning: 'Sir, we have gained a great victory; but we have lost Lord Nelson.'[34] Marsden was profoundly shocked but also acutely aware of his position as 'the only person informed of one of the greatest events recorded in our history'.[35] As soon as the news arrived, he went to wake the First Lord, Lord Barham, who was not asleep in the state bedroom but in the adjoining boudoir. Barham was 79 years old but had spent his entire adult life in the Royal Navy and was instantly alert, his ability to cope with nocturnal interruptions deeply ingrained. He simply said, 'What news, Mr M?'[36]

And what news it was. Just two hours later, it had reached the Prime Minister and, at seven in the morning, the King.

Captain R. Strachan to W. Marsden, 4 November 1805

Lapenotiere set off on 26 October with his weighty packet of letters but there was still one more important dispatch to be sent to London and that was Richard Strachan's account of the battle he fought on 4 November off Cape Ortegal on the north-western tip of Spain.

The enemy fleet, Rear-Admiral Dumanoir's van division from Trafalgar, consisted of four powerful ships of the line, an exact match for Strachan's battleships, but the British also had four frigates that were used to great advantage to chase, harass and then overpower the French ships, all of which were taken.

CÆSAR WEST OF ROCHFORT 264 MILES
4ᵀᴴ NOVᴿ 1805 WIND SE

Sir

Cæsar
Hero
Courageux
Namur

Bellona, } *far to*
Æolus } *Leeward*
Santa Margarita } *in the SE*

Being off Ferrol working to the Westward with the Wind Westerly, On the Evening of the 2ⁿᵈ we observed a Frigate in the NW making Signals, made all Sail to join her before Night, and followed by the Ships named in the Margin, we came up with her at 11 at night, and at the moment she joined us, we saw six large Ships near us, Captain Baker informed me he had been Chaced by the French Rochfort Squadron then close to Leeward of us, we were delighted.* *I desired him to tell the Captains of the Ships of the Line astern to follow me, as I meant to Engage them directly, and immediately bore away in the Cæsar for the purpose, making all the Signals I could, to indicate our movements to our Ships, the Moon enabled us to see the Enemy bear away in Line abreast closely form'd, but we lost sight of them when it set, and I was obliged to reduce our Sails, the Hero, Courageux and Æolus being the only Ships we could see. We continued steering to the ENE all Night, and in the morning observed the Santa Margarita near us, at 9 we discovered the Enemy of Four Sail of the Line in the NE under all Sail. We had also every thing set and came up with them fast, in the evening we observed three Sail astern, and the Phœnix spoke me at Night. I found that Active Officer Captain Baker had delivered my Orders, and I sent him on to assist the Santa Margarita in leading us up to the Enemy, at Day light we were near them and the Santa Margarita had began in a very Gallant manner to fire upon their Rear, and was soon joined by the Phœnix.*

A little before Noon, the French finding an Action unavoidable, began to take in their small Sails and form in a Line of bearing on the Starboard Tack, We did the same, and I communicated my intentions by hailing to the Captains "that I should Attack the Centre and Rear", and at Noon began the Battle, in a short time the Van Ship of the Enemy tack'd, which almost directly made the Action Close and General, the Namur joined soon after we tacked, which we did, as soon as would get the Ships round, and I directed her by Signal to Engage the Van, at half past 3 the Action ceased, the Enemy having fought to Admiration and did not Surrender 'till their Ships were unmanageable. I have returned thanks to the Captains of the Ships of the Line and the Frigates, and they speak in high terms of approbation of their respective Officers and Ships Companies. – if any thing could add to the good opinion I had already formed of the Officers and Crew of the Cæsar, it is their Gallant Conduct in this Day's Battle. the Enemy have suffered much, but our Ships not more than is to be expected

---

* Ever after this dispatch was published, Strachan was known as 'the Delighted Sir Dicky' for this phrase. *Mariner's Mirror*, 34 (1948), 151.

on these occasions. – You may judge of my Surprize, Sir, when I found the Ships we had taken were not the Rochfort Squadron but from Cadiz.

I have the honor to be

with sincere respect

Your very humble and

Obedient Servant

The captured ships, which were taken back to England, had a disproportionate effect on the way that Trafalgar was perceived by the public because so many of Collingwood's prizes were sunk off the coast of Spain. Indeed, of the Allied ships captured at Trafalgar, only the French *Swiftsure* and the Spanish *Bahama* and *San Ildefonso* made it back to England, and they did so weeks after the battle. The very first physical evidence of the great confrontation that could be viewed and admired by the mob was therefore Strachan's prizes. Not only did this victory complete Nelson's dream of annihilation but it also provided the public with the physical proof of the might of British seapower that they craved.

One of Strachan's prizes, *Duguay-Trouin*,[37] went on to enjoy a particularly distinguished career. She served in the Royal Navy under her new name, *Implacable*, and became a training ship in her twilight years. Indeed, she lasted so long that she became famous as the second oldest ship in the Royal Navy, after *Victory,* and as the only surviving French or Spanish ship from Trafalgar. It was a particular shame, therefore, that she was deliberately sunk in 1949 because of excessive maintenance costs in the post-war economic slump, the French also having refused to maintain her as a museum. Parts of her do remain, however, notably the towering stern gallery that confronts visitors as soon as they enter the National Maritime Museum in Greenwich, but her absence is a painful cross to bear for the heritage industries of both Britain and France. It is fitting that the motto of the World Ship Trust, an international organisation dedicated to the preservation of historic ships, is 'Implacable, never again', though the WST's goals are constantly challenged by the logistical and political problems which conspire against the survival of such ships.

Captain R. Strachan to his squadron, 6 November 1805

Strachan's dispatch is disappointingly bland for one who was known by his crew as 'Mad Dick' for his ungovernable temper and violent cursing. His men claimed that 'when he swore he meant no harm, and when he prayed he meant no good'.[38] Strachan in turn, and in good humour, knew his crew as 'damned mutinous rascals'. They were extremely fond of him and he of them. He was always lenient when presiding over courts martial and was always a sought-after commander. This was still a time, remember, when sailors, within reason and given certain restrictions, could choose to follow a commander from ship to ship like a tribe. One contemporary claimed, 'I do not believe he has his fellow among the Admirals, unless it be Pellew, for ability, and it is not possible to have more zeal and gallantry'.[39] Nevertheless, this letter of thanks to his crews offers a glimpse, albeit a brief one, of the warmth that Strachan felt for his men who had fought for him so bravely.

GENERAL MEM^D

Having returned thanks to Almighty God for the Victory obtained over the French Squadron, the Senior Captain begs to make his grateful Acknowledgements for the support he has received from the Ships of the Line and the Frigates. — And requests the Captains will do him the honor to accept his thanks, and communicate to their respective Officers and Ships Companies, how much he Admires their Zealous and Gallant Conduct —

Cæsar at Sea
6th Novr 1805

R. J. Strachan

To
THE RESPECTIVE CAPTAINS
AND COMMANDERS

Although he was happy at sea with his naval family, Strachan's career fell apart when, in 1809, he was placed in charge of the naval contribution to a vast amphibious operation aimed at the Dutch island of Walcheren. The volatile Strachan soon fell out with the commander of the army, John Pitt, the operation ended in failure and it was Strachan who was hung out to dry. It was a sorry end for a man so well liked and so grateful to those who reciprocated his love and trust.

The impact of Trafalgar on the war is not what one might expect from a battle with such a dominant position in British history. If one adds the ships taken by Strachan to those taken by Collingwood, only five of the original fleet of 33 Allied ships of the line were still in Allied hands and, of those that reached Cadiz, one was laid up as a hulk and the others kept in harbour until they were surrendered to the Spanish in June 1808. The Royal Navy had achieved its dream of destruction. But did the victory stop Napoleon in his tracks as Nelson had believed? Not at all.

The battle did not prevent an invasion of England because Napoleon had already changed his strategy and his Grande Armée had marched inland. It soon won crushing victories at Ulm, in which the French captured an entire Austrian army under the command of the incompetent General Mack (pp. 170–1), and at Austerlitz, where a Russo-Austrian army, commanded by the Tsar, was routed, effectively ending the Third Coalition. In the immediate aftermath of Trafalgar, therefore, Austria was crushed, the Holy Roman Empire destroyed and Napoleon's ambition only encouraged. The French dominated central Europe for another decade.

French naval strategy, however, changed significantly. British maritime dominance now made it too risky to launch ambitious trans-oceanic campaigns such as the invasion of Egypt in 1798 or Hispaniola in 1803. The French therefore turned towards smaller raiding squadrons, cunningly located where they could cause the most disruption to British trade. This strategy was partnered by a direct economic assault on Britain via Napoleon's Continental System, a structured embargo of British trade by a pro-Napoleonic alliance of European powers.

The Spanish navy, already in decline, was dealt a blow at Trafalgar from which it never recovered; between 1798 and 1853 not a single Spanish warship was launched. There was neither money nor political support for a maritime strategy. The unhappy Spanish alliance with Napoleon had been the death of its navy and

Russia soon took Spain's place as Europe's third largest naval power. The Spanish naval threat had all but disappeared but now the Baltic, once again, became a theatre of naval war.

In the aftermath of Trafalgar the Royal Navy was thus faced with a new Baltic threat, with the continuing challenge of blockading French ports, with countering French raiding squadrons and with launching its own operations in support of the land campaigns against Napoleon. By no means could the Royal Navy stand down after Trafalgar. Her sailors were sent back to fight in the iron chill of the Baltic, the deep blue of the Atlantic, the silvery stillness of the Mediterranean and the turquoise waters of the Caribbean.

San Domingo
Santo Domingo

6 February 1806

' ... it is impossible for Language to convey an adequate sense of my feelings ... '

Admiral John Duckworth, 7 February 1806

AT A GLANCE

DATE:
6 February 1806

NAVIES INVOLVED:
British and French

COMMANDING OFFICERS:
Vice-Admiral J. Duckworth and Contre-Admiral C. Leissègues

FLEET SIZES:
British, 7 ships of the line; French, 5 ships of the line

TIME OF DAY:
10.00 – 12.00

LOCATION:
Off Santo Domingo. 18°18′N 70°03′W

WEATHER:
Light north north-westerly breezes

RESULT:
3 French ships of the line captured, 2 destroyed

CASUALTIES:
British 338; French 1,510

BRITISH COURT MARTIALS:
None

DISPATCHES CARRIED HOME BY:
Commander Nathaniel Cochrane

The Sextant

Eighteenth-century sextants are not rare but one, in the collections of the National Maritime Museum in Greenwich, is unique. It is not an elaborate object; there are no engravings of an owner's initials, dates or images; but it is a working piece, made of polished brass, with a plain, wooden handle. It has obviously seen some use. Its tangent screw, a critical piece of its mechanism, is bent. It has no accompanying box. Its three sunshades, two red and one green, are slightly marked. It used to belong to Vice-Admiral John Duckworth.

A sextant measures the angle between two objects, usually between the midday sun and the horizon to establish one's latitude but, if near land, it can also be used horizontally to measure the angle between two landmarks. The sextant therefore partially answers one of the two principal questions that mariners are repeatedly posed: 'Where am I?' and 'In which direction do I need to go?'

For a naval officer in 1806 the first problem was much simpler than the second. After the invention in the 1760s of the marine chronometer, which was used to help plot one's longitude, an experienced navigator could discover his location with impressive precision given accurate instruments and helpful atmospheric conditions. The answer to the second question, however, was not necessarily so easy to discover.

Captains and admirals were issued with orders, but those orders all allowed for a certain degree of initiative, simply because they had to. Communication was excruciatingly slow, to the point that the verb 'to communicate', with its implication of a two-way exchange, is rather unhelpful. On some stations it could take *months* to send a message and receive a reply, by which time the immediate strategic situation would inevitably have changed. While a commander was at sea and out of touch, governments could fall, administrations could be restructured, politics could shift one way or another, and the course of wars could derail or suddenly assume an entirely new aspect. He therefore had to use his wits. 'In which direction do I need to go?' could effectively mean 'Which direction would the Lords of the Admiralty expect me take, given the extant circumstances?' for a sea officer would always be required to explain himself and the end did not always justify the means. The decisions of sea officers who were hundreds, if not thousands, of miles away were regularly used to make telling political or strategic blows at home.

All this is important to bear in mind when considering the Battle of San Domingo. It is particularly relevant because Duckworth's sextant is one of the very few of his personal possessions to have survived and it reminds us never to take the location of a sea battle for granted. Yes, Duckworth won a great victory over the French at San Domingo in 1806, but what on earth was he doing in the Caribbean at all? What went through his mind when he peered through those charming red and green sunshades, shot the position of the sun and then plotted his course to the Leeward Islands where, quite by chance, he came across a French squadron? He was supposed to be blockading Cadiz.

The Survivors

In the aftermath of Trafalgar, the British squadrons off the coasts of France and Spain resumed their blockade. The combined fleet had been beaten at Trafalgar but Spain was still allied with France and there was still a powerful French fleet in Brest – which had missed the entire Trafalgar campaign – a smaller force in Rochefort and another combined force of French and Spanish ships in Cadiz. The French and Spanish still had a colonial presence in the Caribbean and the East Indies, and Napoleon still had ambitions for a significant campaign in the eastern Mediterranean which, in his eyes, had only been temporarily frustrated by Nelson's great victory at the Nile. Moreover, British colonial possessions and the arteries of British trade remained isolated and vulnerable.

British economic security, therefore, still had to be maintained by preventing French and Spanish forces from making any threatening moves. Napoleon also had to shore up his own colonial possessions and that could only be done with, or via, the exercise of seapower. Guadeloupe and Martinique were now relatively secure but Saint Domingue was a problem. This once-thriving French colony had fallen to a slave revolt in 1791 and there had been fierce fighting ever since. The charismatic ex-slave leader Toussaint L'Ouverture had been defeated and shipped back to prison in France. However, his powerful position had been seized by another impressive leader, Jean Jacques Dessalines, who, after a successful campaign, proclaimed the new, free Republic of Haiti, the first post-colonial, black-led nation in the world. Then, mimicking Napoleon, Dessalines declared himself Emperor of Haiti with the power to anoint his successor and, among other innovative laws, banned white people from owning property. Napoleon was deeply unhappy with the loss of such a valuable colony and was determined to send troop reinforcements to strengthen the weak position of his forces on the island.

As the autumn of 1805 turned to winter, therefore, the British task of containing French seapower was a complex and demanding one. In the filthy winter weather it soon also became a grim one, particularly off Brest. The coastline of Brittany is plagued by fog at all times of year and its waters run with fierce and challenging currents over hidden rocks. The great fetch of Biscay allows Atlantic swells to rear up and toss ships mercilessly in the teeth of the prevailing south-westerly winds. Keeping the sea ceaselessly throughout the winter was all but impossible and, on 13 December 1805, the blockading British ships headed for home.

The cold and exhausted British sailors took their weather-beaten ships to Torbay in the belief that the weather would provide more than the level of discouragement needed to keep the demoralised French in port. It was a bad misjudgement. A powerful fleet, consisting of 11 ships of the line, four frigates, a corvette and two dispatch vessels in two separate squadrons under the combined command of Contre Admirals Jean-Baptiste Willaumez and Corentin de Leissègues, was waiting for just such an opportunity. They broke out and headed first west and then south. Initially Willaumez steered for the South Atlantic and Leissègues for San Domingo, but both had detailed orders to attack British trade once their primary tasks had been completed.

Almost immediately they stumbled into a British convoy, whose escort raced back to Britain with the shocking intelligence that a large French force was loose. The Admiralty quickly ordered two separate squadrons to sea to search them out, one under Rear-Admiral John Warren and the other under Rear-Admiral Richard Strachan. Duckworth, meanwhile, was off Cadiz and he heard from a separate source that the French were at sea. He wrongly assumed that it was the French squadron from Rochefort but their specific identity had little relevance to his next move. He had clear orders to blockade Cadiz but what should he do now? Should he pursue the enemy and negate those orders? If so, would his absence from Cadiz simply make it more likely that *another* enemy squadron would get to sea unnoticed, destination unknown?

It would have been wrong to assume that Duckworth would catch up with, or even find, the enemy squadron. Once past the familiar landfalls and regular traffic of the European Atlantic seaboard, it was far more likely that a French squadron, intent on escape, would disappear. It was not a matter, therefore, of weighing up the disadvantages of abandoning Cadiz with the advantages of finding and then catching an elusive enemy squadron. There was always a great deal of uncertainty in the finding, chasing and defeating of any enemy.

Moreover, if Duckworth *did* chase, how long should he chase for? Should he head into the Atlantic for one day, maybe two, and then return to base or to his blockade? Or should he take his pursuit further, to the Caribbean or the East Indies? Should he even pursue his enemy *wherever* it took him? Such liberal orders were not unheard of, but they were always issued in a specific and known strategic situation such as Nelson's madcap trans-Atlantic pursuit of Villeneuve in the spring and summer of 1805, or his Mediterranean hunt for the French in 1798 prior to the Battle of the Nile. In both instances, Nelson had been chosen to chase, had been ordered to chase and, by chasing, had not endangered the integrity of a more broadly conceived British naval strategy. Duckworth had no such orders, however. Even if the enemy was caught and brought to battle, there was, as yet, no way of knowing if the French escape was part of another more complex scheme to draw British blockading forces away from the coast of Europe and hence enable the main strike of a new offensive to fall elsewhere. And if that was the case, then to chase the unidentified enemy squadron was to play directly into the enemy's hands.

Duckworth was certainly placed in an awkward situation and he had no recourse to higher authority, but by no means all British naval officers would have done what he did. To understand the reasons for his decision to abandon his station and head for the mid-Atlantic, we must peer into Duckworth's past.

The Aspirant

The only images of Duckworth that have survived are copies of a famous portrait made shortly after San Domingo (fig. 20), in which he wears the medals he received for The Glorious First of June as well as for the later battle. He is captured almost in motion, his sword tucked under his arm as if hurrying off to an urgent appointment, his eyebrows slightly raised, possibly in surprise, probably in confusion. He appears slightly ridiculous.

Duckworth was the son of a parson. His family was long-settled in Lancashire but had no titles or honours to its name. Nelson was also a parson's son and Duckworth had seen Nelson's star rise from plain old Horatio Nelson to the extraordinary title that is now inscribed on his tomb in St Paul's:

> The Most Noble Lord Horatio Nelson, Viscount and Baron Nelson, of the Nile and of Burnham Thorpe in the County of Norfolk, Baron Nelson of the Nile and of Hilborough in the said County, Knight of the Most Honourable Order of the Bath, Vice-Admiral of the White Squadron of the Fleet, Commander in Chief of his Majesty's Ships and Vessels in the Mediterranean, Duke of Bronté in the Kingdom of Sicily, Knight Grand Cross of the Sicilian Order of St Ferdinand and of Merit, member of the Ottoman Order of the Crescent, Knight Grand Commander of the Order of St Joachim.

In February 1806 John Duckworth had achieved equal rank to Nelson, becoming a Vice-Admiral of the White, and had also received a KB for successful operations in 1802 against Swedish and Danish possessions in the Caribbean. However, he had also been frustrated in 1798 after the recapture of Minorca when he had made it painfully and unsubtly clear that he had expected a KB, if not a baronetcy, for his conduct. The Admiralty had been riled by his pretension 'on which St Vincent, representing the matter to Lord Spencer, threw a sufficiency of cold water'.[1] Duckworth had been competent at Minorca, but he had done nothing more than follow his superiors' orders and nothing sufficiently dramatic to deserve such a reward.

Duckworth was therefore aggressively pursuing a dream of social advancement in a way that made many of his powerful political and professional superiors uncomfortable, if not irritated. In fact, he had rather a poor reputation and had already been court martialled three times.

The first two occasions, curiously, were over the same offence, though the charges were different. Serving in America in the early 1770s, he was first lieutenant of the frigate *Diamond*. Returning from a cruise, in which she had sailed with her guns loaded, the *Diamond*, according to custom, was required to fire a salute. Duckworth supervised the unloading of the cannon and counted the shot before giving the order to fire the salute, but one of the cannon had been double-shotted. The forgotten shot, fired from its gun, slammed into the hull of a nearby British ship and killed five men.

Duckworth was court martialled for neglect of duty and then, in an entirely separate court martial designed to head off action in the civil courts, was tried for murder. He was acquitted of both charges but his reputation was stained by the incident. His third court martial resulted from a decision he took during his command of the Jamaica station in 1804. Duckworth had installed a protégé as captain of a frigate and then sent it back to Britain laden with building goods for his new house just outside Exeter, apparently contravening several articles of war in the process. Yet again, however, he was acquitted, although his actions raised several troubling questions. Was he suited to high command? Was he irresponsible? Was he, even, corrupt?

His experience of fleet battle is also relevant. Duckworth joined the navy aged only 11, and served in Edward Boscawen's flagship, *Namur*. Boscawen was a dashing fellow, a true precursor of Nelson. With the young Duckworth aboard in the summer of 1759, he chased and defeated a squadron of French ships off Lagos in one of the navy's more dramatic victories. Duckworth then found himself transferred to the flagship of Edward Hawke, another fine model and another worthy precursor of Nelson. In Hawke's service, Duckworth fought at the battle of Quiberon Bay in November 1759, a thunderous and overwhelming victory over a French fleet in coastal waters, at night, and during a storm.

Duckworth was thus blooded, very early on, in a type of naval warfare that emphasised spontaneity, intense violence and overwhelming victory. In the subsequent years, however, he took part in only one of the numerous fleet battles of the War of American Independence or the Revolutionary or Napoleonic Wars when he commanded the 74-gun *Orion* at The Glorious First of June. Crucially, however, he missed Trafalgar, the greatest battle of his generation, through no one's fault but his own. Just before the battle, he had been appointed to replace the Earl of Northesk as Nelson's third in command, but had refused to sail until his favourite band of musicians arrived, an extraordinary self-indulgence. So

Duckworth had a record of thirsting for glory; he had experience of battle resulting from dramatic chases launched by fleet commanders in spur of the moment decisions; and he was frustrated at missing Trafalgar.

Duckworth's flag captain, Richard Keats, was also frustrated. He had had an impressive fighting career in frigates and frigate squadrons and had fought with great skill during an impressive victory over the French and Spanish on 12 July 1801 at the Battle of Algeciras. He had, however, fought in none of the major large-scale fleet victories so far described. This must have grated for such a talented and aggressive officer who was highly regarded by Nelson. Indeed, at a meeting with Keats in the days before Nelson left for Cadiz before the Battle of Trafalgar, Nelson promised him the prestigious position of being his 'second' in any forthcoming battle, and a surviving order of battle issued before Trafalgar confirms this. The *Superb* is listed as second in line, astern of the *Temeraire* and immediately ahead of Nelson's *Victory*.[2] After Nelson's chase of Villeneuve, however, Keats had been sent home to refit the *Superb*. She was ready in time to participate in Trafalgar but she had been chosen as Duckworth's new flagship and so her departure from Portsmouth was delayed as he waited for his band. So Keats missed Trafalgar solely because of his association with Duckworth. This is likely to have been a cause of the subsequent falling out between the two men. When they finally sailed together for Cadiz, they barely spoke and occasionally communicated in writing to avoid contact with each other.

Moreover, there were several other frustrated officers in Duckworth's squadron. Foremost of these was Rear-Admiral Thomas Louis.[*] As a young officer, Louis had seen significant fleet action during the American War at the Battle of Ushant in 1778 and at Rodney's celebrated destruction of a Spanish squadron in the Moonlight Battle of 1780. Louis had then served in Nelson's Mediterranean squadron at the Battle of the Nile. Nelson considered Louis a close friend and his ship, the 80-gun *Canopus*, formed an important part of Nelson's fleet as it whiled away the time off Cadiz just before the Battle of Trafalgar. Then, on 11 October, 10 days before the battle, Nelson ordered Louis to Gibraltar to secure water and supplies for the fleet and to escort an eastward-bound troop convoy past the Spanish naval base of Cartagena. Louis was horrified and reproached Nelson:

---

[*] Whose grandfather, according to family tradition, was an illegitimate son of Louis XIV.

'You are sending us away, my Lord – the enemy will come out, and we shall have no share in the battle.'[3] Nelson characteristically turned the curse of unwanted duty into a compliment and replied: 'I look upon *Canopus* as my right hand, and I send you first to insure your being here to help to beat them.'[4] But the *Canopus* did not return in time for the battle and Louis never saw his friend again.

Among Duckworth's other captains, Captain Pulteney Malcolm of the *Donegal*, the nephew of the famous naval warrior Thomas Pasley (pp. 64–7), had missed every single major battle of his time, as had the young Captain Samuel Pym of the *Atlas*, while Robert Stopford of the *Spencer* had fought at The Glorious First of June but had missed everything since. Indeed, the only captain in Duckworth's squadron with significant recent battle experience was Edward Berry in the *Agamemnon*.

Duckworth, his flag captain, his rear-admiral and most of his captains were therefore champing at the bit to fight the French, wherever they could be found. And so, when Duckworth heard news of a nearby French squadron causing havoc among British convoys between Madeira and the Canary Islands, he immediately abandoned his post off Cadiz and chased. Having found nothing, he made his way back towards Cadiz, frustrated again. On that return journey, however, he heard news of yet another French squadron, which he erroneously believed to be the Rochefort squadron but which was, in fact, Willaumez sailing from Brest and bound for South America. Duckworth hared off after him, chasing another rumour.

The Goose Chase

This time Duckworth did find his prey, which he chased for 30 hours until his flagship was within only seven miles of the enemy. Both fleets were by now very strung out, with the sternmost of the British fleet as much as 45 miles behind Duckworth, who was in the lead. Although this was a significant distance, it was not unusual for a chasing fleet to find itself so spread out and there was a solution to the tactical problem it posed.

Duckworth could continue with his chase and harry the enemy rear in the hope of disabling one or even two enemy ships. As the fresh British ships then came up, the disabled enemy ships could be overwhelmed. To attack the enemy rear was thus to put the tactical onus on the commander of the escaping fleet. Should he continue with his escape or turn to protect his rearmost ships? If he did the latter, he would almost certainly bring about a general action. To attack the rearmost ships of the enemy was therefore to challenge both the escaping admiral's sense of honour and to test his orders. Had he been ordered to avoid battle at all costs or, if threatened, was he permitted to fight?

Duckworth, however, did nothing. With the enemy in sight, and a gap of no more than six or seven miles between the leading British ship and the sternmost of the French, he abandoned his chase. In the fluid world of orders, expectation, honour and duty, his decision to abandon the chase was undoubtedly wrong because he had lost the opportunity of explaining or justifying his abandonment of Cadiz. He later expressed his concern that his flagship would be overwhelmed if the enemy chose to turn and fight, a curious mindset for someone who had invested so heavily in such a chase.

The result of this abandoned pursuit was that Duckworth was now deep in the Atlantic, far closer to the Caribbean than to his station off Cadiz, and he was running out of water. The French fleet had escaped, its destination unknown. Duckworth therefore headed for the Caribbean, arriving at Barbados in the second week of January, and then moved his squadron further north to St Kitts, where he met with the commander in chief of the Leeward Islands, Alexander Cochrane. Duckworth's squadron of seven ships of the line now contained no less than three flag-officers, an extraordinary concentration of high-ranking officers for such a small force.

Eight days later, the squadron which had sailed from Brest under Leissègues, and not the squadron under Willaumez which Duckworth had just chased, arrived at San Domingo and unloaded 1,800 troops to reinforce General Ferrand in his continuing war against Dessalines. Word soon reached St Kitts that the French were nearby and Duckworth, seizing an opportunity to justify his presence in the Caribbean, hared off, for the third time, after a French squadron. The general intelligence that Duckworth had received was accurate but the detail was not. He believed that the force at San Domingo was only one part of a French fleet, the rest of which was somewhere to leeward.

This gave even greater impetus to this new chase because Duckworth was anxious to get at the French before they could unite. When the fleets finally sighted each other, they were both flying at eight knots, the maximum speed possible in the conditions and eight times faster than the speed at which most of the British ships attacked at Trafalgar. It was the most dramatic attack of any of the battles of the Revolutionary and Napoleonic Wars. Hitherto, they had all been ponderous, with both sides willing, if not entirely prepared, to fight. San Domingo was different, a pure chase. The French were trying desperately to escape to the safety of a nearby bay protected by shore batteries and the British were trying to stop them.

The French fleet was led by *L'Impérial*, an absolute monster of a ship, one of the *Ocean* Class of French First Rates built to inspire awe of the French military machine wherever they went. *L'Impérial* was larger than the mighty four-decked Spanish *Santissima Trinidad* and far larger than anything that the British had ever built, let alone anything in Duckworth's fleet. The largest British ship at San Domingo was the 80 gun *Canopus* with a displacement of 2,258^{77}/$_{94}$ tons,[5] and a crew of 700. The 118-gun *Impérial*, in contrast, had a displacement greater by 671 tons, a crew of well over 1,000, and carried 3,265 square metres of canvas. Her sails blocked out the sun.

Laid down by the zealous revolutionaries of the early Republic, she was christened *Peuple* and then, in the aftermath of The Glorious First of June, became the *Vengeur du Peuple* in honour of the ship of that name which had fought so dramatically and sunk without surrender (pp. 67–8, fig. 4). In March 1805, three months after Napoleon had crowned himself Emperor, she was renamed again, this time as *L'Impérial*, the very embodiment of Napoleonic imperial ambition, majesty and pride. She was noteworthy among her class of huge First Rates because she was the first to carry 18-pounder cannon on her third deck, rather than the usual 12-pounders, a significant increase that set the standard for all subsequent First Rates.

The British had nothing to compare. British shipbuilding policy had focused in recent years on the construction of smaller ships in greater numbers. When the fleets met at San Domingo, the entire Royal Navy had only two First Rates of more than 100 guns, the recently launched 110-gun *Hibernia* and the 110-gun *Ville de Paris*, and both were far smaller than *Impérial*. The navy was still waiting for her first First Rate ship of 120 guns, HMS *Caledonia*, which had been ordered in 1794 but had still not been completed. Indeed, in 1806, the majority of British First Rates were from an altogether different generation: *Britannia* (1762), *Victory* (1765), *Royal Sovereign* (1786), *Royal George* (1788) and *Queen Charlotte* (1790). *L'Impérial*, therefore, was a ship of an altogether greater order. She would make a fine prize indeed and would sate the thirst for glory that pervaded Duckworth's squadron.

The Dispatches

The Duckworth letters are interesting for their variety. Duckworth's account of the battle is distinctive because there is such a contrast between the steady, elegant and flowing hand in which it is written and the rambling stream of consciousness it conveys. Duckworth's secretary, Robert Sconce,[6] a man of patience, thoughtfulness and stoicism, was responsible for the writing; and Duckworth, an over-excitable man in search of glory, was, unfortunately, responsible for the thinking. On the other hand, Duckworth's letter of thanks to his fleet (p. 324) is both thoughtful and erudite. It is interesting that a man who could gather and express his thoughts when thanking his men was left floundering with the more demanding task of narrating a complex event.

Admiral J. Duckworth to W. Marsden, 7 February 1806

Duckworth begins his account of the battle with an acknowledgement that his behaviour and current location require some serious explanation. He goes on to describe the battle in breathless fashion, appropriate for and reflective of the style in which the battle was fought, but rather unhelpful in an official dispatch. One of Duckworth's sentences is 231 words long and includes 19 commas, five semi-colons, one colon, and two dashes. Anyone who can make sense of this letter should win a prize.

SUPERB, OFF TOWN OF ST. DOMINGUE
FEBY 7TH 1806

As I feel it highly momentous for His Majestys Service that the Lords Commissioners of the Admiralty should have the earliest information of the movements of the Squadron under my Command and as I have no other Vessel than

the Kings Fisher that I feel justified in Dispatching, I hope neither their Lordships or Vice Admiral Collingwood will deem me defective in my Duty towards His Lordship by addressing you on the happy event of yesterday: and as you will receive my Letter of the 3ᵈ Instant herewith, I shall only say I lost not a moment in getting through the Mona Passage,* and on the 5ᵗʰ in the Afternoon was joined by the Magicienne with a further corroboration from various Vessels Spoken of an Enemys Force of ten Sailes of the Line; with as many Frigates, & Corvettes being in these Seas. I therefore continued under easy Sail for the Night in my approach off the Town of Santa Domingue, having given Orders to Captain Dunn of the Acasta (whose zeal, and activity I have experienced for a series of years) to make Sail with the Magicienne Captain Mckenzie two Hours before Day Light to reconnoitre when at 6 OClock the Acasta to our great Joy, made the Signal for two of the Enemy's Frigates, and before 7 for 9 Sails at an Anchor, at half past that they were getting under weigh: The Squadron under my Command then in close order with all Sail set, and the Superb bearing my Flag leading and approaching fast so as to discover before 8 o' clock that the Enemy were in a compact Line under all Sail going before the Wind, for Cape Nisao to windward of Ocoa Bay; and as they consisted of only five Sail of the Line, two Frigates, and a Corvette (which hereafter shall be named) I concluded from the information I was in possession of that they were endeavouring to form a junction with their remaining force, and in consequence shaped my Course to render abortive such intention, which was compleatly effected by a little after nine, so as to make an Action certain. I therefore Telegraphed the Squadron that the principal Object of Attack would be the Admiral, and His Seconds and at three Quarters past nine for the Ships to take stations for their mutual support, and Engage the Enemy as they got up. and a few minutes after to Engage as close as possible, when at a short period after ten the Superb closed upon the Bow of L'Alexandre the leading Ship and commenced the Action, but after three Broad Sides she sheered off, the Signal was now made for closer Action, and we were enabled to Attack the Admiral in L'Imperial (formerly Le Vengeur) the Fire of which had been heavy upon the Northumberland bearing the Honᵇˡᵉ Rear

---

* A strait between Hispaniola and Puerto Rico that connects the Atlantic with the Caribbean. An awkward passage full of tidal currents and sandbanks.

Admiral Cochranes Flag. By this Time the movement of L'Alexandre had thrown her among the Lee Division, which Rear Admiral Louis happily availed himself of, and the Action became general and continued with great severity till half past Eleven when the French Admiral much shattered, and compleatly Beat hauled direct for the Land, and not being a mile off, at 20 minutes before noon ran on Shore, Her Foremast then only standing which fell directly on her Striking, at which time the Superb being only in 17 Fathoms water was forced to haul directly off to avoid the same Evil; but not long after the Diomede of 84 Guns pushed on Shore near His Admiral when all His Masts went, and I think it a Duty I owe to Character, and my Country to add from the information of Captain Berry after she had Struck, and the Agamemnon desisted from Firing into Her; from the Captain taking off His Hat and making every token of surrender; and Captain Dunn assures me both the Ensign, and Pendant were down, to comment upon which I leave the World! – About 50 Minutes After eleven the Firing ceased, and upon the Smoke clearing away; I found Le Braave bearing a Commodore's Pendant, L'Alexandre, and Le Jupiter in our possession – When I contemplate on the result of this Action, and that five Sail of the Line had Surrendered or were apparently destroyed in less than two Hours; I cannot though Bound to Pay every Tribute to the noble, and gallant Efforts, of the Honble Rear Admiral Cockrane, Rear Admiral Louis, the Captains, Officers Seamen, and Royal Marines under my Command to suppose that without the aiding Hand of Providence such result could have been effected, and with a Loss so comparatively small, and though I shall ever sympathize with the connections of those that fell; the reflection on the cause will I hope afford much consolation – To speak individually to the conduct of any one would be injurious to all, for all were equally animated with the same zealous ardour, in support of their King, and Country: yet possessed of those feelings, I cannot be Silent, without Injustice to the firm, and manly support for which I was indebted to Captain Keats; and the effect that the system of Discipline, and good Order in which I found the Superb must ever Produce; and the Preeminence of the British Seaman could never be more highly conspicuous than in this Contest. After the Action (the Water being to deep to Anchor in the Bay of Sainte Domingue) it was requisite to bring to with the Prizes, to repair Damages put the Ships in a manageable State, and shift the Prisoners,

which took me till this Afternoon when I detached the Honble Captain Stopford in
the Spencer with the Donegall, and Atlas, which latter had lost her bowsprit with
the Prizes to Jamaica; and being anxious with Rear Admiral Cockrane that He
should return to His Command, where His Services must be wanted, a Jury Main
Mast is fitting to the Northumberland to enable Her to get to Windward, when I
shall order the Agamemnon which is staying by her to accompany the Rear Admiral
to His Station and am now proceeding with the Canopus R: A: Louis, Acasta,
and Magicienne, off Sainte Domingue to make certain of L'Imperial being completely
Wrecked. After which I shall repair to Jamaica, and with the utmost Dispatch
move towards my Station off Cadiz or as circumstances of Service may point out
but certainly sending Rear Admiral Louis and the Ships that require Docking to
England —Having recited the Transactions of this glorious combat, which will fairly
add another Sprig of Laurel to our naval History! I am Sir!
      Your Obedient
        humble Servant

    J. T. Duckworth

What Duckworth is trying to describe is how the French fleet split into two
divisions, the ships of the line forming a line of battle and the smaller ships, the
frigates and corvettes, forming another group. The British, meanwhile, formed into
three divisions: two of ships of the line and, like the French, a separate division
of frigates and smaller ships. As the French fled, Duckworth, leading one division
of ships of the line, sought to cut them off by sailing directly across the bows of
the leading ship. The other division of British ships of the line, led by Louis, was
approaching from the rear when the structure of both fleets fell apart and the
action became general.

The French fought fiercely but their defensive efforts were drowned by the
sustained aggression of the British. Two French ships, the mighty *Impérial* and
the *Diomède*, ran aground on the shoals between Nizao and Point Catalan, their
hulls stove in by the sharp Caribbean coral. The guns of the *Diomède* continued
to fire sporadically but neither ship played any part in the rest of the battle. Both

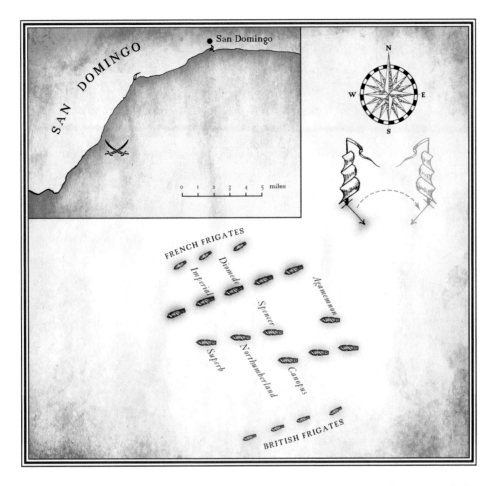

vessels were, however, close enough to a French shore position for many of the ships' stores and crewmen to be saved and, by the time that the British boarded the *Impérial*, they found her almost deserted. The *Diomède* was another matter, however, and the British took her captain and 150 members of her crew prisoner, an event that is described in one of the most confused passages in Duckworth's dispatch. Something here has clearly riled Duckworth and, if unpicked, it becomes clear that it is a matter of honour concerning acceptable behaviour in battle, as defined by unwritten rule and convention.

The nub of the problem was that the captain of the *Diomède* ran his ship aground when Duckworth believed she had already surrendered. Duckworth considered that the French captain had deliberately denied British sailors their lawful prize as well as providing the French prisoners the opportunity to escape. This is what causes him to erupt in a characteristically garbled phrase: 'to comment upon which I leave the World!' It took several weeks for Duckworth to realise and accept that the *Diomède's* ensign had been shot away rather than struck and that she had not, therefore, surrendered (p. 327). Both grounded French ships were subsequently burned by the British, though their destruction had already been ordered by the French in case the British made any attempt at salvage.

Duckworth goes on to name those high-ranking officers who particularly shone in the battle, notably Richard Keats, a reminder that these men, at odds in the run-up to the battle, could still appreciate each other's zeal in the presence of the enemy. In traditional fashion, Duckworth also mentions his second and third in command, the Rear Admirals Louis and Cochrane. Otherwise the dispatch is unremarkable apart for a subtle but unmistakable tone of self-congratulation and self-promotion that did Duckworth no favours at all because, if there was one battle in this period that the British could have expected to win, then this was it. The frigate divisions of both fleets played no part in the main battle, which was contested by seven British ships of the line against five French, the only one of all of these engagements in which the British had a significant numerical advantage. The French had also been surprised by the British. There is some suggestion that they were repairing damages they had sustained in a storm and that many of the French officers were not even on board when the British arrived. Nevertheless Duckworth is still anxious to argue that it would not have been won 'without the aiding Hand of Providence'. He goes on to finish his letter by describing *his own* action as 'glorious' and declaring that it would 'add another Sprig of Laurel to our naval history!' Certainly it was an impressive victory but Duckworth's dispatch lacked the modesty of the finest such documents and its self-important and self-serving tone was tactless.

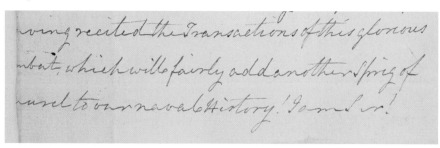

The last few lines of Duckworth's self-congratulatory dispatches.

The French and British lines of battle, 7 February 1806

Duckworth included in his dispatch a breakdown of both lines of battle and the fates of the French ships.

The fleet breakdown illustrates how his fleet was divided. The *Acasta*, *Magicienne*, *Kingfisher* and *Epervier* are all frigates or sloops while the ships of the line are divided into two divisions, one led by Duckworth's flagship the *Superb,* and the other by Rear-Admiral Louis in the *Canopus*. The decision to divide his fleet into two divisions is perhaps a conscious, though curious, imitation of Nelson's attack at Trafalgar, when the fleets of both sides had been at least five times larger, and when such a tactic had a tangible benefit. Although the British fleet went into battle in this formation, the fighting, inevitably for two such small fleets, swiftly became general and unstructured.

		ENGLISH LINE		
ACASTA · MAGICIENNE · KINGFISHER & EPERVER	Weather Division {	SUPERB NORTHUMBERLAND SPENCER AGAMEMNON	CANOPUS DONEGAL ATLAS }	Lee Division

	FRENCH LINE			
1	L'ALEXANDRE	84	Capitaine Garreau	taken
2	L'IMPERIAL	120	Contre Amiral Leissegues / Capitaine Le Bigot	on shore and destroyed
3	LE DIOMEDE	74	" Henry	
4	LE JUPITER	74	" Laignal	taken
5	LE BRAVE	74	" Caudé	
	LA COMETTE	Frigates		escaped to the Southward
	LA FELICITE			
	LA DILIGENTE	Corvette		

The difference between the names of the French ships of the line and the frigates is instructive. The names of the ships of the line all represent men or virile masculine attributes such as gods, kings, emperors or legendary soldiers, while the names of the frigates represent more feminine virtues. These names and virtues were reflected in their figureheads: ships of the line had male figureheads and frigates female.[7] The fate of the French ships describes the result of the battle in the clearest possible terms, something which is not at all obvious in Duckworth's narrative. The ships of the line were all taken or destroyed but the three French frigates all escaped. We know that Duckworth was under the impression that another French squadron was in the offing but it remains a fair observation that a different admiral might well have unleashed the unemployed British frigate squadron to attack the French. The victory could have been even more complete.

The killed and wounded of the British and French fleets, 7 February 1806

These figures are revealing for a number of reasons. There is a huge difference between the numbers of French and British killed and wounded. Indeed, there are so many killed and wounded on the French ships that the exact numbers are not known as they are in the British, but are rounded up. The French table, moreover, has a column for killed, a column for wounded and then a central column for 'killed and wounded' if the individual figures are not known.

In the respective flagships, there are 61 dead or injured aboard Duckworth's *Superb* and an estimated 500 aboard the *Impérial* – roughly half of her crew. As in other battles that produced similar results, the difference in casualty figures is explained by superior British gunnery, superior British guns, particularly the devastating carronades for close-quarter engagements, and the relative strength and weakness of British and French ship design. The French ships were designed for speed and manoeuvrability at the expense of strength and the sides of the *Impérial* were notably thin; it simply became a death trap in close action against British broadsides.

The casualty figures of the British fleet vary considerably. The figures for the *Northumberland*, flagship of Rear-Admiral Cochrane, are particularly high because she took an absolute pounding from the *Impérial* when, at a crucial stage in the action, Cochrane deliberately put his ship between the French giant and Duckworth's *Superb*. It was a gesture of great generosity, courage and tactical nous for which Duckworth was extremely grateful. We know that one of the *Northumberland*'s casualties was Lieutenant Seymour, son of Lord Hugh Seymour, who was wounded by a piece of grape shot which 'penetrated his jaw and tore away part of his teeth'.[8] Cochrane's personal staff were particularly unlucky: his cook, Alexander Sapenack, and two of his secretary's clerks all died. Cochrane himself had a lucky escape when his hat was shot off by a piece of grape shot.

Several of the casualties aboard the *Spencer* are likely to have been caused by friendly fire from the *Northumberland* and the *Superb*, which were surprised by a sudden manoeuvre by the *Spencer*, which was in turn responding to a sudden move by her opponent, the *Alexandre*. In the smoke and confusion, the *Spencer*'s manoeuvre, which placed her under the guns of the *Northumberland* and *Superb*, was not noticed for several minutes. This was not the only example of confusion in the British fleet: at one stage the *Atlas* and *Canopus* collided.

One of the ships with the fewest killed and wounded was the *Agamemnon*, whose captain was the infamous Edward Berry. Just as he had at Trafalgar, Berry spent his time at the Battle of San Domingo drifting around clear of the action and clear of danger, occasionally firing his cannon but at such a distance from the enemy that he had no control over its effectiveness. Well meaning and well liked, Berry just never got it right. After San Domingo he was quietly dropped from the active list, even though he had a service record of battle experience unlike any other naval officer of his time.

GENERAL RECAPITULATION			
	KILLED	WOUNDED	TOTAL
SUPERB	6	55	61
NORTHUMBERLAND	21	79	100
CANOPUS	8	22	30
SPENCER	18	50	68
DONEGAL	12	33	45
ATLAS	8	9	17
AGAMEMNON	1	16	17
TOTAL KILLED	74		
TOTAL WOUNDED		264	
TOTAL KILLED AND WOUNDED			338

French Ships				
	Killed		Wounded	
L'Imperial	200		300	
L'Alexandre	"	400	"	
Le Diomede	80	–	150	
Le Brave	–	300	–	
Le Jupiter	–	200	–	

The casualties of the British ships *Spencer* and *Canopus*

Included with Duckworth's bundle of letters was a breakdown of the men wounded on each ship. This list was subsequently published,[9] along with Duckworth's dispatches, giving relatives and friends the opportunity to ascertain the fate of their loved ones, a practice far more commonly associated with 20th-century warfare. The list of those injured on the *Canopus* and *Spencer* is reproduced below.

The figures for the killed and wounded in these detailed lists do not match up with those given in Duckworth's 'General Recapitulation' of the casualties (p. 319). The total figures for *Canopus* here are 10 killed and 26 wounded, as opposed to eight and 22 above and the figures for *Spencer* are 18 and 27 as opposed to 18 and 50 above. To confuse matters further, the number of names entered in *Canopus's* list below does not even match the totals given for *Canopus* at the bottom of the list. There are, in this list, eight sailors killed and 28 wounded, not 10 and 26. It is a reminder that the administration of a warship's crew shattered by battle was a tricky process and that figures of killed and wounded, if taken in the immediate aftermath of battle, should always be considered approximate.

One of the *Canopus's* men lucky enough not to be on this list was her captain, Francis Austen, brother of Jane Austen, and widely believed to have been the inspiration for Captain Wentworth in her novel *Persuasion* (1818). In that book, Austen describes how Wentworth had been 'made commander in consequence of the action off St Domingo, and not immediately employed, had come into Somersetshire, in the summer of 1806'. There he met and wooed the gorgeous second daughter of Sir Walter Eliot. Francis went on to become Admiral of the

Fleet and another naval brother, Charles Austen, went on to reach the rank of Rear-Admiral.

NAMES OF THE KILLED & WOUNDED ON BOARD THE CANOPUS					
KILLED			**KILLED**		
Thos Barnet	Pvte Marine		Paul Lovele –	Pvte Marine	
Wm Slee	Seaman		Peter Vewas –	Dº Dº	
Wm Bowen	Dº		Joseph Bosley –	Dº Dº	
Wm Wedgery	Dº		Edward Brien –	Seaman	
WOUNDED					
Jno Hallwood	LM	badly	Peter Neal –	Seaman –	Slightly
Chas Blake	Sergt Marine	Dangly	James Stanton	Dº	Dº
Jas. Griffiths	SM	badly	Wm Stephens	Pvte Marine	Dº
Wm Massey	Dº	Dº	Jno Bradley	Seaman	Dº
Jno Mc Mullen	Dº	Dº	Joseph Cooper	Pvte Marine	Dº
Isaac Gardina	Dº	Slightly	John Diffat	Seaman	badly
Mark Whitton	Pvte Marine	badly	Tomas Lowe	Pvte Marine	Slightly
John Dunthorne	LM	Slighy	Jno Desmond	Seaman	Dº
Geod Johns	Dº	Dº	Mr Wm Edwards	Masters Mate	badly
Richd Ellworth	Dº	Dº	Jno C Donnell	Seaman	Slightly
Jno Truby	Dº	Dº	James Shaw	Seaman	Dº
Francis Essex	Pvte Marine	Dº	Peter Howell	Pvte Marine	Dº
Michl Dennison	Dº Dº	badly	Saml Woodward	Dº Dº	Dº
Jno Mc Carty	LM	Slighy	John Brown (2)	Seaman	Dangerly
			Total Killed	10 [sic]	
			" Wounded	26 [sic]	
			36		

SPENCER

KILLED		KILLED	
Martin Oates	Boatsn	William Allen	1st Seaman
James Wallace	Qr Mr	James Murtaught	D⁰
John Styles	Seaman	Thos Lloyd	D⁰
Thomas Edwards	D⁰	Patrick Sullivan	D⁰
James McDonald	D⁰	John Johnson 3d	D⁰
John Rodgers	D⁰	John Mclain	D⁰
Danl Frau	D⁰	John Fowler	D⁰
James Church	Private	John Martin	D⁰
Stephen Jones	D⁰	Antonio Fengos	Private

WOUNDED			
Honble Robert Stofford	Capt.	James Fallos	Seaman
James Harris	Lieut.	Reuben Brown	"
Wm Neame	Mid	Pat: Coffee	"
Charles Pearson	D⁰	Thos. Cleave	"
Jas Cuthberson	Lt Marines	Rd Goss	"
James Daley (2)	Bos Mate	John Gaddis	"
Wm Gibson	D⁰	James Barragay	"
Edwd Johnson	Qr Mast.	Thos. Jowell	"
Thos. Triscott	QrMr Mate	John Tucker	"
John Smithers	Gunn Mate	Bartw Fenny	"
John Mason	Qr Gunner	Michl Casey	"
Jacob Watson	Seaman	John Johnson (2d)	"
Wm Hancock	"	Edwd Donavon	"
John Gingham	"	John James Curtis	"
Jas. Butterworth	"	Thos. Curtain	"
Wm Jones	"	Peter McQuart	"
Francs Brittain	"	Michl Flynn	"
Wm Finch	"	Jas. Marshal, 2,	"

Thos Sherry	Seaman		
John Shanks	"	MARINES WOUNDED	
Thos Lee	"	Geo Wilcox	Corpl
James Poole	"	Wm Dunn	Private
Thos Carroll	"	Sal. Cristofalo	"
Rd Hoskin	"	Robert Halford	"
Pat. Rabbitt	"	Wm Taylor	"
Josh Henderson	"	Thos. Smith	"
Pat. Brannon	"	John Glower	"
John Watson	"	David Walters	"
Wm Murphy	"		
David Brofy	"		
Zach: Warne	"		
Pat: Counell	"		
John Lannon	"		
Henry Webster	"		
John Featherstone	"		
Jasper Rosia	"		
Thos Limerick	"		
Wm White	"		
John Couchee	"		
James Savoury	"		

Duckworth's letter of thanks to his men, 7 February 1806

The next letter offers a powerful contrast with Duckworth's battle narrative. It was written aboard his flagship on the same day, and one can sense the relief flooding out of him that he can now address his men. Duckworth knew that this audience would not question his decisions or his courage. It is emotional, fluent and carefully composed, a charming letter of thanks that would have touched everyone who heard it.

SUPERB, OFF ST DOMINGUE FEBY. 7. 1806

As it is impossible for Language to convey an adequate sense of my feelings to the Honorable Rear Admiral Cochrane for the noble Support rendered me by the Northumberland, or to Rear Admiral Louis and the Captains of the Squadron under my command for the bravery and judgment displayed in the Service of their King and Country, by effecting a complete victory in as short a period as our naval annals can produce I can only therefore with a Heart impressed by the highest sense of Admiration and Approbation beg to offer to the Honorable Rear Admiral Cochrane, Rear Admiral Louis, the Captains, Officers and Seamen, and to the Officers Non Commissioned Officers and Seamen of the Royal Marines, my warmest thanks; and I desire that the Captains will convey those my Sentiments of Admiration and Approbation, with thanks, in the most Gratifying manner to the Officers, Seamen, and Royal Marines, as a proof my high sense of their Services in the Battle of yesterday.

Signed

J. T. Duckworth

To
THE HONBLE REAR ADMIRAL COCHRANE, REAR ADMIRAL
LOUIS, THE CAPTAINS, OFFICERS, SEAMEN, AND ROYAL
MARINES OF THE SQUADRON.

Duckworth remains a confusing figure, but this letter is instructive. Every commanding officer had two separate, but equally significant, personas. Nowhere is this clearer than in the contrast between Duckworth's dispatch to the Admiralty and the letter of thanks to his men. The commanding officer not only had to be able to speak to politicians and administrators but also to his men, to inspire in them a loyalty that would lead them to fight and, perhaps, to die. Nothing in these dispatches suggests that Duckworth was unable to do the latter. Indeed, there is plenty of evidence that his enthusiasm for battle and thirst for glory were both infectious and appreciated.

In one of the preliminary engagements before The Glorious First of June, he had taken his ship *Orion* through the enemy line when others had faltered, and his crew were so animated that, as she broke the line, they 'gave three hearty cheers' while 'shot passed thick everywhere'. Earlier in the day, some members of this high-spirited crew had 'jumped up in the rigging to huzza, & Captn Duckworth hauled them down by their legs'.[10] When the two fleets met again on 1 June, Duckworth insisted his men lay still, withholding their fire even as some of his crew were killed by French shot. The untimely deaths of the two British sailors

> ' … so exasperated our men that they kept singing out – 'For God's sake Brave Captain let us fire! Consider Sir two pour souls are slaughtered already' – but Captn Duckworth would not let them fire till we came abrest of the ship we were to engage, when Capt Duckworth cried out 'Fire my Boys. Fire', upon which our enraged Boys gave them such an extraordinary warm reception that I really believe it struck the rascals with the panic.'[11]

This is clearly a captain who was deeply respected, a man who was cool-headed and courageous in battle and who could control a nervous crew with nothing more than a word or two. The very fact that this episode survives in a diary is evidence that his crew, in turn, were proud of their captain and that they celebrated his sangfroid. When the *Orion* returned from that battle and her crew mutinied, flooded with relief, adrenaline and too much booze, Duckworth was understanding and lenient when he could have been ferocious. One sailor recalled how he 'had them before him to-day & said that as he was of a forgiving nature he gave them into the hands of the ships company, that he restores them with love for the services they had done him.'[12]

At the Battle of San Domingo we know that Duckworth chose to signal nothing more than 'This is Glorious' as he piled headlong into an engagement with the massive 118-gun *Impérial* and her two powerful seconds, the 80-gun *Alexandre* and the 74-gun *Diomède*. In a piece of theatre which may well be unique in naval warfare, he did so with his band playing 'God Save the King' on the poop deck and with a portrait of Nelson hanging from the mizzen stay, put there by Keats.[13] Such behaviour suggests a unique commander with a unique sense of shipboard community. Sailors appreciated uniqueness more than many other traits: it glued a crew together and made it possible for them to endure the terrors and horrors of battle.

If Duckworth's thirst for battle was undoubted and renowned, so too was the degree to which he cared for the welfare of his men and it is important to realise its full extent. Duckworth was not just another officer who was thoughtful and kind, but one who actively promoted new schemes for the welfare, training and education of young gentlemen. He was, in fact, instrumental in creating a production line of fine officers and seamen that were central to British naval success. An example of his attention to detail, regardless of the expense, was that he insisted that the ships' boys all slept in cots, rather than hammocks, believing that hammocks were bad for growing boys.[14] It is no coincidence that one of the finest of the post Trafalgar generation of flag-officers, Admiral of the Fleet Sir William Parker, was trained, protected, nurtured and educated by Duckworth. This caring nature was matched in his private life, in which he was well known for his benevolence and compassion.

The fact that Duckworth was a caring and zealous officer may well, however, have been the reason for his ultimate failure, since it meant he was promoted beyond his abilities. Most at home when training the navy's future officers or when fighting an enemy directly in his path, he was lost when considering wider strategies or making important executive decisions. The naval administration did not match the man with his strengths, and in this regard Duckworth merits some sympathy.

Admiral J. Duckworth to W. Marsden 16 February 1806

Duckworth's final letter is written more than a week after his first burst of correspondence. The adrenaline rush of battle has now cooled, though the energetic Duckworth is still sufficiently fired with enthusiasm to begin with a bang: 'Sir!'

This letter concerns the confusion over the behaviour of the *Diomède* described so awkwardly in Duckworth's first dispatch. Did her captain, as Duckworth believed, surrender his ship before deliberately running her ashore in a calculated move to spite the victors? The answer now appears to be that he did not and it is not surprising that the man at the source of the confusion is the bungling Sir Edward Berry.[15] Indeed, the confusion seems to have arisen as a result of Berry's account of the surrender of an altogether different ship, the *Brave*, which he appears to have later misidentified as the ship which had run aground alongside the unmistakable *Impérial*. Duckworth finished his letter with a grumbling apology 'feeling that Character is much more valuable than Life'. Well-meant maybe, but unfortunately for Duckworth this whole episode was yet more proof of the impulsiveness that had characterised his several chases, the ensuing battle and his subsequent description of it. This letter, designed to save the reputation of an enemy officer, undermined that of its author.

SUPERB PORT ROYAL JAMAICA FEBY 16TH 1806

 Sir!

> Captain Henry of the french ship Diomede which ran on Shore, and I afterwards ordered to be burnt being with His Officers among the Prisoners rescued the afternoon of the 9th before that event took Place He approached to offer Captain Keats His Sword which He from the Report that had been made to me by Sir Edward Berry, and except in the Act of Hailing confirmed by Captain Dunn that the Ship had Struck before She ran on shore, it was disdainfully refused. This or of course made explanation necessary on my Sides & I acquainted Captain Henry, that I had marked His dishonourable Conduct in my publick Letter, when feeling as He appeared to do like a Man of Honor, & referring to His Officers & L'Equipage they gave the strongest Testimony that the Pendant was always Flying though the Ensign was Shot away, and this from strict investigation since my arrival Here, appears to be the case, and as Sir Edward is not present to refer to and the commander in the Brave allows He Hailed the Agamemnon, and what has been recited passed between them I begin to have no doubt that the Diomede has been mistaken for the Brave by Her Ensign Being Down & therefore Sir, feeling that Character is much more valuable than Life, am to beg the heavy Charge on Captain Henry may be done away in such manner as in their Lordships Judgment may appear most proper. I am Sir
> > Your Obedient
> > humble Servant

J. T. Duckworth

TO WILLIAM MARSDEN ESQR
SECRETARY &CO &CO &CO ADMIRALTY

The Battle of San Domingo was a tidy little victory, though the British participants were mightily aggrieved that the magnificent *Impérial* could not be brought back to Portsmouth: the victors only had the satisfaction of watching her burn on the shores of San Domingo. Duckworth's victory was wildly celebrated in the Caribbean, where British merchants had been quaking at the prospect of a powerful French raiding squadron in their waters, and Duckworth himself was immediately presented with a Sword of Honour by the Jamaica House of Assembly.

Once home, he was granted a substantial pension of £1,000 from the Commons, which he later described with some bitterness as 'my dirty annuity', and he was awarded the Freedom of the City of London, another award created with the backing of powerful merchants. But he never received the title he so desired. His victory was tainted by the abandonment of his post at Cadiz, which had forced Collingwood to divert valuable resources from his Mediterranean command, though too late to prevent the escape of a frigate squadron from Cadiz. In fact Collingwood, who was Duckworth's commander-in-chief, was seriously unimpressed. It is now widely accepted that, had it not been for his victory at San Domingo, Duckworth would probably have faced his fourth court martial for failing to engage Willaumez, the enemy he had unsuccessfully chased halfway across the Atlantic.

Duckworth's victory at San Domingo must be placed alongside Hyde Parker's at Copenhagen; both were operations in which the fleet commanders failed to perform as expected. British politicians and senior naval figures, however, were not in the business of showering apparently successful naval officers with awards regardless of the detail of their performance. The Royal Navy was an exacting profession. Yes, advancement and employment went hand in hand with personal or political influence, but only those deemed professionally worthy were lauded. Duckworth thus never received the peerage he expected, although his subordinate, Thomas Louis, received a baronetcy and his third-in-command, Alexander Cochrane, became a Knight of the Bath.

Significant doubts about Duckworth's professional ability remained but, in accordance with the accepted rules of automatic promotion, he was promoted over time and became Vice-Admiral of the Red in 1808 and Admiral of the Blue in 1810. Rather surprisingly, he remained in employment, and was even chosen to lead a significant but logistically doomed expedition to the Dardanelles in 1807.

He continued to believe he had been poorly treated after San Domingo and sent 'folios of grievance'[16] to St Vincent who, however, was unmoved and maintained that Duckworth was not entitled to a British peerage. Nonetheless, the Battle of San Domingo created temporary security for British possessions and trade in the West Indies, which in turn secured the financial foundations that allowed Britain to continue the war. The captured ships did not make as much difference as they could because the *Brave* foundered off the Azores on the way home and the *Alexandre* was too badly damaged to be of any use and was broken up. Of the five French ships of the line at San Domingo, only the *Jupiter* went on to enjoy a career in the Royal Navy. The French frigates that escaped all made it safely back to France.

Duckworth's victory caused no significant strategic alteration, either to British or French strategy. Willaumez enjoyed some success on a cruise that took him to the Cape of Good Hope, back into the South Atlantic and then into the Caribbean. Napoleon continued to pour money into shipbuilding to provide his growing empire with an appropriate scale of seapower, which he envisaged to be somewhere between 100 and 150 ships of the line, and to force Britain into a parallel shipbuilding programme that would threaten her economic stability. His Continental System, meanwhile, continued to impose more economic pressure on the British war machine. In 12 years of warfare, the British had won seven major fleet victories but, by 1806, the French empire was as large and aggressive as it had been at any stage in its troubled history.

CONCLUSION

———

The Paradox

Here is an interesting question. If two fleets were to meet miles away from anywhere and destroy each other with no survivors or witnesses, and therefore no dispatches, would the battle's impact on history be the same as if dispatches had been written? Or, to put it another way, what exact role do dispatches have in the formation of history?

Battles at sea have consequences, and they do so regardless of whether their course is subsequently related by admirals or others directly involved in them. Ships and sons fail to return home. The detritus of battle washes ashore. What is less obvious, though by no means less important, is that such documents may influence history and its interpretation more widely, and in ways that are only partially connected with the battle they describe. There are, after all, many ways to describe an event, and even the most apparently straightforward fact can be interpreted in a variety of ways.

These dispatches describe history, of course, but they also shape it, even now, and both that power and that process remain enigmatic. Besides, at the heart of this material lies a paradox. It was collated in an era of peace to celebrate the achievements of an earlier, war-mongering generation. The association between peace and war is explicit. The generation of naval officers, politicians and administrators who ran the navy in 1821, when the dispatches were first collated, and later in 1859, when they were bound into their magnificent velvet volume, knew an unprecedented period of peace. This was the age of *Pax Britannica*, when the size of the Royal Navy was as small as it had been for two generations. In 1812 there were 98 ships of the line crewed by 130,000 men. By 1817 no more than 13 ships of the line carried just 20,000 men.[1] The once mighty British battle fleet was reduced to small squadrons of gunboats policing distant colonial coasts. Tristan de Cunha, Ceylon, Ascension Island, Trinidad, Tobago, St Lucia and Australia were all British territories from 1815. But those men who now ran the Admiralty also knew the preceding era of war, an apocalyptic age of violence and blood-letting. For them, the association between the one and the other, between war and peace, was transparent.

For us it is not so clear. Indeed, if one stops to consider, this collection of dispatches defies its own myth. By recording a generation of naval battles that ended almost a decade before the end of the war, it argues not for the triumph of naval battle, but for its ineffectiveness. It is, in fact, powerful proof that naval battles did not win wars.

By studying these battles in sequence, we can make new connections and we can appreciate the sheer scale of the challenge that faced the Royal Navy as the fortunes of war shifted and as new theatres of operations opened where others had been closed. We can see, for example, how the war turned sharply against Britain in the autumn of 1794 in spite of the victory on 1 June. We can see how Spain recovered sufficiently from defeat at St Vincent in 1797, and France from defeat at the Nile in 1798, to pose a significant Allied threat at Trafalgar in 1805. We can see how the destruction of the Spanish at St Vincent eased the naval threat in the Atlantic but encouraged a new theatre to open in the North Sea. We can see how the Battle of Copenhagen in 1801 was irrelevant to the progress of the war and we can see how a crushing victory for Britain at Trafalgar did nothing to prevent France from sending powerful squadrons to sea in the following months, which in turn led to new naval threats in the Caribbean and East Indies and to battle at San Domingo in 1806.

The question that arises most forcefully from these dispatches, therefore, concerns the role of fleet battle in the shaping of history and, by demonstrating as it does the inability of decisive battle to bring about lasting peace, the collection necessarily draws our eye *away* from naval battle. Wars in this period were never brought to an end by apocalyptic battle but by negotiation. Military victories on land secured positions of strength from which to negotiate. Territory was the currency of war and it was armies and their soldiers that robbed the banks. The invasion threat under which the British laboured almost constantly between 1794 and 1815 can be understood in these terms. To seize a slice of British territory was not an end in itself but a desperate attempt by the French to secure a powerful bargaining chip. The very ability to wage such war, moreover, was governed by international politics and alliances which, themselves, were governed by money. Alliances were rarely offered freely but were purchased through vast subsidies.

So how does successful fleet battle fit into this picture? The Battle of the Nile had perhaps the most clearly defined strategic results. The British destroyed Napoleon's invasion fleet and thus prevented his army from receiving the maritime support it needed to wage a successful campaign in Egypt. But most of the others have less obvious military results. The Battle of Copenhagen, it can be argued, was fought for nothing. The Tsar, who had pressured the Danes into joining an Armed Neutrality, was already dead. The remaining battles fit somewhere between these extremes and what they share must be measured in less clearly defined terms.

As a general rule, British naval victory made it more difficult for her enemies to secure their own maritime trade and to target that of other nations, which in turn made it more difficult for them to fund the war. British success also made it more difficult for her enemies to launch amphibious operations to secure the territory required to force a peace. British naval victory therefore strangled her enemies' ability to wage war and to negotiate from a position of strength. British trade, meanwhile, became more secure. With more money to hand, more troops could be raised, more alliances bought and more ships built. Moreover, control of the sea lanes in turn increased the ability of the Royal Navy to launch military operations overseas.

Naval victories were, if you like, starbursts in a war of attrition that enabled the war to be won. It is no coincidence that the eight naval victories in this book were followed by Wellington's 15 land victories, without a defeat, in Spain. The undeniable public attraction of those naval starbursts, meanwhile, generated its own influence on events. Everyone in Britain loved naval victory; they could never get enough of it. Every naval victory was appreciated by the public because it made both them as individuals and the nation feel more secure. The Navy kept them safe; the Navy kept them free; the Navy kept them British. The victories were also understood in terms of wealth; naval victories secured trade and trade generated money. Naval victory therefore generated public support for the navy and public support translated into political support. Money was found and infrastructure improved and ships were built. The relationship was symbiotic. Go and visit the great surviving naval dockyards at Plymouth or Chatham and you will be amazed by the facilities constructed: the rope walks, the dry docks, the victualling yards. Yes, these facilities were the foundation of British naval victory but they were also created *because* of British naval victory.

The relationship between the Navy and the public is central to the influence of naval victory upon history. As you sit and read the Admirals' letters, imagine yourself as a direct descendant of a member of the public sitting and reading the published versions of these letters in 1794 or 1805, when everything was fresh and raw and a general and detailed perception of the battle was still elusive. What actually happened in the battle was far less important than what the dispatch described. The dispatch had already acquired an agency of its own.

That said, one of the most significant characteristics of these dispatches is their inaccuracy, an inaccuracy sometimes wilfully achieved. More often than not the fog of war has insufficiently cleared for numbers of captured ships or casualties to be accurate, but occasionally one's gaze is deliberately drawn in certain directions. Collingwood's Trafalgar dispatch is a masterpiece of such manipulation, giving as it does the false impression of absolute cohesion. In some respects, therefore, to search for the 'truth' behind the casualty figures or to plot with utmost care the track of a particular ship is rather to miss the point of naval battle and the dispatches that describe it. Naval battle was infinitely intricate, governed by the relationship between unpredictable bursts of wind and miles upon miles of rigging, and manipulated by thousands of men, each with their own motivation, desires and fears. But the *story* of naval battle was a blunt, unsubtle, instrument of propaganda. It did not necessarily matter if a dispatch was inaccurate; indeed, these dispatches support the argument that it is impossible to fight a war and tell the truth at the same time. The detail was always far less important than the overall message of absolute and repeated British victory.

The Uncertain

An inevitable casualty of such a broad message is any sense of doubt in the narrative we read, for here are seven battles and here are seven overwhelming British victories. One can be easily forgiven for presuming that, after the first one or two, the result was somehow viewed as inevitable; that in some way these battles were won even before they were fought. There is, of course, some value in this approach because it encourages us to appreciate the roles of the bureaucrats and administrators, the manufacturers and suppliers who rode the tides of paperwork to ensure that the ships were repaired, manned and victualled and the men fed, clothed and healthy. It was these individuals and organisations that laid the foundation for British naval victory.

Yet the dispatches themselves often highlight precisely what was uncertain, what was not inevitably to lead to naval victory. They emphasise the unpredictable role of wind, weather and damage; they remind us of the occasions when random events tipped the battle one way or another; above all, they remind us of the presence of an enemy intent on preventing the British from having their own way. The letters are clearly written by men who have fought a fierce and prolonged duel against a proud enemy. One can sense the adrenaline coursing through their bodies as they composed the letters; one can appreciate their relief at being alive and their delight at being victors. All of this helps to freshen our perspective of the battles by highlighting the choices that were available to the participants, the uncertain paths, the tumbling circumstance that guided the results.

How, therefore, can we reconcile this perspective of unpredictability and uncertainty with our understanding of how these victories were won? This is where the detail of battle has its value because the deeper one digs, the more uncertain the picture becomes. When we talk of gunnery, do we mean long distance or point blank? Is the enemy to windward or to leeward? How did developments in chemistry alter the potency of the gunpowder for each fleet? How did changes in gunnery equipment impact on gunnery efficiency? When we talk of seamanship, are we talking about repairing ships in action or the ability to maintain cohesion in fog? Are we talking about the ability to manoeuvre a ship with a disabled foremast, or the ability to engage from the lee position? In terms of leadership, are we talking about admirals commanding captains across vast expanses of ocean, about petty officers commanding sailors in the darkness of the gun decks or even about the leadership of seamen with no official rank but who nonetheless acted as natural leaders?

Each battle must be considered in its own right, each individual duel within each battle, even each ship on its own. Every ship was after all manned to varying degrees of completeness. For example, while a ship could be numerically well-manned, a large portion of her men could be soldiers or inexperienced landsmen rather than trained sailors. A portion of her crew might be suffering from a debilitating illness, be it typhus or scurvy. Nonetheless, even if we bear in mind that exceptions to every one of these following statements can be found in the seven battles in this book, it is generally the case that British gunners could fire with more accuracy and for longer than their enemies; that British hulls could better withstand a broadside than their enemies'; that British sailors could better cope with the carnage surrounding them; and that British sailors could repair their ships with greater efficiency both during and after battle. Most importantly of all, it seems that British sailors themselves knew all of this. They had come to recognise it in the previous war, the War of American Independence, and they had had their suspicions confirmed in 1794 in the first of these actions, The Glorious First of June. Simply put, British sailors knew that, if they could engage their enemy close enough and for long enough, the enemy's guns would, eventually, fall silent.

And yet all of this was soon to change. Seapower certainly changed the nature and direction of the Napoleonic wars but the Napoleonic wars also changed the nature of seapower.

The Change

Napoleon's war against Britain continued after 1806 and he began new wars: against Portugal in 1807, Spain in 1808 and Russia in 1812. In that period the Royal Navy continued to fight the French, but it also fought the Danish, Russian and Ottoman navies. Lest we forget, Britain also went to war with America between 1812 and 1815. None of those conflicts, however, produced another fleet battle on the scale of those fought between 1794 and 1806. Too many people had tried to play with fire and been burned. No one was willing to spend the money on constructing a fleet and then, of all things, risk it in pitched battle with the British. Before very long, however, the coming of steam propulsion changed everything all over again, consigning the entire age of sailing warfare, rather than just the story of British dominance, to the past.

Steam-powered ships became bigger and armoured and their guns fired explosive shells unimaginable distances. Changes in technology also began to affect the way that military campaigns were reported. In 1850 the first under-sea telegraph cable was laid between Dover and Calais, allowing news to be passed rapidly to and from the continent. Five years later a cable linked Sweden, Denmark and Germany, and three years after that another was laid across the Atlantic. The ease with which a fleet's activities could be reported over great distances was therefore changing although, surprisingly, we are still uncertain of the identity of the first naval battle reported by telegraph. It is likely to have been one of the naval battles of the Crimean War (1853–6), depending on the capability of the Russian telegraph system in different locations. We are on firmer footing with radio. Thomas Edison filed a patent as early as 1885 which described the 'Means for transmitting signals electrically', and the first battle between fleets to make significant use of wireless was fought 20 years later, when the Japanese destroyed the Russian battle fleet at Tsushima in 1905.

The last letters in this collection, therefore, mark neither the end of sailing warfare nor the end of the era of handwritten dispatches. However, they *do* mark the last significant fleet battle between British and French fleets in a war that had, by then, lasted 13 years and which was part of a longer tradition of naval warfare between the two countries that can be traced back over a century through the War of American Independence (1775–82), the Seven Years War (1755–62), the War of the Austrian Succession (1739–48) and the War of the Spanish Succession (1702–13) to the Nine Years War of 1688 to 1697. Moreover, none of the fleet battles that followed San Domingo in 1806, and very few that preceded The First of June in 1794, stands comparison with any of those fought between 1794 and 1806. It was an intense sliver of history, a period of unmatched ferocity at sea, a period that characterised and shaped the history of the world and a period populated by men whose achievements and sacrifices deserve the widest possible recognition.

POSTSCRIPT

———•——

The Photograph

The volume of dispatches, with its definitive beginning and end, encourages us to perceive an era that is both self-contained and dislocated from the present day or, indeed, from other periods of history. If we are ever going to value fully this collection and the achievements it describes, however, we must learn to recognise and appreciate the links between past eras as well as the strands of history that connect us directly to the past.

Last year, on a trip to Brighton, I visited one of my favourite shops, The Lanes Armoury. Crammed with arms and armour of every possible description, it is one of the finest sources of antique militaria in Europe. There, in a display case, hidden among the samurai swords, cutlasses and flintlocks, was a battered picture frame about the size of a hardback book. I glanced at the framed objects: a gilt medal below a faded photograph of an elderly man peering mistrustfully out of the picture. He was wearing a dark-coloured mid-Victorian jacket decorated with two medals. His right hand rested on a walking stick and his left hand made a curious gesture beneath his medals, as if to underline them (p. 339).

The picture was clearly taken in the early years of photography, a science that was not widespread until the 1850s. One of the earliest conflicts to be captured by photographers was the Crimean War of 1853–6 but this man was clearly too old to have been active then. A little puzzled I looked more carefully at the medal and saw, to my astonishment, that it was decorated with a fleet of sailing warships. Quite extraordinary. This was, unmistakably, Alexander Davison's Nile Medal (fig. 13), issued to commemorate Nelson's great victory at the Battle of the Nile in 1798, the fourth of the great battles described in this book.

At that time no official medal system existed but, in a magnificent and philanthropic gesture, Davison, Nelson's chosen Prize Agent, had this medal designed, struck and issued to every participant, in gold to Nelson and his captains, in silver to lieutenants and warrant officers, in gilt metal to petty officers and in copper to seamen and marines. The lack of an official rewards system was not remedied until 1847 when Queen Victoria introduced the Naval General Service Medal. It is likely, therefore, that the two medals shown in the photograph are Davison's medal alongside the Naval General Service Medal.

No information about the man or his medal survives, though it is clearly made of gilt, so we can assume that he was a petty officer.[2] The photograph was probably taken in the mid-1850s at the earliest, and he was perhaps 20 or so when serving as a petty officer. He is likely, therefore, to have been in his early 80s when the photograph was taken, just one of a generation of men who had fought in the great age of sail but who went on to experience the extraordinary technological and social changes of the 19th century. HMS *Victory*'s last Trafalgar veteran actually died in 1876, aged 92, but the last known survivor of the Battle of Trafalgar, a Spaniard named Pedro Martínez who had been a cabin boy on the 74-gun *San Juan*, died in Dallas, Texas in 1898, aged 109, some 40 years *after* this photograph was taken.

Let's now fit my great-grandfather into the mix. He was 'launched' in 1894, fought at Jutland in 1916, enjoyed a lengthy and varied career in the navy and was finally 'broken' up in 1982. However briefly, therefore, the life of my great-grandfather, who knew both 20th-century World Wars, overlapped the life of at least one veteran of Trafalgar. Now *his* son, my grandfather, is very much alive. Derek Willis, a naval veteran of World War II, the nuclear tests on Christmas Island in 1956 and the Cod War, is full of stories of his father and of his father's time.

My experience is by no means exceptional. The strands of history run through us all. Perhaps you are related to Walter Hewen, one of the cold and tired sailors who lost his bedding, a shirt, a pair of trousers and a black silk handkerchief in the storm of war at Camperdown (p. 149); to William Kelson, a drummer who was wounded by flying splinters in 'cheek and eyeball' (p. 143); or to one of the four women and one girl mustered aboard the *Hercules* in the same battle (p. 353)? Or are you related to Rear Admiral Alexander Cochrane's cook who died at San Domingo in 1806? Perhaps you are even related to one of the admirals: to Howe, Hood, Duncan, Jervis, Nelson, Hyde Parker, Collingwood or Duckworth.

Every time that we uncover a link we are drawn closer to the past, and every time we are drawn closer to the past we are encouraged to think about it anew.

That is the real value of these dispatches, the real reason that they should not lie forgotten. The past is not an alien time and place, a disconnected world to be studied with scientific objectivity. It is *our* past inhabited by *our* relatives. They are simply waiting to be found and hoping to be understood.

The Appeal

These letters describe a period central to the creation of the British Empire and of British identity and a flashpoint in the history of the world. To view those battles through the original sources is to peer over the shoulders of the Lords of the Admiralty and the King as they learned the fate of nations and the future of their world. It is a profoundly powerful experience and, as was always intended by the Lords of the Admiralty, both in 1821 when the documents were first collated, and in 1859 when they were bound together, it is one that can and must be shared as widely as possible. This collection of dispatches is a cornerstone of British history and culture and should have its place on display in the 'Treasures of the British Library' permanent exhibition, alongside documents as various as the Lindisfarne Gospels, Magna Carta and John Lennon's scribbled lyrics.

It is important, though, to point out that the current inaccessibility of the dispatches does not result from a nation turning its back on its maritime past. Although one should never be satisfied, numerous projects of great worth have been conducted around the country in recent years. My personal favourite was Bill Fontana's remarkable sound sculpture *Wave Memories*, which transmitted a live feed of the sound of the sea off Cape Trafalgar through the public address system in Trafalgar Square, creating a direct link between the location of the battle and its cultural monument. It was quite fantastic: how inappropriate for the ordered space of Trafalgar Square to be interrupted by the real Trafalgar! I am now particularly fond of the efforts being made by National Historic Ships,* a public body devoted to preserving British historic vessels. Nonetheless, we have failed when it comes to these dispatches.

---

* www.nationalhistoricships.org.uk

The Appeal

It seems appropriate to end with the words of Lord Nelson himself. He would have been horrified, though not perhaps surprised, to find that the wishes of the Lords of the Admiralty of 1859 have not been met. On 7 November 1803 he wrote to one of his captains and close friend, Sir Alexander Ball: 'It is the custom, and a very bad one, for the English, never to tell their own story.'[3] Surely the time has come for us to prove the great man wrong. Let us get the dispatches back where they should be, on permanent display, an antidote to our collective amnesia. We are immensely lucky still to have one of the most significant series of documents of world history in our possession and even more blessed that it survives in magnificent condition. Let us therefore cherish it, display it and advertise it as one of our finest national treasures.

Every reader, from first-time dabblers in naval history to career scholars of the age of sail, will, I hope, discover something new here. My favourite letter is from Collingwood to Vice-Admiral Don Ignatio Maria D'Alava in the aftermath of Trafalgar (p. 289). Alava, injured, has escaped to Cadiz and Collingwood writes courteously to remind him that, actually, he had already surrendered and that he should consider himself a prisoner of war. Unsurprisingly, Alava, who was now happily at home, took a different view. I was particularly surprised that William Bligh, famed for the mutiny on the *Bounty*, fought at both Camperdown (1797) and Copenhagen (1801) (p. 134 and p. 238) and I was chilled by Rear-Admiral Thomas Pasley's shaky signature, added to the foot of his dictated narrative of The Glorious First of June (p. 67) when barely able to hold a quill because one of his legs had been blown off only hours before. What, then, is your favourite letter? What did you find most surprising or shocking? Let me know at www.sam-willis. com or on Twitter @navalhistoryguy. Let's get a debate started. And do, please, signal your support for my petition to have the dispatches made accessible to the public once again.

APPENDIX I

The Secretaries of the Admiralty

PHILIP STEPHENS (1723-1809)
18 June 1763 – 3 March 1795

Born on 11 October 1723 in Essex, the third and youngest son of Nathaniel Stephens and Ellis Deane, Stephens may have followed his eldest brother Tyringham into the navy's victualling office, but certainly worked in the Navy Office from July 1739, beginning as a clerk of storekeepers' accounts. He continued in the Navy Office for over 10 years, having transferred to the ticket office in January 1741. He became secretary to George Anson, perhaps after impressing the Commodore by resolving payroll problems following Anson's recent voyage around the world.

Stephens became First Clerk of the Admiralty in April 1751, having been chosen over other clerks with many more years' experience. In 1752 he accompanied Anson, who had been charged with escorting the King across the Channel, and the two worked together again for four months in 1758 when Anson commanded the Channel Fleet. During this time Stephens worked on behalf of others as a prize agent, a role in which he accumulated a substantial personal fortune.

In October 1759 Stephens was made Second Secretary of the Admiralty and in June 1763 he was promoted to First Secretary. During his 21 years in this pivotal role, he served 10 of the Admiralty's First Lords and enjoyed responsibility both within the office and in the regulation of the business that went to the board. Lord Sandwich became dependent on his diligent Secretary, turning to Stephens at the first hint of crisis. The Secretary's power and influence annoyed Charles Middleton, Comptroller of the Navy, but Sandwich continued to rely on Stephens. In 1781, for example, when the French and Spanish fleets united in the Channel, it was Stephens who drafted the admirals' orders following a house call from Sandwich. As a high-ranking official, Stephens inevitably attracted negative attention, and was involved in political scuffles with Samuel Barrington and, in 1778, with future First Lord Augustus Keppel.

Stephens was MP for Liskeard from December 1759 to 1768, and then represented Sandwich from 1768 until 1806. He was known for taking good care of his constituents, but preferred to keep out of the spotlight. Indeed, no record exists of Stephens having spoken in the House in 45 years.

Stephens was an influential figure in the field of exploration, beginning with the first voyage of James Cook. It was he, with the assistance of Hugh Palliser, who made Cook's selection possible. The botanist Joseph Banks used Stephens's unusual influence to sidestep the unhelpful Sir Edward Hawke, then First Lord, during preparation of the *Endeavour*. His support of the expedition was recognised by the naming of Cape Stephens and Stephens Island in New Zealand's Cook Strait. The explorer George Vancouver also named an island after him in Chatham Sound.

In March 1795, aged 71, Stephens resigned his Secretaryship and was subsequently created a baronet. His membership of the Board of Admiralty fell during a period of political instability, particularly the administration of Lord St Vincent, in the course of which both Secretaries tried to resign at once. His wealth of experience led to the King's 1804 request to Viscount Melville, recently appointed First Lord, to keep Stephens on as Commissioner, despite his advanced age.

After 67 years of service, Stephens's administrative stamina was finally exhausted and he resigned his post in October 1806. He received a yearly pension of £1,500. Stephens died three years later, on 20 November 1809. He remained a bachelor throughout his life, but fathered two illegitimate children, both of whom died prematurely. His son died in a duel aged 20 in 1790 while his daughter Charlotte died in childbirth in 1805. With no living descendants, the baronetcy became extinct. Stephens was buried next to his daughter in Fulham.

SIR EVAN NEPEAN (1752-1822)
3 March 1795 – 21 January 1804

Born on 19 July 1752 at St Stephens, near Saltash, Cornwall, the second son of Nicholas Nepean and his second wife Margaret Jones, Nepean joined HMS *Boyne* as a civilian clerk in December 1773, and in October 1775 was made Purser aboard the *Falcon* at Boston. The next year he joined Admiral Molyneux Shuldham and returned with him to Spithead in February 1777. In April of that year Nepean became Purser and secretary to Lord Shuldham in the *Ocean*. Rather than continue with Shuldham on his appointment as Port Admiral in Plymouth, by special resolution of the Admiralty Board Nepean joined the *Achilles* as Purser in February 1778. He then served on the *Hero* and the *Foudroyant,* where he remained until June 1782. In that month Nepean married Margaret (or Harriett) Skinner, who bore him six sons and two daughters.

In March 1782 Nepean enjoyed a radical promotion by Lord Shelburne, becoming Under-Secretary of State at the recently established Home Office. Such major career advancement suggests that he had undertaken some intelligence work as well as fulfilling his duties as a purser. In his new role, Nepean was involved in planning botanical expeditions, notably Bligh's breadfruit quest in the *Bounty*, as well as being responsible for matters such as Irish governmental regulation and arrangements for the first convict settlement in New South Wales. Nepean was nominally responsible for the money paid for Foreign Secret Service, though the actual payments were made by the Chief Clerk, William Pollock. During the 1780s Nepean also appointed William Clarke and 12 others to keep an eye on potential dissidence in London.

An extensive workload with wide-ranging responsibilities was detrimental to Nepean's health and, from 1789, he required annual periods of convalescence at Bath or in the country. Two sinecure appointments had Nepean first as Naval Officer in Grenada, Dominica and Barbados and, subsequently, in the better-paid position of Clerk of the Peace and Chief Clerk of the Supreme Court in Jamaica, a title that remained with him until 1819. The Jamaican appointment had been secured by Lord Grenville, both in appreciation of Nepean's dedication and out of concern for his health. In the Home Office Nepean was relieved by the division of labour afforded by the addition of William Huskisson and John King. Nepean maintained personal friendships with both William Pitt and Henry Dundas, and worked closely with King George III, who valued his discretion.

In 1794 Nepean left his post at the Home Office to join Dundas and Huskisson in the new Department of War and Colonies. The indefatigable Nepean was appointed Secretary of the Admiralty in 1795, but remained an influential figure in foreign and home secret service. In 1797, for example, he was chosen by the King to take sole charge of the nautical arrangements for a secret plot to invade Spanish settlements in South America.

Nepean entered parliament for Queenborough in 1796 and went on to represent Bridport from January 1802 until 1812. In July 1802 he was created a baronet and two years later became a privy councillor. Nepean's involvement in the 1803–4 conspiracy to depose Napoleon met with naval disapproval. His 1804 appointment as Chief Secretary to the Lord Lieutenant of Ireland also proved unsuccessful. Nepean lacked parliamentary experience and this was exacerbated by his unpopularity with Lord Hardwicke, who accused Nepean of indecision and criticised his intimacy with the King. Nepean left Ireland in May 1804 and in September returned to the Admiralty as a junior Lord.

Nepean's official career ended in February 1806, but he remained a privy councillor and in 1812 accepted the Governorship of Bombay. Seven years as Governor were advantageous to his botanical interests and gave him the opportunity to correspond with the botanist Sir Joseph Banks about samples of plants and seeds sent to England, including the best varieties of teak and any number of flowering plants from India's western coast. In May 1820 Nepean became a Fellow of the Royal Society. He died on 2 October 1822 and was buried at Loders Court, near Bridport.

WILLIAM MARSDEN (1754-1836)

21 JANUARY 1804 – 24 JUNE 1807

Born on 16 November 1754 in County Wicklow, Ireland, to John Marsden, a banker and shipping merchant, and his second wife Eleanor Bagnall, Marsden was classically educated in Dublin and intended for a career in the church. Instead he joined his eldest brother, John, as a Writer in the service of the East India Company at Fort Marlborough in Sumatra. Marsden arrived in Sumatra in May 1771 and began his career in the Secretary's office. In January 1774 he assumed full secretarial duties to the East India Company's Sumatran government but formal appointment only came in October 1776. Marsden resigned his post and returned to England in December 1779, where he began to dedicate his time to the arts, as well as to parliament and the law courts.

In March 1780 Marsden became acquainted with the botanist Sir Joseph Banks, the scientist Charles Blagden and the hydrographer Alexander Dalrymple among others, and was invited to attend meals and meetings at the Royal Society, as well as regular breakfasts hosted by Banks at his Soho Square residence. In 1783, inspired by the intellectual milieu at Soho Square, he published his *History of Sumatra*, a book based on his own records from his service at Fort Marlborough. The *History* established Marsden as an able writer and displayed a scholarly treatment of zoology, linguistics and botany.

In 1783 Marsden formally left the East India Company. In January 1783 he became a Fellow of the Royal Society and in December 1785 a Fellow of the Society of Antiquaries. That year also saw him involved in the foundation of the Royal Irish Academy and in June 1786 he received an honorary doctorate in civil law at Oxford. Marsden became a member of the Royal Society Club in August 1787 and held the position of Treasurer from 1788 until 1804. A dedicated orientalist, he studied several languages and used vocabulary lists brought to England by ships' officers on return voyages to supplement his knowledge.

In February 1795 Marsden accepted the Second Secretaryship of the Admiralty, but remained committed to his intellectual pursuits; he was elected to the Literary Club in 1799, and in 1803 became Treasurer of the Royal Society. Then, in 1804, Marsden postponed his retirement to become First Secretary. In this role he reported the victory at Trafalgar and the death of Nelson to Lord Barham, then First Lord of the Admiralty. An enthusiastic numismatist, Marsden made a significant addition to his collection of oriental coins in September 1805 with the purchase of Sir Robert Ainslie's Kufic coin collection. Marsden resigned from the Admiralty in June 1807 and in August married Elizabeth, daughter of Sir Charles Wilkins who was to become librarian of the East India Company and shared Marsden's interest in oriental languages and literature. The marriage produced no children.

In November 1810 Marsden gave up his roles as Treasurer and Vice-President of the Royal Society. That year he had moved to his residence at Edge Grove in Hertfordshire, and went on to spend his married years writing and publishing works including his *Dictionary of the Malayan Language* (1812) and *The Travels of Marco Polo* (1818), the latter a translation from the Italian, and two volumes of *Numismata orientalia illustrata* (1823 and 1825). In 1827 Marsden arranged for the printing of a catalogue of his own library entitled *Bibliotheca Marsdeniana philological et orientalis*, a work intended to further the study of oriental languages and literature. Works on Polynesian languages and lexicography followed, and he also wrote papers for academic journals. From 1831 Marsden gave up his annual Admiralty pension of £1,500, as he felt he had amassed enough in the way of personal wealth for a comfortable life. In July 1834 he gave his enormous oriental coin collection to the British Museum, and the contents of his library were presented to King's College, London in January 1835.

Marsden died on 6 October 1836 of apoplexy, and was buried in Kensal Green cemetery. He was survived by his wife, who went on to edit and publish the wonderful *A brief memoir of the life and writings of the late William Marsden* (1838).

APPENDIX II

---·◆·---

The Royal Navy's Prizes

This appendix provides a list of all the enemy's ships of war taken by the Royal Navy between 1794 and 1806 in the actions in this book and registered as such by the Admiralty. 'Prize' is understood in the contemporary sense of taken, sunk, burnt, or destroyed, including those that escaped after capture. The prizes are listed here in alphabetical order by battle.

The Glorious First of June, 1794

Achille (74)

Dispatch folio 12 Name in dispatches *L'Achilles* Taken by *Brunswick* and *Ramillies* Built and launched December 1777 to January 1779, Brest, as *Annibal*; launched 5 October 1778 Size 1478 / 1500 / 2939 tonnes; 1818⁵⁸⁄₉₄ tons BOM Armament (from 1793): 28x36, 30x18, 16x8 + 4x36 obusiers + 6x1 perriers Complement 11–17 officers, 690/734 men Complement in the action 800 men under Guillaume-Jean-Noël la Villegris Casualties 36 killed, 30 wounded 'Nature of the prize' 74 guns Purchased for £7,964 0s 6d Bounty awarded £4,000 0s 0d Prize money awarded £60,000 for the *Sans Pareil*, *Juste*, *Impéteux*, *Achille*, *América*, and *Northumberland* to the warrant officers, petty officers and foremastmen, 'in part of the money to be paid for the purchase and for the bounty due to the captors', by royal warrant of 22 June 1794 Brought to Portsmouth Crew confined at Plymouth (*Prudent*) Fate Purchased, October 1794 but repairs estimated at £40,231 and 13–14 months so never fitted for sea by the RN; broken up at Plymouth, February 1796. Notes Name changed in 1786. Sister ship of the *Northumberland*. Sources ADM 2/272; ADM 7/354; ADM 18/121; ADM 43/33; ADM 43/80; ADM 103/503; ADM 106/2219; ADM 106/2220; HCA 8/89; *London Gazette* no. 14055 (16 October 1797); Gardiner, *Fleet Battle and Blockade*; Demerliac; Lyon; Roche; Winfield.

América (74)

Dispatch folio 12 Name in dispatches *L'Amerique* Name in RN service *Impeteux* (see Fate) Taken by *Leviathan* Built and launched end 1786 to 1789, Brest; launched 21 May 1788 Size 1537 / 1550 / 3069 tonnes; 1884²⁶⁄₉₄ tons BOM Armament (in 1793/4): 28x36 (30 ports), 30x18, 16x8 + 4x36 obusiers + 6x1 perriers Armament in RN service (in 1796): LD 30x32, UD 30x18, QD 2x18 + 14x32cr, FC 2x18 + 4x32cr, RH 6x18cr 'Nature of the prize' 74 guns Complement 13–17 officers, 690/706 men Complement in the action 720 men under Pierre Lhéritier Complement in RN service 640 Casualties 134 killed, 110 wounded Purchased for £25,778 12s 6d Bounty awarded £3,600 0s 0d Prize money awarded £60,000 for the *Sans Pareil*, *Juste*, *Impéteux*, *Achille*, *América*, and *Northumberland* to the warrant officers, petty officers and foremastmen, 'in part of the money to be paid for the purchase and for the bounty due to the captors', by royal warrant of 22 June 1794 Brought to Portsmouth Crew confined at Plymouth (*Prudent*) Fate Renamed *Impétueux* 14 July 1795 after the captured *Impétueux* burned by accident 24 August 1794; purchased, September 1794; repaired and fitted for sea, July 1795 to November 1796, and served until 1813, when she was put in Ordinary at Chatham; broken up, December 1813. Notes Also appears in the Admiralty records as *Amerique*. Not to be confused with the *Impétueux*. Sources ADM

2/272; ADM 7/354; ADM 18/121; ADM 43/33; ADM 43/80; ADM 103/503; ADM 106/2219; HCA 8/89; HCA 34/61; *London Gazette* no. 14055 (16 October 1797); Demerliac; Gardiner, *Fleet Battle and Blockade*; Roche; Winfield.

Courrier (10)

Built and launched March to September 1792, Boulogne; launched 7 September 1782 as *Courrier des Indes* **Size** 50 / 50 / 113 tonnes; 120 tons BOM **Armament** 4–10 (calibre unknown) **Complement in the action** 31 men under Jacque Nicolas Joseph Brisout (or Canot) **Bounty awarded** £155 0s 0d **Fate** Sunk by order of Lord Howe before the battle. **Notes** Lugger, captured 23 May. Name changed 1793; in the Admiralty records as a cutter, *Courrier de l'Orient*. Sister ship of the *Vanneau*, captured by the *Colossus* in 1793 and in RN service until 21 October 1796. Roche has her under Canot. (Size in BOM is of the *Vanneau*.) **Sources** ADM 18/121; ADM 43/33; ADM 43/80; Roche; Winfield.

Impétueux (74)

Dispatch folio 12 **Name in dispatches** *L'Impetueux* **Taken by** *Russell* **Built and launched** July 1786 to June 1790, Rochefort; launched 25 October 1787 **Size** 1537 / 1550 / 3069 tonnes; 1879⁶/₉₄ tons BOM **Armament** (from 1793): 28x36, 30x18, 16x8 + 4x36 obusiers 'Nature of the prize' 74 guns **Complement** 13–17 officers, 690/706 men **Complement in the action** 713 men under Louis Douville **Casualties** 100 killed, 75 wounded **Prize money awarded** £60,000 for the *Sans Pareil, Juste, Impéteux, Achille, América,* and *Northumberland* to the warrant officers, petty officers and foremastmen, 'in part of the money to be paid for the purchase and for the bounty due to the captors', by royal warrant of 22 June 1794 **Purchased for** £26,956 10s 11d **Bounty awarded** £3,565 0s 0d **Brought to** Portsmouth **Fate** Purchased, but burnt by accident at Portsmouth on 24 August 1794, and the name given to the captured *América*. **Sources** ADM 2/272; ADM 7/354; ADM 18/121; ADM 43/33; ADM 43/80; HCA 8/89; HCA 34/61; *London Gazette* no. 14055 (16 October 1797); Gardiner, *Fleet Battle and Blockade*; Demerliac; Lyon; Roche; Winfield.

Inconnue (12)

Taken by *Audacious* and *Niger* **Built and launched** May 1793 to March 1794, Dieppe; launched *c.* 30 December 1793 **Size** 220–280 /

220 / 475 tonnes; 346⁴⁹/₉₄ tons BOM **Armament** 12x12 **Complement in the action** 136 men under Jean Duchart **Bounty awarded** £680 0s 0d **Fate** Burnt by order of Lord Howe before the battle. **Notes** Variously described as a brig, corvette or sloop, captured 25 May. The British measurements are of the *Belette, ex-Belliqueuse,* a sister ship built at Dieppe at the same time. Five brigs of this design were built at Dieppe and Honfleur; all were taken by the RN, and while in RN service captured twelve enemy ships. The *Mutine*, commanded at the Nile by Hardy, was one of these. **Sources** ADM 18/121; ADM 43/33; ADM 43/80; HCA 8/89; James; Demerliac; Roche; Winfield.

Juste (80)

Dispatch folio 12 **Name in RN service** *Juste* **Taken by** *Invincible* **Built and launched** *c.* July 1782–85, Brest; launched 13 or 17 September 1784, as *Deux Frères* **Size** *c.* 1900 / 1900 / 3800 tonnes; 2143¹⁸/₉₄ tons BOM **Armament** (from 1794): 30x36, 32x24, 18x8 + 4x36 obusiers **Armament in RN service** 84 guns: LD 30x32, UD 32x18, QD 2x24 + 14x32cr, FC 6x12 + 2x32cr 'Nature of the prize' 80 guns **Complement** 13–17 officers, 839 men **Complement in the action** 877 men under Antoine Blavet **Complement in RN service** 738 **Casualties** 100 killed, 145 wounded **Purchased for** £25,929 14s 2d **Bounty awarded** £4,385 0s 0d **Prize money awarded** £60,000 for the *Sans Pareil, Juste, Impéteux, Achille, América,* and *Northumberland* to the warrant officers, petty officers and foremastmen, 'in part of the money to be paid for the purchase and for the bounty due to the captors', by royal warrant of 22 June 1794 **Brought to** Portsmouth **Crew confined at** Plymouth (*Prudent*) **Fate** Purchased, August 1794; served from August 1795; part of Calder's squadron in 1801; laid up at Plymouth, April 1802; broken up there, February 1811. **Notes** Name changed September 1792. **Sources** ADM 2/272; ADM 7/254; ADM 18/121; ADM 43/33; ADM 43/80; ADM 103/503; ADM 106/2219; HCA 8/89; *London Gazette* no. 14055 (16 October 1797); Demerliac; Gardiner, *Fleet Battle and Blockade*; Lyon; Roche; Winfield.

Northumberland (74)

Dispatch folio 12 **Taken by** *Orion* **Built and launched** 24 February 1779 to July 1780, Brest; launched 3 May 1780 **Size** 1478 / 1500 / 2967 tonnes; 1811²/₉₄ or 1827⁸⁷/₉₄ tons BOM

Armament (1793): 28x36, 30x18, 16x8 + 4x36 obusiers + 6x1 perriers 'Nature of the prize' 74 guns Complement 11–17 officers, 690/734 men Complement in the action 700 men under François-Pierre Etienne Casualties 60 killed, 100 wounded (Demerliac and the *Gazette*); 100 killed, 200 wounded (Roche) Purchased for £16,313 7s 4d Bounty awarded £3,500 0s 0d Prize money awarded £60,000 for the *Sans Pareil, Juste, Impéteux, Achille, América,* and *Northumberland* to the warrant officers, petty officers and foremastmen, 'in part of the money to be paid for the purchase and for the bounty due to the captors', by royal warrant of 22 June 1794 Brought to Portsmouth Crew confined at Tenterden, Tavistock, Plymouth (*Prudent*); February 1796 Ashburton, April 1796 Ashford Fate Purchased October 1794 but never fitted for sea by the RN; broken up at Plymouth, November 1795. Notes Sister ship of the *Achille*. Named for the *Northumberland* (64), captured off Ushant in 1744 and in French service until wrecked (as the *Atlas* store ship) off Ushant in 1781. Sources ADM 2/272; ADM 7/354; ADM 43/33; ADM 43/80; ADM 103/503; ADM 106/2219; HCA 8/89; *London Gazette* no. 14055 (16 October 1797); Demerliac; Gardiner, *Fleet Battle and Blockade*; Lyon; Roche; Winfield.

Républicain (18/20)

Dispatch folio 8 Name in dispatches *Républicaine* Taken by *Audacious* and *Niger* Built and launched 1793 to November 1794, Bordeaux; launched September 1793 Armament 18x8 (20 ports) Complement 5–9 officers, 136/140 men Complement in the action 125 men under Jean Bouyer Bounty awarded £625 0s 0d Fate Burnt by order of Lord Howe before the battle. Notes Corvette, captured 25 May. Not to be confused with the *Républicain* (110), which fought the *Queen Charlotte* and survived the battle. Sources ADM 18/121; ADM 43/33; ADM 43/80; James; Demerliac; Roche.

Sans Pareil (80)

Dispatch folio 12 Name in dispatches *Le Sans Pareil* Name in RN service *Sans Pareil* Taken by *Royal George* Built and launched October 1790 to September 1793, Brest; launched 8 June 1793 Size 2000–2034 / 2000 / 3868 tonnes; 2242²²⁄₉₄

tons BOM Armament 30x36, 32x24, 18x12 + 4x36 obusiers + 6x1 perriers Armament in RN service GD 30x24, UD 30x24, QD 2x24 + 12x24cr, FC 2x24 + 4x24cr 'Nature of the prize' 80 guns Complement 17 officers, 839 men Complement in the action 814 men under Jean François Courand Complement in RN service 738 Casualties 264 killed (260 *Gazette*) and 120 wounded Purchased for £33,978 18s 8d Bounty awarded £4,070 0s 0d Prize money awarded £60,000 for the *Sans Pareil, Juste, Impéteux, Achille, América,* and *Northumberland* to the warrant officers, petty officers and foremastmen, 'in part of the money to be paid for the purchase and for the bounty due to the captors', by royal warrant of 22 June 1794 Brought to Portsmouth Fate Purchased, August 1794; fitted for sea, June 1794 to April 1795; served as the flagship of Lord Hugh Seymour in the Channel, 1795–98; in the Caribbean, 1799–1801; prison ship at Plymouth, 1807; sheer hulk there, 1810–38; broken up there, October 1842. Notes One of eight sister ships designed by Sané; six were taken by the British. Also appears in the Admiralty records as the *Sans Paraille*. Sources ADM 2/272; ADM 7/34; ADM 18/121; ADM 43/33; ADM 43/80; ADM 106/2219; HCA 8/89; *London Gazette* no. 14055 (16 October 1797); Demerliac; Gardiner, *Fleet Battle and Blockade*; Lyon; Roche; Winfield.

Vengeur du Peuple or *Vengeur* (74)

Taken by *Brunswick* Built and launched February 1763 to November 1767, Toulon; launched 16 July 1766 as *Marseillais* Size 1550 / 1550 / *c.* 2900 tonnes Armament (from 1793): 28x36, 30x18, 16x8 + 4x36 obusiers 'Nature of the prize' 74 guns; 'afterwards foundering with great part of her crew' Complement 12–17 officers, 706/713 men Complement in the action 'at least' 700 men under François Renaudin Casualties 456 (total) or 267 (Demerliac) or 277 (Roche) survived (*Gazette*: '320 sunk') Bounty awarded £3,500 0s 0d Fate Sank shortly after the battle from the damage received. Notes Renamed in February 1794. Bounty paid for 700 men. Sources ADM 2/272; ADM 7/354; ADM 18/121; ADM 43/33; ADM 43/80; Demerliac; Roche.

Bridport's action, 23 June 1795

Alexandre or *Alexander* (74)

Dispatch folio 148 Name in dispatches *Alexander* Name in RN service *Alexander* Taken by *Queen Charlotte* Built and launched April 1774 to December 1778, Deptford; launched 8 October 1778 Size *c.* 1400 / 1400 / *c.* 2700 tonnes; 1621 tons BOM Armament 28x32, 28x16, 18x9 Armament in RN service LD 28x32, UD 28x18, QD 14x9, FC 4x9 Complement 16 officers, 650 men Complement in the action 666 men under François Guillemet Complement in RN service 550 Casualties 220 killed and wounded 'Nature of the prize' 74 guns Purchased for £12,369 15s 1d Bounty awarded £3,330 0s 0d Brought to Portsmouth Crew confined at Plymouth (*Prudent*) Fate Served in the Channel and Mediterranean, and at the Nile under Alexander Ball; lazarette at Plymouth, 1805; broken up there, November 1819. Notes Originally captured from the British off the Scillies by the *Jean Bart*, 6 November 1794. Not to be confused with the *Alexandre* (80) captured by Duckworth in 1806. Sources ADM 2/276; ADM 7/354; ADM 43/34; ADM 43/80; ADM 103/503; HCA 8/89; Gardiner, *Fleet Battle and Blockade*; Demerliac; Roche.

Formidable (74)

Dispatch folio 148 Name in RN service *Belleisle* Taken by *Barfleur* and *London* Built and launched August 1791 to June 1794, Rochefort; launched 29 April 1794 as *Marat* Size 1537 / 1550 / 3069 tonnes; 1889⁷⁄₉₄ tons BOM Armament (1794): 28x36 (30 ports), 30x18, 16x8 (+ perhaps 4x36 obusiers from October) Armament in RN service GD 30x32, UD 30x24, QD 2x9 + 14x32cr, FC 2x9 + 2x24cr, RH 6x24cr Complement 17 officers, 690/706 men Complement in the action 717 men under Charles-Alexandre Durand-Linois Complement in RN service 700 Casualties 320 killed and wounded 'Nature of the prize' 80 guns Purchased for £24,789 9s 6d; and £6,861 9s 8d for the stores of the *Tigre* and *Formidable* Bounty awarded £3,585 0s 0d Brought to

Plymouth Crew confined at Plymouth (*Prudent*) Fate Purchased, September 1795; served in the Channel Fleet from 1801, including as the flagship of Sir William Cornwallis, and in the Mediterranean; was in the lee column at Trafalgar under William Hargood; in 1806 was at the destruction of the *Impétueux* (74), in 1809 at the capture of Martinique, and in the Walcheren expedition; in Ordinary at Plymouth, 1809, broken up there, 1814. Notes Originally *Lion*; September 1793, *Marat*; May 1795, *Formidable*. Bounty apparently paid only to the *London*. Not to be confused with the *Formidable* (90), launched at Chatham in 1777, which served until 1813. Sources ADM 2/276; ADM 7/354; ADM 18/122; ADM 43/80; ADM 103/503; ADM 106/2220; HCA 8/89; Gardiner, *Fleet Battle and Blockade*; Demerliac; Roche; Winfield.

Tigre (74)

Dispatch folio 148 Name in RN service *Tigre* Taken by *Queen* and *London* Built and launched October 1790 or January 1791 to August 1793, Brest; launched 8 May 1793 Size 1537 / 1550 / 3069 tonnes; 1886⁶⁷⁄₉₄ tons BOM Armament 28x36 (30 ports), 30x18, 16x8 + 4x36 obusiers Armament in RN service LD 28x32 + 2x68cr, UD 28x18 + 2x68cr, QD 4x18 + 10x32cr, FC 2x18 + 2x32cr, RH 6x18cr 'Nature of the prize' 74 guns Complement 17 officers, 690/706 men Complement in the action 726 men under Jacques Bedout Complement in RN service 640 Casualties 130 killed and wounded Purchased for £24,352 14s 2d; and £6,861 9s 8d for the stores of the *Tigre* and *Formidable* Bounty awarded £3,630 0s 0d Brought to Portsmouth Fate Purchased, September 1795; served extensively, including under Sir Sidney Smith at Acre, until paid off in August or September 1815; powder hulk at Plymouth until broken up there, June 1817. Sources ADM 2/276; ADM 7/354; ADM 43/34; ADM 43/80; ADM 106/2220; HCA 8/89; James; Demerliac; Gardiner, *Fleet Battle and Blockade*; Roche; Winfield.

Cape St Vincent, 14 February 1797

Salvador del Mundo (112)

Dispatch folio 153 Name in RN service *Salvador del Mundo* Taken by *Orion* Built and launched unknown – 1787, El Ferrol; launched 1786 Size 2200 tons; 2397⁴⁷⁄₉₄ tons BOM Armament 30x36, 32x24, 30x12, 20x8 Armament in RN service GD 30x32, MD 32x24, UD 32x12, QD 12x9, FC 6x9 Complement 40 officers, *c.* 850 men Complement in RN service 839 Complement in the action 819 men Casualties 5 officers killed, 3 wounded; 37 artillerists, seamen and soldiers killed, 121 wounded Purchased for £42,286 11s 1d Bounty awarded £4,148 14s 11d Brought to Plymouth, 5 October 1797; paid off, December 1797 Fate Purchased, December 1797; served as a receiving ship at Plymouth, then the flagship of four admirals, including Sir Robert Calder; broken up there, February 1815. Sources ADM 43/40; ADM 43/80; ADM 106/2223; *London Gazette* no. 13987 (3 March 1797); Gardiner, *Fleet Battle and Blockade*; Harbron; Lyon; Winfield.

San Isidro (74)

Dispatch folio 153 Name in dispatches *San Ysidro* Name in RN service *San Ysidro* Taken by *Excellent* Built and launched 1786, Ferrol Size 1835⁷⁸⁄₉₄ tons BOM Armament in RN service GD 28x32, UD 30x18, QD 8x9, FC 6x9 Complement 590 Complement in the action 525 men Casualties 4 officers killed, 8 wounded; 25 artillerists, seamen and soldiers killed, 55 wounded Purchased for £21,257 16s 10d Bounty awarded £2,659 9s 0d Brought to Plymouth, 5 October 1797 Fate Purchased, December 1797; hulked at Plymouth as a prison ship, October 1797; sold, 3 November 1814. Sources: ADM 43/40; ADM 43/80; ADM 106/2223; *London Gazette* no. 13987 (3 March 1797); Gardiner, *Fleet Battle and Blockade*; Harbron; Lyon; Winfield.

San José (114)

Dispatch folio 153 Name in dispatches *San Josef* Name in RN service *San Josef* Taken by *Captain* Built and launched 1783, Ferrol Size 2163 tons; 2456²⁴⁄₉₄ tons BOM Armament 32x36, 30x24, 32x12, 18x8, 6x24 mortars for grapeshot Armament in RN service GD 32x32, MD 32x24, UD 32x12, QD 12x9, FC 6x9 Complement 839 Complement in the action 917 Casualties 2 officers killed, 5 wounded; 44 artillerists, seamen and soldiers killed, 591 wounded Purchased for £46,142 17s 9d Bounty awarded £4,645 3s 6d Brought to Plymouth, 5 October 1797, fitted for sea, June 1799 to January 1801 Fate Purchased, December 1797; served at sea in the Napoleonic War, in the blockade of Brest as the flagship of Vice-Admiral Sir Charles Cotton, in the Walcheren Expedition under Richard Dunn, in the Channel Fleet as the flagship of Admiral Lord Keith; in action against the French off Toulon 5 November 1813 as the flagship of Rear Admiral Sir Richard King. Variously in Ordinary and a flagship at Plymouth 1815–37. Gunnery training ship at Plymouth from January 1837. Paid off 1846 and broken up at Plymouth, May 1849. Sources ADM 43/40; ADM 43/80; ADM 106/2223; *London Gazette* no. 13987 (3 March 1797); Gardiner, *Fleet Battle and Blockade*; Harbron; Lyon; Winfield.

San Nicolas (82)

Dispatch folio 153 Name in RN service *San Nicolas* Taken by *Captain* Built and launched 1769, Cartagena Size 1942 tons BOM Armament in RN service GD 30x32, UD 32x18, QD 14x9, FC 6x9 Complement in the action 630 Complement in RN service 719 Casualties 4 officers killed, 8 wounded; 140 artillerists, seamen and soldiers killed, 51 wounded Purchased for £28,260 4s 5d Bounty awarded £3,191 6s 10d Brought to Plymouth, 5 October 1797 Fate Purchased, December 1797; hulked at Plymouth as a prison ship, August 1798; in service, 1801–2 and 1804–11; sold at Plymouth, 3 November 1814. Sources ADM 43/40; ADM 43/80; ADM 106/2223; *London Gazette* no. 13987 (3 March 1797); Gardiner, *Fleet Battle and Blockade*; Harbron; Lyon; Winfield.

Camperdown, 11 October 1797

Admiraal Tjerk Hiddes de Vries (64)

Dispatch folio 183 Name in RN service *Admiral de Vries* Built and launched 1781, Harlingen Size 1360⁵⁴⁄₉₄ tons BOM Armament 26x32, 26x18, 14x8 Armament in RN service LD 28x24, UD 28x18, QD 8x9, FC 8x9; as a troopship, LD none, UD 24x18, QD 8x9, FC 8x9 Complement in the action 448 men under Jan Barent Zegers Complement in RN service 491 (250 as troopship) 'Nature of the prize' Captain Zegers; 68 guns, 450 men Purchased for £16,539 4s 10d Bounty awarded £2,269 8s 0d Brought to Chatham, 7 January 1798 Fate Purchased, December 1797; transport service, March 1798, and fitted as a troopship, July 1798; prison ship at Jamaica, December 1799; sold there, February 1806. Notes Rear squadron (Rear-Admiral Bloys). The largest of the Dutch 68-gun ships. Sources: ADM 7/354; ADM 43/40; ADM 43/80; ADM 106/2223; *London Gazette* no. 14055 (16 October 1797); James; Gardiner, *Fleet Battle and Blockade*; Lyon; Winfield.

Alkmaar (56)

Name in RN service *Alkmaar* Taken by *Monmouth* Built and launched 1783, Enkhuizen Size 1040⁸³⁄₉₄ tons BOM Armament 24x18, 24x12, 8x8 Armament in RN service (from 12 March 1801): UD 18x9, QD 6x9; as a storeship, UD 12x9, QD 4x6 Complement in the action 321 men under Jan Willem Kraft Casualties 26 killed, 62 wounded 'Nature of the prize' Captain Kraft; 56 guns, 350 men Purchased for £11,593 5s 9d Bounty awarded £1,626 1s 3d Brought to Sheerness, 20 October 1797 Fate Purchased, December 1797; troopship, 1798; flagship of Rear-Admirals Holloway and Totty at Sheerness, 1800 and 1801; hospital ship at Portsmouth, 1801; storeship for the Downs, 1805; laid up, 1807; in Ordinary at Sheerness, 1812; sold there, 30 November 1815. Notes Van squadron (Vice-Admiral Reyntjes). Sources ADM 2/283; ADM 7/354; ADM 43/40; ADM 43/80; ADM 106/2223; *London Gazette* no. 14055 (16 October 1797); Gardiner, *Fleet Battle and Blockade*; Winfield.

Delft (64)

Dispatch folio 183 Taken by *Monmouth* Armament 24x18, 24x12, 8x8 Complement in the action 355 men under Gerret Vandooren Casualties 43 killed, 76 wounded 'Nature of the prize' Captain Verdoorn; 56 guns, 350 men; 'afterwards sunk' Bounty awarded £1,798 5s 11d Fate Sank after the battle (14 October). Notes Van squadron (Vice-Admiral Reyntjes). Not to be confused with the *Hercules*. Sources ADM 7/354; ADM 43/40; ADM 43/80; *London Gazette* no. 14055 (16 October 1797); James; Gardiner, *Fleet Battle and Blockade*; Lyon; Winfield.

Embuscade (32)

Name in RN service *Helder* Built and launched 1794–95, Rotterdam; launched 23 April 1795 Size 770 tons BOM (surveyed for purchase as 769⁶²⁄₉₄) Armament in RN service UD 26x12, QD 4x6 + 4x24cr, FC 2x6 + 2x24cr; as floating battery, UD 24x24cr, QD 18x8cr Complement in RN service 244; 155 as floating battery 'Nature of the prize' Captain-Lieutenant Huys; 32 guns, 270 men; 'afterwards escaped & got into the Texel' Value awarded £9,615 0s 0d (including £451 16s 3d for masts and spars, £470 0s 0d for copper bolts, sheathing, braces, and pintles, and £1,763 3s 9d for furniture and stores) Fate Escaped, but was part of the squadron that surrendered to Admiral Mitchell's squadron, 30 August 1799. Purchased, April 1800; added as *Ambuscade* but renamed *Helder*, 25 March 1803, before entering service. Floating battery in the Humber, 1803–4; sold at Sheerness, June 1807. Notes Rear squadron (Rear-Admiral Bloys). Originally *Jonge Willem*, purchased from the Dutch East India Company on the stocks in January 1795. Not to be confused with the *Helder*, Dutch *Heldin* (28), taken in the Nieuwe Diep with twelve other ships, an Indiaman, and a sheer hulk, by the *Circe* of Admiral Mitchell's squadron on 28 August 1799. The value of the *Heldin* was £7,287 18s 6d. The total value of the ships taken by the *Circe* on 28 August was £37,413 13s 5d and the total value of the ships taken on 30 August was £206,432 10s 14d. Sources ADM 7/354; ADM 106/2226; *London Gazette* no. 14055 (16 October 1797); James; Gardiner, *Fleet Battle and Blockade*; Winfield.

Gelikheid (68)

Dispatch folio 183 Name in RN service *Gelikheid* Built and launched 1788, Amsterdam as *Prins Frederick Willem* Size 1304⁴⁷⁄₉₄ tons BOM Armament 26x32, 26x18, 16x8 Armament in RN service LD 26x24, UD 26x18, QD 10x9, FC 4x9 Complement in the action 447 men under Hendrick van der Ruijsch Complement in RN service 491; 73 as hulk Casualties 40 killed, and many wounded 'Nature of the prize' Captain Ruysen; 68 guns, 450 men Purchased for £18,982 17s 6d Bounty awarded £2,264 6s 8d Brought to Sheerness, October 1797, then Chatham, 8 January 1798 Fate Purchased, December 1797; prison ship at Chatham, 1798–1800; flagship of Rear-Admiral Thornborough in the North Sea, 1803, then in November a guardship in the Humber; sheer hulk at Falmouth, 1807; hulk at Portsmouth, 1813; sold there, 1 September 1814. Notes Rear squadron (Rear-Admiral Bloys). Name changed 1795. Sources ADM 2/283; ADM 7/354; ADM 43/40; ADM 43/80; ADM 106/2223; *London Gazette* no. 14055 (16 October 1797); James; Gardiner, *Fleet Battle and Blockade*; Lyon; Winfield.

Haarlem (64)

Name in RN service *Haerlem / Haarlem* Built and launched 1785, Amsterdam Size 1324²²⁄₉₄ tons BOM Armament 26x24, 26x18, 16x8 Armament in RN service LD 28x24, UD 28x18, QD perhaps 2x9, FC 2x9; as troopship: LD none, UD 24x18, QD perhaps 2x9, FC 2x9 Complement in the action 445 men under Olfort Wiggerts Complement in RN service 491; 250 as troopship 'Nature of the prize' Captain Wiggerts; 68 guns, 450 men Purchased for £18,205 17s 4d Bounty awarded £2,254 4s 0d Brought to Sheerness, October 1797, then Chatham, 8 January 1798 Fate Purchased, December 1797; troopship, 1798; to Egypt, 1801; Mediterranean, 1802; in Ordinary at Chatham, 1804–05; to Customs *c*. 1807; receiving ship, Chatham, 1811; sold there, 2 May 1816. Notes Van squadron (Vice-Admiral Reyntjes). Sources ADM 2/283; ADM 7/354; ADM 43/40; ADM 106/2223; *London Gazette* no. 14055 (16 October 1797); James; Gardiner, *Fleet Battle and Blockade*; Lyon; Winfield.

Hercules (64)

Name in RN service *Delft* Taken by *Venerable* Built and launched 1781, Dort Size 1266⁴³⁄₉₄ tons BOM Armament 26x32, 26x18, 14x8 Armament in RN service (as troopship): LD 26x24, UD 28x18, QD 4x9 + 8x24cr, FC 4x9 + 2x24cr Complement in the action 449 men, 4 women, 1 girl under Van Rysoort Complement in RN service 491 (250 as troopship) Purchased for £18,434 16s 4d Bounty awarded £2,274 9s 3d Brought to Sheerness, October 1797, then Chatham, 8 January 1798 Fate Purchased, December 1797; troopship, 1799; powder hulk at Chatham, 1802; sunk as a breakwater at Harwich, 19 September 1822. Notes Rear squadron (Rear-Admiral Bloys). Surrendered after she caught fire; it was extinguished but all her gunpowder had been thrown overboard. Renamed 30 August 1798; not to be confused with the *Delft*. Sources: ADM 2/283; ADM 43/40; ADM 43/80; ADM 106/2223; *London Gazette* no. 14055 (16 October 1797); James; Gardiner, *Fleet Battle and Blockade*; Lyon; Winfield.

Jupiter (74)

Name in RN service *Camperdown* Taken by *Monmouth* and *Russell* Built and launched Amsterdam; launched April 1782 Size 1558⁵⁴⁄₉₄ tons BOM Armament 28x32, 28x18, 12x12, 6x8 Armament in RN service LD 28x32, UD 28x18, QD 2 x18 + 10x32cr, FC 2x18 + 4x32cr Complement in the action 540 men under Vice-Admiral Harmanus Rentjes Complement in RN service 590 (73 as prison ship) 'Nature of the prize' Vice-Admiral Reyntres, Rear-Admiral Meures; 74 guns, 550 men Purchased for £17,264 16s 4d Bounty awarded £2,735 8s 9d Brought to Chatham, 10 January 1798 Fate Purchased, December 1797; prison ship at Chatham, 1798–1800; powder magazine there, 1802; sold to be broken up, 10 September 1817. Notes Van squadron (Vice-Admiral Reyntjes). Sources ADM 43/40; ADM 43/80; ADM 106/2223; *London Gazette* no. 14055 (16 October 1797); James; Gardiner, *Fleet Battle and Blockade*; Lyon; Winfield.

Monnikendam (44)

Taken by *Powerful* Built and launched 1782, Enkhuizen Armament 26x24, 26x18, 14x8 Complement 270 Complement in the action 254 men under Thomas Lancaster 'Nature of the prize' Captain Lancaster; 44 guns, 270 men **Bounty awarded** £1,286 13s 4d **Fate** Lost after the battle. **Notes** Van squadron (Vice-Admiral Reyntjes). **Sources** ADM 7/354; ADM 43/40; ADM 43/80; *London Gazette* no. 14055 (16 October 1797); James; Gardiner, *Fleet Battle and Blockade*; threedecks.org.

Vrijheid (74)

Dispatch folio 183 **Name in RN service** *Vryheid* **Taken by** *Venerable, Triumph, Ardent, Director* **Built and launched** 1782, Amsterdam **Size** 1562 tons BOM **Armament** 28x32, 28x18, 18x12 **Armament in RN service** LD 28x32, UD 28x18, QD 12x12, FC 4x12; as prison ship, none **Complement in the action** 538 men under Loderyk Willem Van Rossum **Complement in RN service** 590 (73 as prison ship) '**Nature of the prize**' Admiral De Winter, Captain Van Rossem; 74 guns, 550 men **Purchased for** £10,780 19s 6d **Bounty awarded** £2,725 6s 1d **Brought to** Sheerness, October 1797, then Chatham, 8 January 1798 **Fate** Purchased, December 1797; prison ship (or possibly hospital ship for prisoners) at Chatham, February 1798; a powder magazine in the Medway, April 1802; sold at Chatham, 11 June 1811. **Notes** Centre squadron (Admiral De Winter). Flagship: surrendered only after all her masts had been shot away. **Sources** ADM 2/283; ADM 7/354; ADM 43/40; ADM 43/80; ADM 106/2223; *London Gazette* no. 14055 (16 October 1797); James; Gardiner, *Fleet Battle and Blockade*; Lyon; Winfield.

Wassenaar (64)

Name in RN *Wassenar* **Taken by** *Triumph* then *Russell* **Built and launched** 1781, Zwindrecht, Rotterdam **Size** 1269^{48}/$_{94}$ tons BOM **Armament** 26x32, 26x18, 14x8 **Armament in RN service** LD 28x24 (none as troopship), UD 28x18, QD 8x9, FC 2x9 **Complement in the action** 446 men under Adolph Holland **Complement in RN service** 491 (250 as troopship) '**Nature of the prize**' Captain Holland; 64 guns, 450 men **Purchased for** £14,393 8s 9d **Bounty awarded** £2,259 5s 4d **Brought to** Sheerness, 28 October 1797 **Fate** Purchased, December 1797; troopship, 1798; flagship of Admiral Peyton in the Downs, February to May 1798; in the Mediterranean, 1800–02; powder hulk at Chatham, 1802–15; sold there for breaking up, 13 August 1818. **Notes** Centre squadron (Admiral De Winter). Captured twice: she briefly rehoisted her colours after being fired on by a Dutch brig. **Sources** ADM 2/283; ADM 7/354; ADM 43/40; ADM 43/80; ADM 106/2223; *London Gazette* no. 14055 (16 October 1797); James; Gardiner, *Fleet Battle and Blockade*; Lyon; Winfield.

The Nile, 1–3 August 1798

Aquilon (74)

Dispatch folio 190 **Name in dispatches** *L'Aquillon* **Name in RN service** *Aboukir* **Taken by** *Minotaur, Vanguard, Theseus* **Built and launched** May or September 1787 to June 1790, Rochefort; launched 8 June 1789 **Size** 1537 / 1550 / 3069 tonnes; 1869^{90}/$_{94}$ tons BOM **Armament** 28x36, 30x18, 16x8 + 6x36 obusiers (obusiers added in 1795) **Complement** 13–17 officers, 690/706 men **Complement in the action** 700 men under Henri-Alexander Thévenard '**Nature of the prize**' 74 guns, 700 men **Casualties** 87 killed, 213 wounded **Bounty awarded** Bounty unknown; and £30,000 for the stores found in all the prizes **Purchased for** £22,428 0s 0d (the total for the six ships including 'the fractional parts of a ton' was £117,465 11s 5d) **Brought to** Plymouth **Fate** Purchased, March 1799; not fitted for sea; broken up at Plymouth, March 1802. **Sources** ADM 2/287; ADM 7/354; ADM 106/2224; ADM 106/2225; *Naval Chronicle*, 14 December 1798; *London Gazette* nos. 15065 (2 October 1798) and 15265 (7 June 1800); James; Demerliac; Roche; Winfield.

Artémise (28)

Dispatch folio 190 **Name in dispatches** *L'Artemise* **Taken by** *Theseus* **Built and launched** December 1791 to November 1794, Toulon; launched 25 September 1794 **Size** c. 600 / 600 / 1100 tonnes **Armament** (1797) 26x12, 10x6 + 4x36 obusiers **Complement** 10 officers, 268 men **Complement in the action** 250 men under Pierre-Jean Standelet '**Nature of the prize**' 36 guns, 250 men; burnt. **Casualties** c. 40 killed and wounded **Bounty awarded** Bounty unknown; and £30,000 for the stores found in all the prizes **Fate** Burnt and abandoned by her crew then blew up. **Sources** ADM 7/354; *London Gazette* nos. 15065 (2 October 1798) and 15265 (7 June 1800); James; Demerliac; Roche.

Conquérant (74)

Dispatch folio 190 **Name in dispatches** *Conquerant* **Name in RN service** *Conquerant* **Taken by** *Audacious* **Built and launched** February 1745 to January 1747, Toulon, to a design by Coulomb; launched 9 or 10 March 1746; rebuilt January 1765 to December 1765 or January 1766, Brest, to a design by Ollivier; launched 29 November 1765 **Size** 1500 / 1500 / 3000 tonnes; 1681¾ tons BOM **Armament** 28x36, 30x18, 16x8 **Complement** 12–17 officers, 715 men **Complement in the action** 700 men under Etienne d'Albarade '**Nature of the prize'** 74 guns, 700 men **Casualties** 125 killed, 85 wounded **Bounty awarded** Bounty unknown; and £30,000 for the stores found in all the prizes **Purchased for** £6,724 0s 0d (the total for the six ships including 'the fractional parts of a ton' was £117,465 11s 5d) **Brought to** Plymouth **Fate** Purchased, March 1799; not fitted for sea by the RN; laid up at Plymouth and broken up there, January 1803. **Notes** In 1798 she was France's oldest surviving 74-gun ship; armament in 1798 was possibly 28x18, 30x12, 16x8. Roche has her in RN service as a hospital ship, Demerliac as a prison ship. **Sources** ADM 2/287; ADM 7/354; ADM 106/2224; ADM 106/2225; *Naval Chronicle*, 14 December 1798; *London Gazette* nos. 15065 (2 October 1798) and 15265 (7 June 1800); James; Demerliac; Roche; Winfield.

Franklin (80)

Dispatch folio 190 **Name in RN service** *Canopus* **Taken by** *Defence* and *Swiftsure* **Built and launched** *c*. November 1794 to March 1798, Toulon; launched 25 June 1797 **Size** 2000–2034 / 2000 / 3868 tonnes; 2258⁷/₉₄ tons BOM **Armament** 30x36, 32x24, 28x12 **Armament in RN service** LD 32x32, UD 32x18, QD 2x18 + 12x32cr, FC 2x9 + 4x32cr **Complement** 17 officers, 849 men **Complement in the action** 800 men under Maurice Gillet **Complement in RN service** 700 '**Nature of the prize'** Blanquet, 1. Contre-amiral; 80 guns, 800 men **Casualties** 120 killed, 180 wounded **Value awarded** Bounty unknown; and £30,000 for the stores found in all the prizes **Purchased for** £31,108 0s 0d (the total for the six ships

including 'the fractional parts of a ton' was £117,465 11s 5d) **Brought to** Plymouth **Fate** Purchased, March 1799; flagship of Admiral Affleck, 1798–99 then in Ordinary, August 1799; flagship of Rear-Admiral Campbell, April 1803, and joined Nelson's fleet in August but as flagship of Rear-Admiral Louis missed Trafalgar; fought with Duckworth at San Domingo, 1806, and the Dardanelles, 1807; in Ordinary, February 1812; fitted for sea and repaired several times until in Ordinary, May 1848; fitted as receiving ship then tender then mooring hulk at Plymouth, 1862–69; sold there, October 1887. **Notes** *Canopus* is the old name for *Aboukir*. Her longevity may be attributed to her being built (like the *Tonnant* and *Spartiate*) of Adriatic oak. **Sources** ADM 2/287; ADM 7/354; ADM 106/2224; ADM 106/2225; *Naval Chronicle*, 14 December 1798; *London Gazette* nos. 15065 (2 October 1798) and 15265 (7 June 1800); James; Demerliac; Roche; Winfield.

Guerrier (74)

Dispatch folio 190 **Taken by** *Zealous* **Built and launched** 3 November 1750 to January 1754, Toulon; launched 9 September 1753 **Size** 1455 / 1500 / 1500 tonnes **Armament** 28x36, 30x18, 16x8 **Complement** 12–17 officers, 660/750 men **Complement in the action** 700 men under Jean-François-Timothée Trullet '**Nature of the prize'** 74 guns, 600 men **Casualties** 130 killed, 90 wounded **Bounty awarded** Bounty unknown; £20,000 paid as compensation for the *Guerrier*, *Heureux*, and *Mercure* being destroyed; and £30,000 for the stores found in all the prizes **Fate** Burnt by the British as too badly damaged to reach England, 18 August. **Notes** Fought at the northern end of the French line, attacked by *Goliath*; not to be confused with the *Peuple Souverain*, in the centre of the line, which was renamed *Guerrier* by the Royal Navy. **Sources** ADM 2/288; ADM 7/354; *London Gazette* nos. 15065 (2 October 1798) and 15265 (7 June 1800); James; Demerliac; Roche; Winfield.

Hercule (bomb)

Dispatch folio 190 **Built and launched** Requisitioned at Marseille and armed at Toulon in January 1798 **Armament** 6x6 + 1x12in mortar **Complement** 2 officers, 90 men under (forename unknown) Favre **Bounty awarded** Bounty not awarded. **Fate** Beached and burnt by the French on 15 August. **Notes** Not officially considered a prize by the Admiralty. Not to be confused with the *Hercule* (74), captured by the *Mars, Ramillies* and *Jason* in 1798. **Sources** Demerliac; Roche.

Heureux (74)

Dispatch folio 190 **Taken by** *Goliath, Theseus, Alexander, Leander* **Built and launched** May 1782 to April 1784, Toulon; launched 19 December 1782 **Size** 1530 / 1530 / 3010 tonnes **Armament** (from April 1794) 28x36, 30x18, 16x8 + 4x36 obusiers **Complement** 13–17 officers, 690/706 men **Complement in the action** 700 men under Jean-Pierre Etienne **'Nature of the prize'** 74 guns, 700 men **Casualties** 100 killed, 150 wounded **Bounty awarded** Bounty unknown; £20,000 paid as compensation for the *Guerrier, Heureux,* and *Mercure* being destroyed; and £30,000 for the stores found in all the prizes **Fate** Burnt by the British as too badly damaged to reach England (16 August in James, 18 August in Nelson's letter of 7 September 1798, 29 August in Demerliac). **Sources** ADM 2/288; ADM 7/354; *London Gazette* nos. 15065 (2 October 1798) and 15265 (7 June 1800); James; Nicolas; Demerliac; Roche.

Mercure (74)

Dispatch folio 190 **Taken by** *Alexander* **Built and launched** August 1782 to 1783, Toulon; launched 5 August 1783 **Size** 1550–1581 / 1550 / c. 3100 tonnes **Armament** (from February 1795) 28x36, 30x18, 16x8 + 4x36 obusiers + 4 perriers **Complement** 17 officers, 690 men **Complement in the action** 700 men under (forename unknown) Cambon **'Nature of the prize'** 74 guns, 700 men **Casualties** 105 killed, 148 wounded **Bounty awarded** Bounty unknown; £20,000 paid as compensation for the *Guerrier, Heureux,* and *Mercure* being destroyed; and £30,000 for the stores found in all the prizes **Fate** Burnt by the British as too badly damaged to reach England (18 August in James and in Nelson's letter of 7 September 1798, 30 August in Demerliac). **Sources** ADM 2/288; ADM 7/354; *London Gazette* nos. 15065 (2 October 1798) and 15265 (7 June 1800); James; Demerliac; Roche.

Orient (118)

Dispatch folio 190 **Built and launched** May 1790 to August 1793, Toulon; launched 20 July 1791 as the *Dauphin Royal* **Size** 2794–2930 / 5095 / 5140 tonnes **Armament** 34x36, 32x24,

34x18, 18x12 **Complement** 21 officers, 1109 men **Complement in the action** 1010 men under Luc-Julien-Joseph Casabianca **'Nature of the prize'** Brueys, Commr. in Chief; 120 guns, 1010 men; burnt. **Casualties** c. 700 killed in the action and 100 in the explosion **Bounty awarded** Bounty unknown; and £30,000 for the stores found in all the prizes **Fate** Exploded during the battle. **Notes** Name changed in September 1792 to *Sans Culotte* and then in May 1795 to *Orient*. 70 survivors of the explosion were picked up by the British. Part of her mast was made into a coffin and presented to Nelson. **Sources** ADM 7/354; *London Gazette* nos. 15065 (2 October 1798) and 15265 (7 June 1800); James; Demerliac; Roche.

Peuple Souverain (74)

Dispatch folio 190 **Name in dispatches** *Le Souverain Peuple* **Name in RN service** *Guerrier* **Taken by** *Defence* and *Orion* **Built and launched** November 1755 to November 1757, Toulon; launched 6 June 1757 as *Souverain* **Size** c. 1536 / 1536 / 2800 tonnes; 1685$\frac{18}{94}$ tons BOM **Armament** 28x36, 30x18, 19x8 + 4x36 obusiers (obusiers added February 1795) **Complement** 12–17 officers, 715 men **Complement in the action** 700 men under Pierre-Paul Raccord **'Nature of the prize'** 74 guns, 700 men **Casualties** 96 killed, 125 wounded **Bounty awarded** Bounty unknown; and £30,000 for the stores found in all the prizes **Purchased for** £5,055 0s 0d (the total for the six ships including 'the fractional parts of a ton' was £117,465 11s 5d) **Brought to** Gibraltar, September 1798 **Fate** Too damaged to proceed further than Gibraltar so receiving ship there, January 1799; purchased, March 1799; served as flagship there, 1803–04; sheer hulk there, 1805; broken up there, August 1810. **Notes** Name changed in c. September 1792 to *Peuple Souverain*. The first to surrender, at about 9pm. Not to be confused with the *Guerrier*, at the northern end of the line. **Sources** ADM 2/287; ADM 7/354; ADM 106/2224; ADM 106/2225; *Naval Chronicle*, 14 December 1798; *London Gazette* nos. 15065 (2 October 1798) and 15265 (7 June 1800); James; Demerliac; Roche; Winfield.

Sérieuse (32)

Dispatch folio 190 **Taken by** *Orion* **Built and launched** March to November 1779, Toulon; launched 28 August 1779 **Size** 600 / 600 / 1100

tonnes **Armament** (from March 1794): 26x12, 6x6 + 4x36 obusiers **Complement** 9–10 officers, 255/275 men **Complement in the action** 250 men under Claude-Jean Martin '**Nature of the prize**' 36 guns, 250 men; sunk. **Casualties** *c.* 60 killed and wounded **Bounty awarded** Bounty unknown; and £30,000 for the stores found in all the prizes **Fate** Dismasted and sunk after the battle by the British. **Sources** ADM 7/354; *London Gazette* nos. 15065 (2 October 1798) and 15265 (7 June 1800); James; Demerliac; Roche.

Spartiate (74)

Dispatch folio 190 **Name in RN service** *Spartiate* **Taken by** *Vanguard* and *Audacious* **Built and launched** *c.* November 1794 to March 1798, Toulon; launched 24 November 1797 **Size** 1537 / 1550 / 3069 tonnes; 1949⁴¹⁄₉₄ tons BOM **Armament** 28x36, 30x18, 16x8 + 4x36 obusiers **Armament in RN service** LD 28x32; UD 30x18; QD 2x18 + 14x32cr; FC 2x18 + 6x32cr **Complement** 16 officers, 690 men **Complement in the action** 700 men under Maxime (or Maurice) Julien Émeriau de Beauverger '**Nature of the prize**' 74 guns, 700 men **Casualties** 64 killed, 150 wounded **Bounty awarded** Bounty unknown; and £30,000 for the stores found in all the prizes **Purchased for** £28,035 0s 0d (the total for the six ships including 'the fractional parts of a ton' was £117,465 11s 5d) **Brought to** Plymouth **Fate** Purchased, March 1799; fitted for sea at Plymouth, July 1801 to April 1803; fought in the weather column at Trafalgar, and served until December 1809; in Ordinary at Portsmouth to 1813, then Woolwich; repaired and served as the flagship on the South American station, 1823–25, then in the Mediterranean, the North Sea and South America; finally paid off, 1836; sheer hulk at Plymouth, August 1842; broken up there, 30 May 1857. **Sources** ADM 2/287; ADM 7/354; ADM 106/2224; ADM 106/2225; *Naval Chronicle*, 14 December 1798; *London Gazette* nos. 15065 (2 October 1798) and 15265 (7 June 1800); James; Demerliac; Roche; Winfield.

Timoleon (74)

Dispatch folio 190 **Taken by** *Theseus* and *Leander* **Built and launched** September 1784 to either 1786 or September 1787; launched 15 September 1785 as *Vaisseau No. 1* **Size** 1537 / 1550 / 3069 tonnes **Armament** (from March 1794): 28x36, 30x18, 16x8 + 4x36 obusiers + 4

perriers **Complement** 13–17 officers, 690/706 men **Complement in the action** 700 men under Louis-Léonce Trullet '**Nature of the prize**' 74 guns, 700 men **Bounty awarded** Bounty unknown; and £30,000 for the stores found in all the prizes **Fate** Beached by her crew to avoid capture; burnt on 3 August and exploded. **Notes** Name changed January 1786 to *Commerce de Bordeaux*, December 1793 to *Bonnet Rouge*, January 1784 to *Timoleon*. **Sources** ADM 7/354; *London Gazette* nos. 15065 (2 October 1798) and 15265 (7 June 1800); James; Demerliac; Roche; Winfield.

Tonnant (80)

Dispatch folio 190 **Name in RN service** *Tonnant* **Taken by** *Theseus* **Built and launched** November 1787 to September 1790, Toulon; launched 24 October 1789 **Size** 2000–2034 / 2000 / 3868 tonnes; 2281¾ tons BOM **Armament** 30x36, 32x24, 18x12 + 4x36 obusiers + 4 perriers **Armament in RN service** LD 32x32, UD 32x18, QD 2x18 + 14x32cr, FC 4x32cr **Complement** 13–17 officers, 839 men **Complement in the action** 800 men under Aristide Aubert Dupetit-Thouars **Complement in RN service** 700 '**Nature of the prize**' 80 guns, 800 men **Casualties** 110 killed, 150 wounded **Bounty awarded** Bounty unknown; and £30,000 for the stores found in all the prizes **Purchased for** £24,090 0s 0d (the total for the six ships including 'the fractional parts of a ton' was £117,465 11s 5d) **Brought to** Plymouth **Fate** Purchased, March 1799; in service, January 1799; in Ordinary, July 1799; under Pellew, March 1803, and in action with Calder's squadron, September 1803; at Trafalgar; flagship of Rear-Admirals Harvey and de Courcy, 1806; alternating repairs and service 1809–14; flagship of Vice-Admiral Cochrane, North America, 1814, and Rear-Admiral Hallowell, Ireland, 1815; in Ordinary at Plymouth, 1818, then broken up there, March 1821. **Notes** Dismasted wreck but was the last to surrender (with 1,600 other survivors on board), on 3 August. Six vessels of the French navy have been named after Dupetit-Thouars. **Sources** ADM 2/287; ADM 7/354; ADM 106/2224; ADM 106/2225; *Naval Chronicle*, 14 December 1798; *London Gazette* nos. 15065 (2 October 1798) and 15265 (7 June 1800); James; Demerliac; Roche.

Copenhagen, 2 April 1801

Charlotte Amalia (26)

Dispatch folio 123 Built and launched 1765, place unknown Armament 26x24 Complement 228 Complement in the action 241 under Hans H. Koefoed Casualties 19 killed, 2 died of wounds, 18 wounded Bounty awarded £30,393 15s 0d for the whole fleet Fate Burnt after her crew abandoned her. Notes Blockship. Sources ADM 43/48; James; Pope; Tracy.

Cronborg (22)

Dispatch folio 123 Built and launched 1781, Nyholm Size 934 tons (Danish) Armament 22x24 Complement 201 Complement in the action 223 under Jens E. Hauch Casualties 18 killed, 2 died of wounds, 7 wounded Bounty awarded £30,393 15s 0d for the whole fleet Fate Burnt. Notes Frigate without masts. Sources ADM 43/48; James; Pope; Tracy.

Dannebroge (60)

Built and launched 1772, Nyholm Size 2020 tons (Danish) Armament 24x24, 24x12, 12x8 Complement 349 Complement in the action 357 under Ferdinand A. Braun Casualties 53 killed, 3 died of wounds, 48 wounded Bounty awarded £30,393 15s 0d for the whole fleet Fate Caught fire during the action and exploded. Notes Blockship, served as Fischer's flagship. Sources ADM 43/48; Pope.

Hayen (20)

Dispatch folio 123 Built and launched 1793, Copenhagen Size 1128 tons (Danish) Armament 20x18 Complement 175 Complement in the action unknown, under Jochum N. Müller Casualties 7 killed, 6 wounded Bounty awarded £30,393 15s 0d for the whole fleet Fate Burnt. Notes Floating battery. Sources ADM 43/48; James; Pope; Tracy.

Hiaelperen (22)

Built and launched 1787, Bodenhoffs Plads Size 852 tons (Danish) Armament 16x36, 2x12, 4x150 [sic] mortars Complement 238 Complement in the action 269 under Peter C. Lillienskjold Casualties 3 died of wounds, 3 wounded Bounty awarded £30,393 15s 0d for the whole fleet Fate Burnt. Notes Frigate in good condition. Sources ADM 43/48; Pope.

Holsteen (60)

Dispatch folio 123 Name in RN service Holstein to 1805, then perhaps to Nassau Built and launched 1772, Nyholm Size 2020 tons (Danish); 1394 7¾/94 tons BOM Armament 24x24, 24x12, 12x8 Armament in RN service GD 26x24, UD 24x18, QD 12x24cr Complement 475 Complement in the action 400 under Jacob Arenfeldt Complement in RN service 491 Casualties 12 killed, 4 died of wounds, 49 wounded Purchased for £16,035 10s 5d Bounty awarded £30,393 15s 0d for the whole fleet Brought to Sheerness, by May 1801; then Chatham, 16 October 1802 Fate Hospital ship until she reached England; purchased, May 1801; commissioned, 1805, and served in the North Sea and at Copenhagen, 1807; prison ship at Chatham, 1810–14; sold there, 3 November 1814. Notes Blockship. Renamed to Nassau only in Lyon. Sources ADM 43/48; ADM 106/2227; James; Lyon; Pope; Tracy; Winfield.

Indfødsretten (64)

Dispatch folio 123 Built and launched 1776, Nyholm Size 2032 tons (Danish) Armament 26x24, 26x12, 12x8 Complement 368 Complement in the action 394 under Albert de Thura Casualties 21 killed, 6 died of wounds, 35 wounded Bounty awarded £30,393 15s 0d for the whole fleet Fate Burnt. Notes Blockship. Sources ADM 43/48; James; Pope; Tracy.

Jylland (54)

Dispatch folio 123 Built and launched 1760, Nyholm Size 2358 tons (Danish) Armament mostly 24 Complement 425 Complement in the action 371 under Eric O. Brandt Casualties 28 killed, 7 died of wounds, 36 wounded Bounty awarded £30,393 15s 0d for the whole fleet Fate Burnt. Notes Blockship. Sources ADM 43/48; James; Pope; Tracy.

Prøvesteenen (58)

Dispatch folio 123 Built and launched 1767, Nyholm Size 3208 tons (Danish) Armament 30x36, 28x24 Complement 382 Complement in the action 529 under Lorentz F. Lassen Casualties 40 killed, 8 died of wounds, 27 wounded Bounty awarded £30,393 15s 0d for the whole fleet Fate Surrendered and burnt.

Notes Blockship with two gun decks. **Sources** ADM 43/48; James; Pope; Tracy.

Rendsborg (22)

Dispatch folio 123 **Built and launched** 1786, Bodenhoffs Plads **Size** 504 tons (Danish) **Armament** 22x24 **Complement** 211 **Complement in the action** 221 under Christian T. Egede **Casualties** 28 killed, 43 wounded, 7 missing **Bounty awarded** £30,393 15s 0d for the whole fleet **Fate** Driven on the shoals and burnt. **Notes** Blockship. **Sources** ADM 43/48; James; Pope; Tracy.

Sælland (74)

Dispatch folio 123 **Built and launched** 1787, Nyholm **Size** 2630 tons (Danish) **Armament** 30x24, 30x18, 14x8 **Complement** 640 **Complement in the action** 553 under Frederik C. L. Harboe **Casualties** 39 killed, 17 died of wounds, 108 wounded, 20 missing **Bounty awarded** £30,393 15s 0d for the whole fleet **Fate** Burnt. **Notes** Unrigged two-decked ship. **Sources** ADM 43/48; James; Pope; Tracy.

Søhesten (20)

Dispatch folio 123 **Built and launched** 1795, Bodenhoffs Plads **Armament** 20x24

Complement 190 **Complement in the action** 126 under Bernhart U. Middelboe **Casualties** 12 killed, 7 died of wounds, 14 wounded **Bounty awarded** £30,393 15s 0d for the whole fleet **Fate** Burnt. **Notes** Floating battery. **Sources** ADM 43/48; James; Pope; Tracy.

Sværdfisken (18)

Dispatch folio 123 **Built and launched** 1764, Gammelholm **Size** 466 tons (Danish) **Armament** 18x24 **Complement** 190 **Complement in the action** 176 under Søren S. Sommerfeldt **Casualties** 18 killed, 4 died of wounds, 15 wounded **Bounty awarded** £30,393 15s 0d for the whole fleet **Fate** Burnt **Notes** Floating battery. **Sources** ADM 43/48; James; Pope; Tracy.

Wagrien (52)

Dispatch folio 123 **Built and launched** 1773, Nyholm **Size** 2020 tons (Danish) **Armament** 52x24 **Complement** 273 **Complement in the action** 261 under Friderich C. Risbrich **Casualties** 21 killed, 7 died of wounds, 35 wounded **Bounty awarded** £30,393 15s 0d for the whole fleet **Fate** Surrendered and burnt. **Notes** Blockship. **Sources** ADM 43/48; James; Pope; Tracy.

Trafalgar, 21 October 1805 and Cosmao-Kerjulien's sortie, 23 October 1805

Achille (74)

Dispatch folio 248 **Nationality** French **Taken by** *Prince* **Built and launched** 5 November 1802 to February 1805, Rochefort; launched 17 or 18 November 1804 **Size** 1505 / not given / 3004 tonnes; 1929 tons BOM **Armament** 28x36, 30x18, 12x8 + 4x36 obusiers **Armament in the action** LD 28x36, UD 30x18, QD 12x8, FC 6x8, poop 4 or 6x36 brass howitzers (or 74 guns: x36, x18, x12) **Complement** 16 officers, 690 men **Complement in the action** 766 men under Louis Gabrielle Denieport or 755 (490 naval, 215 infantry, 50 marine artillery) (Adkin) **Casualties** 480 (Roche) or 516 (Demerliac) or 621 (testimony of the survivors) killed **Bounty awarded** £3,873 1s 9d; and £300,000 'for the use of the officers and seamen who had been engaged in the late glorious battle off Trafalgar' **Fate** After five or six hours in action she caught fire and exploded, with 158 survivors (Adkin, Demerliac and Roche) or 145 (testimony of the survivors) or about 100 (Gardiner) saved by the boats of the *Prince* and others. **Sources** ADM 43/53; Hansard, 23 May 1806 vol. 7 c349; Adkin; Demerliac; Gardiner, *Campaign of Trafalgar*; Goodwin; Roche.

Aigle (74)

Dispatch folio 248 **Nationality** French **Taken by** *Defiance* **Built and launched** December 1794 to February 1801, Rochefort; launched 6 July 1800 **Size** 1537 / 1550 / 3069 tonnes; 1929 tons BOM **Armament** 28x36, 30x18, 16x8 + 4x36 obusiers **Armament in the action** LD 28x36, UD 30x18, QD 14x8, FC 6x8 (or 74 guns: x36, x18, x8) **Complement** 17 officers, 690/706 men **Complement in the action** 729 men under Pierre Paulin Gourrèges (495 naval, 215 infantry, 45 marine artillery) (Adkin) **Casualties** 400 killed and wounded **Bounty awarded** £3,686 0s 1d; and £300,000 'for the use of the officers and seamen who had been engaged in the late glorious battle off Trafalgar' **Fate** Driven onto the rocks off Puerto Santa Maria on 25 October, with 50–100 sailors on board. The wreck was sold for 5,825 piastres. **Sources** ADM 43/53; Hansard, 23 May 1806 vol. 7 c349; Adkin; Demerliac; Goodwin; Roche.

Algésiras (74)

Dispatch folio 248 **Name in dispatches** *Algeziras* **Nationality** French **Taken by** *Tonnant* **Built and launched** 20 July or August 1801 to 27 August or September 1804, Lorient; launched 8 July 1804 **Size** 1480 / not given / 2900 tonnes; 1896²²⁄₉₄ tons BOM **Armament** 28x36, 30x18, 16x8 + 4x36 obusiers **Armament in the action** LD 28x36, UD 30x24, QD 12x8, FC 4x8, poop 4x36cr **Complement** 17 officers, 706 men **Complement in the action** 755 under Laurent Le Tourneur (490 naval, 215 infantry, 50 marine artillery) (Adkin) **Casualties** 77 killed, 142/3 wounded **Fate** The prize crew released the French crew in the night of 22/23 October to save the ship and she was brought to Cadiz, the prize crew becoming prisoners; 14 June 1808 taken by the Spanish and renamed *Algeciras*; accidentally holed below the waterline while being careened at Cadiz, 1826. **Sources** Adkin; Demerliac; Gardiner, *The Campaign of Trafalgar*; Goodwin; Roche.

Argonauta (80)

Dispatch folio 248 **Name in dispatches** *Argonaute* **Nationality** Spanish **Taken by** *Belleisle* **Built and launched** 1798, Ferrol **Armament** 30x24, 32x18, 14x8, 4x8, poop 4x18cr **Armament in the action** LD 30x32, UD 32x18, QD 8x12, FC 2x12, and 8x32cr (or 92 guns: x36, x18, x12, inc. 14cr x24 and x32) **Complement** 802 **Complement in the action** 745 men under Antonio de Pareja or 798 (458 naval, 279 infantry, 61 marine artillery) (Adkin) **Casualties** 100 killed, 200 wounded **Bounty awarded** £3,766 18s 1d; and £300,000 'for the use of the officers and seamen who had been engaged in the late glorious battle off Trafalgar' **Fate** Scuttled between 28 and 30 October by the *Ajax*. **Notes** Not to be confused with the

French *Argonaute*, which escaped. De Pareja commanded the *Perla* at St Vincent. **Sources** ADM 43/53; Hansard, 23 May 1806 vol. 7 c349; James; Adkin; Gardiner, *The Campaign of Trafalgar*; Goodwin; Harbron.

Bahama (74)

Dispatch folio 248 **Nationality** Spanish **Taken by** *Colossus* **Built and launched** 1784, Havana **Size** 1786⁷⁵⁄₉₄ tons BOM (surveyed for purchase as 1772¹⁵⁄₉₄) **Armament in the action** LD 28x24, UD 30x18, QD 14x8, FC 4x8, poop 4x18cr (or 74 guns: x24, x18, x8) **Armament in RN service** LD 28x32, UD 30x18, QD 6x12 + 2x32cr, FC 2x12 + 2x32cr **Complement** 510 **Complement in the action** 650 men under Dionisio Alcalá Galiano **Complement in RN service** 640 **Casualties** 75 killed, 67 wounded (Adkin), or 100 killed, 150 wounded (Harbron), or 400 killed and wounded (Gardiner) **Purchased for** £11,077 5s 0d (including copper sheathing and nails at £1,503 and anchors and iron ballast at £634 5s 0d) **Bounty awarded** £3,286 11s 3d; and £300,000 'for the use of the officers and seamen who had been engaged in the late glorious battle off Trafalgar' **Brought to** Portsmouth, then Chatham, 12 June 1806 **Fate** Towed to Gibraltar by the *Orion*; purchased, August 1806, but repairs estimated at £35,000 and not fitted for sea by the RN; hulked at Chatham as a prison ship, April 1807; paid off, October 1814 and broken up there, December 1814. **Notes** Also known as *San Cristobal*. Galiano had commanded the *Desaibierta* for Malaspina's circumnavigation. **Sources** ADM 2/310; ADM 43/53; ADM 106/2239; Hansard, 23 May 1806 vol. 7 c349; Adkin; Gardiner, *The Campaign of Trafalgar*; Goodwin; Harbron; Winfield.

Berwick (74)

Dispatch folio 248 **Nationality** French **Taken by** *Achilles* **Built and launched** May 1769 to 19 May 1778, Portsmouth; launched 18 April 1774 **Size** c. 1400 / 2700 / c. 2700 tonnes; 1622⁵⁶⁄₉₄ tons BOM **Armament** 28x32, 28x16, 18x9 **Armament in the action** LD 28x36, UD 30x24, QD 12x8, FC 4x8, poop 4x36cr (or 74 guns: x32, x16, x9) **Complement** 16 officers, 650/690 men **Complement in the action** 728 men (including 391 soldiers) under Jean Gilles Filhol-Camas or 755 (495 naval, 215 infantry, 45 marine artillery) (Adkin) **Casualties** 51 killed, c. 200 wounded **Bounty awarded** £3,680 19s 0d; and £300,000 'for the use of the officers and seamen who had been engaged in the late glorious battle off Trafalgar' **Fate** Towed by *Britannia* but cast off, 23 October, and wrecked off San Lucar, 27 October, when her prisoners cut her cables; 61 were saved by boats of the *Donegal* but about 200 died. **Notes** Originally captured by a French squadron off Cape Corse, 7 March 1795. **Sources** ADM 43/53; Hansard, 23 May 1806 vol. 7 c349; James; Adkin; Demerliac; Gardiner, *The Campaign of Trafalgar*; Roche; Winfield.

Bucentaure (80)

Dispatch folio 248 **Nationality** French **Taken by** *Conqueror* **Built and launched** 22 November 1802 to January 1804, Toulon; launched 13 or 14 July 1803 **Size** *c.* 1800 / 2000 / 3750 tonnes **Armament** 30x36, 32x24, 18x12 + 6x36 obusiers **Armament in the action** LD 30x36, UD 32x24, QD 12x8, FC 6x8, poop 6x36 howitzers **Complement** 17 officers, 849 men **Complement in the action** 853 men under Jean-Jacques Magendie or 888 (580 naval, 248 infantry, 60 marine artillery) (Adkin) **Casualties** 197 killed, 85 wounded (Demerliac), or 209 or 400 killed and wounded (Gardiner, Roche); around 500 survivors were rescued by the *Indomptable* but many died in her wreck **Bounty awarded** £4,312 19s 7d; and £300,000 'for the use of the officers and seamen who had been engaged in the late glorious battle off Trafalgar' **Fate** Retaken from the prize crew but 'driven on shore and wrecked near the Tower of Cadiz', 23 October. **Notes** Demerliac records that the final toll after the wreck of the *Indomptable* was 274 dead including 209 in the action. **Sources** ADM 43/53; Hansard, 23 May 1806 vol. 7 c349; Adkin; Demerliac; Gardiner, *The Campaign of Trafalgar*; Goodwin; Roche.

Fougueux (74)

Dispatch folio 248 **Name in dispatches** *Feugeux* **Nationality** French **Taken by** *Temeraire* **Built and launched** October 1782, Lorient; dismantled February and March 1783; rebuilt November 1784 to end 1785; launched 21 July 1785 **Size** 1537 / 1550 / 2996 tonnes; 1886 tons BOM **Armament** 28x36, 30x18, 16x8 **Armament in the action** LD 28x36, UD 30x18, QD 14x8, FC 6x8, poop 4x36cr (or 74 guns: x36, x18, x8 and 4x36cr) **Complement** 13–17 officers, 690/706 men **Complement in the action** 682 men under Louis-Alexis Baudouin or 755 (495 naval, 215 infantry, 45 marine artillery) (Adkin) **Casualties** 546 killed and wounded; 560

or 562 killed in total after she sank (including 30 men from the *Temeraire*), with 120 survivors **Bounty awarded** £3,448 7s 3d; and £300,000 'for the use of the officers and seamen who had been engaged in the late glorious battle off Trafalgar' **Fate** Wrecked on the reefs of Santi-Pietri, 22 October. **Notes** The oldest French ship at Trafalgar, and the first prize to be lost. **Sources** ADM 43/53; Hansard, 23 May 1806 vol. 7 c349; Adkin; Demerliac; Gardiner, *The Campaign of Trafalgar*; Goodwin; Roche.

Indomptable (84)

Dispatch folio 248 **Nationality** French **Built and launched** September 1788 to February 1791, Brest; launched 20 December 1790 **Size** 2000–2034 / 2000 / 3868 tonnes **Armament** (from 1800) 30x36, 32x24, 18x12 + 4x36 obusiers + 6x1 perriers **Armament in the action** LD 30x36, UD 32x24, QD 12x12, FC 12x12, poop 6x36cr **Complement** 17 officers, 866 men **Complement in the action** 800 men under Jean-Joseph Hubert or 887 (580 naval, 247 infantry, 60 marine artillery) (Adkin) **Bounty awarded** £4,045 0s 0d by Treasury order; and £300,000 'for the use of the officers and seamen who had been engaged in the late glorious battle off Trafalgar' **Fate** Escaped the battle but sortied on 23 October and sank off Rota on 24 October with the loss of around 1,000 men (from her crew and from the *Bucentaure*); about 180 survivors. **Notes** Not usually considered a prize but included here because the Admiralty paid head money for her. **Sources** ADM 43/53; Hansard, 23 May 1806 vol. 7 c349; Adkin; Demerliac; Roche.

Intrépide (74)

Dispatch folio 248 **Name in dispatches** *Intrepide* **Nationality** French **Taken by** *Orion* **Built and launched** 1788–90, Ferrol, as *Intrepido*; transferred to the French under the Treaty of San Ildefonso **Size** *c.* 1450 / not given / 2784 tonnes **Armament** 28x24, 30x18, 16x8 **Armament in the action** LD 28x24, UD 30x18, QD 12x8, FC 4x8, poop 4x36cr (or 74 guns: x24, x18, x8) **Complement** *c.* 17 officers, 700 men **Complement in the action** 637 men under Louis Antoine Cyprian Infernet or 745 (480 naval, 215 infantry, 50 marine artillery) (Adkin) **Casualties** 200 (Demerliac) or 242 (Adkin) or 306 (Gardiner) killed and wounded **Bounty awarded** £3,220 16s 7d; and £300,000 'for the use of the officers and seamen who had been engaged in the late glorious battle off Trafalgar' **Fate** Burnt and sunk, 24 October, by the *Britannia*. Infernet was unharmed in the action; he was taken prisoner, exchanged six months later and decorated with the Grand Cross of the Legion of Honour. **Notes** Struck her colours with eight feet of water in the hold. **Sources** ADM 43/53; Hansard, 23 May 1806 vol. 7 c349; James; Adkin; Demerliac; Gardiner, *The Campaign of Trafalgar*; Goodwin; Harbron; Roche.

Monarca (74)

Dispatch folio 248 **Name in dispatches** *Minorca* **Nationality** Spanish **Taken by** *Bellerophon* **Built and launched** 1794, Ferrol **Armament** 28x24, 30x18, 14x8, 4x8 **Armament in the action** LD 28x24, UD 30x24, QD 14x8, FC 4x8, poop 4x18cr (or 74 guns: x24) **Complement** 510 **Complement in the action** 640 men under Teódoro de Argumosa or 667 (370 naval, 243 infantry, 54 marine artillery) (Adkin) **Casualties** 100 killed, 150 wounded **Bounty awarded** £3,236 0s 0d; and £300,000 'for the use of the officers and seamen who had been engaged in the late glorious battle off Trafalgar' **Fate** Ran onshore at Arena Gordos with 170 Spanish on board, 25 October. **Notes** She first struck to the *Tonnant* but drifted away and re-hoisted her colours. Also appears in the Admiralty records as *Monorca*. **Sources** ADM 43/53; Hansard, 23 May 1806 vol. 7 c349; Adkin; Gardiner, *The Campaign of Trafalgar*; Goodwin; Harbron.

Neptuno (80)

Dispatch folio 248 **Nationality** Spanish **Taken by** *Minotaur* and *Spartiate* **Built and launched** 1795, Ferrol **Size** 1753 tons BOM **Armament** 28x24, 30x18, 14x8, 4x8 **Armament in the action** LD 30x32, UD 32x18, QD 8x12, FC 2x12, and 18cr (or 84 guns) **Complement** 642 **Complement in the action** 800 men under Cayetano Valdés y Flores Bazán (445 naval, 285 infantry, 70 marine artillery) (Adkin) **Casualties** 12 killed, 47 wounded (Harbron), 42 killed, 47 wounded (Gardiner); 37 killed and 47 wounded when she struck (Valdés) **Bounty awarded** £4,045 0s 0d; and £300,000 'for the use of the officers and seamen who had been engaged in the late glorious battle off Trafalgar' **Fate** Retaken by sortie, 23 October; wrecked in Cadiz Bay, and burnt, 31 October. **Notes** Not to be confused with the French *Neptune*. Valdés commanded

the *Pelayo* (74) at St Vincent. The *Neptuno* was the last to surrender. **Sources** ADM 43/53; Hansard, 23 May 1806 vol. 7 c349; Adkin; Gardiner, *The Campaign of Trafalgar*; Goodwin; Harbron.

Rayo (100)

Dispatch folio 248 **Nationality** Spanish **Taken by** *Donegal* **Built and launched** 1749, Havana, as the *San Pedro* (80) **Armament** (as 80): 30x36, 30x28, 20x8; (as 100): 30x36, 32x18, 10x18, 16x8, 6x8, 6x18cr **Armament in the action** LD 30x36, UD 32x18, spar deck 10x18, QD 16x8, FC 6x8, poop 6x18cr (or 94 guns: x36, x24, x8, x6) **Complement** (as 80): 670: (as 100): 830 **Complement in the action** 812 men under Enrique MacDonnell (407 naval, 362 infantry, 61 marine artillery) (Adkin), 812 at the time of her capture **Casualties** 1 killed, 11 wounded (Harbron); 18 casualties (Gardiner) **Bounty awarded** £4,105 13s 6d; and £300,000 'for the use of the officers and seamen who had been engaged in the late glorious battle off Trafalgar' **Fate** Escaped the battle but sortied on 23 October; captured on the 24th; wrecked on the 26th near San Lucar, and burnt 31 October. **Notes** Rebuilt as a 100-gun ship, 1803. The oldest ship at Trafalgar, and the only First Rate in the van division. Testimony to the prize court: 'sailed from Cadiz on the nineteenth day of October . . . were engaged by a British fleet [and] after an engagement of nearly six hours they restor'd and got into Cadiz; that the twenty third day of October they were again ordered out to assist some of the ships of the Combined Fleet that were dismasted, in the execution of which, they were attacked' and taken on the 24th by the *Donegal*, which had been sent to Gibraltar for water and so missed Trafalgar. **Sources** ADM 43/53; Hansard, 23 May 1806 vol. 7 c349; Adkin; Gardiner, *The Campaign of Trafalgar*; Goodwin; Harbron.

Redoubtable (74)

Dispatch folio 248 **Nationality** French **Taken by** *Victory* and *Temeraire* **Built and launched** January 1790 to December 1792, Brest; launched 31 May 1791 as *Suffren* **Size** 1537 / 1550 / 3069 tonnes; 1929 tons BOM **Armament** 28x36, 30x18, 16x8 + 6x36 obusiers + 6x1 perriers **Armament in the action** LD 28x36, UD 30x18, QD 14x8, FC 6x8, poop 4x36cr (or 86 guns: x36, x18, x8 inc. 14 carronades) **Complement** 13–17 officers, 690/706 men

Complement in the action 643 men under Jean-Jacques Etienne Lucas (403 naval, 200 infantry, 40 marine artillery) (Adkin) **Casualties** 490 killed, 81 wounded (Demerliac) or 474 killed, 70 wounded (Gardiner); Lucas reported 300 killed and 222 seriously wounded **Bounty awarded** £3,257 3s 4d by Treasury order; and £300,000 'for the use of the officers and seamen who had been engaged in the late glorious battle off Trafalgar' **Fate** Badly damaged in the battle and on 22 October in tow of the *Swiftsure*; 119 men were saved by her boats between 5 and 5.15pm, before high seas prevented further rescue, and she sank about 10pm; 192 drowned including 18 men from the *Swiftsure*. Survivors were found on three rafts on 23 October; 169 (in total) escaped including 134 wounded, the greatest loss of any Trafalgar ship. **Notes** Name changed to *Redoutable* in May 1794. Lucas was exchanged in 1806 and awarded the Gold Cross of the Legion of Honour. **Sources** ADM 43/53; Hansard, 23 May 1806 vol. 7 c349; Adkin; Demerliac; Gardiner, *The Campaign of Trafalgar*; Goodwin.

San Agustín (74/80)

Dispatch folio 248 **Nationality** Spanish **Taken by** *Leviathan* **Built and launched** 1768, Guarnizo, near Santander **Armament** 28x24, 30x18, 14x8, 4x8 **Armament in the action** LD 28x24, UD 30x18, QD 14x8, FC 4x8, poop 4x18cr (or 80 guns: x36, x30, x18, x8) **Complement** 642 **Complement in the action** 620 men under Felipe Jado Cajigal or 711 (413 naval, 243 infantry, 55 marine artillery) (Adkin) **Casualties** 150 killed, 200 wounded (Harbron), or 180 killed, 200 wounded (Gardiner), or 184 killed, 201 wounded (Adkin) **Bounty awarded** £3,134 17s 6d; and £300,000 'for the use of the officers and seamen who had been engaged in the late glorious battle off Trafalgar' **Fate** 'Set on fire and burnt' by the *Leviathan* and *Orion* on 30 October. **Notes** Struck her colours after being boarded by the *Leviathan* three times. **Sources** ADM 43/53; Hansard, 23 May 1806 vol. 7 c349; Gardiner, *The Campaign of Trafalgar*; Goodwin; Harbron.

San Francisco de Asis (74)

Dispatch folio 248 **Nationality** Spanish **Built and launched** 1767, Guarnizo, near Santander **Size** 1740 tons BOM **Armament** 28x24, 30x18, 14x8, 4x8 **Armament in the action** LD 28x24, UD 30x18, QD 14x8, FC 4x8, poop 4x18cr

Complement 510 **Complement in the action** 657 under Luís Antonio de Flores (370 naval, 234 infantry, 53 marine artillery) (Adkin); estimated for head money as 700 **Casualties** 5 killed, 12 wounded **Bounty awarded** £3,236 0s 0d; and £300,000 'for the use of the officers and seamen who had been engaged in the late glorious battle off Trafalgar' **Fate** Sortied and sank off Rota, 23 October; the crew got on shore. **Notes** Not usually considered a prize but included here because the Admiralty paid head money for her. **Sources** ADM 43/53; Hansard, 23 May 1806 vol. 7 c349; Adkin; Goodwin; Harbron.

San Ildefonso (74)

Dispatch folio 248 **Nationality** Spanish **Name in RN service** *Ildefonso* **Taken by** *Defence* **Built and launched** 1784; launched 22 January 1785, Cartagena **Size** 1815.5 tonnes (2756.83m³); 1751⁶²⁄₉₄ tons BOM (surveyed for purchase as 1751⁵⁰⁄₉₄) **Armament** 28x24, 30x18,16x8, 2x4 pedreros **Armament in the action** LD 28x24, UD 30x24, QD 10x30 and 6x24 obusiers, FC 2x4 pedreros (or 74 guns: x24 inc. 10x30 and 6x24 howitzers, and 6x8) **Armament in RN service** GD 28x32, UD 30x18, QD 6x12 + 8x32cr, FC 2x12 + 2x32 **Complement** 505 **Complement in the action** 724 men under José Ramón de Vargas y Varáez or 716 (420 naval, 244 infantry, 52 marine artillery) (Adkin) **Casualties** 34 killed, 148 wounded **Purchased for** £10,486 15s 8d (including £1,728 12s 11d for stores) **Bounty awarded** £3,660 14s 6d; and £300,000 'for the use of the officers and seamen who had been engaged in the late glorious battle off Trafalgar' **Brought to** Portsmouth **Fate** Considered by the Spanish to be a very fine sailer; purchased, August 1806, but repairs were estimated at £41,003 and she was not fitted for sea by the RN; fitted at Portsmouth as a victualler, March to June 1808; provision depot ship at Spithead, 1812–14; in Ordinary at Portsmouth, July 1814; broken up there, July 1816. **Notes** When surveyed in England she was estimated to be fourteen years old. Also recorded as *Il Defonso*. **Sources** ADM 2/310; ADM 43/53; ADM 106/2239; ADM 106/2239; Hansard, 23 May 1806 vol. 7 c349; Adkin; Harbron; Lyon; Winfield.

San Juan Nepomuceno (74)

Dispatch folio 248 **Name in RN service** *San Juan* **Nationality** Spanish **Taken by** *Dreadnought*

Built and launched 1766, Guarnizo, near Santander **Size** 1740 tons BOM **Armament** 28x24, 30x18, 14x8 **Armament in the action** LD 28x24, UD 30x18, QD 14x8, FC 4x8, poop 4x18cr (or 70 guns, x36, x18, x8, and 12 carronades, x36 and x24) **Armament in RN service** LD 28x32, UD 30x18, QD 6x12 + 2x12cr, FC 2x12 + 2x32cr **Complement** 510 **Complement in the action** 650 men under Cosmé Damián Churruca or 693 (431 naval, 212 infantry, 50 marine artillery) (Adkin) **Complement in RN service** 640 (34 as sheer hulk) **Casualties** 100 killed, 150 wounded (Harbron), 300 (Gardiner) **Purchased for** £13,797 11s 1d **Bounty awarded** £3,286 11s 3d; and £300,000 'for the use of the officers and seamen who had been engaged in the late glorious battle off Trafalgar' **Fate** Base ship at Gibraltar, 1805–8, then prison ship; flagship, 1813–14; sold, January 1816. **Notes** Provisionally renamed *Berwick* after her capture. Purchased, October 1806 to serve as a sheer hulk at Gibraltar in place of the *Guerrier*. Also listed in Admiralty records as *St John de Nepomuceno*, *St John Nepomuceno*. **Sources** ADM 2/310; ADM 43/53; Hansard, 23 May 1806 vol. 7 c349; Adkin; Gardiner, *The Campaign of Trafalgar*; Harbron; Lyon; Winfield.

Santa Ana (112)

Dispatch folio 248 **Nationality** Spanish **Taken by** *Royal Sovereign* **Built and launched** 1783; launched 29 September 1784, Ferrol **Size** 2200 tons (Spanish); 2208 tonnes (3504.70m^3) **Armament** 30x36, 32x24, 30x12, 18x8 **Armament in the action** LD 30x36, MD 32x24, UD 32x12, QD 10x8, FC 10x48 and 2x32 and 6x24 howitzers, poop 4x4 howitzers **Complement** 848 men, 40 officers (peacetime) **Complement in the action** 1,053 under José Gardoquí, or 1,189 (720 naval, 383 infantry, 86 marine artillery) (Adkin) **Casualties** 59 killed, 169 wounded (Harbron), or 97 killed, 141 wounded (Gardiner and Adkin); 97 dead and 141 wounded by 30 October **Bounty awarded** None; but £300,000 'for the use of the officers and seamen who had been engaged in the late glorious battle off Trafalgar' **Fate** Retaken by sortie, 23 October, and escaped to Cadiz; convoyed to Havana with the *Principe de Asturias* by HMS *Implacable* (ex-*Duguay Trouin*), September to November 1810; sank there, 1817; sold there, 1820 but not recovered by 1834. **Notes** Present at all the actions of the Spanish

navy. Name ship of her class of seven (including the *Salvador del Mundo*), often considered the finest three-deckers of the eighteenth century. Gardoquí commanded her again in 1809–10. **Sources** Hansard, 23 May 1806 vol. 7 c349; Adkin; Gardiner, *The Campaign of Trafalgar*; Goodwin; Harbron; Hierro.

Santísima Trinidad (136)

Dispatch folio 248 **Name in dispatches** *Santissima Trinidad* **Nationality** Spanish **Taken by** *Prince* **Built and launched** August 1767; launched 2 March 1769, Havana **Size** launch, 4902 tonnes (7443.69m^3); in 1796, 2475 tonnes (3758m^3) **Armament in the action** LD 34x36, MD 34x24, UD 34x18, QD 18x8, waist 6x4cr, FC 10x24cr (or 126 guns: x36, x24, x12, x8, inc. 16 carronades) **Complement** 1,071 and 25 servants **Complement in the action** 1,015 men under Francisco Javíer de Uriarte y Borja or 1,048 (604 naval, 382 infantry, 62 marine artillery) (Adkin) **Casualties** 205 killed, 103 wounded **Bounty awarded** £5,132 1s 10d; and £300,000 'for the use of the officers and seamen who had been engaged in the late glorious battle off Trafalgar' **Fate** Foundered, 24 October, about twenty-five miles south of Cadiz; many of her crew were rescued by boats from the *Neptune*, *Ajax* and *Prince* but many of the wounded (around 30 in British sources, around 80 in Spanish) died with her. **Notes** Built as a 120-gun three-decked ship but converted to a four-decked 136-gun ship at Cadiz, 1797, the only four-decked ship then in existence. She may have struck her colours to the *Excellent*, *Blenheim*, *Orion*, and *Irresistible* at St Vincent, but was rescued by four Spanish ships. Borja died at eighty-nine in 1842, the longest lived of the Spanish Trafalgar captains. **Sources** ADM 43/53; Hansard, 23 May 1806 vol. 7 c349; Adkin; Gardiner, *The Campaign of Trafalgar*; Harbron; Hierro.

Swiftsure (74)

Dispatch folio 248 **Name in RN service** *Irresistible* **Nationality** French **Taken by** *Colossus* **Built and launched** May 1784 to May 1787, Deptford; launched 4 April 1787 **Size** *c.* 1400 / not given / 2700 tonnes; 1621^{23}/$_{94}$ tons BOM (surveyed for purchase as 1636^{27}/$_{94}$) **Armament** 28x32, 28x16.5 [sic], 20x9 + 2cr and 6cr English, calibre not stated **Armament in the action** LD 28x36, UD 30x24, QD 12x8, FC 4x8, poop 4x36cr (or 74 guns: x32, x18, x8) **Complement** 16 officers, 650/690 men **Complement in the action** 690 men under Charles l'Hôpitallier-Villemadrin or 755 (495 naval, 215 infantry, 45 marine artillery) (Adkin) **Casualties** 68 killed, 123 wounded (Demerliac, Adkin); 250 (Gardiner) **Purchased for** £12,466 14s 5d (including £1,481 for copper and nails and £1,168 for anchors and iron ballast) **Bounty** awarded £3,488 16s 3d; and £300,000 'for the use of the officers and seamen who had been engaged in the late glorious battle off Trafalgar'

Brought to Portsmouth **Fate** Purchased, August 1806, but repair estimated at £30,000 and not fitted for sea by the RN; prison ship at Chatham, March 1808 to 1813; broken up there, January 1816. **Notes** Originally captured by the French in the Mediterranean, 24 June 1801; when retaken named *Irresistible*, there being a *Swiftsure* in service. **Sources** ADM 2/310; ADM 43/53; ADM 106/2239; ADM 106/2239; Hansard, 23 May 1806 vol. 7 c349; Adkin; Demerliac; Gardiner, *The Campaign of Trafalgar*; Winfield.

Sir Richard Strachan's action, 4 November 1805

Duguay Trouin (74)

Dispatch folio 274 **Name in dispatches** *Du guay Trouin* **Name in RN service** *Implacable* then *Foudroyant* **Taken by** *Caesar* **Built and launched** 15 November 1794 to November 1800, Rochefort; launched 24 March 1800 **Size** 1505 / 1550 / 3004 tonnes; $1896^{22}/_{94}$ tons BOM **Armament** 28x36, 30x18, 16x8 + 6x36 obusiers **Armament in the action** LD 28x36, UD 30x24, QD 12x8, FC 4x8, poop 4x36cr (at Trafalgar) **Armament in RN service** LD 30x32, UD 30x18, QD 2x12 + 12x32cr, FC 2x12 + 2x32cr **Complement** 16 officers, 690 men **Complement in the action** 550 men under Claude Touffet or 755 (490 naval, 215 infantry, 50 marine artillery) (Adkin) **Complement in RN service** 640 **Casualties** 150 killed and wounded in the action (+ 12 killed and 24 wounded at Trafalgar) **Purchased for** £34,059 2s 4½d (including furniture and stores at £740 12s 6d) **Bounty awarded** £2,780 18s 9d **Brought to** Plymouth, 10 November 1805 **Fate** Purchased, April 1806; in commission from 1808 and served in the Baltic; 1810, flagship of Rear-Admiral Keats in the Mediterranean; paid off, 1812, and in Ordinary, 1815–39; recommissioned, 1839, and served off Syria, 1840; in Ordinary, 1840–55; training ship in the Hamoaze, 1855–1908; 1912 to Falmouth for preservation; renamed *Foudroyant*, 1943; paid off, January 1947, and finally scuttled in the Channel off Selsey Bill with British and French ensigns flying, 2 December 1949. **Notes** A 1949 film of her end is at www.britishpathe.com/record.php?id=27323 **Sources** ADM 2/309; ADM 43/53; ADM 106/2238; Adkin; Demerliac; Goodwin; Roche; Winfield.

Formidable (80)

Dispatch folio 274 **Name in RN service** *Brave* **Taken by** *Hero* **Built and launched** August 1794 to October 1795, Toulon; launched 17 March 1795 as *Figuieres* **Size** 2034 / 2000 / 3868 tonnes, $2248^{55}/_{94}$ tons BOM **Armament** (from 1803) 30x36, 32x24, 28x12 + 4x36 obusiers **Armament in the action** LD 30x36, UD 32x24, QD 12x12, FC 6x12, poop 6x36cr (at Trafalgar) **Armament in RN service** LD 32x32, UD 30x18, QD 2x12 + 14x32cr, FC 2x12 + 3x32cr **Complement** 17 officers, 866 men **Complement in the action** 810 men under Jean-Marie Letellier (for Trafalgar, 840: 550 naval, 235 infantry, 55 marine artillery) (Adkin) **Complement in RN service** 690 **Casualties** 200 killed and wounded (+ 22 killed and 45 wounded at Trafalgar) **Purchased for** £19,708 13s 7¼d (without furniture and stores) **Bounty awarded** £4,095 11s 3d **Brought to** Plymouth, 11 November 1805 **Fate** Purchased, April 1806; prison ship at Plymouth, January 1808 to 1813; powder hulk, 1814; broken up there, April 1816. **Notes** Named *Formidable* from November 1794, then *Figuieres*, then from May 1795 *Formidable*. A report by her second in command gave a return of 1,090 rounds fired (either at Trafalgar or in both actions), 430 x 36, 620 x 24, 40 x 12. **Sources** ADM 2/309; ADM 43/53; ADM 106/2238; Adkin; Demerliac; Goodwin; Roche; Winfield.

Mont Blanc (74)

Dispatch folio 274 **Name in RN service** *Mont Blanc* **Taken by** *Courageux* **Built and launched** July 1789 to March 1793, Rochefort; launched 13 August 1791 **Size** 1537 / 1550 / 3069 tonnes; $1886^{44}/_{94}$ tons BOM **Armament**

28x36, 30x18, 16x8 + 6x36 obusiers + 8
perriers Armament in the action LD 28x36,
UD 30x24, QD 12x8, FC 4x8, poop 4x36cr
Armament in RN service LD 30x32; UD
30x18; QD 2x12 + 12x32cr; FC 2x12 + 2x32cr
Complement 13–17 officers, 690/706 men
Complement in the action 786 men under
Guillaume-Jean-Noël de Lavillegris or 755 (495
naval, 215 infantry, 45 marine artillery) (Adkin)
Casualties 180 killed and wounded (+ 20 killed
and 24 wounded at Trafalgar) Purchased for
£10,649 15s 6d (including furniture and stores
at £480 13s 5d) Bounty awarded £3,974 4s
3d Brought to Plymouth, 10 November 1805
Fate Purchased, April 1806; not fitted for sea
by the RN; powder hulk at Plymouth, 1811–15;
sold, for £5,510, 8 March 1819. Notes Named
Pyrrhus; January 1793, renamed *Mont Blanc*;
April 1794, renamed *Trente et un Mai*; April
1795, renamed *Républicain*; January or February
1796, renamed *Mont Blanc*. Struck her colours
with seven feet of water in the hold. Sources
ADM 2/309; ADM 43/53; ADM 106/2238;
Demerliac; Roche; Winfield.

Scipion (74)

Dispatch folio 274 Taken by *Courageux* Built
and launched September 1798 to September
1801, Lorient-Caudan; launched 29 March
1800 Size 1505 / 1550 / 3004 tonnes; 1887³⁹⁄₉₄
tons BOM Armament 28x36, 30x18, 16x8 +
4x36 obusiers Armament in the action LD
28x36, UD 30x24, QD 12x8, FC 4x8, poop
4x36cr Armament in RN service LD 30x32, UD
30x18, QD 2x12 + 12x32cr, FC 2x12 + 2x32cr
Complement 16 officers, 690 men Complement
in the action 700 men under Charles Bérenger or
755 (490 naval, 215 infantry, 50 marine artillery)
(Adkin) Casualties 200 killed and wounded (+
(or inc.) 17 killed and 22 wounded at Trafalgar)
Purchased for £25,986 5s 0d (including furniture
and stores at £220 4s 8d) Bounty awarded
£3,539 7s 6d Brought to Plymouth, 10 November
1805 Fate Purchased, April 1806; commissioned,
July 1809; 1810 flagship of Rear-Admiral
Stopford; in the East Indies, and at the capture of
Java, September 1811; Mediterranean, 1812; in
Ordinary at Portsmouth, 1814; broken up there,
January 1819. Sources ADM 2/309; ADM 43/53;
ADM 106/2238; Demerliac; Goodwin; Roche;
Winfield.

San Domingo, 6 February 1806

Alexandre (80)

Dispatch folio 285 Name in RN service
Alexandre or *L'Alexandre* Taken by *Spencer*
Built and launched May 1793 to October 1799,
Brest; launched 8 July 1799 as *Indivisible* Size
2000–2034 / 2000 / 3868 tonnes; 2231⁴⁹⁄₉₄ tons
BOM; surveyed at Jamaica as 2255⁵⁴⁄₉₄ tons
Armament (from 1803): 30x36, 32x24, 18x12 +
14x36 obusiers Armament in RN service GD
28x32, UD 28x18, QD 4x12 + 10x32cr, FC 2x12
+ 2x32cr, RH 6x18 Complement 17 officers,
849 men Complement in the action 820 men
under Pierre-Elie Garreau Casualties 300 killed
and wounded Purchased for £23,136 11s 7d
(including £1,700 for copper sheathing, £34 for
the stumps of the lower masts, and £2,992 12s
4d for stores) Bounty awarded £4,146 2s 6d
Brought to Port Royal, Jamaica, 12 February,
then Plymouth, 11 May 1806 Fate Purchased,
January 1807; repairs estimated at £35,000
and not fitted for sea by the RN; hulked, 1808,
at Plymouth as a powder ship; sold there for
£4,600, May 1822. Notes Name changed to

Alexandre, February 1803. Registered in the RN
from 24 February (see *Brave*). Sources ADM
2/310; ADM 43/53; ADM 106/2240; James;
Demerliac; Lyon; Roche; Winfield.

Brave (74)

Dispatch folio 285 Name in dispatches *Braave*
Name in RN service *Le Brave* Taken by *Donegal*
Built and launched August 1793 to July 1795,
Lorient; launched 2 July 1795 as *Cassard* Size
1537 / 1550 / 3069 tonnes; 1890 tons BOM est.
(Winfield); surveyed at Jamaica as 1828⁸⁄₉₄ tons.
Armament 28x36, 30x18, 16x8 + 4x36 obusiers +
6 perriers Complement 13–17 officers, 690/706
men Complement in the action 660 men
under Louis-Marie Coudé Casualties 260 killed
and wounded Purchased for £25,147 7s 6¼d
(including £65 0s 0d for fishes for masts and boats
and £2,231 6s 3d for stores) Bounty awarded
£3,337 2s 6d Brought to Port Royal, Jamaica Fate
Foundered near the Azores on her way to Britain,
12 April 1806 (all survived). Notes Name in April
1795 was *Dix Août*, changed in February 1803

to *Brave*. Also in the Admiralty records as *Braave*. Duckworth put the *Brave*, *Alexandre*, and *Jupiter* into commission without authority but they were retrospectively registered by an instruction of 13 June 1806, the *Brave* from 21 February. **Sources** ADM 2/310; ADM 43/53; ADM 106/2240; James; Demerliac; Roche.

Diomède (74)

Dispatch folio 285 **Name in dispatches** *Diomede* **Taken by** *Agamemnon* **Built and launched** September or October 1794 to February 1800, Lorient-Caudan; launched 1 August 1799 as *Union* **Size** 1537 / 1550 / 3069 tonnes **Armament** 28x36, 30x18, 16x8 + 4x36 obusiers **Complement** 13–17 officers, 690/706 men **Complement in the action** 620 men under Jean-Baptiste Henry **Casualties** 250 killed and wounded **Bounty awarded** £3,134 17s 6d **Fate** Ran herself aground; the British took 51 prisoners then burnt the wreck. **Notes** Name changed to *Diomede*, February 1803. **Sources** ADM 43/53; James; Demerliac; Roche.

Imperial (118)

Dispatch folio 285 **Taken by** *Canopus* **Built and launched** October 1793 to February 1804, Brest; launched 1 October 1803 **Size** 2929 / 5095 / 5140 tonnes **Armament** 32x36, 34x24, 34x12, 18x8 + 6x36 obusiers (Demerliac), 34x36, 32x24, 34x18, 18x12 (Roche) **Complement** 21 officers, 1,109 men **Complement in the action** 1,500 men under Julien-Gabriel Bigot **Casualties** *c.* 500 killed and wounded **Bounty awarded** £7,584 7s 6d **Fate** Ran herself aground; burnt and 'totally destroy'd' by the *Canopus*, 8

February. **Notes** Begun as the *Peuple*, renamed *Vengeur*, July 1794; renamed *Imperial*, February or March 1805. Listed by the British as 136 guns. Her complement in the action given in the court documents probably included the soldiers she carried to reinforce General Ferrand at Santo-Domingo. **Sources** ADM 43/53; James; Demerliac; Roche.

Jupiter (74)

Dispatch folio 285 **Name in RN service** *Le Jupitre* and *Maida* **Taken by** *Donegal* and *Atlas* **Built and launched** February 1794 to May 1796, Lorient-Caudan; launched 28 September 1795 as *Viala* **Size** 1537 / 1550 / 3069 tonnes; 1899 tons BOM (surveyed for purchase as 1898⁸⁰⁄₉₄ tons, and surveyed at Jamaica as 1911¹¹⁄₉₄ tons) **Armament** 28x36, 30x18, 16x8 + 6x36 obusiers + 6 perriers **Armament in RN service** GD 30x24, UD 30x24, QD 2x24 + 12x24cr, FC 2x24 + 2x24cr **Complement** 13–17 officers, 690/706 men **Complement in the action** 660 men under Gaspard Laignol **Casualties** 200 killed and wounded **Purchased for** £13,075 0s 1d (including £616 2s 0d for masts and yards, and £3,914 1s 6d for stores) **Bounty awarded** £3,337 2s 6d **Brought to** Portsmouth, 6 May 1806 **Fate** Purchased, January 1807; repairs estimated at at least £40,000; served in the Copenhagen expedition of 1807; in Ordinary at Portsmouth, March 1808; sold for £4,700, August 1814. **Notes** Name changed to *Voltaire*, December 1795; *Constitution*, February 1803. Registered in the RN as *Le Jupitre* [sic] from 24 February 1806 (see *Brave*). **Sources:** ADM 2/310; ADM 43/53; ADM 106/2239; ADM 106/2240; James; Demerliac; Lyon; Winfield.

Notes

Size: the first and third French figures are from Demerliac and are 'port', the maximum weight of the load (armament, stores and merchandise) that the hull could carry, and 'déplacement en charge', the load displacement (the mass of the ship), in tonnes of 978.78kg; the second figure is from Roche, and is his calculation of 'port' in tonnes of 1,000kg. Spanish figures are from Hierro. Tons BOM is a calculated measure of volume in British tons of 2,240lb, and for ships surveyed by the RN is taken from Winfield, except where shown; other values are calculated by Goodwin. French authorities assume ships to the same plan are identical; surveys of these

ships in Britain usually produce different BOM values (and as can be seen different surveys of the same ship give different values). Danish figures are from Pope, Spanish figures are from Harbron. The Copenhagen pound was 0.94 English, the Madrid pound was 0.99.

Armament: designed armament, in weight of shot in pounds; 'cr' are carronades. French armament is from Demerliac unless stated; armament in the action is from Goodwin or Hierro. Figures in brackets are from the testimonies of the survivors in the prize courts. Obusiers (Sp. obuses) were 'the early French answer to the British carronade', 'a bronze howitzer mounted on a slide carriage' (Winfield). The French 36lb howitzer, however, was a land-service piece mounted on a sea-service carriage. Perriers were breech-loading swivel guns; pedreros threw a stone ball. The French pound was 1.08 English.

Complement: the official, established or designed complement including officers.

Complement in RN service: the established complement (which included the fictitious widows' men).

Complement in the action: the main figure is the number of people 'living on board and belonging to' the ship at the beginning of the action, a total sworn to in the prize court to by survivors. The death toll in fleet actions means the survivors were sometimes quite low in rank (the *Imperial's* figures were given by illiterate seamen) and may not be exact; but Admiral Villeneuve swore to the numbers for *Indomptable*, *Bucentaure*, and *Redoutable*. The figures for Copenhagen are from Pope; the head money for the action was paid for 6,000 men taken as a total for the whole fleet. The second figure, for Trafalgar, is from

Adkin. His numbers for the French include his estimated distribution of the 4,000 troops to be landed at Naples and his numbers for the Spanish are 'based on Admiral Gravina's report on the manning of his fleet dated 19 October 1805'.

Casualties: figures are from Demerliac or as stated; occasionally these are at odds with the testimony of survivors given to the prize court.

'Nature of the Prize': as recorded in ADM 7/354.

Purchased for: the value of a ship's hull, at a price per ton BOM, typically £5 to £8, as surveyed by the officers of the dockyard to which the prizes were brought, agreed with the prize agent, and proposed by the Navy Board to the Admiralty, and sometimes also of its furniture and/or stores; the money was paid by government to the prize agent and distributed by him to the captors in proportions established by an Order in Council.

Bounty awarded: head money, paid by government to the captors, based on the number of people alive on board at the commencement of the action as sworn to by the chief surviving officers.

Brought to: the port of first arrival then the first permanent station, if known.

Sources

Admiralty records in the National Archives, Kew (TNA: PRO copy)
ADM 2/–: Letters from the Admiralty to the Navy Board ADM 7/354: an anonymous Admiralty document entitled 'List of Prizes', from 15 February 1793 to 8 December 1799 ADM 18/–: Promiscuous Bill Books of the Navy Board ADM 43/–: Head Money vouchers ADM 103/503: French prizes, 1796–1810 ADM 106/–: Letters from the Navy Board to the Admiralty HCA 8/89: Prize court assignation books, June to July 1794 HCA 34/61: Sentences in Prize Causes, 1793–96

Secondary Sources
Adkin, Mark, *The Trafalgar Companion* (Aurum Press, London, 2005)
Demerliac, Alain, *Nomenclature des navires français de 1792 à 1799* and *1800 à 1815* (Éditions Omega, Nice, 1999)
Gardiner, Robert, *Fleet Battle and Blockade* (Chatham Publishing, London, 1996); *The Campaign of Trafalgar* (Chatham Publishing, London, 1997)
Goodwin, Peter, *The Ships of Trafalgar* (Conway Maritime Press, London, 2005)

Harbron, John D., *Trafalgar and the Spanish Navy* (Conway Maritime Press, London, 1988)
Haythornthwaite, Philip J., *The Napoleonic Source Book* (Arms and Armour Press, 1990)
Hierro, José Ignacio González-Aller; Cruz Apestegui; Jorge Pla; Carmen Zamarrón, *Modelos de Arsenal del Museo Naval*, trans. Richard Rees (Lunwerg Editores, Barcelona and Madrid, 2004)
James, William, *The Naval History of Great Britain* (Richard Bentley, London, 1837)
Lyon, David, *The Sailing Navy List* (Conway Maritime Press, London, 1993)
Nicolas, Nicholas Harris, *The Dispatches and Letters of Lord Nelson* (Henry Colburn, London, 1844)
Pope, Dudley, *The Great Gamble* (Simon and Schuster, New York, 1972)
Roche, Jean-Michel, *Dictionnaire des bâtiments de la Flotte de guerre française de Colbert à nos jours*, tome 1: *1671–1870* (Groupe Rezotel – Maury Millau, 2005)
Tracy, Nicholas, *Nelson's Battles* (Chatham Publishing, London, 1996)
Winfield, Rif, *British Warships in the Age of Sail 1793–1817* (Chatham Publishing, London, 2005)

GLOSSARY

abeam, In the direction at right angles to the ship's centreline.

aboard, 1. On board a ship. 2. Alongside, touching another ship.

Admiral of the Red, White, Blue, The officer nominally commanding ships of the Red, White or Blue squadron, ranking in seniority in that (descending) order.

astern, Behind a ship, in the direction from which she is moving.

athwart, Across.

back, *vb*. 1. To trim the sails so that they catch the wind on the wrong side and check the ship's way. 2. (Of the wind) to change in an anti-clockwise direction.

backstay, Ropes which support a mast by running downwards and backwards from the masthead to the chainwales.

battery, 1. The broadside guns mounted on one deck, or one side, of the ship. 2. A group of guns mounted ashore. 3. **floating —**, a stationary raft or hulk mounting heavy guns.

beam, 1. The width of the ship. 2. The direction at right angles to the centreline. 3. A timber running from side to side of a ship to support a deck.

beak-head, The timbers that form the ship's head.

bear, *vb*. 1. To lie or point in a particular direction. 2. **— away**, to bear up, to turn downwind. 3. **— down**, to bear up. 4. **— up**, to turn downwind.

bend, *vb*. To make a sail fast to its yard, mast or stay.

bilge, 1. The angle of the ship's hull between side and bottom. 2. **— and bilge**, close alongside, touching.

bits, Large timbers fixed perpendicularly in the fore-part of the ship that are used to secure the anchor cables.

boatswain, A ship's officer responsible for sails, rigging and ground tackle. 2. **—'s call**, A whistle used to convey orders.

bobstay, A rope used to secure the bowsprit downwards to the stem, used to counteract the force of the foremast stays, which pull it upwards.

boom, 1. A light running spar, particularly one extending the foot of a sail. 2. A floating barrier protecting a harbour.

bow, Either side of the foremost part of the ship's hull, as it widens from the stem. **on the —**, said of a ship or object on a bearing somewhere between right ahead and abeam.

bowline, **bowling**, Rope which holds the edge of a square sail tight against the wind.

bowsprit, A spar projecting over the bows, spreading various items of rigging and one or more sails.

brace, A rope used to traverse the yards on a horizontal plane.

broadside, 1. The side of the ship. 2. The number of guns mounted or bearing on one side. 3. The simultaneous fire of those guns. 4. The total weight of shot fired by all the guns of the ship. 5. **— on**, of a ship showing her broadside at right angles to the observers line of sight, or to a named point of reference.

bulkhead, A vertical partition within the ship.

bulwark, A barrier around the side of a deck.

bumpkin, A short boom projecting from the bow, used to extend the lower edge of the foresail to windward.

buntlines, Ropes fastened to the foot of a square sail to furl it up towards the yard.

by the board, Overboard.

cable, 1. A large rope or hawser, particularly the anchor cable. 2. The standard length of an anchor cable, 120 fathoms.

capstan, *sb.* A mechanical device for hauling in cables, consisting of a vertical revolving drum turned by bars inserted in its rim.

carronade, A type of short gun, of heavy calibre but small charge and short range.

cartridge, A cloth or paper bag containing the propellant charge of a gun.

cat head, Strong pieces of timber extending outwards from the bow, on each side of the bowsprit. Used as a sort of crane to suspend the anchor clear of the ship's bows.

chain plate, A metal plate used to fasten a shroud or stay to the hull.

channels, Planks projecting horizontally from the ship's side abreast of the masts, used to extend and anchor the shrouds.

chase, 1. The pursuit of one ship or squadron by another. 2. The ship pursued. 3. — **gun**, a gun mounted to fire ahead or astern. 5. **general** —, order to a squadron to pursue a beaten enemy without regard to order. 6. **stern** —, pursuit in which the pursued lies dead ahead of the pursuer.

clamps, 1. Thick planks in a ship's side, used to sustain the ends of the beams. 2. Small crooked plates of iron which keep the cannon secured to their carriages.

clew lines, Ropes fastened to the clues – the lower corners of the foresail and mainsail, used to truss up the sails when furling.

clew garnets, Serve the same purpose as clew lines but are common to all square sails.

close-hauled, *adv.* Steering as nearly towards the wind as possible.

course, 1. The direction of ship's movement. 2. The foresail or mainsail, the lowest square sails.

cringle, An eye sewn into a sail.

crosstrees, Horizontal struts at the top of topmasts, used to anchor the topgallant stays.

deck, A floor or platform within a ship. 2. — **head**, the underside of the deck overhead. 3. **gun** —, the deck carrying the main battery (seventeenth–nineteenth century). 4. **half** —, the after end of the main deck, below the quarterdeck. 5. **lower** —, a) the gun deck or (in a two- or three-decker)

lowest gun deck; b) the ratings of the ship's company as a whole, those who berth on the lower deck. 6. **main** —, the highest deck running the whole length of the ship. 7. **quarter** —, a deck above the main deck over the after part of the ship. 8. **spar** —, a light deck connecting quarter deck to forecastle. 9. **upper** —, a continuous weather deck incorporating quarterdeck and forecastle. 10. **weather** —, a deck exposed to the sky.

dead, Directly, straight.

double, **double on**, *vb.* To attack a ship or squadron from both sides.

draught, 1. The depth of water required to float a ship. 2. A plan or chart. 3. The drawings showing the design of ship.

fish, *vb.*, To strengthen a damaged spar or mast by lashing spars to it in the manner of splints.

flag, 1. An admiral's distinguishing flag. 2. — **captain**, the captain of a flagship. 3. — **rank**, admiral's rank. 4. — **ship**, the admiral's ship.

flotilla, 1. A group of small warships. 2. Coastal warships considered as a whole.

forecastle, A deck built over the forward end of the main deck.

foretopsail, The topsail on the foremast.

freeboard, The minimum height of the ship's side above the waterline.

frigate, A cruising warship with an unarmed lower deck, mounting her battery on the main deck.

furl, *vb.* To bundle up a sail to its yard, mast or stay.

gammoning, A rope used to bind the inner quarter of the bowsprit to the ship's stem.

gangway, A light bridge connecting forecastle and quarterdeck.

gangboard, A board or plank with cleats nailed onto it to allow safe embarkation or disembarkation of a ship or boat.

get the wind, *vb.* To gain the weather gage.

grapeshot, Anti-personnel shot consisting of small shot that scatters on firing.

gun, 1. A piece of artillery. 2. — **deck**, see **deck**. 3. — **lock**, a flintlock firing mechanism for a great gun. 4. — **port**, a port cut to allow guns mounted below decks

to fire out. 5. — **shot**, the range of a gun. 6.
— **tackle**, tackle rigged to run out the gun
after firing. 7. **chase** —, see **chase**.

halliard, A rope used to hoist or lower any
sail on its yard or stay.

hawser, A large rope. Smaller than a Cable.

hawse-pieces/hause-pieces, A name given
to the foremost timbers of a ship.

hawse-holes, Cylindrical holes cut through
the bows of a ship on each side of the stem,
through which the anchor cables pass.

head rails, Curved rails that project from
the bows to support the knee of the head,
where the figure-head rests.

heave-to, To stop by backing some of
the sails.

heel, *vb.* (Of the ship) to incline or be
inclined to one side or the other.

hold, The lowest internal space of a ship,
below all the decks.

jack, A type of national flag flown forward,
particularly by warships.

jeers, Tackles used to raise or lower the yards.

jib, A triangular headsail hoisted on a stay set
between the foretopmast and the bowsprit.

jibboom, An extension to the bowsprit.

keel, The timber lying centrally along the
length of the bottom of the ship, forming a
spine upon which other parts of her frame
are erected.

knee, *sb.* A timber angle-bracket connecting
two or more ship's timbers. **Lodging**
—, fixed horizontally to the ship's frame.
Hanging —, fixed vertically to the ship's
frame.

knight-head, One on each side, secures the
inner-end of the bowsprit.

landward, *adv.* Towards the land.

langridge, Anti-personnel and dismasting
shot made up of irregular pieces of iron,
nails etc.

larboard, Relating to the port or left-hand
side of the ship.

large, Relating to a course with the wind
abaft the beam.

league, Three miles.

lee, 1. The direction towards which the wind
is blowing. 2. The water sheltered from the
wind by the land or by a ship. 3. —
shore, a coastline towards which the

wind is blowing.

leeches, The borders of edges of a sail, which
are either sloping or perpendicular.

leeward, Relating to the direction towards
which the wind is blowing.

Leewardly, (Of a ship) Tending to drift
rapidly to leeward when trying to sail close-
hauled.

leeway, The extent to which the wind blows
a ship to leeward of her apparent course.

lift, Ropes that run from the mast-head to
the extremities of the yard below, used to
support the weight of the yard.

limber head, Timbers around the limber-
holes, which are cut into the ship's floor
near the keel, creating a channel which
communicates with the ship's pump.

line, 1. — **abreast**, A formation in which
the ships of a squadron sail on the same
course abeam of one another. 2. — **ahead**,
a formation in which one or more ships
follow a leader, imitating his movements. 3.
— **of battle**, a fighting formation in which
the ships of a fleet form a straight line in a
predetermined order. 4. — **of bearing**, a
formation in which a squadron of ships lie
in a straight line diagonal to their course.

longboat, The largest of the ship's boats,
designed for carrying heavy weights.

loose, *vb.* To hoist or let drop sails, to
make sail.

lugger, A small sailing vessel with lugsails.

mast, 1. A vertical spar or spars supporting
sails, rigging and other spars. 2. **fore** —, the
foremost mast. 3. **lower** —, the lowest and
principal element of fore, main or mizzen
mast, on which the topmast is stepped. 4.
made —, a mast made up of more than one
tree assembled together. 5. **main** —, the
tallest (usually second) mast. 6. **mizzen** —,
see **mizzen**. 7. **topgallant** —, **top** —, see
topgallantmast, topmast. 8. — **dock**, see
dock. 9. — **head**, the top of a lower, top
or topgallantmast.

maintopsail, The topsail on the mainmast.

master, The warrant officer responsible for
navigation.

midshipman, A boy or young man hoping to
become a commissioned officer.

middle deck, On a three-decker, the deck

between the lower deck and the
upper deck.

mizzen, 1. The aftermost mast of a ship
or ketch. 2. — **peak**, the upper end of
the mizzen yard or gaff. 3. **mizzentop**,
see **top**. 4. — **yard**, the yard of the
lateen mizzen sail (seventeenth to mid-
eighteenth century).

moor, *vb.* To secure a ship by two anchors, or
by making fast to a buoy.

the Nore, An anchorage in the mouth of the
Thames near the entrance to
the River Medway, which led to Chatham
naval dockyard.

outboard, *adv.* Relating to, towards, the
outside of the ship.

orlop (deck), The lowest deck.

pay, *vb.* (Of a ship in stays) To fall off on to
one or other tack.

pitch, *vb.* To dip head and stern alternately
into the waves.

plank sheers, Pieces of plank laid over the
timbers of the quarter deck, forecastle, and
round house.

poop, A short deck built over the after end of
the quarterdeck.

pontoon, A low, flat vessel often fitted with
cranes and tackles.

port, 1. An opening cut in a ship's side. 2.
gun —, a port out of which a gun is fired.
3. — **timber**, the wood used in the
construction of a gunport.

preventer stay, Serves the same purpose as
a stay but is used as a temporary expedient
when excessive force is expected.

quarter, 1. The sides of the ship's stern. 2.
(*pl.*) Each man's post or station in action. 3.
Mercy, safety on surrender. 4. — **deck**, see
deck. 5. **on the** —, in a direction between
abeam and right aft, diagonal to the ship's
course. 6. — **gallery**, a balcony projecting
from the stern and quarter of large ships,
accessed via the admiral's or captain's cabin.

rake, *vb.* To fire down the length of an enemy
ship from ahead or astern.

reach, *vb.* To sail with the wind abeam.

reckoning, 1. A calculation of the ship's
position. 2. **dead** —, an estimate of the
ship's position without the benefit of
observations, by calculating course, speed

and drift from a known point of departure.

reef, 1. A tuck taken in a sail to reduce
its area. 2. A line of submerged rocks.
3. — **point**, a short length of line secured
through a sail in order to be made fast
around the yard or boom to take in a reef.

reef, *vb.* To shorten sail by bundling part of
the sail against yard or boom.

reef tackle pendants, Ropes used to lighten
the sail when reefing by pulling the unused
sail up towards the yard.

rideau/radeau, Derived from the French
radeau meaning raft. A naval gun platform.

riders, Interior ribs that strengthen a
ship's frame.

rigging, *sb.* 1. The ropes supporting and
controlling the masts and spars. 2. **running**
—, rigging controlling the movement of sails
and movable spars. 3. **standing** —, rigging
supporting the masts.

royal, A small square sail flown above
the topgallant.

sail, 1. A piece of cloth spread aloft by
masts and rigging to catch the wind and
propel a ship. 2. Some number of ships.
3. — **cloths**, heavy canvas for sails. 4. —
plan, an arrangement of sails. 5. **easy** —,
a reduced sail plan, for slow speed. 6. **fore**
—, the fore course, the lowest square sail
set on the foremast. 7. **head** —, a sail set
forward of the foremast. 8. **main** —, the
main course, the lowest square sail set on
the mainmast. 9. **stay** —, a triangular sail
set on one of the stays supporting a mast
from ahead. 10. **studding** —, a light sail
temporarily spread outboard of a square
sail in light airs. 11. **top** —, a square sail
hoisted on the topmast, above the course.

sail, *vb.* 1. (Of any sort of ship) To move, to
proceed. 2. **make** —, to hoist, spread sail.
3. **shorten** —, to reduce, take in sail.

sheet, A rope or tackle controlling the clew
of a sail.

sheer hulk, An old vessel fitted with sheers
to assist in the stepping or striking of masts.

shift, *vb.* 1. To exchange, replace or move. 2.
— **flag**, (of an admiral) to change flagship.

shot, 1. A bullet or (non-explosive) projectile
fired from a great gun. 2. **canister** —,
see **canister**. 3. **chain** —, hollow shot

Glossary

formed in two halves containing and linked by a length of chain, designed to damage rigging. 4. **dismantling** —, one of a number of types of shot designed to damage masts and spars. 5. **grape** —, see **grape**. 6. **fire** —, hollow shot filled with an incendiary compound.

shroud, A stay supporting a mast from the side.

skids, Long vertical timbers fixed amidships to the ship's side to protect the hull when heavy items are hoisted or lowered.

slip (a cable), To cast off; especially to sail without weighing anchor, in which case the anchor cable is let slip and buoyed for later retrieval.

sloop, A small cruising warship, having only one internal deck, and mounting her main battery on the upper deck.

sound, *vb.* To take a sounding, to measure the depth of water beneath a ship.

spar, 1. A mast, pole or boom. 2. — **deck**, see **deck**.

spirketting, The timber between the decks and the gun ports.

Spithead, An area of the Solent, off Portsmouth.

spring, A hawser led from the capstan, out of the ship aft and made fast some way along the anchor cable, hauling on which will cant an anchored ship to bring her broadside to bear as desired.

spring, *vb.* (Of a mast or spar) to split along the grain.

spritsail, 1. A sail set on a yard below the bowsprit. 2. — **topsail**, a sail set on a small mast stepped on the end of the bowsprit.

standing, *adj.* Fixed.

stantions/stanchion, A small pillar of wood or iron used as a support for various purposes in a ship: they can be used to support the decks, quarter-rails, awnings etc.

starboard, Relating to the right-hand side of the ship.

stay, *vb.* 1. To tack. 2. **in stays**, of a ship pointing into the wind while in the process of going about. 3. **miss stays**, *vb.* in tacking, to fail to turn into the wind and to fall back on to the original tack.

staysail, see **sail**.

step (a mast), To place a ship's mast.

stern, 1. The after end of the ship. 2. — **post**, a straight timber erected on the after end of the keel, supporting both the rudder and the structure of the stern. 3. — **chaser**, a chase gun pointing aft.

strike, *vb.* 1. To lower a mast, spar, sail etc. 2. To strike colours, to surrender. 3. To run aground.

studdingsail, A light sail temporarily set outboard of a square sail in light airs.

surge, Bodily movement of the ship ahead or astern.

sway, Bodily movement of a ship from side to side.

tack, 1. A rope or tackle serving to haul down the clew of a square sail. 2. The course held by a ship beating to windward. 3. **larboard** —, **port** —, the tack on which the wind blows from the left-hand side of the ship. 4. **starboard** —, the tack on which the wind blows from the right-hand side of the ship.

tack, *vb.* 1. To shift tacks, to go about, to turn into the wind and so onto the opposite tack. 2. To beat to windward by successive tacks.

tiller, *sb.* A bar inserted in the head of the rudder by which the ship is steered.

top, 1. A platform built at the head of the lower masts, serving to spread the shrouds of the topmast and provide a space for men working aloft. 2. — **gallant**, see **topgallant**. 3. — **hamper**, ship's structure or equipment carried high up, tending to increase windage or reduce stability. 4. — **man** (likewise **foretopman** etc.), a seaman skilled in working aloft. 5. — **mast**, a mast fitted to the top of the lower mast and extending it. 6. — **sail**, see **sail**. 7. — **sides**, the upper part of the ship's structure, clear of the water-line. 8. — **timber**, a structural timber forming the uppermost section of a frame on each side. 9. — **weight**, the weight of ship's structure or equipment carried high, hence tending to reduce stability. 10. **fore** —, **main** —, **mizzen** —, a) the platform built at the head of the foremast, mainmast, mizzenmast; b) the fore, main or mizzen topmast head, the head of the topmast or topgallantmast.

topgallant, 1. A square sail set on the topgallantmast, above the topsail. 2. — **mast**, a mast fitted to the top of the topmast and extending it. 3. — **yard**, the yard set on the topgallantmast, spreading the topgallant.

taffrail, Bulwark at the after end of the poop or quarterdeck.

top (of a mast), A platform built at the top of the lower mast.

treenail, **trenail**, A wooden peg or pin used to fasten together the parts of the hull of a wooden ship.

truss, Secures a yard to its home mast.

trussle tree/trestle-tree, Strong horizontal timbers that support the mast top.

tumblehome, The inward slope of the ship's side above the waterline.

tye, A thick runner securing a tackle to a yard or gaff.

unhandy, Unmanoeuvrable, clumsy.

unmoor, *vb.* To weigh anchor, to cast off a mooring.

upperworks, The upper portion of the ship's structure.

van division, The leading division of a fleet or squadron divided into van, centre and rear.

vice-admiral, A flag officer ranking below admiral and above rear-admiral.

wake, The track of the ship's passage through the water astern.

wear, *vb.* 1. To alter course from one tack to the other by turning before the wind. 2. To fly a particular flag or carry some distinguishing mark.

weather, 1. Relating to the direction from which the wind is blowing. 2. — **gage**, the windward position in relation to another ship or fleet.

weather, *vb.* To get to windward of something.

weatherly, *adv.* (Of a ship) tending to ship seas easily.

wind, 1. The direction from which the wind blows. 2. The windward position, the weather gage. 3. **head** —, a wind coming from ahead, one making progress on that course impossible. 4. **off the** —, *adv.* sailing with the wind abaft the beam. 5. **on the** —, *adv.* sailing close-hauled.

windward, *adj.* Relating to the direction from which the wind is blowing

woolding, a rope wound numerous times around a mast to support it if it is split or if the mast is composed of numerous pieces of timber and requires such support.

yard, 1. A spar hung horizontally from a mast to spread the head or foot of a square sail. 2. An establishment to build, repair and supply warships. 3. — **arm**, the extreme ends of a yard. 4. **main** —, the yard spreading the mainsail.

yaw, Deviations from side to side of the ship's course under pressure of wind and sea.

NOTES

Introduction

[1] The impressive few are: Warner, O., *The Glorious First of June* (London: 1961) and *The Life and Letters of Vice Admiral Lord Collingwood* (London: 1968); Krajeski, P.C., *In the Shadow of Nelson: The Naval Leadership of Admiral Sir Charles Cotton, 1753–1812* (London: 2000); Hore, P., 'John Richards Lapenotiere and HM Schooner *Pickle* and their Fifteen Minutes of Fame' *Mariner's Mirror*, 91, no. 2 (2005) pp. 284–93; Duffy, M. and Morriss R., 'The Battle of the Glorious First of June 1794' in Duffy M. and Morriss R. (eds.), *The Glorious First of June 1794: A Naval Battle and its Aftermath* (2001), pp.1–12 and Blake, R., *Evangelicals in the Royal Navy, 1775–1815: Blue Lights & Psalm-Singers* (Woodbridge, 2008).

[2] J.B. Bourchier, ed., *Memoir of the Life of Admiral Sir Edward Codrington*, vol. 1 (London: 1873), 68.

[3] The criteria for inclusion remains an interesting question. James Saumarez's action in the Gut of Gibraltar in July 1801, in which two Spanish First Rates of 112 guns were destroyed and a French Third Rate of 74 guns was captured, is the most notable exclusion. His level of success equalled, if not exceeded, Bridport's tally of three enemy 74-gunners captured or destroyed at Groix in 1795, the smallest of the British victories in the collection. The reason for the exclusion of Saumarez's action is therefore curious. Perhaps it is because a total of three enemy ships taken or destroyed was, by 1801, an insufficient measure of victory even if two of those ships were magnificent Spanish First Rates. Or perhaps it is because of the nature of their destruction; in the chaos of battle those ill-fated Spaniards fired into each other, believing each to be an enemy ship, until they both exploded.

[4] N.H. Nicolas, ed., *The Dispatches and Letters of Lord Nelson*, vol. 2 (London: 1845), 63.

[5] Bridport's action off Groix in 1795 might be added to this list but it is important to remember that although Bridport was criticised within the navy for failing to press his victory, the public were delighted and considered him a hero.

[6] N.A.M. Rodger, *The Command of the Ocean: A Naval History of Britain 1649–1815*, vol. 2 (London: 2004), 608, 639.

[7] But note that Saumarez's capture and destruction of three enemy ships in the Gut of Gibraltar on 12 July 1801 is not included in the collection of dispatches. Even if it is included in this calculation the gap is still four years and three months.

[8] M. Lewis, *A Social History of the Navy 1793–1815*, (1960), p 440–443.

[9] See for example FF235, 236, 238, 240, 245, 246, 248, 250, 252, 254, 255 published in Nicolas, *The Dispatches and Letters of Lord Nelson*, V, (1845), pp. 215–27, but they are badly transcribed and heavily edited.

[10] J. Sugden, *Nelson: A Dream of Glory* (London: 2005), 703.

[11] J.D. Davies, 'Adam, Viscount Duncan,' in *British Admirals of the Napoleonic Wars: The Contemporaries of Nelson*, ed. P. Le Fevre and R. Harding (2005), 62.

[12] Quoted in T. Jenks, *Naval Engagements: Patriotism, Cultural Politics, and the Royal Navy 1793–1815* (Oxford: 2006), 27.

[13] W. Marsden, *A Brief Memoir of the Life and Writings of William Marsden* (London: 1838), 126.

[14] Rodger, *Command of the Ocean*, 187.

15 For example, his comment on Captain William Parker's letter, describing his action before 1 June 1794, notes: 'Let him [i.e. Parker] know it [has] been communicated to their Lships who have great satisfaction in the account he has given of the exemplary conduct of the officers and ship's company on the occasion.'

1. The Glorious First of June

1 N. Hampson, *Prelude to Terror: The Constituent Assembly and the Failure of Consensus 1789–1791* (Oxford: 1988), x.

2 *The Task* by William Cowper, 1785. For more on this see E. Royle, *Revolutionary Britannia? Reflections on the Threat of Revolution in Britain 1789–1848* (Manchester: 2000), ff.13.

3 H. Gough, *The Terror in the French Revolution* (Basingstoke: 1998), 54.

4 O. Warner, *The Glorious First of June* (London: 1961), 63.

5 R.J.B. Knight, 'Richard, Earl Howe, 1726–1799'. In *Precursors of Nelson: British Admirals of the Eighteenth Century*, edited by P. Le Fevre and R. Harding (London: 2000), 285.

6 Knight, 'Earl Howe', 292.

7 J.B. Bourchier, ed., *Memoir of the Life of Admiral Sir Edward Codrington*, vol. 1 (London: 1873), 18.

8 The French fleet consisted of 26 ships.

9 Nelson to Howe 8 Jan 1799, N.H. Nicolas, ed., *The Dispatches and Letters of Lord Nelson*, vol. 3 (London: 1845), 230.

10 Bourchier, ed., *Memoir*, 18–22.

11 R. Bevan and W.G. Kemble, 'Narrative of the Engagement between the Brunswick and the Vengeur, 1 June 1794,' in *The Naval Miscellany*, vol. III, ed. W.G. Perrin, (London: NRS Vol. 63, 1927), 163; Also see NMM: STT/3.

2 St Vincent

1 N.H. Nicolas, ed., *The Dispatches and Letters of Lord Nelson*, vol. 1 (London: 1845), 309.

2 J.S. Corbett, ed., *Private Papers of George, Second Earl Spencer, First Lord of the Admiralty, 1794–1801*, vol. 2 (London: NRS Vol. 48, 1914), 58.

3 S. Howarth, ed., *Battle of St Vincent 200 Years: Selected Papers from the Bicentennial International Naval Conference* (Shelton: 1998), 72.

4 John Jervis, Earl of St Vincent, *ODNB*.

5 Nicolas, ed., *Nelson Letters*, vol. 2, 229.

6 The ships which came from the home fleet were *Prince George*, *Orion*, *Namur*, *Irresistable*, and *Colossus*.

7 The three-decked *Principe de Asturias* captured at Passaro in 1718 does not count because she was not a First Rate; in fact she was a captured British Third Rate, the *Cumberland*; and the First Rate destroyed on the stocks at Havana in 1762 never made it to sea.

8 Nicolas, ed., Nelson Letters, vol. 2, 335.

9 Ibid., 325.

10 Ibid., 313.

11 J. Sugden, *Nelson: A Dream of Glory* (London: 2005), 709.

12 J. Ross, *Memoirs and Correspondence of Admiral Lord de Saumarez*, vol.1 (1838), 173.

13 Howarth, ed., *Battle of St Vincent 200 Years*, 15.

14 Nicolas, ed., *Nelson Letters*, vol. 2, 337.

15 C. White, *1797: Nelson's Year of Destiny* (Stroud: 1998), 75.

16 E.A. Hughes, ed., *The Private Correspondence of Admiral Lord Collingwood* (London: NRS Vol.98, 1957), 81.

17 Nicolas, ed., *Nelson Letters*, vol. 2, 337.

18 R.J.B Knight, *The Pursuit of Victory: The Life and Achievement of Horatio Nelson* (London: 2005), 230.

19 J.S. Tucker, *Memoirs of Admiral the Right Hon. The Earl of St Vincent*, vol. 1 (London: 1844), 254.

20 Rodger, *Command of the Ocean*, 439.

21 S. Howarth, ed., *Battle of St Vincent*, 42.

22 C.C. Lloyd and R.C. Anderson, *St Vincent and Camperdown* (New York, 1963), 63–4.

23 Knight, *Pursuit*, 221.

24 Sugden, *Nelson: A Dream of Glory*, 690.

25 Hughes, ed., *Collingwood Correspondence*, 49.

26 Described in Jervis's first biography, J. Tucker's *Memoirs of Admiral the Right Hon. The Earl of St Vincent* (1844).

27 Though he later received £500 from the 'Patriotic Fund', a charity established by members of Lloyd's Coffee House for the relief of injured sailors and their dependants.

28 Sugden, Nelson: *A Dream of Glory*, 707.

29 T. Sturges Jackson, ed., *Logs of the Great Sea Fights, 1794–1805*, vol.1 (London: NRS Vol.16, 1981), 233.

30 Knight, *Pursuit*, 219.

31 John Jervis, Earl of St Vincent, *ODNB*.

3 Camperdown

1 T.W. Tone, *Memoirs of Theobold Wolfe Tone*, vol. 2 (London: 1827), 231.

2 R. Camperdown, *Admiral Duncan* (London: 1898), 111.

3 C.C. Lloyd and R.C. Anderson, *St Vincent & Camperdown* (New York: 1963), 118.

4 Camperdown, *Admiral Duncan*, 92.

5 Lloyd and Anderson, *St Vincent & Camperdown*, 129.

6 Ibid., 141.

7 Sir Richard Onslow, *ODNB*.

8 L. Brockliss, J. Cardwell, and M. Moss, *Nelson's Surgeon: William Beatty, Naval Medicine and the Battle of Trafalgar* (Oxford: 2005), 113; Lloyd and Anderson, *St Vincent & Camperdown*, 147.

9 B. Vale and G. Edwards, *Physician to the Fleet: The Life and Times of Thomas Trotter, 1760–1832* (Woodbridge: 2011), 28.

10 J. Ralfe, *The Naval Biography of Great Britain*, vol. 4 (London: 1828), 160.

11 The bottoms of British warships were covered in copper, which reduced the growth of weed and barnacles, increased speed and performance and reduced the frequency of hull repair and maintenance.

12 Nicolas, ed., *Nelson Letters*, vol. 6, 216.

13 Nicolas, ed., *Nelson Letters*, vol. 2, 446 n.

4 The Battle of the Nile

1 A.T. Mahan, *The Life of Nelson*, vol. 2 (London: 1897), 154.

2 See *Gentleman's Magazine*, lxxi, 659; and lxviii, 104.

3 A true lightning conductor not only provides a route to earth when struck but also reduces the probability of a strike by discharging the cloud before it has become sufficiently charged to arc and strike.

4 J.S. Corbett, ed., *Private Papers of George, Second Earl Spencer, First Lord of the Admiralty, 1794–1801*, vol. 2 (London: NRS Vol. 48, 1914), 446.

5 Knight, *Pursuit*, 278.

6 One of them, Sir John Orde, then Rear Admiral of the White and thus significantly superior to Nelson, was particularly incensed. Orde bore a grudge that festered for several years before he erupted in a fit of bile, hounded St Vincent and demanded a duel. Orde only stood down after he had received a direct order from his irritated sovereign.

7 J.A. Davis, *Naples and Napoleon: Southern Italy and the European Revolutions* (Oxford: 2006), 75.

8 A different version of F194 is in BL Add. MS. 34907.

9 Nicolas, ed., *Nelson Letters*, vol. 3, 74.

10 G.P.B. Naish, ed., *Nelson's Letters to His Wife and Other Documents* (NRS Vol.100, 1958), 184.

11 T. Coleman, *Nelson* (London: 2001), 163.

12 Nicolas, ed., *Nelson Letters*, vol. 3, 55.

13 J. Ross, ed., *Memoirs and Correspondence of Admiral Lord De Saumarez*, vol. 1 (London: 1838), 228.

14 Knight, *Pursuit*, 641.

15 For more on this see M.K. Barritt, 'Nelson's frigates May to August 1798', *Mariner's Mirror*, vol. 58, no. 3 (1972), 281–295.

16 *Copies of original letters from the army of General Bonaparte in Egypt, intercepted by*

the fleet under the command of Admiral Lord Nelson (London: 1798), xviii.

17 Nicolas, ed., *Nelson Letters*, vol. 6, 71.

5 Copenhagen

1 Knight, *Pursuit*, 352.

2 Ibid., 360.

3 D. Bonner-Smith, ed., *Letters of Admiral of the Fleet the Earl of St. Vincent*, vol. 1, (London: NRS Vol. 55, 1922), 86.

4 A powerful squadron did, in fact, weigh on 2 April but strong southerly winds prevented them from beating out of Karlskrona.

5 NMM: CRK/10.

6 C. White, *Nelson: The New Letters* (Woodbridge: 2005), 119.

7 We know that Parker and Nelson met during this storm to discuss the attack. Nelson's sailors were so concerned about the safety of their one-armed admiral that they refused to let him climb down the side of the ship in the traditional fashion. Instead, he clambered into the ship's launch as it lay on the booms in the centre of the weather deck and then the launch, with Nelson sitting in it, was hoisted up, swung overboard and then lowered into the sea.

8 The 74-gun, Third Rate *Elephant* drew 15 inches less water than the 98-gun Second Rate *St George*, a crucial tactical advantage in shallow water.

9 P. Le Fevre, "'Little Merit Will Be Given to Me': Admiral Sir Hyde Parker (1739–1807) and the Diplomatic Build-up to the Battle,' in *Battle of Copenhagen 1801: 200 Years*, ed. S. Howath (Shelton: 2003), 25.

10 Knight, *Pursuit*, 382.

11 Her full complement was 550.

12 J. Ralfe, *The Naval Biography of Great Britain*, vol. 4 (London: 1828), 161.

13 He was a renowned swimmer who, during his service life, saved nine men from drowning and, aged 60 and crippled, swam 14 miles for a 'small wager'.

14 J. Ward, *Zion's Works: New Light on the Bible from the Coming of Shiloh, the Spirit of Truth, 1828–37*. Compiled by C.B.

Holinsworth, 17 vols (London, 1899–1904).

15 T. Sturges Jackson, ed., *Logs of the Great Sea Fights, 1794–1805*, vol. 2 (London: NRS Vol. 18, 1981), 102.

16 A.M. Broadley and R.G. Bartelot, *The Three Dorset Captains at Trafalgar* (London: 1906), 63.

17 Knight, *Pursuit*, 362.

18 Nicolas, ed., *Nelson Letters*, vol. 4, 353.

6 Trafalgar

1 A.T. Mahan, *The Life of Nelson: The Embodiment of the Seapower of Great Britain*, vol. 2 (London: 1897), 44.

2 T. Coleman, *Nelson: The Man and the Legend* (London: 2001), 303.

3 Knight, *Pursuit*, 629.

4 It is possible that the change of heart came when the Allies heard that Nelson's fleet was temporarily reduced in numbers because he had sent Thomas Louis to Gibraltar with six ships of the line to get supplies for the fleet. Louis was furious and thought that he was going to miss the coming battle. Nelson insisted he would not, but Louis did not return in time to take part. He did, however, take part in Duckworth's victory at San Domingo (see Chapter 7).

5 Nicolas, ed., *Nelson Letters*, vol. 7, 91.

6 Ibid., 150.

7 Some modern historians have an irritating habit of spelling his name Lapenotière, but he never used accents when writing his own name.

8 See Appendix I.

9 G.L. Newnham, *Collingwood, A Selection from the Public and Private Correspondence of Vice-Admiral Lord Collingwood*, vol. 2 (London: 1828), 138.

10 E. Desbrière, *The Naval Campaign of 1805: Trafalgar*, trans. C. Eastwick, vol. 2 (Oxford: 1933), 129-32.

11 Rodger, *Command of the Ocean*, 539; N. Tracy, *Nelson's Battles: The Art of Victory in the Age of Sail* (London: 1996), 181.

12 All of the captured allied officers were taken to the *Euryalus* to surrender their swords.

Midshipman Joseph Morre was particularly impressed by the size of the pile their swords made on her quarterdeck.

13 Nicolas, ed., *Nelson Letters*, vol. 7, 80.

14 Newnham, *Collingwood Correspondence*, 413.

15 Nicolas, ed., *Nelson Letters*, vol.7, 147.

16 Six different orders of sailing, issued before the battle, are known to exist, the variety in the lists explained by the frequent arrivals and departures to and from Nelson's fleet as it grew with reinforcements and he sent ships out on reconnaissance or watering missions. This list, compiled from a variety of sources, is taken from M Duffy, ' ... All Was Hushed Up: The Hidden Trafalgar,' *Mariner's Mirror*, XCI, no. 2 (2005): 222.

17 Duffy, ' ... All Was Hushed Up: The Hidden Trafalgar,' 227.

18 Many thanks to Mark Barker of the Inshore Squadron for this.

19 E. Fraser, *The Enemy at Trafalgar: An Account of the Battle from Eye-Witnesses' Narratives and Letters and Dispatches from the French and Spanish Fleet* (London: 1906), 191.

20 P. Mackesy, *War in the Mediterranean 1803–10* (London: 1957), 75–6.

21 J.B. Bourchier, ed., *Memoir of the Life of Admiral Sir Edward Codrington*, vol. 1 (London: 1873), 63.

22 Which can be found in P. Goodwin, *The Ships of Trafalgar: The British, French and Spanish Fleets October 1805* (London: 2005).

23 Duffy, ' ... All Was Hushed Up: The Hidden Trafalgar,' 232.

24 It seems to have been a favourite phrase: Nelson also called Thomas Louis his right hand. Nicolas, ed., *Nelson Letters*, vol. 7, 63.

25 C. Hibbert, *Nelson: A Personal History* (London: 1995), 361.

26 Bourchier, ed., *Memoir*, 64; Duffy, ' ... All Was Hushed Up: The Hidden Trafalgar,' 217, 236.

27 Some unverified figures are offered here: A.H. Taylor, 'The Battle of Trafalgar,' *Mariner's Mirror*, 36, no. 4 (1950) 320.

Goodwin, *The Ships of Trafalgar: The British, French and Spanish Fleets October 1805* (London: 2005) is also useful. M. Duffy and R. Mackay, *Hawke, Nelson and British Naval Leadership 1747–1805* (Woodbridge: 2009), 9 claims that 4,530 French were killed and wounded, and 2,408 Spanish.

28 Alessandro Malaspina circumnavigated the world twice, in 1786–8 and then his major five-year voyage of scientific discovery 1789–94. The Galiano expedition was part of the second Malaspina circumnavigation. Galiano and Valdés explored the Strait of Juan de Fuca, now the international boundary between America and Canada on the Pacific coast. Galiano and Valdés met the British explorer George Vancouver during their survey and they shared the work.

29 This relates to a new law that was passed in March 1805, which expanded legal powers over ships coming from countries infected with 'epidemical diseases'. This was particularly relevant to the British fleet because an unknown 'plague' was then ravishing southern Iberia. The relationship between Britain, the sea and infectious diseases is best followed in J. Booker, *Maritime Quarantine: The British Experience, c.1650–1900* (Aldershot: 2007). For the 1805 law, see ff.304.

30 She had joined up to serve alongside her husband. She was naked when rescued but soon fitted out with female clothing that was kept aboard the *Victory* for amateur dramatics.

31 Perhaps part of the answer lies in the identity of Collingwood's flag captain, Edward Rotherham, who Collingwood disliked and described as fat and stupid. T. Voelcker, *Admiral Saumarez Versus Napoleon: The Baltic, 1807–12* (Woodbridge: 2008), 130. Hardy, Nelson's flag captain, was now struggling with the damaged *Victory* on his own and the frigates were busy towing damaged British ships and their prizes.

32 D. Allen and P. Hore, *News of Nelson: John Lapenotiere's Race from Trafalgar to London* (Brussels: 2005), 68.

[33] It is still an excellent pub.

[34] W. Marsden, *A Brief Memoir of the Life and Writings of William Marsden* (London: 1838), 116.

[35] C.I. Hamilton, *The Making of the Modern Admiralty: British Naval Policy-Making, 1805–1927* (Cambridge: 2011), 6.

[36] Marsden, *A Brief Memoir of the Life and Writings of William Marsden*, 116.

[37] Named for René Duguay-Trouin, a famous French privateer of the 17th Century.

[38] W. Richardson, *A Mariner of England* (London: 1908), 220.

[39] Sir Richard Strachan, *ODNB*.

7 San Domingo

[1] Sir John Duckworth, *ODNB*.

[2] Service Historique de la Marine V MS236 Nelson.

[3] Nicolas, ed., *Nelson Letters*, vol. 7, 63.

[4] Ibid.

[5] This is a Builders Measurement (BM), a technique of estimating a ship's capacity. It was calculated by the formula keel x breadth x ½ breadth ÷ 94, hence why fractions of a ton are quoted in ninety-fourths.

[6] A fascinating man who left us some account of his life in Sconce, R. C., *The Life and Letters of Robert Clement Sconce,* 2 vols (London: 1861).

[7] A particularly fine and very rare example of a French frigate's female figurehead is preserved at the Musée de la Marine in Paris.

[8] *Naval Chronicle*, XV, 243.

[9] See *Naval Chronicle*, XV, 254 ff.

[10] M. Duffy and R. Morriss, eds., *The Glorious First of June 1794: A Naval Battle and Its Aftermath* (Exeter: 2001), 86.

[11] Ibid., 87; NMM: BRK/14; E.A. Hughes, ed., *The Private Correspondence of Admiral Lord Collingwood* (London: NRS Vol. 98, 1957), 47.

[12] NMM: PAR/50; TNA: ADM 52/2812.

[13] It is not too far-fetched to believe that this was done deliberately to spite Duckworth whose faffing in Portsmouth (see p. 306) had prevented Keats from sailing into battle at Trafalgar as Nelson's second.

[14] A. Phillimore, *The Life of Admiral of the Fleet Sir W. Parker*, vol. 1 (London: 1876), 56.

[15] See pp. 278 and 319.

[16] E.P. Brenton, *Life and Correspondence of the Earl St. Vincent*, vol. 2 (London: 1838), 285.

Conclusion

[1] N.A.M. Rodger, *The Admiralty* (Lavenham: 1979), 94.

[2] A list of those who actually received the medal in 1847, including their rank and ship, does exist however, and is reproduced in K.J. Douglas-Morris, ed., *The Naval General Service Medal Roll, 1793–1840* (London: 1982), but we have no way of knowing which of those men he is. The Roll can also be searched online here, entering 'Nile' for 'clasp':

http://www.dnw.co.uk/medals/resources/medalrolls/navalgeneralservice/

[3] Nicolas, ed., *Nelson Letters*, vol. 5, 284.

FURTHER READING

I f you have enjoyed reading these original letters and would like to read more, there is no better home for you than the Navy Records Society which, for over a century, has regularly published volumes of significant letters relating to British Naval History. You can find out more online: www.navyrecords.org.uk. One of their volumes is particularly important for this period and subject, though it goes no further than Trafalgar. I am also fond of it because it was the first book on naval history that I ever bought: T. Sturges-Jackson's *Logs of the Great Seafights*, 2 vols (1981). Other significant NRS volumes are Brian Lavery's *Shipboard Life and Organisation* (1998), Julian Corbett's *Fighting Instructions 1530–1816* (1905) and his companion volume *Signals and Instructions 1776–1794* (1909).

For biographies there is no better place to start than the *Oxford Dictionary of National Biography*, which has many fine essays on British naval officers. Peter Le Fevre & Richard Harding's *British Admirals of the Napoleonic Wars: The Contemporaries of Nelson* (2005) is indispensable. For Nelson in a single volume, see Roger Knight's *The Pursuit of Victory* (2005); for his early life see John Sugden's *Nelson: A Dream of Glory* (2005); for his ability as a commander, see Colin White's *Nelson the Admiral* (2005).

For a general introduction to the ships of the period and life at sea, Brian Lavery's *Nelson's Navy* (1989) is still excellent and Nicholas Blake's *Steering to Glory* (2005) dissects a ship's day in all the detail you will ever need.

For tactics and command, see Creswell's *British Admirals of the Eighteenth Century: Tactics in Battle* (1977); my *Fighting at Sea in the Eighteenth Century: The Art of Sailing Warfare* (2008); and Duffy & Mackay's *Hawke, Nelson and British Naval Leadership 1747–1805* (2009).

For the ships see Brian Lavery's *The Ship of the Line*, 2 vols (1983) and Robert Gardiner's *The Line of Battle* (1992). For a particular focus on Trafalgar see Peter Goodwin's *The Ships of Trafalgar* (2005). Rif Winfield's *First Rate: The Greatest Warships of the Age of Sail* (2010) is a lively study of the largest ships of the era. For seamanship there is still no rival to John Harland's *Seamanship in the Age of Sail* (1985).

For more on the Admiralty, its infrastructure and its relationship with the State, see Nicholas Rodger's *The Admiralty* (1979); C. Hamilton's *The Making of the Modern Admiralty: British Naval Policy Making 1805–1927* (2011); Clive Wilkinson's *The British Navy and the State in the Eighteenth Century* (2004); and, best of all, Roger Morriss's *The Foundations of British Maritime Ascendancy: Resources, Logistics and the State, 1755–1815* (2011).

Each battle has its own significant bibliography but my *The Glorious First of June* (2011) showcases the latest research for that battle; Colin White's *1797: Nelson's Year of Destiny* (1998) and Lloyd and Anderson's *St. Vincent and Camperdown* (1968) are good for the battles of 1797; Lavery's *Nelson and the Nile: The Naval War against Napoleon 1798* (1998) is excellent for the Battle of the Nile and the campaign preceding it, and for a French perspective see Battesti, M., *La Bataille D'Aboukir 1798: Nelson Contrarie La Stratégie de Bonaparte* (1998); Copenhagen is best followed in Ole Feldbæk's *The Battle of Copenhagen* (2002); Trafalgar in Lavery's *Nelson's Fleet at Trafalgar* (2000) and in the relevant chapter in Knight's biography of Nelson *The Pursuit of Victory* (2005), though I am particularly fond of a much older collection of translated French and Spanish narratives in Edward Fraser's *The Enemy at Trafalgar* (1906). Piers Mackesy's *War in the Mediterranean 1803–10* (1957) still provides an excellent strategic overview of the various campaigns. The Battle of San Domingo does not, yet, have a book dedicated to it, and one must look around for scraps. William James's *The Naval History of Great Britain*, 6 vols (1886) and Laird Clowes's *The Royal Navy: A History from the Earliest Times to the Present*, 7 vols (1897–1903) both provide narratives of San Domingo and, indeed, of all of the battles in this book. Similar French works are Troude, O., *Batailles Navales de la France* (1867) and Roncière, C., *Histoire de la Marine* (1920).

For surgeons and medicine, see L. Brockliss's *Nelson's Surgeon: William Beatty, Naval Medicine and the Battle of Trafalgar* (2005) and Haycock & Archer's *Health and Medicine at Sea, 1700–1900* (2009).

For a detailed study of the journey of an officer sent home with dispatches, turn to D. Allen and P Hore, *News of Nelson: John Lapenotiere's race from Trafalgar to London* (2005) and John Fisher's *The Pickle at Trafalgar: The Graphic Story of the Trafalgar Way…* (2005).

For those interested in the change from the written word to radio, see T. Sarkar's *History of Wireless* (2006) and Tom Standage's entertaining *The Victorian Internet: The Remarkable Story of the Telegraph and the Nineteenth Century's On-line Pioneers* (1998).

For a thorough study of the entire period, see Nicholas Rodger's *The Command of the Ocean* (2005) and for a much shorter though excellent recent study, see Jonathan Dull's *The Age of the Ship of the Line* (2009).

NOTE ON THE AUTHOR

———•—•———

Dr Sam Willis is a maritime historian and archaeologist, a Fellow of the Royal Historical Society and a Fellow of the Society of Antiquaries. He is the author of the bestselling Hearts of Oak Trilogy and the Fighting Ships series. Sam is an experienced square-rig sailor and his books are infused with his knowledge and experience of seamanship. He has consulted on history for many clients including the BBC, Channel 4 and Christie's and regularly comments on history in the national press and on TV. Sam is proud to live in the best county in England (Devon) and spends as much of his time as possible by, in, or on, the sea. For more information, please visit: www.sam-willis.com and follow Sam's unpredictable ramblings and discoveries on Twitter @navalhistoryguy.

INDEX

Index

Index

Index

Index

Index

Index

Index

Index